MW01088524

"Theraplay® is a cherished g
gift is deceptively simple and ...
foundation for establishing or deepening attachment bonds. The approach is
playful, engaging and safe, and designed to create positive shared memories of
warm and attuned physical and emotional experiences between parents and
children. This book took my breath away in its congruence with the Theraplay
approach: it is engaging to read, it provides ample and strong structure for
the Theraplay practitioner, it challenges us to weave attachment theories with
unique responses to clients and it nurtures and encourages practitioners to
provide the best possible assistance they can. Vivien Norris and Dafna Lender's
expertise shines through as they provide a 'virtual supervisor' type of guidance
to the reader, answering many of the questions that we practitioners have as
we negotiate our daily practices. Not only is this book a remarkable addition to
the literature on Theraplay, it also succeeds in integrating current neuroscience
and research to further guide and strengthen interactive clinical nuances. I
will be reading this book multiple times because there are layers of important
information to guide us in our work. I am left speechless with gratitude. It's
been many years since I've been so enlightened and re-energized by a book with
such heart and substance!"

—*Eliana Gil, PhD, Gil Institute for Trauma Recovery and Education*

"In *Theraplay®—The Practitioner's Guide*, Vivien Norris and Dafna Lender
skillfully and comprehensively explain the essential principles of Theraplay.
Theraplay is an efficient mode of therapy for children that seamlessly
incorporates within a play environment several elements that are shared with
models of psychotherapy. In this guide, we learn about efficient exercises
that are effective in enhancing the child's ability to regulate state that can be
delivered as games; we learn that Theraplay is rooted in developmental science
(e.g. attachment theory) and is consistent with contemporary neuroscience
(e.g. Polyvagal Theory). From a Polyvagal perspective Theraplay respects the
biobehavior state of the child, applies therapist-initiated social engagement
strategies to trigger a state of safety in the child and promotes synchronous
reciprocal interactions as a neural exercise that increases social flexibility and
improves emotion regulation. It is through this development of the child's
ability to feel safe and secure that is key to Theraplay's efficacy and functionally
illustrates the attributes of Theraplay as a model therapy for children."

—*Stephen W. Porges, PhD, Kinsey Institute, Indiana University, Bloomington
and Department of Psychiatry, University of North Carolina at Chapel Hill*

"I have found the Theraplay® approach to healing distressed children to be at the leading edge of humanistic, experiential and evidence-based treatments. What this clear volume offers are step-by-step precise protocols for assessment and treatment using this vital method. Various activities and exercises are simply described and can be applied to many therapeutic situations. This book is a rich contribution, not only for practitioners of Theraplay, but also as a gift to all clinicians working to alleviate the suffering of troubled children."

—*Peter A. Levine, PhD, author (with Maggie Kline) of* Trauma Through a Child's Eyes *and* Trauma-Proofing your Kids

Theraplay®
The Practitioner's Guide

Theraplay®
The Practitioner's Guide

Vivien Norris and Dafna Lender

Foreword by Phyllis Booth

Jessica Kingsley Publishers
London and Philadelphia

First published in 2020
by Jessica Kingsley Publishers
73 Collier Street
London N1 9BE, UK
and
400 Market Street, Suite 400
Philadelphia, PA 19106, USA

www.jkp.com

Library of Congress Cataloging in Publication Data
A CIP catalog record for this book is available from the Library of Congress

British Library Cataloguing in Publication Data
A CIP catalogue record for this book is available from the British Library

ISBN 978 1 78592 210 7
eISBN 978 1 78450 488 5

Printed and bound in Great Britain

Clinical practice protocols change over time and no technique or recommendation is
guaranteed to be safe or effective in all circumstances. The information and guidance
in this book is intended as a resource for professionals practicing in the field of
psychotherapy and mental health and is not a substitute for appropriate training and
supervision. Neither the publisher nor the authors can guarantee the complete accuracy,
efficacy or appropriateness of any particular recommendation in every respect.

MIX
Paper from
responsible sources
FSC
www.fsc.org   FSC® C013056

*To Phyllis Booth
and in memory of Ann Jernberg*

Contents

Part 5: Resources

Activities

Foreword

A message from Phyllis Booth to all of you who have been introduced to Theraplay[1] *and have chosen this book to help you put Theraplay into practice.*

I would like to tell you the story of how Theraplay came into being.

You have been introduced to Theraplay at a stage in its development when it is solidly established as a successful, evidence-based intervention model for helping families and their children with a wide range of presenting issues, from mild behavior problems and unhappiness to difficult, puzzling behaviors stemming from severe developmental trauma. It has also been used successfully for people of all ages, from very young to very old. Vivien, Dafna and I thought it a good idea that you hear my story about the beginnings of Theraplay so that you will understand the richness of the approach and how it grew to be what it is today.

Theraplay grew out of a long collaboration between Ann Jernberg and me. It was Ann who had the courage to try a new and innovative approach in order to help the children she was working with. Just after Theraplay was launched, I joined her in her efforts to understand and explain why this natural, playful approach was working so well.

But to go back to the beginning. Ann and I met in 1949 at the University of Chicago Nursery School. I was a newly minted "headteacher" and Ann Marschak was my assistant teacher. We were both in our early twenties. In 1950, my husband and I left Chicago to join the faculty of a liberal arts college in Indiana where he taught English and I was headteacher in the cooperative nursery school on campus. As time went by, I found myself advising parents about how to handle various issues with their children. I soon realized that I needed to get more training in order to do that well, so I made plans to go back to grad school. In 1962, my family—by then including our three children—and

---

1 A registered service mark of The Theraplay Institute, 1840 Oak Avenue, Suite 320, Evanston, Illinois 60201.

I returned to the University of Chicago where I pursued my studies toward a degree in clinical psychology. Ann had stayed in Chicago, completed her doctorate in clinical psychology, married Pete Jernberg and had two little girls.

In 1967, Ann was appointed head of Psychological Services for the city-wide Chicago Head Start program. Learning that I was back in Chicago, she called to ask me to join her team of psychological consultants. Our plan was to go into Head Start classrooms, observe the children and consult with the teachers in order to identify children who needed psychological help. During that first summer, we found more than 200 children who needed help. The second step of the plan was to refer the children to the appropriate social agencies, public and private, for treatment. But we faced a big problem: there were no agencies in all of Chicago that were prepared to treat that many preschool children.

Not satisfied with having identified the need and then doing nothing to meet it, Ann came up with the innovative idea that we recruit and train lively, engaging people to go into the schools and work individually with each child who needed help. Ann had worked as a psychologist at Michael Reese Hospital in Chicago and was still in touch with many of the staff there. One of the staff, Dr. Viola Brody, told Ann about a young woman, Ernestine Thomas, who had been hired for clerical work at the Dysfunctioning Child Center, an outpatient clinic at Michael Reese. Ernestine was so good at helping children that she had been encouraged to work with them therapeutically. She interacted with the children in a relaxed, playful and respectful way that drew them out of their fearful shells and brought them to life.

Viola Brody's unconventional manner of working also influenced Ann's approach to treatment. A former music teacher, now a trained child therapist, Vi held the children and rocked and sang to them until they settled and were calm. Ann believed that we could meet the needs of the Head Start children by using a similar direct, interactive model, so clearly based on what parents do naturally and comfortably with their own children. Ann hired Ernestine Thomas as the first Head Start therapist. Soon she hired other non-professionals, including a few Head Start parents.

In 1969, in order to demonstrate to the world the effectiveness of this playful, face-to-face, relationship-based approach, Ann made an award-winning film called *Here I Am*. Three years later, she was able to add a follow-up section. She found two of the children and filmed them as they interacted in a lively, cooperative way with their peers. The changes which the teachers had observed after just two months of treatment had been maintained over the years.

As time went on and the program grew, we contacted everyone we knew— my younger daughter, by then a senior in High School, joined the team. My husband, a professor in the English department at the University of Chicago, worked with three little boys at a nearby Head Start. Soon we found that we had to go beyond the limited number of people we knew, so we put an advertisement in the Chicago newspaper asking people to apply for the job. In order to recruit the liveliest, most sensitive and attuned people, we organized "interview days" at our Michigan Avenue Head Start office. A dozen or so people gathered, mostly in their early twenties. We asked them to role-play what they might do with a child they wanted to get to know and to help. We hired those who had an easy, playful manner and showed the most sensitivity and creativity.

We asked them to work one on one with each child assigned to them and to respond to the children in a natural, spontaneous manner, face to face, with no need for props or toys, simply inviting the child to join them in joyful, interactive play, and calming and comforting them when needed. We counted on the new recruits' natural, instinctual abilities to engage the children and to create a better experience for them.

They met with each child two or three times a week, taking them out of the classroom to any quiet place they could find within the school building. I often found myself working with a child in the space under a stairway or between the entry doors to the school building. Occasionally there was an empty classroom I could use. In those days, we didn't have pillows and blankets but we brought along bean bags or other small items from the classroom. Mostly we improvised activities that didn't require any materials at all.

We met in weekly supervisory sessions with Ann and Ernestine as our supervisors. We talked about our experiences. We role-played interactions that had been difficult and tried to find better ways to manage. Although I had a lot of experience with children as a nursery school teacher, I needed these opportunities to talk about and fine tune my work as much as the new recruits. One day I found myself stuck on the idea of the "adult takes charge," in a way that ended in a tugging match with my role-playing partner over who would take off her socks—a scenario that had played out that week in one of my Head Start sessions. Ernestine, in her supervisory role, came along and deftly diverted the struggle: "Let's see who can get the other one's sock off fastest?" The mood instantly changed: the socks came off, and we moved on to another playful activity.

We often found that as we played with the children, we gathered ideas for games and activities from our own childhood experiences. Or together we came up with new activities that we could use to engage and delight the children as well as to calm and comfort them. Sometimes, new activities grew out of our interactions with the children we worked with. For example, the Bean Bag Drop game, which has become a stand-by in our repertoire of activities, grew out of my effort to connect with a little boy who frantically tried to avoid all interactions, with anyone in the classroom and certainly with me, a stranger coming in from the outside. I found myself crawling under tables and around chairs trying to get near him as he fled from my approach. Finally, I got close enough to but a bean bag on his head. As I had expected, he ducked his head and I caught the bean bag. I smiled and put it back on his head. He ducked again, but this time when I caught it, he looked up, just a little bit interested. When I put it on my head, he glanced up to watch it drop into my hands. Soon he joined the game, taking turns with me catching the bean bag. This bit of improvised activity was the beginning of several months of play which ended at the year-end "graduation party" where he boldly volunteered to stand up and smash the piñata in front of the whole class and his proud father.

As part of our weekly supervisory sessions, we helped each other reflect on our own and the children's emotional responses in order to be more attuned to each child's needs. We needed this understanding in order to provide a new and enticing experience for them that would be reassuring and helpful. We were creating a team of sensitive, attuned and lively people who began to make a difference in the lives of the Head Start children they worked with.

Soon, teachers began to see changes in the children we were working with. Sad, withdrawn, frightened children became livelier and more outgoing; angry, aggressive, acting-out children calmed down and were able to engage with others in a friendly, cooperative way. We averaged 15 sessions for each child, a relatively quick change for children who had seemed so hard to reach or so out of control.

But I have skipped ahead a bit in telling my story. I was not actually in Chicago in 1969–70 when the program was launched and the first part of the film made. I was in London, studying at the Tavistock Centre where I was introduced to attachment theory through weekly lectures by John Bowlby, whose first book, *Attachment and Loss*, was published in 1969. Each week, James and Joyce Robertson presented their films, which documented the devastating effects of loss on young children. And I attended case conferences with Donald Winnicott, whose work is a wonderful reminder of the healing power of relationships as well as the importance of play.

When I returned to Chicago, Ann showed me the film, *Here I Am*, and the newly remodeled office space designed for Theraplay sessions. It had two observation rooms and equipment for filming sessions. I was excited and was soon swept up in the Theraplay approach. This was the room in which we held our supervision sessions for Head Start mental health workers, where we taught our first Theraplay courses and ran a private clinic for families who sought help for their children. The room was filled with wonderful, big pillows, soft mats on the floor and very little else.

Although we had not been able to include many Head Start parents in our sessions with their children, we always included parents in our work at the clinic. Ann would sit with them in one of the observation rooms and help them understand what was happening with their child as Chuck West and I, or any of a number of other Theraplay practitioners over the years, were doing with their child. The parents would join us in the Theraplay room when we called for them.

Fresh from my introduction to Bowlby's attachment theory and the work of Donald Winnicott, I found myself applying what I had learned to our work with the Head Start children. I remember saying to Ann, "We are providing Winnicott's holding environment," by which I meant that we were creating the safe, supportive and engaging relationship that the children needed. We were changing the children's "inner working models" (a Bowlby concept), their view of themselves and the world, from negative to positive. Our team of mental health workers were creating a new, more positive experience for each child. Each child learned that they were valued, competent and delightful in the eyes of their mental health worker, their teachers and their parents. They could count on people being kind, responsive and warm. The world was no longer a frightening, threatening place. Our effort to replicate the positive interactions of parents with their babies was paying off. It was some years later that I found Bowlby's statement, which supports our clinical application of attachment theory. He says, "The pattern of interaction adopted by the mother of a secure infant provides an excellent model for the pattern of therapeutic intervention..." (Bowlby, 1988, p.126).

Over the 50 years since we first began working with the Head Start children, there has been an outpouring of research stimulated by attachment theory. The focus initially was on aspects of the parent-child relationship: What kinds of interaction lead to secure attachment? What makes it possible for parents to respond in these good ways? The interaction between parents and babies has been looked at closely to see the nuances of the interactive dance. There is a strong emphasis on the importance of co-regulation between a parent and young baby that leads to the gradual development of self regulation. More recently, neuroscience has made it possible to understand the powerful effect these early interactions have on the developing brain of the child.

Much of this research confirms our sense that we were on the right track when we took the healthy parent-child model for our therapeutic work. It has also given us new insights into how to understand the responses of children and parents and how to fine tune our work.

Having told you my story of Theraplay, I want now to talk about this book and how you can make use of it. Your interest in adding Theraplay to your set of skills for working with children indicates that you are open to new ways to provide the best possible experience for the children who come to you for help. You are the next generation of young—all of you are young from my point of view—people who are ready to provide the attuned, sensitive, engaging and calming experiences that our children need in order to become whole and happy people.

You have taken Level One Theraplay training and made the decision to put the training into practice. We cannot offer you the weekly, in person, supervision sessions which we had the good fortune to be able to provide in the old Theraplay office in Chicago. But Vivien and Dafna wrote this book to give you the detailed guidance that will help you get started. It shares the wisdom and experience of the many practitioners around the world who have used Theraplay to help children and families.

We also hope that you will find ways to get together with others in our Theraplay family to share ideas and learn from each other. If Theraplay is a good fit for you, we strongly recommend that you enter the practicum program to get the supervision that will help you become a certified Theraplay practitioner.

Phyllis Booth

Acknowledgements

This book has developed over a long period and has been influenced by our work with many colleagues and clients and we are very grateful to them all. Thank you to our wonderful colleagues in the international Theraplay community, The Theraplay Institute and The Family Place. Thank you to colleagues who have provided invaluable comments on individual chapters (Fiona Peacock, Julie McCann, Erika Lyons), and in particular to Sandra Lindaman for detailed feedback on the theory chapter. Thanks to several colleagues who kindly reviewed the whole text (Charlotte Elliott, Andrea Bushala, Katherine Lott and Gillian Engberg), to Annie Keirmaier, Nicole Charney and Mandy Jones for their contribution to Chapter 9 and to Jennie Forsyth for her contribution to Chapter 18. Thank you to Andrea Bushala (again) for compiling the Theraplay activities in Chapter 23. We are very grateful to the Theraplay student and the family she worked with who generously consented to share the anonymized supervision notes contained in the book.

We took on the task of writing this book in the spirit of collaboration across continents. The experience of co-writing without meeting face to face has been surprisingly straightforward with the use of email and Skype. Our disparate backgrounds (Malaysia, UK, Israel, US) had no bearing on our ability to share the richness of our Theraplay worlds. We have both hugely appreciated each other's support in the joint endeavor.

We deeply appreciate our partners, Michael and Jonathan, for their support—and our children, for their patience while we have been unavoidably preoccupied.

Lastly, we want to express our sincere gratitude to Phyllis Booth who painstakingly reviewed all of the chapters and provided invaluable feedback and gave us the encouragement and support needed to complete the book.

Introduction

Chapter 1

Introduction

Theraplay is an intervention that focuses on enhancing the connection, trust and joy between a child and a parent. The method involves interactive, playful activities using simple face-to-face reciprocal interactions, and involves using all of the senses, including rhythm, movement and touch.

In writing this book, we have searched for a structure that will both faithfully represent the Theraplay approach in practice and be of most use to the reader. The basic Theraplay "method" may seem straightforward and yet within sessions the practitioner is faced with frequent decision points that may have a wide range of impacts, unique to each child-parent pair. The effort of trying to understand and helpfully respond to a child's moment-to-moment reactions in any given interaction is as complex a task as in any in-depth therapy process.

The paradox of Theraplay is its combined simplicity and complexity. The simple activities and structured framework allow people to quickly access the model and understand the core elements. Theraplay can in some cases be impactful without an in-depth understanding of why it works, and this makes it highly accessible. At the same time, the attention to detail and observation of constantly shifting moments allows endless possibilities in terms of understanding the complexity of relational interaction.

It can be helpful to differentiate between the "nuts and bolts" of Theraplay, how it is set up, the structure of sessions, the activities and so on from the reflection and constant adjusting that is going on in the practitioner's mind behind the scenes. Where the practicalities may be seen as the "method," what lies behind this—the theory, reflection, deepening of skill development of the practitioner—is the power house. Our focus in this book is to try to build a picture of the power house that feeds into this apparently simple approach. This book focuses on work with children and their parents, though Theraplay itself can be used with a wide range of populations. We have kept a practical and practitioner-based focus throughout the book while embedding theoretical constructs and reflection into our discussion and we hope that this captures the spirit of Theraplay as it actually happens.

It is not possible to cover all areas or eventualities in one book and we refer you to other publications where relevant, including your Level One Theraplay training handout.

Who is the book for and how is it organized?

This book is intended as a guide to practitioners who have completed the core Theraplay training provided by accredited Theraplay Institute trainers. It could also be helpfully used as an accompaniment to the training. Our aim is to deepen your understanding about the key principles involved in Theraplay practice and to add insight for those of you who wish to understand the Theraplay approach in more depth. It is not an alternative to undertaking the training but, we hope, a useful addition. The book may also be of interest to therapeutic practitioners working in different modalities and to those who wish to know more about Theraplay practice. We have approached writing this book by asking ourselves the kinds of questions we might ask during and following a session or in supervision, such as:

- What do I think the child might be experiencing in this moment?

- How about the parent?

- Why did I decide to do that activity in that way?

- What was I hoping for and how did it go?

- Do I think my response helped the child feel more or less comfortable? What makes me think that?

- What was it about the way I adjusted my responses in that moment that might have had the impact?

- Are the child's non-verbal body responses congruent with what the child seems to be expressing verbally?

This list could go on. A great deal of the work in developing sensitive Theraplay practice involves very close observation of the child and parent and a high level of self-reflection in terms of our own responses and behaviors. Theraplay practice makes significant use of video recording of sessions for reflection, unpicking what may be going on moment to moment, trying to build a picture by tracking patterns and sequences, noticing "moments of meeting" between the child and practitioner or child and parent and trying to understand elements of strength and vulnerability for all involved. As the practitioner becomes more skilled in the process of delivering Theraplay and in this micro-analysis of interactions, she becomes more able to be highly attuned within the sessions and to adapt and provide work with sensitivity and purpose. Much of the work relies on practitioner intuition, getting a "feel" for what might be helpful, as well as being able to develop and learn through the training and supervision process. People differ widely in their capacity to do this. We hope that this book brings to life some of the reflection behind the scenes and the dilemmas, challenges and joys of participating in Theraplay.

The book is divided into different parts. Part 1 covers the overarching Theraplay principles. We have woven a range of theoretical constructs into our summary of the principles that guide the work.

Part 2 considers the "nuts and bolts" of Theraplay in practice and reflects on these elements. Starting with the Marschak Interaction Method (MIM) assessment (a structured observational assessment that forms the initial part of a Theraplay intervention) and moving on to how to set up the room, choose activities and manage a wide array of situations with both children and parents, our aim is to provide a sense of the lived experience of engaging in Theraplay. Throughout this section of the book we have included some typical practice questions and case examples.

Our case examples are used to enliven the discussion and are drawn from both specific experiences we have had in sessions or supervision and also invented examples based on experience. All examples are anonymized. In most examples, we talk in the first person, as if we were actually in the room at the time, to help create a feeling of "in the moment reflection" about how the situation is unfolding. We hope this gives an experience as close as possible to live supervision.

Part 3 looks at the development of a Theraplay practitioner and considers the typical developmental phases a practitioner might go through when learning about the Theraplay approach. There are parallels, too, in the experiences reported by children and parents. We then move on to look at the supervision process.

Part 4 provides some examples of completed supervision forms. The Theraplay approach rests on some basic underlying assumptions that can challenge prior expectations about what therapeutic help might look like. For this reason, it can be experienced as quite a shift in approach.

Part 5 provides a range of different useful resources, including checklists and handouts for parents, examples of sessions for different age groups and an up-to-date list of Theraplay activities.

Notes on terminology

"Parent" is used throughout the book to describe the range of caregivers who provide an everyday parenting role for the children they are caring for, including birth parents, foster carers, adoptive parents and residential workers—anyone who is caring for children in a parenting capacity.

"Child" refers to children of all ages. When referring to children, we have alternated between male and female throughout the book. We acknowledge that there are children who are non-binary in their gender identity.

"Practitioner" is the term used to describe the professional who is delivering the Theraplay intervention. The practitioner may have a wide range of additional core qualifications. When referred to in the text the pronoun we use is "she."

"Student" refers to someone who is learning about Theraplay and is not yet fully qualified. Within this context, the Theraplay student will already be a professional working with children with a range of other qualifications.

The case examples of work presented come from a range of sources. Some are invented for the purposes of illustrating a point, others are amalgamated examples from our practice, all heavily disguised.

We have described a wide range of activities and perspectives throughout this book. We would like to acknowledge that the way in which families interact and play and the roles professional helpers may take differ greatly across families and cultures. We are inevitably influenced by our own culture and appreciate that adaptations may be needed to suit different contexts.

In writing this book, we have drawn on the work of a wide range of academic and clinical professionals. We have included a full reference list at the back and refer to specific authors when their work is first mentioned within the introductory section of the book, which is more focused on theoretical links. We have not repeated referencing in the more discursive section of the book as it breaks the flow of discussion. We acknowledge the deep influence others have had on our thinking.

Chapter 2

Theraplay® Guiding Principles

--- CHAPTER PLAN ---

This chapter will discuss the following areas:

Theory base summary

Safety and reciprocal social engagement

- The social engagement system primer

Attunement and co-regulation

- Use of face-to-face play
- Provision of care and nurture
- Intersubjectivity—emotional communication about us
- Relationship repair following breaks in connection

Creating more positive inner working models and attachment patterns

- Attachment system
- Shifting intimacy demand
- Activation of the attachment system
- Gentle challenge of unhelpful patterns of relating

Guiding principles in practice

- Making sense of the child's responses and behavior in the context of relationships
- Theraplay® attitude
- Using the Theraplay® dimensions as a framework
- Following the Theraplay® protocol
- Including parents
- Keeping the non-verbal focus

- Tracking sequences and patterns
- Creating predictability
- Building in success
- Adapting to cultural differences

Adaptations to Theraplay® practice

Theraplay® research

Summary

Theraplay is an experience of safety, social engagement, regulation and security. The key to Theraplay's efficacy is not the activities! The activities are just the vehicle that facilitate connection. The key is that we lend the child, and teach the parents to lend their child, our *whole selves* to help them organize into healthier, happier people. How does this happen? Theraplay changes a child's perception of himself and what it is like to be with another person through relationship. The playful interactions are the method, the "delivery system" that the practitioner or parent uses to facilitate this change. For example, when a child is upset in a Theraplay session and pushes you away with his legs, you say, "Boy, you've got strong legs! I bet you can't push me over with these legs on the count of three!" and then hold his two feet in the palms of your hands, count to three, the child pushes and you rock backwards with a big "OOOOHHHH" sound. When you come back up, you see that the child's face has changed from defensive dysregulation to a moment of proud delight. What just happened? By reframing and organizing his rejection into a moment of reciprocal play, you have given the child an opportunity to experience himself as strong, clever and, most importantly, still *connected* to the adult, rather than bad, rejected and isolated. You have given him new meaning for what it means to be him. *That is Theraplay.*

This chapter will discuss the key principles and attitudes that underpin Theraplay practice. You need a solid understanding of these principles and the theory underlying them in order to work in a focused, purposeful and sensitive way. Each child, family and practitioner is, of course, unique but these principles are common to all coherent Theraplay practice. The following discussion is not designed to be a comprehensive explanation of the theory underlying our guiding principles, but rather to link theory and principles in an accessible way without losing sight of the depth of theoretical understanding they are based on. We will start by summarizing the core theoretical links and then move on to the principles and discussion.

If you are new to Theraplay you may prefer to concentrate on the practical applications to begin with (see Part 2). If you are more experienced you are likely to find the links between Theraplay application and theoretical constructs helpful. A detailed description of the theoretical base can be found in Lindaman and Hong (2020) and a summary can be found in Norris and Rodwell (2017).

This chapter will discuss the underpinning theoretical ideas from a practical perspective. We will then move on to look at the guiding principles and attitudes of Theraplay. We minimize the use of terminology, and a glossary is provided at the end of the book.

Theory base summary

From the very beginning, Theraplay took as its model the patterns of interaction found in healthy, secure parent-child relationships. It was found that interactive, relationship-based play helped children to become calmer, more engaged and more outgoing. Over the 50 years since then, the understanding of how and why Theraplay is effective has developed significantly and draws on a range of overlapping theories and clinical experience. With this new understanding, we summarize our understanding of the Theraplay process below.

Theraplay provides a progressive experience first of safety and reciprocal social engagement (Porges, 2011; Porges and Dana, 2018), then of co-regulation, where the parent attunes closely to the child and uses her body to help regulate the child, repairing when things go wrong (affective synchrony and interactive repair (Schore, 2003)). This culminates in the creation of more positive ways of relating (inner working models (Bowlby, 1988)) and attachment patterns (Ainsworth, 1969; Schore, 2001; Crittenden *et al.*, 2014). We will now look at each of these stages in more detail.

Safety and reciprocal social engagement

The most basic requirement for healthy development is that the caregiver, through her own physiological state and actions, engenders a state of safety and receptivity in the infant. Interactions with a newborn focus on the regulation of basic functions linked to the most primitive part of the brain, the autonomic nervous system. This includes regulation of breathing, heart rate, respiration, responses to pain, body temperature, sleep, feeding, digestion and elimination. Infants cannot regulate themselves and need their parent to help them—this process is known as co-regulation. Co-regulation can only develop in a context of safety.

In order to survive, all humans constantly make an unconscious and split-second threat analysis of their surroundings and interactions to see if they are safe. We scan for safety first before doing anything else. A positive assessment results in a "felt sense" of safety (this is known as "neuroception" of safety (Porges, 2011)). In this state, you are open to trusting others and to connecting; you are more able to tolerate emotions, to learn and to use your highest level of skills. You are in an "optimal state of arousal." This "open and engaged" state is what we are hoping to facilitate in Theraplay.

This system that we use to signal and perceive safety in other humans is described as the social engagement system (Porges's polyvagal theory, 2011). For infants and children, the message of safety is conveyed through the facial expressions, vocal tone, gesture and contact provided by the parent. A felt sense of safety and the effective use of the social engagement system are the building blocks in the formation of trusting relationships. Before we can think about attachment patterns and about how better to provide co-regulation for children, we must recognize when they are not feeling safe and find ways to create a sense of safety for them.

In contrast to an open and engaged state, if a child assesses a situation as dangerous, this results in a defensive state of hyperarousal which can lead to active attempts to fight or flee the situation (the fight-flight response). The child will not be able to trust or connect in this state. Going further, if the child assesses the situation as a life threat, this results in another kind of defense and a withdrawal of movement and energy to a shut down, even a frozen lack of response (freeze response). Again, they will not be able to trust or engage in this state.

Most children who come to us for therapeutic support will be very vulnerable to being triggered into these hyper- or hypoaroused states. As a child's neural system develops (through relationship) we see emerging patterns or bias towards more active (linked to the sympathetic nervous system) or more passive (the parasympathetic nervous system) responses which can be triggered when in a state of fear. For one child, therefore, stress may be displayed via hyperactivity, hypervigilance and hostility, whereas another child will become disconnected and lethargic. Some children can rapidly switch between states, going from frenetic activity to collapse.

When considering how we can be of help, we need to think about the contexts that can enhance feelings of safety and optimal arousal and provide the child with more of these experiences. Polyvagal theory describes two positive areas which are very relevant to Theraplay:

1. How experiences of play and care can help the social engagement system develop and support a state of optimal arousal.

2. How resilience develops by moving between states of greater and lesser arousal and between states of safety.

The Theraplay process gives both the child and the caregiver *new ways* to enter and stay in a safe, socially engaged state and to practice moving between states of arousal (Lindaman and Mäkelä, 2018). This process is illustrated below in Figure 2.1.

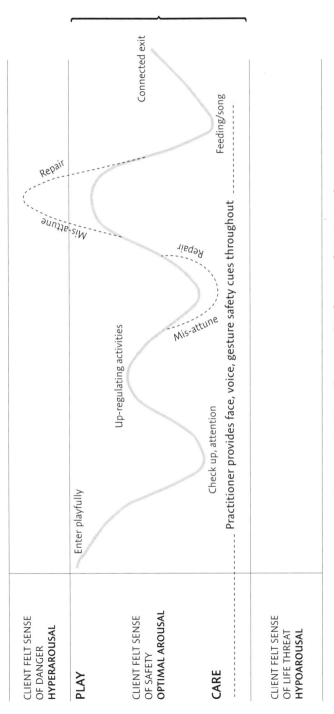

1 Practitioner observes the parent-child interaction (MIM) and plan intervention accordingly
2 This chart is about the child in sessions. The practitioner uses her safe face, voice and gestures to create a felt sense of safety for the child
3 Practitioner attunes and synchronizes with the child during guided reciprocal play and care (Structure, Engagement, Nurture, Challenge)
4 When mis-attunement and other factors result in dysregulation, the practitioner repairs and helps the child regain optimal arousal
5 Over time, this improves regulation and promotes resilience and more secure attachment patterns

Windows of tolerance

CLIENT FELT SENSE OF DANGER **HYPERAROUSAL**

PLAY

Enter playfully

Repair

Mis-attune

Up-regulating activities

CLIENT FELT SENSE OF SAFETY **OPTIMAL AROUSAL**

Repair

Mis-attune

Connected exit

Feeding/song

CARE

Check up, attention

Practitioner provides face, voice, gesture safety cues throughout

CLIENT FELT SENSE OF LIFE THREAT **HYPOAROUSAL**

Figure 2.1: The Theraplay process (Lindaman and Norris, 2019)

The Theraplay model has always acknowledged the importance of the practitioner's social engagement through facial, vocal and gestural, proximity and contact cues, and because we now have science to support our practice, we will spend a bit more time describing this central feature.

The social engagement system primer

Theraplay is about social engagement, connection and reciprocity. We all know people who seem to have the magic touch when it comes to relating to others. They have a way of calming a tense situation and putting people at ease and can instantaneously connect with clients. It's great to have that just-right timing and manner that gets a sullen teenager to crack a smile and that helps calm a wary client.

Voice prosody

The basis of the social engagement system (known as the SES) is the connection of the vagus nerve with nerves that supply the muscles we use in the actions of looking, facial expressions, vocalizing, listening, chewing, sucking, swallowing, breathing and gesturing with the head. This forms a link between body sensations and vocalization, facial expression and head movements. One outcome is that the nervous system can be calmed or aroused by the facial expressions and vocalizations of another person.

Prosody consists of the timing, phrasing, emphasis and intonation of sound, which all help convey aspects of emotional meaning and make our speech lively, convincing and engaging. It is conveyed by raising and lowering the pitch of voice, speeding up or slowing down the rhythm of our sentences and varying the loudness of our voice. Even the frequency of breathing can convey a sense of urgency or calmness. The effective use of prosody creates a sense that you're really attending to and understanding another person. It's also a feature of storytelling that keeps listeners interested and curious, holding their attention and thereby organizing and calming their nervous system. Although Theraplay is primarily non-verbal, voice prosody still impacts hugely.

Imagine a father chatting with his baby while dressing her on the changing table. The "dialogue" goes something like this:

Father: (pulling the arm out of the baby's pajama shirt) Where's Bella's arm? Ooooh, there it is! You're getting so biiigggg.

Bella: Ba!

Father: (in a high-pitched, excited tone) That's right! Big! Who's a big girl?

Bella: (making a gurgling, babbling noise with her lips) Brrrrrrrrrrrr.

Father: (putting the shirt over Bella's head, speaking with increasing volume and inflection in his voice) Where did you go? Where did you go, Bella? (pulls shirt to discover baby's eyes) Boo!

Bella: (looking momentarily startled, then smiling wide, wiggling her whole body and squealing as she giggles)

Father: You're so silly. You're so silly. I got your tummy (leans down to blow raspberries on baby's belly). I got your belly!

Bella: (kicks legs and lets out another, louder squeal)

Father: You're so funny, aren't ya, little girl?

Later, when they're in the kitchen, Bella's father uses the coffee grinder, and Bella is startled by the growling, loud noise. She gasps in shock and then lets out a shrill cry.

Father: (speaking with quick, urgent breaths) Oh! Oh, Bella! Come here (picks her up from high chair). Oh, that startled you, didn't it? Cos you didn't know what that was (shifts to speak in soft, cooing, slow voice as he rocks her). You were looking at your banana, and then Daddy made that loud grrrrrrrr noise from the coffee grinder, and you didn't know what that was. I'm sorry, baby. It's okay.

Bella: (quickly shifts from a scream to a whimper and then sighs as she settles her head on her father's shoulder)

This parent-infant dialogue is the essential foundation for prosody in human beings. Humans use that voice instinctively while tending to babies because babies are biologically programmed to hear higher-pitched tones, which lilt up and down. They capture the baby's attention and make her calmer, more organized and more amenable to the parents' suggestions and handling. Conversely, babies experiencing felt safety, as in our example, aren't so able to interpret the lower-pitch, grumbly noises that naturally signal danger (like a lion's roar) or the monotonous sounds, usually lower in pitch, that seem controlled and unemotional.

Most successful therapeutic practitioners, regardless of theoretical orientation, make good use of their prosodic voice as an essential component of conveying empathy.

Resonance
Related to prosody, another factor that elicits trust is resonance. From a therapeutic perspective, resonance is about connecting with and amplifying the other person's vitality affects, their feelings. It helps the person you're

communicating with to feel convinced that you understand the intensity of their feelings (Malloch Trevarthen, 2009). You accurately attune and help regulate the other person's affective state (Fosha, Siegel and Solomon, 2009). This feature of communication is important when a client is feeling intense emotion and is frightened by that intensity and the negative effect it might have on the relationship.

From a physiological perspective, resonance involves using the body to vibrate in sympathy with the sound of your voice. It comes when you open up your lungs (breathe deep), open up your throat (yawn) or sing with a smile, as this raises your soft palate, which helps stimulate the vagal system and relaxes your jaw (Porges, 2011). The more relaxed you are and the more space you create in your body cavity, the more resonance you'll produce. Singing, especially in company, amplifies this effect. Much like in music, when you pluck one string and a nearby string vibrates, when you are able to synchronize and match the affect of the client you are with, it is as if you're vibrating at the same frequency as your client to show, "I understand you" (Schore, 2001).

The combination of the above helps create the possibility of close attunement that can be experienced in a bodily way. This is routinely used within Theraplay as a way to catch the focus of the child you are with by matching the state they are in in some way—for instance, using a faster and more animated voice if they are being very active.

Picture an angry teenager who's been given the ultimatum of going to you for therapy or having his screen time taken away indefinitely. He's resentful, hostile and defensive as he sits in your office. He stares sullenly at the wall, and when you try to connect with him, he lets out a tirade: "I don't know why I have to come to this stupid place every week! I only came because my mom told me she'd take my phone! I know you're the one who told her to do that!" An outburst like this can cause even the most experienced therapist to momentarily retreat inward in defense. This position will constrict your throat and lungs, and you'll produce a thinner, more monotonous vocal tone, which may contribute to the client getting more upset. Why? Because he sensed your retreat, and his worst fear—that he's no good—is confirmed.

The emphasis in Theraplay is on maintaining an open and engaged stance, even in the face of provocative behavior. The movement and activity inherent in Theraplay help the practitioner to regulate and take a deep breath so that they can produce a more convincing response.

Facial expressions

A second aspect of communication in the social engagement system is the use of facial expressions to elicit trust. The facial expressions that evoke positive social states include having a genuine smile, a focused, curious look in your eyes, and a wide, smooth (unfurrowed) brow and forehead.

As an example, in a genuine smile, the eyes close a little as the muscles around the eyes tense, wrinkles appear on the sides of the eyes because the face muscles pull the cheeks up and make them bigger, and the skin under the lower lip tightens so the bottom teeth get covered up. In other words, you're smiling with your eyes. By evoking a warm smile on greeting a reluctant child, you are unconsciously affecting their brain, signaling the message "Give it a chance; it could turn out all right." In effect, you are overriding their own internal message and choosing an incongruent response of, "Yes, I know you're fearful, but I'm still open to you."

Another powerful message of safety is signaled through your eyebrows and forehead, which play an important role in indicating true acceptance and curiosity about another person's negative feeling states. When children or parents have been exposed to high levels of judgment and negative evaluation, they can be hypersensitive to pensive looks or a furrowed brow. Managing the muscles around your eyes, ears and forehead can help correct that effect, so that you can send your preferred message: "I'm truly open and curious about you." A more open, smooth browline and forehead signals receptivity rather than suspicion or judgment.

Another key illustrator of safety is the use of gestures, both of the head and hands, as well as one's overall posture. All of us are reassured when body language is congruent with the emotion that is being communicated. As an example, leaning forward is a sign of intense interest and can be used mindfully to show focus and investment in the client.

Hand gestures go along with body posture. The degree to which we use gestures to convey or emphasize a point varies from culture to culture (Italian more, Scandinavian less). However, it's universally accepted that using gestures can set the listener's brain at ease because it helps make your message congruent and clear. Non-verbal gestures are used routinely in Theraplay to provide clarity about what is going to happen next (e.g. holding hands together to catch a bean bag) as well as to express emotion (e.g. cheering, arms up, when something has been achieved).

Eye contact and touch

When interacting with another person, we tend to look in a sustained way at the speaker to show our interest and attention. But beyond that, what in your eyes lets people know you're really interested? What produces bright eyes, rather than a dull look? One answer can be found in the difference between the meaning of the two words looking and gazing. Looking simply refers to the act of directing your eyes in a particular direction, whereas gazing refers to the act of looking at something in a steady way, usually for a longer time. Additionally, the pupils in the eyes of a listener who is really engaged will dilate or get larger. Although this is imperceptible to the naked eye, the brain registers this subtle difference as a signal of genuine interest. Many Theraplay activities involve this very close attention to the other person and expressions of deep interest, such as looking into their eyes to see their color or singing in a personalized way.

Finally, the therapeutic use of touch is a powerful signaler of safety when applied in an attuned way. Touch is incorporated into the Theraplay modality from start to finish and there is a significant literature to support the fundamental importance of touch to development and well-being (Field, 1990). Even for adults or clients who are wary of touch, there's a strong argument to be made for incorporating calming or reassuring touch. With permission and awareness of the client's physiologic responses, you can integrate touch into activities and can gently press a client's hand or place a hand on the client's shoulder. Even approximating warm touch when direct contact isn't appropriate can be effective. For example, preparing a warm mug of tea for clients to grasp, having plush throw blankets of various textures available for them to hold or drape around their shoulders, or having various weighted pillows for them to clutch can provide tremendous comfort to calm and contain feelings of vulnerability.

Theraplay® is founded on your social engagement system

The most elegant way to put all these social engagement mechanisms to use is through sequences of play and care.

Porges considers play an important neural exercise in practicing detecting trust versus danger in relationships. A game of hide and seek illustrates this learning perfectly. Since the hider can't see the seeker, she is unable to pick up on the safety cues of the seeker's face and voice. This creates uncertainty in the hider. The tension rises as the seeker comes closer, until she finally finds the hider and calls, "Got you!" This produces a startling effect in both players. But after the initial discovery, the players show warm facial expressions and a gentle voice to re-establish connection and safety. Lots of Theraplay games produce similar surges of energy, risk and connection.

Take, for example, the Feather Pass game, in which two people stand face to face and one blows a fluffy feather up and toward her partner, and the partner blows it back. The volley continues for as long as possible before the feather hits the ground. The feather floats and dodges in funny ways as it is passed, so each player has to really attune to the other's movements and engage in quite a bit of acrobatics to continue the exchange. Sometimes the partners are so invested that they dive to the floor to keep the sequence going. The net effect is that of joy and amusement as the pair experiences their shared investment in the silliness of the joint endeavor. This type of activity is priceless in family therapy when a sullen or depressed child is unwilling to engage in any conversation. Play shouldn't be limited to young clients and their families. The power of play can be harnessed to create movement and healing in adult clients when more conventional methods aren't doing the trick.

Attunement and co-regulation

A great deal of focus in any Theraplay interaction will be on maintaining a manageable state of regulation, for the child, for the parent and for you as the practitioner. When everyone is calm and well regulated, all sorts of possibilities open up.

Co-regulation develops in the context of relational safety and close attunement to the infant's physiological and emotional state. A sensitive and closely attuned parent will naturally synchronize with the baby or child in a myriad of unconscious ways (including tempo, rhythmic choice of words, timbre and the matching of pitch intensity and affect) and will pick up on the infant's subtle cues. The adult's state of regulation and sensitive attunement supports the baby's state (known as co-regulation). When the synchrony and connection are disrupted for any reason, the parent will try to find a way to reconnect (interactive repair). The ability to self-regulate (physiologically, emotionally and behaviorally) develops from the foundation of this responsive early years care. Our early experiences have a profound impact on our ability to cope with stress and on the development of our emotional and sensory processing systems. Children who have experienced trauma typically struggle to self-regulate across environments. They have not had enough experiences of safe shifts in state and experience life through a "fear lens" (Perry, 2001), making it hard for them to trust or rely on others.

Theraplay can be understood as a "moment-to-moment" experience of co-regulation of both physiological and affective states (Lindaman and Mäkelä, 2018). The practitioner attunes and establishes synchrony with the child's state and leads the child and parent through a sequence of playful (up-regulating) and soothing (down-regulating) activities. As illustrated in Figure 2.1, this sequence creates opportunities for many joyful and quiet moments and the practitioner will quickly try to repair the connection with the child if they mis-attune and lose this connection. Your aim as a Theraplay practitioner is to develop a detailed understanding of and feeling for the child's regulation state, to become aware of whether they need up or down regulation and to find ways to help them remain within their window of tolerance.

Use of face-to-face play

The way we work on attunement and regulation is via a particular kind of play and care. Many child therapies use play. The play of Theraplay is distinguished by face-to-face, synchronous interactions using movement, proximity and touch, all characteristics of what Porges calls "polyvagal play" (Lindaman and Mäkelä, 2018). This kind of play is reciprocal and the practitioner is constantly aware of the responses and regulatory state of the child. Via the play, the practitioner engages the social engagement system of the child and provides repeated practice opportunities for up and down regulation. The practitioner provides a range of social cues to try and support the child to remain in a regulated state and avoid triggering a stress response. The aim is that the child will begin to connect and be more able to form a relationship rather than reacting defensively. This kind of play sequence might be described as a "neural exercise" in state regulation (Porges, 2011; Lindaman and Mäkelä, 2018).

Provision of care and nurture

Equally important is the provision of care and comfort which helps calm and soothe the nervous system. Helping a child to genuinely relax and to sink into moments of calm and comfort is often a key aim in our work and is hugely beneficial to the child.

The care or nurture aspects of Theraplay are unique in child therapy and include singing, rocking, feeding, paying attention to the body and caring for hurts. These activities help to calm the neural system (Panksepp, 2005; Porges, 2011) and help children experience safe provision of comfort. This combination of sequences up-regulating and down-regulating elements of Theraplay, in the context of safety, is a core strength of the approach.

Theraplay provides a wide range of activities that have different regulatory impacts, and the way in which you do an activity can also create a specific impact. For example, blowing bubbles randomly will evoke excitement and energy, perfect for an under-aroused child, whereas blowing an individual bubble, placing it on a wand and asking the child to pop it with their elbow provides a calming structure, which is good for a child who needs organizing. Once you are feeling confident that you understand a child's particular needs well enough and are able to influence shifts in their state, then you can stretch them a little, extending an activity or trying something a little more risky. More specific guidance on Theraplay adaptations with respect to sensory regulation can be found in Chapter 18.

Intersubjectivity—emotional communication about us

Intersubjectivity is a connected but different concept to attachment and refers to the to and fro connected experiences of relating, which are also crucial in the development of strong relationships. Intersubjective connection requires attunement, shared attention and shared intention (you are both focusing on something with a shared purpose). Intersubjective relationships are symmetrical in that both parties (e.g. adult and child) are equal members in the dialogue, with one person's response impacting on and amplifying the others. You make a funny face, your child begins to laugh, you do the funny face again, they laugh more and this amplifies your pleasure and you continue with ever sillier faces. This example illustrates "primary intersubjectivity," which is the developmental stage of reciprocity based on two people interacting directly with each other without a third play object (like a toy). The emphasis in Theraplay on "here and now" connection (in the moment and focused on the people involved in the interaction) stems from our understanding that primary intersubjectivity is an early developmental building block on which later development rests.

Babies learn intersubjectivity via play with their parent (playing peeping games, singing during diaper changes, mirroring). As the baby matures, they master the ability to focus on something outside the dyad, and begin to do things like point at objects (and their parent will look too) or drop things in the delight that their parent will retrieve them. This ability to share attention and intention with another person about a third object (e.g. baby and parent look together at the dog and laugh) is known as secondary intersubjectivity. Within Theraplay, the main focus is on primary intersubjectivity, and many activities involve simple and direct face-to-face engagement. Other activities use simple props (e.g. foil, feathers) and there may be a combination of primary and secondary intersubjective experience taking place—for example, you are making a foil sculpture of the child's hand and everyone is focusing intently on this (secondary intersubjectivity), then you admire what you have made and focus on the child and notice how amazing they are (primary intersubjectivity).

The reason it is helpful to be familiar with this concept is that children who have missed out on the basic development of primary intersubjective connection (for whatever reason) will need to go back to this way of connected playing in order to naturally progress. It doesn't matter what age the child is. You may, for instance, meet an older child who can seemingly play well, they may appear able to use symbolic play and toys (usually this play will be on their own terms and be quite repetitive) and yet when you try to connect with them in a more intimate way (e.g. join in with new ideas), the child will not be able to tolerate this. The play is not reciprocal. You are likely to find that this child finds spontaneous to and fro very hard, and that they don't know how to relate using primary intersubjectivity. This can then become the focus of your Theraplay work and you will explore ways to help this child relax and engage in a genuinely intersubjective manner with you.

Relationship repair following breaks in connection

Unlike many other child-based interventions, Theraplay focuses squarely on the parent-child relationship. Since children develop within the context of their primary relationships with their parents, this makes intuitive sense. It can also present a range of new challenges as described in more detail in Chapter 7, which focuses on the work with parents. One of the practical applications of attachment theory is our strong focus on safety within the relationship. When things go wrong (in whatever small way) it is our responsibility as the practitioner to notice and repair this with the parent or child. All strong relationships are characterized by a sequence of relationship rupture and repair; over and over we mis-time a response, notice the mistake and then apologize. The repair element is very significant because it gives the message that we have noticed that something wasn't quite right and are committed to finding a way to recreate safety and rebuild our connection. This becomes a routine way of working, and, once a trusting relationship has been established with the child and the parent, it allows mistakes to be made and recovered from.

Creating more positive inner working models and attachment patterns
Attachment system

Over time, the micro-experiences of the first year of caregiving culminate in attachment patterns and internal working models that influence the way the child sees themselves and others and directly impacts on the way they relate. When children have not, for whatever reason, developed a secure way of relating, they interpret others' responses through the lens of their early experiences. Theraplay aims to gently challenge unhelpful patterns via play and in a context of safety.

The term "attachment" is often used in a broad way and it can lose its meaning. There are some interconnected concepts in terms of relationship development and learning that can be useful to differentiate.

The attachment system refers to the process by which children seek proximity to their main carer at times of stress. It is fundamentally a system to help keep infants and children safe by looking to a key adult to help them. This is an asymmetrical relationship between the child and parent in which the child is looking towards the adult for help and not the other way around. The parent has emotional needs that are met via the relationship with their child but this is different in quality. A range of authors have explored attachment concepts in depth; some focus more on the importance of seeking safety and comfort and others more on the avoidance of threat (Hrdy, 2009; Crittenden *et al.*, 2014). For the purposes of this discussion, we are thinking about how the child typically looks towards his parent for safety cues, and for care and comfort when stressed. When parenting goes well, the child will turn to his parent when stressed and she will understand the world and how to adjust things to keep him safe and help him feel comforted. This can be seen in many everyday examples; a child is playing happily, a door slams, he immediately stops and looks towards his mother to check he is safe, she reassures him with a look and he settles down again to play. Without safety, a child cannot relax and explore the world, and so finding ways to help a child or their parent feel safe within their relationship with you is fundamental to any other work.

When a child is able to express distress and this is picked up by a sensitive adult who then provides soothing, several different systems begin to develop. The child's regulation system is being fed as the parent rocks, comforts and helps the child's internal state to calm. The child is experiencing safe reliance on an adult, which will lead to greater capacity for learning from them and a feedback loop is set in motion whereby "feelgood" hormones are released in both parent and child, who experience a state of well-being.

In terms of practical application in Theraplay, you will provide safe organization (Structure dimension), a confident lead and sensitive adjustment of demands (Challenge dimension) so that the child can feel confident that you are someone they can safely rely on. We model this approach to parents and hope that when stressed the child will seek comfort from their parent (or from you) and that you will be able to facilitate the provision of comfort (Nurture dimension). The care or nurture aspects of Theraplay are integrated into all sessions and include singing, rocking, feeding, paying attention to the body and caring for "hurts." These activities relate to the natural soothing and comfort apparent across all mammals and are crucial in calming the nervous system. Everything is done with sensitive engagement. (Panksepp, 2005; Porges, 2011).

Shifting intimacy demand

It is also helpful to know how to manage the levels of intensity of the connection you are trying to develop with a child. Primary intersubjective connection is intense and direct. For some children, it can initially be too much, and you will need to find ways to reduce the level of intensity to make it more manageable. In this situation, using props and choosing activities that lessen the intensity (by shifting the play towards secondary intersubjectivity or to parallel play) will help the child. When you gain experience about what activities work, you will find that you begin to actively use shifts in intimacy demand as a way to regulate and re-engage children.

Activation of the attachment system

Given that our aim within Theraplay is to help deepen the relationship between a child and their parent it can be disconcerting when what you are trying to helpfully provide seems to trigger the child. For example, you try to provide comfort and the child seems to find it unpleasant. This is a very common dilemma for parents of vulnerable children. What do you do when you try to provide closeness and comfort to a child but they seem to be actively working against you, and they withdraw when you try to comfort them, and especially seem to struggle with intimacy?

Remember that the attachment system is activated by fear. A clear example of when comfort and fear come together is when children have experienced relational trauma. When children have experienced early trauma "within the nest"—in other words, they suffered harm at the hands of the adults closest to them during childhood—they may experience care and personal engagement as threatening. If the adults who are supposed to protect and comfort a young child instead hurt, frighten or do not adequately respond to him then it is understandable that he will try to find ways to survive without this care. Later provision of care may elicit a range of aversive experiences for him, no matter how much he may want or need it. He may adapt in a range of ways to try and cope and typically you see under- or over-activation of the attachment system. For instance, he may become self-sufficient and display little distress when hurt, and may even not appear to feel pain. This can be described as a dampening or shutting down of the usual attachment behaviors. Alternatively, he may become increasingly dramatic, appearing to escalate situations so that he can elicit an adult response, yet when the adult comes to provide the care, the child may subtly thwart the adult's overtures. Whatever his self-protective reaction, one of the things that he misses out on is an experience of relying on and receiving nurturing care from his parent, and his parent will not have the experience of successfully providing it. This process of providing and receiving care is fundamental to the development of relationships and therefore any approach that can help refocus these behaviors in a healthy direction will be useful. The approach will need to be manageable for the child, so that he can gradually gain confidence that experiencing care is safe and pleasurable, and it will also need to be gently persistent in order to make lasting shifts in this dynamic. The parent will also need sensitive support.

Gentle challenge of unhelpful patterns of relating

One of the core aims of Theraplay is gently and persistently to find ways to challenge unhelpful attachment patterns in a context of safety (to challenge the internal working model). For children who are very self-reliant (who withdraw specifically when stressed and find provision of nurture and comfort very difficult), we will often focus on safe ways to promote comfort and safety seeking from the child and to provide support to help this feel more comfortable for them. In practice, this will often mean adjusting the intimacy demands being placed on the child (usually relating to the Engagement and Nurture dimensions) to make them less intense and so more manageable for the child.

It is worth noting here that the ordinary functioning of the attachment system and ability to relate in a relaxed manner can also be "knocked off course" by a range of contexts other than parental neglect and abuse. For instance, prematurity, early or extended medical interventions, parental absence (e.g. through illness or bereavement), experience of pain that cannot be soothed (e.g. severe eczema or reflux) or developmental issues such as autism can lead to a disrupted expression of attachment behaviors and relating. There is a tendency to link difficulties in attachment and relating with poor parenting and this is not necessarily the case.

It is also important to remember that difficulties with intersubjective connection (e.g. a child who shows a still face to their parent) deeply impact the parent in a two-way process. Most adults will have better developed cognitive abilities to make sense of their experiences, but prolonged exposure to a child who cannot manage reciprocity will impact the resilience of the parent (Baylin and Hughes, 2016).

Guiding principles in practice

This section draws the theoretical concepts together to address the question of what we do in practice. In addition to the active use of the practitioner's own social engagement system and the focus on close attunement and repair of breaks in relationship, the specific tools of Theraplay are a particular kind of play, the offering of direct care, the involvement of parents and the use of a clear framework and attitude, as described below.

Making sense of the child's responses and behavior in the context of relationships

In order to use Theraplay-based ideas in a thoughtful and effective way, you need to understand as fully as possible what is underlying the child's responses.

It is very easy to misinterpret behavior, especially when children find it hard to communicate clearly. A typical example of misinterpretation is when a child's difficult behavior is described as "controlling" or "resistant." Both descriptions have pejorative implications, when the reality is that the child is highly anxious and fearful. Since the children we work with often find it hard to put words to their experiences, making sense of their non-verbal responses is even more critical. A central priority in our Theraplay approach is the careful observation of the interaction between the parent and child, and the ongoing efforts to understand these interactions. This is the focus of the Marschak Interaction Method (MIM) assessment and should be kept in mind throughout ongoing work with the family.

The following is a list of questions you could ask yourself as the intervention progresses:

- What is going on now between us or between the child and the parent?

- Was there anything that I just did that led to their response?

- If the child is uncomfortable or dysregulated, is there something I can do right now to help make him feel more at ease?

- Looking back, why did I select that activity or way of interacting?

Don't expect to know the answer straightaway; you may have to come back to the behavior again with a new understanding another week. Children are generous as regards our ignorance. They will keep giving us opportunities to understand their communication until we do get it.

Your answers to these questions will be influenced by your level of experience and training as well as your own personal style. Consider the following questions:

- Did you do a comprehensive assessment?

- Do you have a solid grounding in child development and experience such that you can differentiate typical from atypical age-related behaviors?

- Are you able to draw on a broad range of theoretical ideas in order to make the best sense of the behavior?

- How self-aware are you?

- Do you have the time, patience and willingness to use videos to observe in detail the interaction that you are participating in?

- Can you separate out the sensations and responses that come from your own personal experience, so that you can respond in ways that are helpful to the child (transference/countertransference)?

- Can you do this reflecting while at the same time managing the here and now of the interaction?

These are all discussions you can bring to supervision.

Theraplay® attitude

There is a recognisable Theraplay attitude that is applied consistently across our work, whether it be with families, parents, children, students or trainees, which brings a strong sense of coherence to our approach. This attitude can be summed up in the simple mantra "no hurts, stick together, have fun and the adult is in charge." "No hurts" means that we are paying attention to everyone's sense of safety and well-being throughout. "Stick together" encapsulates the idea that we are working collaboratively and that we will do whatever we can to help things go well and to repair when there are ruptures in connection. "Have fun" is all about the joy, delight and healing power of reciprocal engagement. "The adult is in charge" is the basic premise that the adult is the one who is responsible for leading the session such that the first three elements of this ethos actually take place. Theraplay is a positive and hopeful approach, focused on exploring what can be possible together.

Using the Theraplay® dimensions as a framework

The four dimensions of Structure, Engagement, Nurture and Challenge (based on the elements present in healthy relationships) provide an organizing framework for all of our work. Each dimension is important and is adjusted according to the needs of the particular situation to provide safety, social engagement, co-regulation and connection for the parents and children.

Theraplay practitioners are trained to lead (Structure) parent-child interactions within safe social connection (Engagement) with up-regulating (Challenge-Play) and down-regulating (Nurture) aspects. All aspects of the Theraplay process can be considered a neural exercise that develops emotional regulation and resilience (Lindaman and Mäkelä, 2018).

Defining the dimensions

The dimensions[1] can be simply defined as follows:

- *Structure*—The adult is a reliable leader, whose actions create environmental regulation via organization, clear boundaries and clear

---

1 More detail about the dimensions is provided in your Level One handouts and in Norris and Rodwell, 2017 and Lindaman and Hong, 2020.

expectations, and relational regulation through pacing, choice of activity and level of arousal. This guidance and regulation form the basis for predictability, safety and co-regulation for the child.

- *Engagement*— Engagement is about the joy of companionship, being connected in the "here and now," being focused on in a personal way and having the sensitivity to pick up on the child's cues. These interactions allow the child to feel connected and experience shared joy.

- *Nurture*—The adult provides gentle, caring and soothing activities per session including provision of food. The adult looks for opportunities to express appreciation and concern and to take care of the child (and parent) throughout the session. These caring activities are down-regulating and stress reducing. They make the child feel valued and loveable.

- *Challenge*—The adult supports the child's development by partnering with the child in playful, physical activities that extend the levels of high and low arousal and encourage the child to try new things. Experiencing successful challenge activities creates a sense of mastery and helps the child feel more competent, confident and courageous.

Following the Theraplay® protocol

The Theraplay protocol provides a standard recommended sequence of events that have been found to be most effective. In order to deliver Theraplay effectively, you need to have attended training and be accessing supervision. It is important to learn how to deliver Theraplay as a stand-alone intervention using the established protocol in order to understand its potential impact—and that is the focus of the rest of this book.

Including parents

In Theraplay, the parent work is just as important as the child work. Theraplay's power comes from the development of social engagement and reciprocity within the parent-child relationship in ways that feel new and safe. The parent is an active participant in all sessions and the focus of the work is the *relationship between* the parent and child.

Keeping the non-verbal focus

Theraplay is principally a non-verbal way of working and we place a lot of emphasis on observation and interpretation of non-verbal responses, beginning with the MIM analysis and during sessions and video feedback. Even though most human communication is non-verbal, accurate observation of non-verbal behavior takes practice, and most practitioners will be more experienced in using language-based approaches. You will develop your skills in observing non-verbal responses such as body posture, facial response, muscle fluidity (e.g. whether the child is moving in a stiff and tense way or is floppy/displaying a drop in muscle tone, or is relaxed) and levels of activity and quiet. As you become more adept at monitoring the child's non-verbal state, you will increasingly be able to notice when there is incongruence. As an example, the child smiles and looks at you warmly but you notice that her arms are stiff and braced to her body. This is a classic example of miscuing (where the child may show one emotion facially while actually feeling another, as expressed in their non-verbal behavior).

Once you are able to pick up on the child's (and the parent's) subtle non-verbal communication and can make some sense of it, you will be able to attune much more closely and in turn be in a better position to provide helpful responses. The development of this awareness begins with very close observation. This is the principal focus of supervision. You will prepare for supervision by looking carefully at the video of one session in detail. Then you and your supervisor may look at small sequences several times or view the video without sound in order to help you develop your observation skills.

Tracking sequences and patterns

Starting with the MIM analysis, you will begin tracking sequences and patterns of behavior and responses. The use of video really helps with this process. When things are difficult in a family, parents often find it hard to see a pattern. Tracking mini-sequences that occur during Theraplay sessions can be extremely powerful. You can begin to build up a detailed picture of what kinds of situations or relational responses are too hard for the child, or you may find those that help and use these examples from sessions to bring the parent's awareness to the ways in which they may be impacting their child and vice versa. When you have seen a family over an extended period of time it is very interesting to return to look at earlier sessions or at the MIM. You will often see that the patterns you have become familiar with as you have got to know the child well have been present in some form from the beginning.

The patterns and sequences that are most important to watch for are those linked to the parent-child relationship; when the child responds to the parent in a particular way, what happens? This level of analysis helps you develop your understanding about the mini-sequences of stress arousal and comfort or co-regulation that can support the development of a more secure attachment pattern. Once you are aware of these sequences you can work towards extending those that are helpful and find ways to avoid or divert those that are not helpful.

Creating predictability

There is a great deal of research and clinical evidence that supports the idea that all mammals develop and learn through patterned, predictable and repetitive experiences (Perry, 2007). When children are able to predict what is going to happen next, they become calmer and more able to relax and engage with the world.

When you work with children and families, you must understand the basic contextual factors that help clients feel safe. These include organizing the work so that it is provided by a consistent worker, at predictable times, ideally in the same place. Most therapeutic models provide these basic predictable structures in any work they offer.

Within the Theraplay model there are many other layers of predictability that we think of as falling under the Structure dimension. These include the overall structure of the sessions and the relational predictability of the practitioner as well as the predictability within specific activities.

The overall structure of sessions is predictable and remains consistent. You may vary this pattern depending on the needs of the child at the moment, but whatever their individual needs within the session, children benefit from a clear and structured framework.

Creating relational predictability

Predictability in terms of the response of the practitioner is central to creating a sense of safety for the child. This is also the basis of effective parenting. Providing a predictable, empathic and congruent way of responding (regardless of what the child or parent presents) has a powerful impact in creating a felt sense of safety. It has been identified as a key factor in effectiveness of all kinds of therapy (Wampold, 2015). The aim is for the practitioner to respond to the child in a consistently warm and clear manner. If you are faced with a very volatile and changeable child, this can be harder to maintain than it sounds. A warm response may initially surprise the child if they are not used to being responded to in this way.

There will obviously be individual differences in style and temperament of the adults involved; however, there are some general relational principles for the practitioner that encapsulate the Theraplay approach and these are summarized in the table at the end of this chapter.

Creating safe surprises

Some children benefit from very high levels of predictability and repetition (to help them feel safe) and others will need more variation to keep them engaged and to help them practice small shifts in state in a safe environment. Within the Theraplay model, predictability (as represented by all elements of the Structure dimension) will often be used alongside small "safe" surprises. The surprise element might be provided by a cue or signal as to when the child begins an activity or may be integral to the activity itself. It is essential to be sensitively attuned to the child at both an affective and somatic level and to be flexible so that you can respond to the child's signals.

ACTIVITY EXAMPLE: USING A CUE

The Bean Bag Drop game begins with a signal: "ready…steady…go." On "go" you drop the bean bag into the child's hands. The pattern is predictable. The child knows when the bag will drop but there is a moment of anticipation followed by an exciting change of pace when the bean bag swiftly falls, and finally a resolution when it lands. For many children, this shift from rhythmic countdown to the object moving through space into their hands creates a feeling of delightful anticipation and excitement. When things go well, this process creates a pleasurable sensation, with a flip in the tummy and a giggle, as well as a clear beginning, middle and ending. This kind of activity helps build a secure base and resilience—from a secure beginning the child experiences an increase in arousal and, with support, a resolution.

You can be very creative in combining the elements of predictability and surprise. Activities can involve simple or complex signals, changes in pace and different facial expressions and emotional matching. There are many details you can adjust that will have a significant impact on how the child experiences the interaction. Here are contrasting examples using the same activity:

- Example of providing a high level of predictability: You place the bean bag on the child's head, hold the child's hands ready to catch and say, "ready, steady, drop," in a steady rhythm, with no pause before the drop. On "drop," the bean bag drops and the adult and child catch the bean bag. The practitioner keeps their vocal tone quite matter of fact and does not shift to an exciting tone when the bean bag drops.

- Example of providing a high level of excitement: You place the bean bag on the child's head, hold the child's hand ready to drop and say, "ready…" (looking at the child with intense excitement and pausing), "steady…" (extending the pause and showing excitement via facial expression and vocal tone), "drop!" (said quite suddenly in an energetic tone). Follow up with laughing and matching of the child's excitement: "Yeah, you got it!"

- Example of extending the element of surprise: More complex and extended cues can be used to build on the experience of anticipation— for example, "You're going to drop the bean bag when I say blue. Red, green, yellow… (add pauses and maintain eye contact) …blue!"

Even in these small examples, you can see that the children will be having different experiences. The first child has a very organized predictable experience, the second child experiences more uncertainty, anticipation and animation. The aim is to provide an experience for the child that is manageable and helpful to them. We don't want them to become overstimulated or to dysregulate but the interaction needs to be appealing and help them expand their tolerance for excitement. Children differ widely in terms of what specific sequence is going to help them feel just right, and this is where the skill of Theraplay lies.

Building in success

When we feel as though we can do something, our confidence and enjoyment increase and we are more able to relax. This idea is encompassed in the Challenge dimension. The idea of "building in success" in Theraplay practice means pitching activities at the right developmental level and subtly judging what the child (or parent) may be able to manage in any given situation. Building in success and focusing on strengths is as important in the parent work as it is in the work with the child. You have to be very sensitive to how you time any feedback, what areas are open to exploration and when and how to involve parents to ensure it goes well. We make extensive use of video feedback and going over scenarios with parents so that they feel informed and confident when we ask them to do something. When you are attuned to the child and family, this principle can help you to gently challenge current patterns while maintaining trust in the relationship.

Adapting to cultural differences

Theraplay is practiced successfully (with some small adaptations) in over 40 countries. However, this does not mean that we believe that there is only one way for parents and children to interact. When using any therapeutic intervention, it is essential to be sensitive to cultural and family differences and how your role impacts on the people you are working with.

Parents come to us for help with their child and therefore there is an inherent power differential in which we hold some power over the client. By putting their family in our hands, the parents are exposing themselves to the lens of our worldview. This puts them in a vulnerable position; if their worldview diverges enough from ours, they may be evaluated as wrong or bad in some way. As practitioners, we may think that we are open and accepting of all types of cultures and families but, in actuality, every perspective we have, no matter how universal it may seem to us, has a cultural bias. Working with a client who has a very different worldview from us can challenge our abilities to balance cultural sensitivity with our professional views or our personal identity. As an example, let's look at the suppositions that underlie attachment theory:

- The preferred way for an infant to be raised is to have two adult caregivers who are primarily responsible for most of the child's upbringing.

- Face-to-face contact with infants in the first few months is crucial to the development of an infant's interpersonal brain.

- It is potentially harmful to the parent-infant relationship for a parent, especially a mother, to be absent from her infant for long periods of time and should be avoided except for extreme necessity.

- An adopted child should learn to depend on his adoptive parents for comfort and connection.

- All children are better off living in a loving, stable nuclear family than in an institutional setting.

- An adult who has an idealized view of their own parents and cannot recognize that their relationship with their parents had faults has an insecure attachment style, which is not the most adaptive.

From our Western perspective, each of the above tenets seem like givens yet they are to some extent culturally biased. One only needs to do a search on "is attachment theory universal?" to get tens if not hundreds of academic papers criticizing the supposition that attachment theory tenets are universal (Rothbaum *et al.*, 2000).

For example:

- There are many places around the world where the biological parents are not the main attachment figures at all or they play only a minor part in the child rearing.

- There are cultures where the baby is held in a dark papoose on the parent's back with virtually no eye contact for the first three months.

- There are immigrants who send their baby to live with grandparents in their home country for two years while they return to America so they can work hard and earn money. The child does not necessarily have ill-effects when returning to the care of his parents.

- There are adopted children who have been conditioned to such an extent by abuse and neglect to not trust parent figures that it would be unrealistic to presume they could ever develop a close, trusting bond with a new caregiver.

- There are many societies where portraying an elder in any type of negative light is disrespectful and it would be inappropriate to acknowledge a parent's mistakes, especially if the parent is deceased.

We use our Western ideas of attachment theory as a guide because it has been effective in directing our thoughts and our interventions for helping clients in our Western cultures, but these values are by no means immutable and it is clearly important to take other cultures into account.

How does this relate to Theraplay specifically? The dimensions themselves are universal in that all children in all cultures need some form of Structure, Engagement, Nurture and Challenge. But when you work with a family from another culture, you will need to explore in an open and reflective way what fits with their own norms: individual, familial and cultural. Let's look at some Theraplay norms from a cultural perspective.

Structure dimension

Theraplay norm: In a Theraplay session, we accept and don't punish the child if he doesn't do what we want him to because the child is showing his internal working model, which needs to be expressed.

Cultural criticism: It may not be acceptable to voice dissent against an adult because it could put the child in danger (e.g. an African American child in the US could receive harsher discipline in school for disrespect or disobedience), and, in certain cultures, being openly disobedient is a dangerous sign of disrespect.

Engagement dimension

Theraplay norm: An anxious child who doesn't like to take risks should be encouraged to play boisterous, loud games like the peanut butter and jelly game or cotton ball fight so they can learn to express themselves with confidence.

Cultural criticism: For certain historically traumatized people, games that are loud or chaotic are risky and destabilizing. Immigrants, refugees and people who have been or are persecuted have had to internalize and submerge their needs. If they do act silly or "crazy," they put themselves in danger. In certain cultures, behaving in a calm and organized fashion is of the highest value, and acting "silly" is forcefully discouraged.

Nurture dimension
Theraplay norm:

- If a child is developmentally younger due to early years trauma, the parent should give him extra nurture and do things with him rather than expect him to do it himself.

- A parent should be supported to feel comfortable feeding her 5-year-old child or putting lotion on her child's feet.

- Feeding a child in a Theraplay session will not lead the child to act more dependent/needy/developmentally younger.

- When a child is anxious, providing empathy is the right thing to do.

Cultural criticism: The assumption that a parent has to be comfortable with physical affection or touch to be a secure attachment figure is false. The measure of attachment security is based on the parent's ability to be attuned, sensitive and responsive to the child's needs, but she can do it many ways that don't involve overt nurturing or touch. Refraining from affection is a cultural norm and is not "avoidant" behavior. Furthermore, there are communities where historical or community trauma has proven time and again that it is not safe to be vulnerable, and children need to grow up quickly. Those parents may feel that encouraging their child to indulge in developmentally younger activities will expose them to more harm in the world.

Challenge dimension
Theraplay norm:

- If developmentally appropriate, it's okay to let the child win two out of three rounds of thumb wrestling.

- If the child is a sore loser due to chronic shame, parents should avoid playing board games with rules and instead play cooperative games.

Cultural criticism: These tenets are seen as indulging a child's immature behavior and can be antithetical to a parent's responsibility to guide a child into a successful and productive citizen.

These are just a few examples which illustrate why Theraplay attitudes may not be congruent with a family's culture. It is important to hold assumptions lightly about why a parent behaves in a certain way, especially when you observe the MIM. If you see a behavior that you think is damaging or unproductive, be mindful that it may be your cultural bias that you are overlaying on the family. If a family culture diverges from your own values, take care not to assume that this indicates insecure attachment or less than optimal health. Similarly, you don't need to avoid engaging in Theraplay as long as your activities do not run counter to the cultural values. We have to be mindful that if a parent or child is not cooperating with a game, it may be because of a certain cultural meaning that you need to learn more about.

The concepts of cultural competence and cultural humility can be useful (Tervalon and Murray-Garcia, 1998). Cultural competency implies that there is a finite set of information about certain cultures and that we as experts can learn enough to deem ourselves sufficiently informed. However, the concept of cultural competency does not acknowledge our inherent cultural bias and the inherent power differential between ourselves as professionals and the people seeking our help. Cultural humility is a more helpful concept because it assumes that no one is free from the bias of their own, unconscious cultural lens (Ortega and Coullborn Faller, 2011; Schuldberg *et al.*, 2012). It therefore guides you to assume a stance of curiosity and not-knowing. It requires you to practice humility by saying out loud that you do not know a particular individual's experience and then to be able to listen without judgment to the client. This position requires constant self-reflection and self-examination. In order to navigate cultural differences, we need to have cultural *humility* rather than cultural competency (Fisher-Borne, Cain and Martin, 2015).

It is especially difficult to have cultural humility when a client's perspective challenges the behaviors, thoughts or morals that are most important to you. A sign that you may be getting triggered might be that you feel panic, rage, defensiveness or helplessness. In those situations, take time to reflect before acting.

With a trusted colleague or supervisor, ask yourself:

- What is my cultural bias that may be conflicting with the client's worldview?

- What can this client teach me?

- Am I approaching this client humbly and with a collaborative mindset?

In session with the client:

- Stop yourself from providing advice or direction as though you are the expert in their lives.

- Use your most receptive communication skills, including open-ended questions and reflective listening.

- Check that your social engagement system (open face, relaxed shoulders, resonant voice, congruent gestures) is communicating openness, non-defensiveness and a posture of "learner" rather than "expert."

Adaptations to Theraplay® practice

In any Theraplay intervention there will be adaptations you will make to fit within the family culture as well as the wider cultural and practical context. As an example, if the child or parent has physical or cognitive limitations you will adjust the activities and select those that are possible and comfortable. Other considerations might include the gender of the Theraplay practitioner, the age of the child or client-specific issues such as how to manage the snack part of the session with a child who has an eating disorder.

Older children, for instance, need more physical space and a different kind of approach so that they do not feel patronized. You will still undertake the work within the same Theraplay framework and purpose but will adjust your style and choice of activities so that they are more in keeping with the young person's age. Similarly, a male practitioner may need to address issues like touch with a higher level of caution than his female colleagues. This is not to say he will not provide nurturing touch (and a male model of nurturing provision can be particularly powerful) but he will give careful thought to consents and the potential for misinterpretation, particularly if working with families with experience of being hurt by a male.

It is not possible to describe every eventuality but the guiding principle is to be sensitive to the unique context and make adjustments to maximize the potential effectiveness of your work while maintaining safe practice. Further detail about different applications and adjustments to practice is available in Lindaman and Hong (2020).

Theraplay® research

At the time of writing this book, there have been many small-scale research studies regarding Theraplay and there are several active research studies about the efficacy of Theraplay, including a randomized controlled trial in the Netherlands.[2]

Theraplay has achieved evidence-based status within the US. It has been accepted by the US Substance Abuse and Mental Health Services Administration

---

2   For the most up-to-date and comprehensive description of research, visit www.theraplay.org.

for inclusion on the National Registry for Evidence-Based Programs and Practices. It was rated *effective* for reducing internalizing problems and *promising* for reducing symptoms related to autism spectrum disorders and conditions. Theraplay is rated as *promising* research evidence by California Evidence-Based Clearinghouse for Child Welfare.

Summary

This chapter has considered a range of overlapping theoretical constructs and principles that have contributed to our understanding of what makes Theraplay effective. You may find different ideas helpful in different contexts. In practical terms, these ideas can be expressed as a series of general Theraplay principles that will recognizably identify the intervention as based on Theraplay.

Keep a relationship focus throughout	Bring the same level of attention and care to the work with parents as you do the work with the child. Work hard to build a trusting relationship with the parent and repair quickly if there is a break in connection.
	Remember your goal is to deepen the parent-child relationship. Find ways to bring the parent and child together in ways that are manageable for both. Ask yourself if what you are doing is helpful to the parent-child relationship.
Focus on safety and the child's well-being	Be aware of the child's sense of safety and monitor their state throughout your contact with them. Close attunement is essential. If you think they are feeling anxious, make a brief comment and adjust the activity.
	Try to keep the child within their window of tolerance.
Make persistent efforts to connect with the child and to find ways to help this feel manageable for them	This includes a wide variety of responses. Try to support the child in ways that "help things work out," by "re-doing" an activity that may have gone wrong, by re-approaching the child even if they have been rejecting, and by adapting the way in which activities are approached.
Show consistent, unconditional and positive regard and warmth regardless of the child's behavior	Find ways to show the child that you enjoy being with them and want to be with them.
	Don't show irritation if things become difficult. Take responsibility for finding different ways through and make this clear to the child—for example, "I'm sorry, I didn't explain that quite right, let's…"
Provide calm and confident leadership and take responsibility for the session	Project a positive self-image and convey your ability to guide and protect. The safety and well-being of the child is your priority throughout.
	Confidently guide and structure the sessions from beginning to end. You do not need to ask permission or wait for approval before acting. Questions such as "Would you like to jump?" communicate to the child that you are uncertain and can create anxiety.

Structure the session so that it is well organized and clearly delineate activities within each session	This requires good planning and organization. Make sure that you have a well-thought-through plan, that your expectations are clear, and that you support the child across transitions. Build up sequences of play within the session that include predictability, rhythm, pattern and clear beginnings and endings.
Be appealing and delightful and make yourself the primary playroom object	Be spontaneous and engaging so that any child will find themselves drawn to join in your games. You—your actions, movements, words and sounds—must be the major and indispensable "prop" of Theraplay. Initiate playful, engaging activities that capture the child's attention and create moments of true connection. Use your whole social engagement system and be very aware of your non-verbal communication. Keep a focus on "in-the-moment" intersubjective connection and resist getting into conversation. Theraplay is not about chatting.
Focus intensively and exclusively on the child. Use every opportunity to help the child see themselves as unique and accept the child just as they are	Use your whole self, all your physical energy and your emotional investment to make a meaningful connection with the child. Whether or not the child can engage in the activities is less important than that they feel seen and appreciated by you and their parent.
Be sensitive and responsive to cues given by the child	Closely attune to the child and in particular to their non-verbal behavior. If the child is enjoying an activity, extend it. When they signal anxiety, notice and respond to it: "Oh that didn't feel quite right." If they are hurt or upset, attend to this and quickly repair if you feel connection has been lost. If the child has a lot of ideas, acknowledge that you appreciate the ideas even if you don't follow them: "You have so many good ideas."
Maintain focus on the "here and now," not on the past	Aim for a feeling of being together in the present without distractions. Draw the child's attention towards "moments of meeting" with you (and their parent) via your intent focus on them and the activity.
Use every opportunity to make eye contact and physical contact in ways that are manageable for the child	This includes touch as it arises naturally in the activities as well as spontaneous touch. Include different kinds of touch: structuring (holding child's hand), engaging (Slippery Slip), nurturing (rocking), challenging (helping child balance). Be aware of the child's sensory sensitivities and adjust your approach to help the child remain within their window of tolerance. If the intensity of the connection is too hard for the child, find ways to reduce this intensity, such as including a prop or moving away from face-to-face contact.
Attend to physical hurts and emotional hurts and provide care and comfort	If a child or parent is hurt, physically or emotionally, stop what you are doing and show concern. When you provide nurture, the priority is to make sure that the child experiences it as genuinely comforting and can relax into it so that they can absorb the feeling of being cared for. This is more important than the actual activity.

cont.

Provide sequences of play that involve small safe surprises and shifts in state	Give the child practice (in a safe and relational context) of lively and quiet activity, anticipation and resolution and support to take mild risks with a return to safety.
Build in success	Pitch activities carefully at an emotional and cognitive developmental level that you know the child can achieve. Provide enough support to assure that activities go well and that the child feels your presence. You want the child to experience "I can do it" and together, "We did it!"
Anticipate the situations the child may find hard and act before, not after, the child shows signs of significant stress	Get to know the child very well. Monitor patterns and subtle triggers so that you can intervene early. End activities clearly before they disintegrate, provide additional support during vulnerable moments. If things go wrong, look back at the sequence on your video to see how you might do it differently in the future.
Make sure that each session contains some gentle challenge to the child's unhelpful ways of relating (negative inner working models)	According to the child's individual needs, begin to extend sequences for longer and increase the relational intensity of activities. Keep responding in ways that may be slightly surprising to the child, for example have another go at an activity that just went wrong: "I know we can do this together." Give a warm response when the child is expecting a critical one.
Make your presence felt throughout the duration of a child's distress or angry outburst	If the child becomes distressed, change focus to help calm and soothe the child (as you would when caring for hurts). The child will need a break from playing, they may want comfort from their parent or a snack, they may want to withdraw and hide or may be screaming and shouting. Give the clear message that you are available to the child and parent—"You are so upset, let's see what will help"—and provide whatever input might be manageable, such as a snack, a blanket and support to the parent. Stay with the child until they calm. Review the video to see whether you could have done anything different to prevent or help manage the distress.

Nuts and Bolts

Chapter 3

Intake

CHAPTER PLAN

This chapter will discuss the following areas:

Structure of the Theraplay® Intervention Program

Intake session

- – Background and history
- – Caregiver-child relationship and parental reflective function
- – The parent's own attachment history
- – Establishing a therapeutic relationship with the parent

Summary

The standard Theraplay intervention proceeds as summarized below. The intake process comprises the initial meeting with the parents and administration of questionnaires as appropriate.

Structure of the Theraplay® Intervention Program

Session 1: Initial interview with caregivers. Administer appropriate questionnaires and standardized measures. The Theraplay Institute uses the Behavior Assessment System for Children, Third Edition (BASC-3) and the Parent Relationship Questionnaire (PRQ). The Family Place uses the Assessment Checklist for Children (Tarren-Sweeney, 2007) and The Carer's Questionnaire (Golding, 2008) among others.

Session 2: One parent and child participate in the Marschak Interaction Method (MIM), a structured technique for intensive observations of the ways parent and child typically interact with one another. The practitioner observes and videos this interaction.

Session 3: Same as 2, except that the other parent participates (if applicable).

Session 4: Feedback session with both parents.

Session 5: Parent Theraplay demonstration session.

Sessions 6, 7, 8: Theraplay sessions with the child and parent begin.

Session 9: Meeting with the parents only to reflect on progress (with video examples from sessions) and discuss issues with the child at home.

Sessions 10, 11, 12: Theraplay sessions, with the parents gradually taking more of the lead role in interacting with the child, with the practitioner's guidance.

Session 13: Meeting with the parents only to reflect on progress (with video examples from sessions), role-play with parents and discuss issues with the child at home.

Sessions 14, 15, 16: Theraplay sessions, with the parents taking more of the lead role in interacting with the child, with the practitioner's guidance.

Session 17: Meeting with the parents only to reflect on progress (with video examples from sessions), role-play with parents and discuss issues with the child at home.

Sessions 18, 19, 20: Theraplay sessions, with the parents taking more of the lead role in interacting with the child, with the practitioner's guidance.

Session 21: Meeting with the parents to evaluate therapy goals, decide on end date and whether to add additional modality or refer for additional intervention.

Sessions 22, 23, 24: Theraplay sessions where the parents are actively involved in planning and leading the sessions.

Session 25: Final "goodbye Theraplay party" or additional sessions as needed. The practitioner re-administers evaluation measures.

Session 26: Re-administering of the MIM. Final meeting with the parents to review goals achieved and areas for future work if necessary. Schedule first follow-up session.

Sessions 27, 28, 29: Theraplay "tune up" sessions scheduled once a month for three months.

Intake session

Some of us work in settings where we are known for our Theraplay work (like The Theraplay Institute in Chicago or specialist centers elsewhere in the world), where potential clients are routinely screened for the appropriateness of Theraplay for the presenting problem and family situation. Other practitioners may be working in services where Theraplay is less familiar or where there is a great variety of interventions offered. Whatever the setting, we should first make the parent aware that Theraplay:

- involves the caregiver playing a central role in every aspect of the intervention

- is not focused on fixing outward behavioral problems of the child, but instead on the relational aspect of the caregiver and child that can be worked on to improve behavior.

We would also consider whether:

- the child's presenting problem suggests that Theraplay is suitable

- the parents are open for a collaborative working relationship

- the parents are stable enough. If parents are active substance users or are severely mentally ill and are not actively engaged in their own treatment, then Theraplay is contraindicated (see Chapter 8).

Theraplay is helpful for a wide variety of presenting issues, such as those related to: developmental trauma, separation and loss, regulation, attention deficit hyperactivity disorder (ADHD), anxiety, sensory processing or even a simple lack of "goodness of fit" between parent and child temperaments. There are many cases where a child or family would benefit from Theraplay, but it is a matter of where Theraplay fits within a sequence of interventions that may be needed. For example, if a child has recently experienced an acute trauma like the death of a close relative or has been assaulted, the first intervention should focus on re-establishing environmental safety at home, putting in place safeguards and rituals to promote calmness, providing the child with an opportunity to integrate the trauma into their narrative and to develop some coping skills through trauma-focused cognitive behavioral therapy or play therapy techniques. Theraplay would come next in the sequence of interventions, to work on:

- deepening trust between current caregiver and child

- regulation issues that may have been caused by the trauma

- re-establishing the role of joy within relationships

- repairing damaged self-esteem.

In a different context, Theraplay may well come before the narrative work.

Finally, there are cases when Theraplay is not appropriate at all (see contraindications in Chapter 8).

Assuming that we feel Theraplay is a good fit, the first session, called the intake session, is flexibly designed to meet the needs of the family. Because there is so much to cover, we recommend allowing one-and-a-half to two hours for this session.

There are a number of areas you should focus on:

1. Background and history of child and family.

2. Caregiver-child relationship and parental reflective function (which is addressed by the intake questions by dimensions provided in the Theraplay training).

3. The parent's own attachment history.

4. Establishing a therapeutic relationship with the parent. You are beginning to form a relationship with the parent and this relationship building is arguably the most important element as it may well determine whether the parent will trust you enough to engage in some work.

We will consider these areas in turn.

Background and history

The information that we are most interested in has to do with the child's development, abuse and neglect history, significant losses, placements, separations from caregivers, hospitalizations, family history of mental illness and family disruptions. One area of child health that is often overlooked and can cause behavior problems is sensory processing difficulties. During the initial history taking, it's important to enquire specifically about whether the child was easy or difficult to soothe as a baby. A parent may, for instance, tell you that her child had reflux, allergies and sleeping difficulties. At this point you should consider screening for sensory processing difficulties by using the short sensory profile (Dunn, 2014).

We ask for any medical, psychological and developmental reports beforehand so we can focus on what is presently concerning the caregivers when they come in. In addition to these standard areas of enquiry, you need to be particularly aware of the parts of the child's story that are missing. There is a great deal of information that we can infer about trauma, abuse and neglect from listening to what the caregivers say they don't know. We also want to listen to what kind of story the parents tell about the reasons their child behaves the way she does. Through this conversation, we will be getting to know the client and will begin to develop some sense of whether we may be able to be of help.

Practice questions:

- What techniques can you use to find out more meaningful and specific developmental or biographic information about the child and family?

- Why is the story the parent tells about the reasons for their child's behavior important?

EXAMPLE: An adoptive mother of a 6-year-old girl from a foreign orphanage comes in with the presenting problem that her daughter is aggressive towards the other children, especially around mealtimes. When I ask about her daughter's early experience in the orphanage, the mother tells me that the orphanage had a good reputation. She describes the facilities as clean and that the caregivers seemed warm and caring with the babies. When she met her daughter, she was a healthy weight. I feel that the mother's description is very general, so I ask her to put herself back in the orphanage and tell me what she saw. The mother then remembers that she witnessed a mealtime scene while visiting. In preparation for mealtime, the orphanage caregiver placed each of the ten 1-year-old girls in walkers with wheels and tied their hands to the frame of the walkers. Then the caregiver sat in the middle of this group of babies with a big bowl of porridge and fed a spoonful to the baby closest to her. After each baby received a spoonful, the caregiver pushed the baby backwards with her foot and the other babies shuffled in to get a spoonful. Then they too would get pushed backwards, until all the babies had had a chance to approach. The mother relays this horrific picture to me in a matter-of-fact manner. I take this picture of feeding time in the orphanage and use it as an opportunity to expand on the traumatic effect it would have had for her daughter's hands to be tied and for her to have to compete to be fed. With this image in mind, the mother and I are able to develop a different story in the mother's mind about why her daughter is aggressive towards her other children around mealtimes.

There are many instances in which a parent will either not know or not remember information about their child's past, but your interactive role as a guide in the intake interview can help a parent expand and become aware of how much they actually do know. For instance, if the parent is speaking in generalities, like the adoptive mother did about the orphanage, it is helpful to ask her to try to put herself back in the orphanage and imagine herself walking through the place.

If you ask them to describe what they are seeing, like a reporter who is visiting a location, you can stimulate the recollection of details that can help you and the parent make more sense of the child's situation. It is more important to focus on getting a few detailed memories than to quickly whizz through a checklist of generic questions about developmental stages.

One also has to be on the alert for details that parents may recount in a "by the way" kind of manner. One adoptive parent said about her son's early experience with his birth mother, "His birth mother was very loving, but she was just too young to take care of him." In the next sentence she said, "When I met him at the age of 1, he couldn't bear any weight on his legs." The practitioner clarified with the adoptive mother that there was a contradiction in those two statements: his birth mother was very loving but if he could not bear weight on his legs as a 1-year-old, it probably meant that he stayed in the crib all that time. Being left in the crib is harmful to a baby both physically and psychologically. The practitioner highlighted this not to blame the birth mother, but to illustrate to the adoptive mother that her son's early upbringing was more neglectful than she had realized. This is important because a great deal of the success of parenting a troubled child hinges on the parent's knowledge about why the child is struggling. If she can understand and empathize that her son did not get the attention and stimulation that he needed as a baby, it can help her understand why he is so sensory seeking and unfocused at age 7.

A parent who is caring for a child who has had previous families (through entering the foster and adoption system or through kinship care or step-parenting) does not have comprehensive information about the child's past experiences. You and the parent may be very reliant on historical records or other people's accounts which give some insight into the child's early years. The written records may be hard to access and can be incomplete, and reports often bunch sibling histories together as if they have had the same experience. These records are also often written in generalities in a similar way to the orphanage example given above. The professional account of a child's traumatic early years may also be written in such a way that it has the effect of minimizing the impact on the child. It may, for instance, state that the child was living in accommodation that was "unsuitable" or that they were exposed to "inappropriate adults." The reality may have been very severe for the child, with the child sleeping on the floor among rubbish and filth and being exposed to regular and unpredictable violence and sexual abuse, but it is often difficult to obtain this information. A detailed history can be invaluable and all attempts should be made to gather the best information possible. The day-to-day notes made by direct carers (e.g. foster carer notes) usually have the most useful information about how the baby and toddler responded to care. Where these notes are incomplete, the parent (with support from professionals) is left to "fill in the gaps" as they try to build up a picture of what the child may have experienced that makes sense in the present. Making the links between the child's early experience and the current difficulties can create a dramatic shift in the parent's perception of the child and their levels of empathy, both of which impact on their ability to support their child.

Caregiver-child relationship and parental reflective function

The "intake questions by dimensions" (Salo and Booth, 2019) that are provided in the Level One Theraplay training as well as Chapter 22 of this book are helpful because they give you information on two levels: what the parent says (positive or negative content) and the quality and manner in which the parent presents the content. Let's take a few relational questions under the Nurture dimension:

- Do you usually think that you know what your child is feeling in a particular situation?

- Can you usually calm your child when he is upset? What is this like for you?

- Do you like holding/soothing/taking care of your child?

- If not, what do you think is difficult about it?

These questions get to the heart of the attachment relationship and are very intimate. The parents' responses may be positive or negative, but it is the way in which the parents answer the questions that may reveal the most about the underlying relationship. That is because these questions are meant to evoke deep feelings in parents. If the parents struggle greatly with those feelings, they may defend against them and not be able to have empathy for their child or have the necessary reflective function skills to do the work of Theraplay. Signs that parents may have difficulties with reflective function include the following:

- Their answers sound vague, flat or generic.

- They use contradictory or covertly hostile language.

- Their answers to questions are focused mainly on how they feel and not a balance between their feelings and also seeing their child's perspective.

Practice questions:

- What does the way a caregiver talk about their child reveal about reflective function?

- How will your conclusions about the caregiver's capacity for reflective function inform your next steps?

EXAMPLE: Chava is a single parent who adopted 11-year-old Nia when Nia was 9 years old. Chava comes to therapy expressing concern about Nia's explosive bouts of anger and lack of interest in engaging with the rest of the family. I ask Chava whether she feels she knows what her daughter is feeling in a particular situation. Chava responds, "Yes, I think I do. Nia doesn't want to engage in anything because she gets bored easily and is not a very curious person. She just likes to play on her phone and nothing is more interesting than that." Chava's response does not sound to me as if she has answered the original question, so I ask it more specifically: "Chava, when Nia has a tantrum and screams and flails about because you told her she can't go outside after dark, do you have any sense of what is going through her mind?" Chava quickly responds, "I think she doesn't like to hear the word 'no' and she is quite controlling, so she gets angry and can't listen to reason at those moments." I move on to the next question: "Do you feel you can calm Nia when she is upset?" Chava spurts out, "I've tried to talk to her and calm her down by reminding her that she can go out again the next day after school. She is so unreasonable at those times and she also cannot use any of the coping skills that she learned from her social worker at school. I usually just leave the room and wait until the storm has passed."

In this example, Chava is describing her daughter's motives in superficial ways. Chava cannot think of possible motives for her daughter's behavior that are empathic to Nia. Chava doesn't express any thoughts or feelings that show she has insight in the way her behavior could influence or interact with her daughter's behavior. Her response of leaving the room and waiting until the storm has passed suggests that Nia is left to deal with her intense feelings on her own.

 EXAMPLE: John and Howard are raising their 4-year-old adopted son Sultan and are finding it very hard to stay consistent with setting limits. Sultan is very active and demanding and his parents feel worn out to the point where they vacillate between giving in to his demands or shouting at him. I ask them if they feel they know what Sultan is feeling in a particular situation. Howard responds, "I feel as if Sultan has a voracious appetite for life. He wants to devour every experience. He is so energetic and curious, which I know is a good thing, but his drive for action is totally upsetting to me because I can't get anything done. We can't let him stay up until 10 o'clock at night and he doesn't understand that. I guess he's too young to comprehend a schedule. I think it frustrates him so much when we tell him to go to sleep. It's as if we've mortally wounded him every time we say it's bedtime." I follow up and ask if they feel they can comfort him when he's upset. John responds, "No, not if he's in full-blown hurricane mode. I can endure his screaming more than Howard and I've often spent an hour trying to calm him down by reading him a book, singing, whatever. But Sultan can be so out of control that he'll throw books and toys at me and won't let me near him. I want to strangle him by the end of the night, and when he's finally asleep, I feel totally defeated and guilty."

As they describe the problems, Howard and John reveal that they can see both their own and Sultan's point of view. They express how hard it is for them to deal with him, but they can also see that his behaviors are due in part to generally positive attributes like curiosity and enthusiasm for life. They also can see that, because of Sultan's age, it is normal for him to be frustrated and they also acknowledge how uncomfortable they are about their own feelings of frustration. This balanced and honest portrayal of the strong conflicting feelings between their needs and their son's needs shows good reflective function abilities.

By listening not so much for the content of the caregiver's answers but more to how the parent answers, you can understand more deeply the underlying state of mind of the parent regarding the parent-child relationship. A vague, distant or dismissive feel to the parent's responses can signal that the parent feels defensive, insecure or very hurt in the situation and is deeply struggling to cope. A parent whose answers are very angry and focused primarily on the effects of the child's behavior on their own functioning suggests that the parent is feeling rejected by their child or ashamed at their own failures as a parent.

These insights, and more, come from the body of research from the Adult Attachment Interview (Hesse, 2008). This structured assessment is an interview for adults that analyzes the speech style evoked by interviewees when they are asked questions about their early childhood relating to their relationship with their parents. While the interview focuses on the adult's relationship with their own parents, the speech patterns revealed in the Adult Attachment Interview can be generalized for using with clients as they speak about other close relationships, like those with their own children.

There are a number of techniques you can use to help parents who are unable to reflect on their own or their child's feelings. Because there are various reasons why reflective function could be low in parents, there is not one method for addressing this issue. Here are several avenues to take for improving reflective functioning, which will be explored in more depth in the following chapters of this book:

- Provide psycho-education on the developmental and trauma explanations as to why the child might behave the way he does.

- Plan to increase the ratio of parent sessions to Theraplay sessions from 1:3 to 1:2 or even 1:1, so that you can have plenty of opportunity to reflect with the parent on the Theraplay session.

- If parents are defensive or remain distant, actively provide empathy for the parents' plights and hardships, so that they begin to feel that you deeply care about them and want to understand them. This might mean you will spend more sessions with them at the beginning of the intervention and you may decide to delay Theraplay sessions. We talk more about this in the parent and complex parent chapters.

If you discover in the intake session that the parents are so hostile and blaming towards the child that you can't imagine how you will be able to proceed with Theraplay, it is still possible to go on to the next step in the assessment process, which is the MIM.

A word about working with parents who are at cross-purposes with one another

You will sometimes find that the parents are at cross-purposes with one another. Be on the lookout for this situation, as it indicates a need to be vigilant to address this phenomenon in your work. Parents may come in and tell you explicitly that they don't see eye to eye on their child's problems. One may even make it clear that they feel that the other parent is the cause of the problem. It is a good thing if the parents are able to say this to you directly and they should be commended for putting this difficult matter on the table. Others will show you through their snide comments inserted as an aside, like "I get Johnny to school every morning by 8am, with teeth brushed, hair combed and face washed, unlike some people I know." Alternatively, their critical feelings are expressed non-verbally, like rolling eyes and laughing sarcastically. Either way, it is necessary for you to identify, address and manage this conflict from the beginning. Theraplay is strongly influenced by the family systems approaches that attend to what each family member is non-verbally communicating, and holds that person responsible to constructively articulate their feelings. You should be direct in naming these dynamics and be firm about stating expectations for open and civil behavior in a parent session. You should also insist that the interfering messages, once addressed, either cease or, alternatively, you can ask one parent to step into the waiting room and you will meet with each of them separately. We talk more about this in the MIM feedback section.

The parent's own attachment history

Exploring the parent's own attachment history to some extent will become a part of any Theraplay intervention, but how it will be done, and to what depth, will vary considerably. A significant part of our parental response to children relates to our own experiences of being parented. Therefore, if we are facing challenges in our parenting, an understanding of our own attachment history and triggers is crucial. A structured way of learning about the parent's attachment history is by using Questions for Parent Self-Reflection (Siegel and Hartzell, 2014) provided in the Theraplay Level One handouts, as part of an extended intake interview. Other practitioners elect to use the Hopes and Dreams interview developed by Daniel Hughes (Hughes, 2011b). Some practitioners elect not to enquire too much about the parent's attachment history at the beginning of the intervention, addressing it in the subsequent monthly parent meetings. When and how the parent's attachment history is explored is variable and depends on your work context and the openness of the parents to this exploration. It is ideal to get to this information at the beginning of your Theraplay intervention. However, reasons to delay this part of the process could be that:

- the parent is too vulnerable and will need time with the work before being able to explore their own experiences

- cultural differences mean that this type of information is seen as private or shaming

- the parent reacts so defensively that the insistence on exploring their history at the beginning stage of the process can lead to them withdrawing from the work.

With vulnerable/defensive parents, we find that through the process of the intake and MIM assessment, the parent begins to develop trust in us, and this, in turn, allows us to more accurately judge when and to what extent we can explore the parent's own history.

Practice questions:

- Why is it important to explore parents' attachment history?

- When is the best time to do this and how?

EXAMPLE: Mari and Kate have been referred for support regarding their adopted child. I invite them to an initial meeting and Mari opens up in a relaxed manner about her daughter's controlling behavior and how this triggers anger in her. She is able to make links with her own childhood experiences of being dominated by much older siblings and appears to find this reflection useful and straightforward. Throughout this conversation, Kate sits quietly. At several points, Mari tries to draw Kate into the conversation and she makes comments about Kate's childhood that clearly create discomfort for Kate. The most important aspect of an initial session is that both parents have a feeling of safety about being with me and about how we may progress with the work.

I therefore state that there is no pressure for us to talk about issues that feel intrusive or difficult, and that while it can be very helpful to make links to the past, we can take it at a pace that feels comfortable to each of them. My aim is to show Kate some empathy (that I can see her discomfort and that it is okay not to speak) and to signal to Mari that there is no need for her to keep bringing Kate in at this point. We move forward with the work, and at a much later point, nearly a year into the work, Kate requests an individual session with me to think through some of her personal triggers. At this attachment-history-focused session (which I deliberately book for two hours' duration), Kate opens up about some early experiences that she feels are impacting her parenting. She clearly expresses that she couldn't have talked in this way earlier, because she didn't know me.

We will hold in mind that there is more work to be done in terms of shifting the parents' perception of the issues but we need to consider carefully when the parent will feel most able to engage in this element of the work and in what format. As in the example above, it would have been very easy to offend Kate such that she would decide not to proceed with the work. Even where we feel strongly that the adult attachment element of the work is a big factor, we need to remember that without the parents' trust and cooperation, we cannot help the child.

Establishing a therapeutic relationship with the parent

One of the main facets of the Theraplay philosophy is that we see the parent as our client as much as we see the child as our client. You can also helpfully think of the relationship between the parent and child as a client. What this means is that we are dedicated to seeing the parent not just in their role as a caregiver and vehicle for change, but as a whole person who has deep needs to feel seen and felt, to be recognized for their uniqueness and have their point of view deeply understood. While this is a basic tenet of the helping professions, it is often forgotten.

Establishing a trusting relationship with parents starts with some basic principles: Be reliable and consistent in communication and be ready on time. Serve them tea or the drink of their choice. Remember how they take their tea and have it ready for them at every parent meeting. Make them feel comfortable in the room, acknowledge how they are feeling. When you greet them for the first time and during the intake session, look at them attentively, nod in acknowledgement, demonstrate empathy and give them time so they feel that you genuinely wish to connect with them.

EXAMPLE: A mother comes in for the intake session looking tired and worn out. I offer her a cup of tea, which she hesitates to accept but I insist. I serve her a cup of tea with a saucer, a little spoon to deposit the used tea bag and a small chocolate just for fun. The mother still has her coat on as she sits down. "It's chilly in this room," I say. "Would you like a blanket?" The mother stares back at me in disbelief. I hand her the mug of tea. She takes a deep sigh and says, "I can't remember the last time someone has served me tea."

This parent was so exhausted and used to managing for herself that she had no expectations of being cared for. She probably assumed that she would be blamed in some way for her child's problems. After the practitioner provided some basic nurturing care she noticeably relaxed and molded into her chair. The practitioner explained that they would just spend some time talking and they reflected together about how hard it was to take care of herself when she was having to work so hard with her child. This beginning set the atmosphere in which she felt valued and the parent and practitioner built a strong relationship within which they were able to grapple with some difficult topics.

Summary

As professionals working with children, we are often inclined to direct our attention and energies towards helping the child and yet it is the parent in the child's life who can have the most profound impact on their care and well-being. The work with parents often has the greatest impact in terms of any therapeutic progress and so this relationship needs to be a priority. The Theraplay dimensions are as useful for supporting parents as they are for children. We provide clear structure by explaining expectations, providing organization, predictability and engagement by showing deep personal interest in the parent and attuning very closely to any signs that they are feeling uncomfortable; we provide nurture, via care and soothing (that many parents need just as much as their children), and challenge when we support them to take risks and stretch themselves beyond their usual limits.

Underpinning all of this is safety. As in our work with their children, we need to find ways to help parents feel safe in working with us. Parenting is our most vulnerable role, and without some level of trust in the relationship between parent and practitioner, it will not be possible to create a context for change. This does not mean that the relationship will be without difficulties, because therapeutic work is hard, but if we attend to the rupture and repair cycle that happens within all relationships, this gives us a strong basis on which to move forwards.

Chapter 4

MIM Administration, Feedback and Parent Demonstration Session

―――――――――――― CHAPTER PLAN ――――――――――――

This chapter will discuss the following areas:

Setting up and administering the MIM

- Scheduling the MIM: Back to back or separate days
- Deciding which parent goes first
- Choosing MIM tasks—when to consider alternatives
- Observing the MIM—alternatives to videoing
- When might you intervene in a MIM?
- Analyzing the MIM and setting intervention goals and objectives

Conducting the MIM feedback session

- Exploring parental feelings whatever approach to feedback you take
- Deciding when to feed back to parents separately
- Deciding whether the parents are ready to move on to Theraplay® sessions

Parent demonstration session

- Choosing your focus for the parent demonstration session

Summary

This chapter looks at the administration and analysis of the MIM, from the organization and administration of it to feedback and the parent preparation session. Our aim is to provide practical and thoughtful discussion on a range of issues as summarized in the chapter plan above. The MIM is a detailed observational assessment, and anyone undertaking it should have attended accredited training.

For more information about the MIM, see Chapters 3, 4 and 6 of the *Clinical Handbook for the Marschak Interaction Method (MIM)* (Salo and Booth, 2019).

Setting up and administering the MIM

The Marschak Interaction Method is the assessment tool that is designed to assess dyadic relationships between caregiver and child and is an integral and essential step of the Theraplay intervention process. It is the basis for beginning all Theraplay interventions. Every effort should be made to administer the MIM even when there are practical issues that make it difficult.

Your Theraplay course provided the basic information about how to administer the MIM, the activities lists and all of the analysis and intervention planning tools necessary for successfully beginning to use the MIM. We will not repeat the administrative information that is included within the MIM training materials here but will focus rather on the range of choices and dilemmas that come up.

Scheduling the MIM: Back to back or separate days

The standard lists include a version for when you have two caregivers and a version for when you have only one. The following relates to choices when there are two parents. You have to decide whether you will be administering both MIMs on the same day, one after the other, or on different days. There are a variety of reasons why each scenario could occur and there is no right or ideal preference.

If you are doing two MIMs back to back, however, there are a few things to keep in mind:

- You should shorten each MIM by removing the last two tasks—"Put funny hats on each other" and "Feed each other"—thereby making each MIM only seven tasks rather than nine tasks (the last two tasks can be done with both parents). The reason for abbreviating each MIM is to reduce the overall time the child is interacting so that they do not become so fatigued that the overall experience becomes developmentally too challenging.

- If both MIMs are done back to back, you have the opportunity to include several tasks for both parents together with the child. This triad portion in the MIM is valuable because it shows you the dynamics that are unique to the chemistry and patterns created by the parental unit in relation to the family system and that can have a big impact on the child's behavior.

There is therefore a clear advantage to having both parents available to participate in this portion of the MIM. The reasons why you might not administer this portion are largely due to logistics. If each caregiver MIM is done on a different day, it may be difficult for the caregiver who is not scheduled for their dyadic MIM to come in an additional time to complete the triadic MIM. When scheduling the MIMs you should be flexible and arrange them in the way that works best for the family.

Deciding which parent goes first

Another question that comes up frequently is: Which parent should do their MIM first? Again, there is no one correct answer. The decision rests on clinical judgment about what will be the most revealing and helpful. But here are two typical scenarios that may occur, especially during MIMs that are done back to back:

- Scenario 1: You know that the child tires very easily, and as she gets more tired, she gets more dysregulated. Parent A has a harder time with the child than Parent B. Which parent should go first? The answer depends in part on what your goal is for the MIM. If you want to see the child in their most difficult state, then have Parent A go second, when the child is more tired. If, however, you feel there is a risk that the child's behaviors might be so disruptive as to cause undue stress on the family, it is better to allow Parent A to go first when the child is fresher, and then let Parent B handle the more fatigued and challenging behaviors.

- Scenario 2: The parents predict that their child will act "like a perfect angel" for the MIM as part of her pattern of what they describe as controlling and manipulative behaviors. Parent A has a harder time dealing with the child than Parent B. In this case, it would be best to let Parent A go second. This is because we would like to do whatever we can to see the child act in the way that is most inherent to their emotional and behavioral challenges. If the child is well mannered and guarded in the first MIM (with the parent who has more success in general), it is likely that the child will show more of her "true colors" during the second MIM with the more challenged parent. One cost of this is that you may get fewer moments of success to show in the MIM feedback with Parent B.

However, the following caveat is true no matter what the child's behavior is predicted to be: if one of the parents feels extremely stressed by the prospect of participating in the MIM, it is better to allow them to have the "easier" of the two positions, even if this means that you will not get to see as many or as intense clinical behaviors as if you did it the other way around.

EXAMPLE: Parents of 4-year-old Joe seek help. The family comes from far away and are eager to get the therapy process going as quickly as possible. Together, his parents and I decide to schedule both MIMs on the same day. During the intake, Joe's parents tell me that he gets silly easily, especially when he is tired, and that he has low frustration tolerance. Both parents agree that Joe has more problems with his father than his mother because his father loses patience with Joe more easily. To help me decide which parent should do the MIM first, I ask the parents whether they think Joe is likely to try to "hold it together" and act more composed because he is in an unfamiliar place and is feeling watched. Joe's parents say that Joe cannot hold it together for very long and they suspect that he will act the way he normally does if he becomes stressed or fatigued.

Throughout the discussion, the practitioner tries to gauge what frame of mind Joe's father is in as part of her consideration of which parent should go first. It appears to her that Joe's father is very worn out and discouraged. The practitioner asks herself: should she put the father second when she knows that Joe will likely be more tired and therefore more dysregulated so that she can see the extreme behavior that Joe sometimes displays at home? Or, should she consider that Joe's father is very stressed and that she does not want to stress him out more than necessary, especially given the fact that Joe will show his difficulties regardless? The practitioner feels that setting up the father to add a possible greater level of difficulty to his already discouraged view of his competencies will not be helpful. She opts to have Joe's father go first so as to not burden him any more than necessary. In Joe's case: With his father, Joe remains focused and cooperative. But by the second MIM he gets tired and overstimulated. He won't stay near his mother for the majority of the activities and even runs out of the room before she gets a chance to stop him. However, the MIM did show the mother's skill in using movement, rhythm and touch to provide structure and regulation. When the practitioner asks the parents if this was typical of their interactions with Joe, the father says yes, it's typical for Joe to be uncooperative and unfocused, but the practitioner's observation is that Joe stayed fairly regulated and was accepting his father's guidance. The mother says that is what Joe acts like in crowded, loud places or when he is very tired. In this case, doing the MIMs back to back was useful since it showed both what the parents were struggling with as well as their coping styles.

EXAMPLE: Sherry is a 14-year-old girl who suffers from depression. She is polite in the outside world, but at home she can be very biting and mean. During the initial phone conversations, Sherry's mother, Matilda, said that she and her husband argue about raising Sherry. She feels that her husband does not support her when Sherry is disrespectful towards her. I decide that we should schedule the MIMs back to back because I want to include the three-person part of the MIM to assess the triadic relationship. In deciding which parent should go first, I took the following information into account: Sherry's mother experiences more conflict with her daughter than her father does. Matilda feels that Sherry is very rejecting and acts in a rather fake way towards her. With her father, Sherry is more relaxed and playful. Sherry is normally "slow to warm up" in new situations. Sherry's parents are afraid that the whole MIM set-up will cause Sherry to be guarded and I will not see her angrier side. I decide that Sherry's father should do the MIM first. My reasons are that since Sherry feels more relaxed with her father, starting with him might help to counteract the guarded, self-conscious tendency that Sherry has in new situations. I believe that this reduction in anxiety will allow me to see a more accurate picture of how Sherry interacts with her mother by the second MIM.

In the example of Sherry above, Sherry and her father did the first MIM. They had a hard time getting things started and Sherry acted in a very rigid and controlled manner. Her father tried many things to entice Sherry to participate, cajoling her and using a jokey, almost pleading manner. By the end of their MIM, her father managed to get Sherry to loosen and warm up a bit but it was clear how hard the father had to work to connect with Sherry. He reported after the MIM was over that it tires him and he too feels rejected by Sherry. With her mother, Sherry did indeed show her hurt, sarcastic side, at one point telling her mother that she "smells" and is "disgusting" when her mother leaned towards her. The mother was satisfied that the practitioner got to see this side of Sherry since she had feared that Sherry would be too controlled to show this angry side of herself. The triad MIM was extremely significant and helpful, in that it showed how the mother withdrew almost immediately from the banter between the father and Sherry and how she showed a great deal of non-verbal negative affect. Doing the three-person MIM was clearly valuable as they were able to use this information very productively in the feedback.

In summary, there is no easy way to decide which parent goes first in each individual case, but either way you can get important information. Either scenario will show important, if different, aspects of the parent-child behavior. In the majority of cases, the structure of the MIM itself will facilitate a successful implementation of this tool. In the minority of cases, however, careful thinking through will be necessary, for example if the child is dysregulated or gets fatigued easily, or if the parent-child relationship is so hostile or stressed that the child acts out or a parent becomes too stressed and gets overwhelmed or angry or shuts down.

Choosing MIM tasks—when to consider alternatives

The list of tasks and alternatives is given in your Theraplay training book, so we won't repeat them here. Always carry out the MIM tasks in the correct order and in full. Some tasks in the MIM are more stressful than others and you need to have a clear ethical rationale for asking families to go through with them. The costs (in terms of their stress and possible distress with you for putting them through it) should be outweighed by the benefits. In most situations, the balance is fine as you are taking your work seriously, spending significant time analyzing and making sense of what you observe, and spending time with the parents feeding back. The whole MIM process is in fact an intervention in itself when done thoroughly, and many parents will find the process enlightening and helpful.

There are some situations, however, in which more consideration is needed about what it is you are asking the family to do. The leave task is discussed in more detail below. Another example is the "Tell the story about when you first came to live with me" task (which is a very important and telling task). This task can be difficult for some foster or adoptive families if they have had traumatic transitions or where the transition is, for whatever reason, not yet easy to talk about. It can be hard to predict this beforehand and in many cases the task brings important information to light. If you are aware that the transition to the family was traumatic then it will be worth letting the parents know that this task is included in the MIM and to think it through beforehand (which is not what we would usually do). The same consideration would be given to the leave task if you know the child is extremely anxious around separation or, for instance, in a very new family placement.

A different consideration is around personal and cultural issues. Three tasks that need some thought are:

- combing—ensure that you have a wide-toothed comb suitable for all hair types. Do not, for instance, use the combing task for someone who wears a headscarf or is bald, wears braids or has dreadlocks (swap with an alternative nurture task)

- lotion—ensure that you have hypoallergenic low or non-perfumed lotion and check during the consent process that this is agreed. Lotion can be hard for children with extreme sensitivity and for those who have experienced sexual abuse using lubricants, and an alternative nurture task can be used instead

- snack—during the consent process, discuss food intolerances and parental preference about the snack. Some parents can be unhappy if you provide their child with sweets without permission, for instance, and dietary issues and eating disorder issues need to be checked beforehand.

Observing the MIM—alternatives to videoing

It is critical that you are able to monitor what is happening in the MIM. If you can't watch the MIM through a one-way mirror or video link, you should at least listen with a baby monitor so you can hear the audio. You can still get a good sense of what's going on in the room. If it is not possible for you to monitor what is going on either visually or by audio, then you should sit in the room behind a barrier of some kind so that you can listen and monitor in that way. Do not sit in plain sight of the dyad as this will interfere with the MIM proceeding in a way that will be of use to the intervention. If you are required by your work setting to be in the room, try to sit as far away as you can or outside the sightline of the dyad and pretend to be occupied reading or writing something.

When might you intervene in a MIM?

The general rule is that we do not intervene in MIMs. We leave the dyad to their own devices. There are rare times when you will have to intervene because a MIM is getting derailed by extremely unhelpful or dangerous behavior, or if the parents lose track of time and go on for much longer than is necessary.

Intervene and stop the MIM for the following reasons:

- There is a question of safety. Safety issues that can occur are: the child hitting or hurting the parent repeatedly or the child doing unsafe things like climbing on tall furniture.

- The parent has gone over the designated amount of time for the MIM (20–45 minutes) or the dyad is taking so long on one activity (more than 10 minutes or so) that they will not be able to complete the other tasks in the allotted time.

- The "leave the room" situation has made the child so distressed that the child is excessively crying or dissociating.

- The parent is so harsh or punitive that forcing the child to get through nine activities with the parent feels like setting them up for emotional abuse.

🖐 **EXAMPLE 1**: Freddy is a 5-year-old boy with moderate autism. He and his mother Ellen start the MIM. As soon as I leave the room, Freddy begins to tug and pull on his mother's arm to try to get her to exit with him. Ellen misses out the first squeaky animal task and tries to get Freddy to focus on blocks but he runs away from her, screaming excitedly. Ellen stands and tries to walk Freddy back to the table. While doing so, Freddy slaps Ellen's arm. Ellen warns him sternly not to hit and he does it again. He then runs from the room and Ellen chases Freddy into the waiting room, where Freddy grabs a toy train. Ellen tries to get him to put it down. She spends three minutes vacillating between cajoling and being stern. She finally picks him up and carries him back into the room. She sits him on the couch and tries to entice him with lotion. He leans back over the armrest of the couch and dangles backwards until only his legs are on it. Ellen grabs Freddy's knees and his foot accidentally bumps Ellen's chin. Ellen lets go and says "Ow" loudly. Freddy runs around the room screaming. After seven minutes, I step in and say to Ellen, "It's okay. I see this is really very hard. Let's call Freddy's father in so you can do a few activities together." I do this because I sense that Ellen will not be able to achieve any sense of order or regulation in this set-up and I know that Freddy's father, Mark, has a strong and calming presence with Freddy. When Mark comes in, he sits on the floor and puts Freddy on his lap facing forward. While holding Freddy's wrists, Mark speaks to Freddy firmly and rhythmically until Freddy calms down enough for the family to try to do the hat activity. They are able to achieve this and the feeding task for several minutes as a triad. I do not ask the father to do his MIM after this, as I sense that not only have I seen enough of the father's skill in the triadic interactions, but the parents are worn out and I do not want to stress them any further.

🖐 **EXAMPLE 2**: Terry and her 8-year-old son Emelio come in for a dyadic MIM. Twenty-three minutes after the MIM has begun, they are only on their second task. In the squeaky animal game, Terry and Emelio create an elaborate imaginary world where the two pigs are going on an adventure to different planets to save endangered creatures that are being eaten by poisonous plants. It starts out collaboratively and I can see the tremendous capacity for Terry to enter Emelio's rich imaginary world. However, by the time 11 minutes have passed, I begin to worry that the entire hour will go by without Terry moving on. This is despite the fact that I have clearly stated that they have nine activities to do and that the MIM usually takes between 25 and 50 minutes to complete. I decide to intervene. I knock on the door, peek my head in and say to Terry, "I think I have a good picture of this activity, you can go on to the next one." Terry looks a little disoriented, as though I have pulled her out of a far away world. When they move on to task number two, "Adult draws a quick picture and encourages child to copy it," Terry has Emelio copy an elaborate picture, which he is all too happy to do. They then begin adding more detail to their pictures, comparing ideas, embellishing aspects of the drawing. I have already seen plenty of Engagement and a lack of Structure. What I am missing are examples of the Nurture dimension, so after 12 minutes of the draw task, I step in again and alert Terry to the fact that we only have about 20 more minutes. Terry affably notes that they have got carried away because they love drawing. I tell Terry that I want them to complete two more tasks. I take five task cards out of the MIM box and leave only "Leave the room" and "Feed each other." We consider "Leave the room" under the Nurture dimension because it shows how the parent prepares the child for separation as well as how they reconnect after the absence. Terry and Emelio proceed with the two tasks I have left. The rest of the MIM takes another 32 minutes, making a total of 50 minutes.

 EXAMPLE 3: Susan and her 5-year-old son Camron come in to do the MIM. During the first five activities Camron acts alternately rejecting, angry and helpless with his mother. Initially, Susan tries to appease and cajole Camron to cooperate, but soon becomes exasperated and frustrated. When Susan reads task number five, "Adult leaves the room for one minute without the child," Camron starts whining, repeating, "I wanna go with you!" Susan hesitates and then attempts to persuade Camron that he will be okay. She offers him gum from her purse, and when none of this works, she gets up quickly and heads for the door. Susan manages to open the door, but Camron, now screaming and sobbing, grabs her leg and will not let go. Susan has a very distressed look on her face and seems unable to move or make a decision. This whole scene since Susan announced the leave task feels as if it's taken hours, whereas in reality it has been about three minutes. After another 36 seconds of Susan standing at the threshold of the therapy room with Camron's tear-streaked face crying, I open my observation room door and approach Susan, who looks alarmed. I tell her that if she feels it is best not to complete this task, it is okay to re-enter the room with Camron and move on. Susan's eyes refocus and she returns into the room with Camron and they proceed to the next task. The whole task of attempting to leave the room took approximately five minutes.

For Freddy and Ellen, the practitioner saw enough in the first seven minutes of interaction to decide that it was too emotionally negative for the dyad to continue. The practitioner let it go on this long because she wanted to see if Ellen had any ways to regulate and engage Freddy that would eventually calm him enough to do even one activity. There is value in being able to witness the child's dangerous and wild behaviors, but only in a limited amount. When the practitioner saw two examples of Freddy's potentially dangerous behavior (kicking his mother, dangling off the couch) and the mother's inability to redirect and calm him, she intervened to stop the MIM.

For Terry and Emelio, the practitioner realized after the first two tasks that Terry gets caught up in the fantasy and is indeed like another child, unable to take on the responsibility for structuring the situation. She did not have an internal structure that would allow her to adhere to the external limits the practitioner had set. This related directly to the problems Terry described during the intake. Entering the room again and again to move things along is disruptive, so the practitioner chose to enter for the third and last time to remove five out of the seven tasks that remained. The practitioner chose two nurture tasks because she had not yet seen sufficient examples of their interaction in that dimension. Another possibility would have been to let the MIM unfold without interruption until the 50 minutes were up and then enter the room to say that even though they hadn't got through all the tasks, the practitioner had enough information to make a good plan for the next session. The practitioner would then end as usual by asking the questions that come at the end of the MIM. Using this option might have left the practitioner no opportunity to see the nurture tasks. Either way, the practitioner would have been able to address Terry's tendency to get swept into imaginative play and relate it to her difficulties in providing structure in Emelio's daily routine.

For Susan and Camron, some might question the wisdom of allowing them to struggle for as long as they did when they were both clearly very distressed. The rationale is that, aligned with attachment theory, the attachment mechanism can only come into focus when the child is in a state of true distress—in other words, they feel anxious, fearful, sick, threatened and so on. This is why Marianne Marschak put the "Leave the room" task into the MIM. This was before Mary Ainsworth, who created the Strange Situation Protocol for classifying attachment categories, used the same task which has become so familiar to us. The guiding principle is that we are striving to recreate a mild stressor in order to activate the attachment system so we can observe the coping style of the dyad and then deeply understand their underlying internal working model. If the "Leave the room" task is stressful for the dyad, the practitioner should make every attempt to let the task unfold without intervening. If, however, several minutes have passed and you have gained enough information about the dyadic response to separation and reunion, you do not have to leave the dyad to struggle on unnecessarily. In general, you should let it unfold to let the dyad show you how they cope.

Keep in mind that:

- this type of occurrence happens routinely in their daily life, for example when the child goes off to school or needs to be put to bed

- the dyad is asking for help for exactly this distressing problem, so it is necessary to observe it to understand it

- you will not be doing this in your Theraplay practice—you only do it once in the assessment phase to determine the nature and scope of the issue.

In Susan and Camron's case, the push/pull nature of their interaction and the lack of structure was evident throughout the first half of the MIM. Therefore it was no surprise that Camron aggressively tried to stop his mother from leaving and that Susan was not reassuring and confident. What was most informative, however, was the non-verbal cues that were evident as the task unfolded. In viewing the video, the practitioner could see that as soon as Susan read the task, her face changed to that of concern and she breathed in a small gasp of alarm. Immediately, Camron said, "What, Mommy?" and started squirming in his chair as if getting ready for action. Susan put the card down slowly and straightened out the pile of cards, as if to buy time. Camron's eyes were getting bigger as Susan gathered her courage to announce the task at hand. The non-verbal cues that Susan gave Camron throughout, culminating in Susan's almost frozen distress while at the door, provided a tremendous amount of insight into her struggle to parent Camron. When Susan saw the video, she was able to talk about her fear that Camron's strong negative responses would be overwhelming. She was aware that her usual response was to freeze: "It feels as if I'm walking through molasses. I just can't move." The cascading effect of her fear of her own immobilization in the face of Camron's demanding tantrums caused her to function even less efficiently. In subsequent parent-only sessions, the practitioner and Susan were also able to explore some of the fears that underlay Susan's immobilization response. These related to the fact that Camron was born prematurely and spent three months in the hospital, during which time Susan felt intensely helpless as she watched her baby feel pain, distress and loneliness. Watching and understanding the "Leave the room" task was the first step in separating and dealing with that traumatic dyadic beginning so that Susan could be freed up to think about Camron's needs in the present moment.

Analyzing the MIM and setting intervention goals and objectives

Analyzing the MIM thoroughly takes time and practice. As covered in your Theraplay training, you will analyze the MIM in stages, first observing verbal and non-verbal interactions and sequences and then answering the MIM analysis questions by dimension form. Finally, you will fill out the "strengths and needs" summary form. These analysis tools will guide you towards what the areas of difficulty are, for both the parent and child, and will lead to your choice of feedback clips and, following the feedback session with parents, your setting of intervention goals and objectives. For detailed information on MIM analysis see Salo and Booth (2019).

Setting clear objectives for your work with the family can be a complex task but one well worth doing as it gives a clear focus for your work. Let's take an example where we move from the MIM analysis to set some objectives.

EXAMPLE: Amir is 5 years old, withdrawn and easily startled. He has been living with his current foster carers for nine months and, though settled, he is still quiet and very compliant. We undertake the MIM, analyze it in detail and draw out the themes below in discussion with his foster carers during the feedback session.

	What Amir needs	What parent needs to do
STRUCTURE	For things to be very simple and clear, with visual prompts.	Reduce tentative questioning. Allow pauses for him to understand what has been asked.
ENGAGEMENT	To feel deep interest without becoming overwhelmed. To increase in confidence so that he can relax and allow experiences in. Developmentally very young games.	Take things slowly, keep games very simple with repetitions. Notice how he is more engaged with non-verbal toddler-type activities. Reduce the surprise element. Avoid sarcasm and too many jokes.
NURTURE	To feel more relaxed receiving nurture. To allow adults to help him when he starts to become stressed (rather than self-soothing).	Find more opportunities to provide manageable nurture (not too intense but don't follow his cues that he wants to be on his own—he is miscuing). Notice when he is starting to become dysregulated and try to repair straightaway.
CHALLENGE	To be tempted towards more intimate exchanges and trying new things (this is a challenge for him, as he is very sensitive and feels alarmed easily). To have experiences that things go well without stress. To gain confidence in keeping going.	Build success into whatever it is he is trying. When you know he can do something and the context is safe, encourage him to persist. As you know the "collapse" thing he does is habitual, differentiate between when to push forward and when he's getting anxious.

How can we move from these helpful descriptions towards an intervention plan? First let's consider the key dimensions that we are concerned about.

- Structure: The practitioner is not concerned about Amir needing more structure. Amir is compliant and can manage well with very low structure. When the sessions start, the practitioner will be able to take a calm pace and be confident that Amir will follow her lead.

- Engagement: This is a high priority in this situation. Amir becomes overwhelmed very easily and shows little spontaneous play or ideas. He doesn't seem relaxed and can't manage loud voices, surprises or humor. He did much better when the play was very simple, non-verbal and physical, the kind of play much more typical of a toddler.

- Nurture: This is another area the practitioner is concerned about. Amir found receiving care difficult and moved his body away from his very sensitive foster carer. Again, he seemed to get overwhelmed easily and wasn't able to relax while being cared for.

- Challenge: Amir doesn't need to be challenged as he just gets stressed and then freezes.

The practitioner's focus therefore in the sessions will be mainly on Engagement and Nurture. She can sense that if she keeps the sessions simple, repetitive and without surprise, she may be able to support Amir to feel safe enough to express some spontaneity and closeness.

Setting goals and objectives

When setting goals for any work it is common to make these goals quite broad. Agencies requesting work will often say things like: help the child to become more securely attached, or help the child to participate more in relationships.

These goals are helpful but it can be more purposeful in terms of your work to set more specific objectives. One way to make the distinction between a broader goal and an objective is to think simply, can I count something? Specific objectives are countable.

Examples of specific objectives that may help for Amir include:

- Increase moments of curiosity and initiative, for example the child will reach out and make a beep-honk noise of his own.

- Increase moments of connected joy and playfulness, for example the child will laugh spontaneously.

- Enable him to be more able to enjoy nurturing touch, for example the child will allow the Weather Report activity for one minute and look relaxed.

- Increase capacity to tolerate small surprises, for example the child will play Peek-a-Boo and have an animated face rather than a frozen look.

You will see that these examples are mainly in the Engagement and Nurture dimensions and are aligned with observations from the MIM.

In addition, it is always helpful to set objectives for parents that clearly reflect the heart of Theraplay. For Amir's foster parents, suitable objectives might be to be able to:

- read his cues more accurately, for example the parent will notice the discrepancy between his smiling face and hunched shoulders

- intervene with reassuring touch when Amir is uncomfortable, for example the parent will put a hand on his knee or back with a firm but gentle touch.

The practitioner discussed these ideas with the parents during the feedback session, agreed them together and included them at the end of the MIM report. This provided a concrete set of goals and objectives to work towards and gave everyone a sense of purpose and direction.

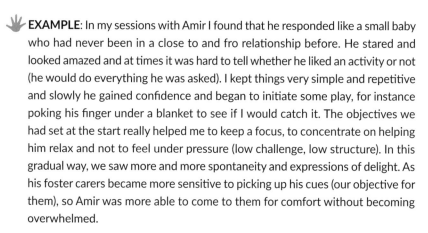

EXAMPLE: In my sessions with Amir I found that he responded like a small baby who had never been in a close to and fro relationship before. He stared and looked amazed and at times it was hard to tell whether he liked an activity or not (he would do everything he was asked). I kept things very simple and repetitive and slowly he gained confidence and began to initiate some play, for instance poking his finger under a blanket to see if I would catch it. The objectives we had set at the start really helped me to keep a focus, to concentrate on helping him relax and not to feel under pressure (low challenge, low structure). In this gradual way, we saw more and more spontaneity and expressions of delight. As his foster carers became more sensitive to picking up his cues (our objective for them), so Amir was more able to come to them for comfort without becoming overwhelmed.

Conducting the MIM feedback session

The primary goal of the MIM feedback is to connect with the parents. So first, check in with yourself: how are you feeling? If you look nervous, ill at ease, worried or tense, it will compound the parents' stress and increase their defensiveness. It is therefore imperative, especially if the MIM was poor, to do exercises for relaxation of body and openness of face—sing a song, stretch, listen to inspiring music. You have to put yourself in a frame of mind where you are the least stressed and most open possible. Be aware that having a computer in front of you will exacerbate your tendency to seem distant or technical. Be sure to have the computer up and running smoothly (with battery charged!) and the video cued exactly to where you want to start so that you do not have to focus on the technology.

The first thing to do, as in every parent-only meeting, is to take care of the parents' comfort by offering to hang their coat, get them a drink, make sure they are comfortable in their seat, offer them anything they need. Provide them with something to write with if they are looking around as if they want to take notes. Once they are settled ask, "How was that for you?" We want to know how stressed, judged or insecure they are feeling when they first come in. If they say that it was hard in any way, respond empathically. "I can understand how stressful it must be if you are already worried about your child and someone videos you. Of course you feel nervous or uncomfortable." Then acknowledge the courage and caring determination they have to engage in this process. Only then do you reassure them that you are not looking to assign blame but to figure out the best way to understand the relationship. If the parents have come in against their will or on the recommendation of a professional and they do not agree that there is a problem, you can frame your goals as you wanting to learn as much as possible about what makes their child tick.

Organizing your approach to the MIM feedback session can be conceptualized as a continuum between a focused, matter-of-fact "reporting your findings" approach on the one end to an open-ended exploratory approach on the other end.

- "Reporting your findings" involves summarizing strengths and areas that need focus and illustrating your points with video examples.

- With an exploratory approach, you present no analysis or assessment findings, but focus instead on asking open-ended questions, such as: "What were you feeling at that moment? Why do you think your child reacted the way she did? Tell me more about why you chose that activity."

With most parents, the balance will be in the middle, with you using a good mix of exploration and supportive/empathic comments while providing your observations about what you see as themes to work on. Let's explore which circumstance would need one end of the continuum or the other.

 EXAMPLE 1: Richard and Ann are an older couple with three grown-up biological children. After their children were grown up, they adopted two severely neglected children, Nico, now four, and Kate, five. After two years of parenting these children, Richard and Ann report that while it is a pleasure parenting Kate, it is hard to relate to Nico because he feels superficial and finds many ways to thwart closeness and true connection with them. Because

they live in a rural area where there are no clinicians specializing in attachment and adoption issues, Ann and Richard have come to our center from across the country for a three-day intensive assessment and therapy program. Ann is a child development specialist and a very grounded person. Despite feeling discouraged about her relationship with her son, she feels competent in many other areas of her life, has a good support system and a great sense of humor. Richard is supportive and warm and the two of them have a secure marital relationship based on support and trust. In the phone intake, Ann has a very well-articulated way of explaining how she feels regarding her son, and her distress is palpable. She enquires as to what specifically I think I can do to help them in three days. She is very focused on gathering as much information and experience as possible so that she can bring back recommendations to the new local practitioner and implement new strategies at home.

I decide to favor the "present your findings" approach for the following reasons: the parents are very secure and are eager for concrete, actionable learning and advice. They have made a grand gesture of coming to me, at tremendous cost and effort. Their need for as much acute information/help as they can get in a concentrated amount of time informs my decision.

I plan my MIM feedback to include as much information as I can. Throughout the MIM, Nico shows signs of being overwhelmed by too much verbal interaction. I feel that he would benefit from more calming, firm touch. In order to help the parents understand this, I prepare a list of video examples which show his signs of insecurity when they ask him questions or turn decisions over to him.

As I have said, the first thing I do when starting any feedback session is to ask, "How was it for you?" But Richard beats me to it by asking, "So, how badly did I do?" I am surprised at his opening comment and I first reassure him that I could see how much he was invested in and dedicated to his boy. I then explore his fear that he has done "badly." Richard responds, "I didn't know what you wanted, so I just did what I normally would do." "That's what I wanted!" I exclaim. "Good, cos that's what you got!" Ann, too, makes some self-deprecating comments but overall seems at ease. As I proceed with sharing the video clips and my observations, Ann and Richard are attentive and open. I show them a clip where their son kicked off his shoe while trying to copy a difficult block task. Ann says, "That's typical. You see how he flipped off his shoe to try to divert attention away from what I was trying to do? He is a master manipulator." I suggest that the reason for the shoe flip was possibly a diversion because he was anxious about completing the task. "Anxious about what?" Ann asked. "About not being able to do it right," I answer. "Why would he be worried about that? We have done nothing but be supportive from the moment he entered our home." Our discussion continues in a detailed and useful manner and I hear more about their difficult feelings.

EXAMPLE 2: Elana is a single mother of 9-year-old Mark who has been in and out of the child psychiatric hospital after being violent at home and school. Several times in the last few months, child protection services workers have come to the home because neighbors have heard Elana and Mark violently screaming at one another. Elana works in a store and has had another child protection services call made about her because she left Mark at home alone for an entire day when he was sick and she could not find childcare. Elana comes to therapy at the recommendation of her newly assigned caseworker to help her find more productive ways of getting her passive, irritable and depressed boy to cooperate with her other than shouting at him and threatening him. During our intake session, Elana reports that she has tried many different parenting and behavioral approaches with Mark, all of which failed because Mark is so negative, gives up easily and lashes out when she urges him. Elana feels that Mark is this way because his birth father, who left them when Mark was two months old, was learning disabled, couldn't keep a job and had a frightening temper. She is afraid that Mark takes after him. She says that all she wants is for Mark to make an effort and do the best he can. Elana questions whether any therapy will help because she has been to three different therapeutic practitioners with Mark, none of whom listened to her.

My sense from the intake is that Elana feels deeply unsupported by the professionals in her life. It is not surprising that she had not come to see me voluntarily. She sounds worn out, discouraged and angry. It is clear that she has a very stressful life. For these reasons, I know that my main message in the MIM feedback should be supportive. I need to communicate that "I accept you for who you are. I believe you love your son and that you are doing the very best that you can." My belief that Elana needs a high level of connection and support is confirmed when I watch the MIM. Elana has a jokey, almost peer-like attitude with Mark. Mark seems reticent and a little lost. Elana tries to tease and cajole him into cooperating with the games. When this doesn't work, at one point she says, "You're no fun," which hurts Mark's feelings. Elana makes the interactions into mini-lectures, turning the draw task into a lesson on the circumference of a circle. Elana asks Mark, "Do you understand what I'm saying?" and when he does not confirm her request, she rolls her eyes a little and mumbles, "Come on, you know this." Mark becomes increasingly shut down until, by the end of the MIM, his facial expression is flat and he looks as if he just wants to get out of the room.

Even though I can attribute many sources of the conflict to Elana's lack of attunement and misattribution of her son's motives, I know I should not start by pointing them out. In fact, I doubt I will get to them in the MIM feedback at all. Elana has no reason to trust me and feels unsupported by everyone. I have to proceed with the MIM by using only a tiny bit of video to elicit conversation about how she feels when she parents Mark so that I can provide a great deal of empathy and understanding for how hard her job is and how hard she has tried and still is trying. No matter how well intentioned my messages, if I go in with my own agenda, there will be little chance that Elana will feel that I am really interested in her experience and point of view.

When she comes in for the feedback session, I offer Elana tea with honey, which is what she drank when we met for the intake. She thanks me but seems tired and remote. I ask her how she is doing today and she gives me a matter-of-fact "fine." She tells me that she prides herself on never being late and that even though the bus was behind schedule, she still got to me early because she thinks it's inconsiderate of other people's time to be late. I wonder if I myself had started the session on time as I sense that there is some underlying complaint against me. I respond that it is so commendable that she is always on time considering how she has so little control over public transport. My attempt at empathy doesn't seem to resonate with her. I had prepared to show her one short clip during the teach task where she was successful in getting Mark to try copying a hand trick by using visual cues rather than words, but first I ask her how it was for her to do the MIM. Elana responds briefly, "It was fine. We don't usually play that way. If anything, we play cards so I couldn't do any game." I try to get her to elaborate: "Oh, you enjoy playing cards! What game do you like to play?" "We play gin rummy but Mark always has a hard time losing so he either tries to cheat or he gets frustrated and walks away." "I see, so Mark has a difficult time sticking to it if things don't go his way?" "Yeah!" Elana perks up. "He acts as if his life is so hard and that if he is not winning all the time, he gets a bad attitude and starts to give up. I keep telling him that he has to learn perseverance because the world is not going to be handed to him on a silver platter." "Gosh," I say, "that sounds pretty tiring if you have to keep convincing him to try hard and not give up." "Yes! It's so tiring and then he gets angry at me when I have to keep telling him over and over again to get his homework done or whatever. It's a constant battle."

Now that I feel as if my empathy is getting through to Elana, I feel I can use the opening to introduce the teach task as an example of how she did get him to participate in the activity without having to cajole or lecture. I show her about 45 seconds where she visually shows Mark the step by step of the hand game. The video shows her clapping, then he in turn claps. She folds her fingers down, then he does. She lifts two fingers up, then he does the same. She turns one hand in the opposite direction and Mark can't seem to copy the movement. Elana takes his wrist and guides his hand in the other direction. It works and he smiles at her. That was the only positive bit I have to show but it makes an impact on Elana. She seems to believe me that I am not out to prove she is a bad mother.

Elana proceeds to tell me about her worries that Mark will need special support at school and won't be able to do well in high school and beyond. She reveals that she is pretty good at maths, had worked as a book-keeper and wanted to go to university to study accounting. She says that marrying Mark's father ruined her life but she wants Mark to have a better future. I respond that now I understand—she is pushing her son because she wants him to have a better life than she did and she is worried! "Yes!" she exclaims. "Can this therapy help at all? I'm willing to do whatever it takes if I knew it would help." "I think it can!" I say. "You see, Mark may be clever, but he may learn differently from you, and if we figure out how he best learns, you can tailor your wonderful teaching to play to his strengths." I show her a piece that I had not planned to show, the draw task, where she rolled her eyes when Mark did not confirm his understanding of the circumference of the circle. "What do you see here?" I ask. "They started geometry last month and I've been practicing this with him during homework. He's looking at me like this is the first time he's heard it." "Let's watch it one more time, Elana. Watch what he is doing when you are explaining it to him." I play that portion again. "What do you see him doing?" Elana looks reflective. "He was using his pencil and tracing it along the exterior of the circle like I was and he was really looking at the picture. I guess he was trying. But then he won't repeat it so I can't tell if he is getting it or not." "Okay," I say. "My sense is that if you watch your son's non-verbal behavior, you will be able to see that he is paying attention and is trying to cooperate with you."

Exploring parental feelings whatever approach to feedback you take

Because they were solid and open, the practitioner felt that she could sit down and present Ann and Richard with "present your findings," yet she still had to spend time exploring their feelings that they were being manipulated by Nico and their resentment and self-doubt that had accrued over the previous two years. Ann had told the practitioner in the intake that she felt guilty that she hadn't been able to connect with Nico when she was so easily able to connect with Kate. Ann felt that perhaps she was giving Kate preferential treatment and that maybe Nico was picking up on that. Yet in the same breath, Ann said she had tried to be as loving as possible and spend as much time with Nico as she can, even taking him on special outings without the other children and implementing an extended bedtime ritual for him that she does not do for Kate. The practitioner spoke to Ann about the concept of blocked care (see Chapter 7) and helped her identify that even though she hadn't got to the point of total discouragement, she was beginning to go down that road.

Deciding when to feed back to parents separately

The MIM feedback is typically done with both parents present, each observing as you discuss the video clips of the other's MIM. Note that the parents do not observe the other parent's MIM while it is happening live. They are together only for the MIM feedback session. However, there are instances when the feedback should be done with each parent separately. Certainly, in cases of contentious divorces or where parents clearly have a great deal of conflict, you would schedule a separate session for each parent feedback. But what about for couples where the conflict is not as overt? During the intake, the parents may have revealed that they disagree and that there is tension between them about the way each of them handles the child's problematic behaviors. More commonly, you may have observed through their non-verbal communication that the parents are critical of one another. If you notice this, you should name it and ask the parent displaying the behavior to make their feelings or their message explicit. If you feel there is a lack of safety, you can ask the parents directly whether they would feel more comfortable doing the MIM feedback separately.

In some cases, you will not have noted anything particularly tense between the parents during the intake and proceeded to conduct the MIM feedback in the typical manner of both parents together. Once you get started, you observe behavior that indicates there is tension. For example, one parent may make side comments, laugh derisively or roll their eyes when you are viewing and discussing an incident that happened in the other parent's MIM. Or you may notice that one parent is not letting the other parent finish their thought or they discount the other's observations. If that happens more than once, you must draw attention to it and talk about it. It is of the utmost importance to be in charge of creating and maintaining a safe climate within your session room. If you notice one parent displaying one of these unhelpful actions, you can start by providing structure in a matter-of-fact way: "I notice you rolled your eyes while your partner was speaking about her experience. In the second part of the session, you will have a chance to express your perspective. But right now I would like to hear from your partner first. Can you hold your feelings inside just for this first part?" The parent will likely say yes and agree. However, they may continue to interfere, only in a different manner, for example they might try to make a "helpful" clarification. If that happens, you need to take a minute in your own mind and decide how you would like to intervene. The most direct action is to state that you have decided that it would be better to conduct the rest of the MIM feedback with each parent separately and invite the interfering parent to sit in the waiting room. While this may seem abrupt, it sends a very clear signal to the parents that you are in charge of safety and it models that you will not tolerate passive-aggressive behavior. Another way to handle the situation is to turn once again to the critical partner and say, "It seems to me that you are really struggling with holding on to your feelings while we watch your partner's MIM video. It's really important that you both have a chance to look at your video examples without interruption. You could wait outside and we can look at your videos separately or I will ask you not to make any comments to show your disagreement with your partner. Which option do you prefer?"

Deciding whether the parents are ready to move on to Theraplay® sessions

There are many instances where you will feel that more than one feedback session is necessary before deciding how to proceed. For example, if a parent reveals that they struggle with depression or the parents show extreme strains in the marriage resulting in a great deal of tension in the home, it is best to ask for another meeting with the parents to explore these issues. You might hesitate to suggest an additional parent-only meeting without doing any actual intervention with the child. When parents bring their child for help, they are focused on the child's problems and they typically hope that you, like a car mechanic, will take the child and "fix" the problem. You need to be clear from the first session that Theraplay focuses on the entire family and that meetings with parents are as valuable and necessary as sessions with the child. It would be clinically imprudent to begin the parent-child work without having the time to explore the terrain on which the entire parent-child system is sitting: the caregiver's functioning. This point cannot be emphasized enough and you must establish this principle not only with the families but also with your managers and colleagues.

Parent demonstration session

The parent demonstration session is scheduled after you have done the MIM feedback and you have all agreed that you are ready to move on to the next stage of intervention, the actual Theraplay sessions. This parent demonstration session is standard in the Theraplay protocol. Even if it "postpones" the work with the child, do not be tempted to skip it on the grounds that the family is impatient. The parent demonstration session is critical to the Theraplay intervention's success.

The parent demonstration session can focus on a range of goals based on the particular needs and characteristics of the parent. The parent demonstration session is essential because:

- the parent is exposed to the experiential aspect of the intervention. It is crucial for the parent to become familiar with what Theraplay feels like in order for the work to be successful

- the parent gains insight into her own responses and ways of coping

- knowing what to expect in a session increases parents' confidence and reduces anxiety

- the parent can think about how her child will react to the experience

- you can illustrate Theraplay concepts such as the four dimensions, regulation, proprioceptive input and so on

- you can gain more insight about the parent's attitude toward attachment and their emotional response to activities that might mirror their early experiences.

With all these goals, it can be difficult to decide how to approach the parent demonstration session and what to focus on. It can be helpful to conceptualize the planning of the parent session as a continuum between experiential versus didactic.

Choosing your focus for the parent demonstration session

Based on the situation, you will make a judgment about how emotionally intense the parent session can usefully be, as illustrated in Figure 4.1. You can approach the session by providing the parent with a pure Theraplay experience (which is more intense) or by using a more psycho-educational approach (less intense).

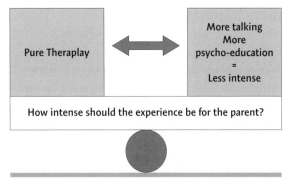

Figure 4.1: Parent demonstration session planning 1

Approaching the parent demonstration as a "pure Theraplay" session would mean that you would plan a session of approximately 20–30 minutes, as you would for a child, including entrance, check-ups, caring for hurts, activities that have up-regulating and down-regulating aspects, and then wrapping-up activities such as sharing a snack, singing the Twinkle Song and an exit activity. During the session, you would stay in the "here and now" and not discuss the meaning, methodology or reason for why you are doing what you are doing. The goal would be for the parent to feel what it is like to be engaged in the here and now, to have fun, to feel relaxed, to be taken care of without having to perform or do anything special. This was the original reason why the parent demonstration session was included in the Theraplay protocol. Only after the official Theraplay portion (20–30 minutes of an hour-long session) was over would you process how the session felt for the parent and answer their questions.

However, a pure Theraplay session might not feel appropriate or the most useful approach for some parents. The parent demonstration session can focus on the other end of the spectrum, away from experiential—taking a didactic approach. Below are some different reasons why you might choose a more didactic approach.

- Parents who are traumatized spend a great deal of effort keeping control of their environment and are frightened of letting go and being in the here and now, so would find it too anxiety provoking.

- Parents who are defensive or ambivalent about being involved in the intervention may be especially wary of having the focus on them.

- You as the practitioner may have a limited amount of time to work with the family, so the scope of the work needs to be curtailed.

These are all legitimate reasons why a skills-based approach could be the most useful. Make sure, however, that you do not choose a didactic approach because you are nervous of the more experiential approach. The experiential option is powerful and the parent will have a genuine understanding of why the approach can help their child.

The more didactic a session is, the more you will focus on mechanical or cognitive explanations. For example, you might play Hand Stack with the parent in several different ways: up/down, slow/fast, with/without touch. The game might last for a couple of minutes. After that you explain the reason for the game and it's variations as they relate to touch, structure and so on. You might ask the parent if they have questions and spend several minutes speaking on a conceptual level or helping the parent by offering applications at home. Then you might go on to demonstrate another activity for a few minutes, and then again offer explanation and discussion about the purpose of the activity within the context of the work with the child. The interaction remains on a cognitive level and does not address how the parent felt themselves when doing the activity. By using the parent demonstration session in this way, the practitioner is appealing to the parent's executive brain systems rather than trying to reach them on an emotional level.

Another way to conceptualize a parent demonstration session is to consider the continuum between focusing on the parent's physiological responses, associations and reactions to the activities and how those reactions relate to their own attachment history, rather than focusing on how their child might react to the activities (see Figure 4.2).

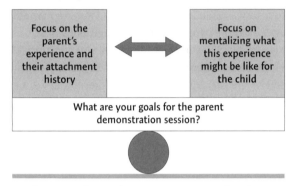

Figure 4.2: Parent demonstration session planning 2

During the intake, MIM and feedback sessions that precede the parent demonstration session, you may become aware of themes that suggest that the parent has reactions to her child based on her own attachment history and that this might be influencing or interfering with the parent's ability to meet her child's needs.

EXAMPLE: In the MIM assessment of Ferhana and her 8-year-old daughter Imani, a strong pattern can be seen whereby Ferhana encourages her daughter to comb her hair by herself (despite the directions saying that parent and child comb each other's hair). She even mocks Imani a bit when Imani struggles to copy Ferhana's picture. In the feedback, I explore this and wonder with Ferhana why she encouraged Imani to comb her hair by herself. Ferhana explains that she believes a child should not have younger developmental needs because her own childhood was difficult and she had to grow up fast and not be too needy. She goes on to reveal that she doesn't like to ask for help or to be the center of attention. When she has a problem, she likes to go away and solve it on her own rather than share her problems with a trusted friend or relative. I validate and empathize with Ferhana's drive to help her daughter grow up and be strong. I then highlight that Imani, because of difficult life circumstances, needs to learn that trusting an adult to help her weather difficult periods is essential, and I suggest that if Ferhana can learn to feel comfortable with depending on another person, she can transmit that feeling to her daughter. I offer Ferhana the opportunity to use the parent demonstration session as a launching point for experiencing what it's like to accept nurture and begin to feel comfortable with it. Ferhana agrees to try it, so I plan an experiential session for next time.

I plan six activities for the experiential portion of Ferhana's Theraplay session: walking in while balancing bean bags on head, Bean Bag Drop, Beep and Honk, Popping Bubbles, Paper Punch and Toss and Powder Prints. I conduct the activities while remaining entirely in the "here and now." The Theraplay portion of the session lasts about 20 minutes. Ferhana alternates between being reciprocal and seeming engaged with me to seeming a bit distant or embarrassed. After finishing the powder print activity, I take a deep breath to signal a transition and announce: "There, you've just had your first experience with a Theraplay session." We move to the couch to chat about what the experience was like for Ferhana.

Ferhana responds, "I felt kind of silly; like, what's the point of playing these little games? I really don't like being the center of attention." I provide empathy and explore Ferhana's sense that the games are "silly." Together we discover that Ferhana feels that when she was a young girl, her playful, silly side was met with scorn and derision from her parents and was seen as a sign of immaturity. She expresses that she felt constantly out of favor for not being able to be tough and stoic. Ferhana has discovered that she cannot fully trust that my intent to play with her is altruistic and benign. Ferhana says, "I always have this sense underneath that if I really let go and be silly or lose composure, someone will use it against me." Providing the direct Theraplay experience in this way is very helpful for Ferhana and opens a level of reflection and discussion that will clearly be helpful in the work with her daughter.

On the other end of the spectrum is using the parent demonstration session as a way of helping the parent explore how their child might experience the activities.

✋ **EXAMPLE**: In the MIM assessment with Mike (aged 6) and his father Josh, Mike shows that he feels anxious when he does not know what is going to happen. During ambiguous moments when his father hesitates about what to do next, Mike seeks reassurance and directions and then takes matters into his own hands and initiates his own idea of what to do. My observation is that he does this so that he can alleviate his anxiety by taking control. Josh shows annoyance at Mike when Mike tries to take over.

When I meet with Josh to give feedback, I try to explain what I have observed but he dismisses the explanation and says that Mike needs to learn to relax. Perhaps this is because Josh is temperamentally so different from his son or maybe Josh was anxious himself as a child and is pushing his son to overcome this same tendency. With this family, it will be useful to demonstrate activities to Josh that strongly illustrate the contrast between providing very clear, strong structure in an activity and a lack of structure—in other words, to approach the parent demonstration session in a more didactic way.

I plan several activities to demonstrate differences in structure—from being very clear and directive to being ambiguous. I do the following activities in contrasting ways and invite Josh to discuss what each version is like for him and how he thinks it might be for Mike.

- "Draw a picture on child's hand" task. The first time I say, "I'm going to draw a picture on your hand. Would you like a flower or a sun?" and the second time, "What do you want me to draw on your hand?"

- Bean Bag Drop with and without saying, "Ready, steady, go."

- Hide and Seek. The first time I am very overt while I am looking for Josh by saying with a lot of vitality "Hmm, where is Josh?" and tapping firmly on the objects in the room as I search so that Josh knows where I am. I find him relatively quickly (within about 30 seconds). The second time I am quiet while looking for Josh and take a longer time to find him (about a minute or so).

After demonstrating the contrasting ways of doing each activity we discuss what they were like. Josh is able to reflect that while he liked the element of surprise in the beanie drop and hide and seek game, he can feel that the tension is bigger in the less structured versions. I point out to him that while he finds the tension pleasurable, his son is physiologically different from him and so that tension causes him distress rather than pleasure. Josh reflects on this difference and begins to appreciate the gap in how he and his son take in the world. He then expresses worry that if he accommodates his son's rigidity, his son will not learn to "roll with the punches" and be flexible as real life demands. This gives me the opportunity to explain that meeting Mike where he is at will help him to learn to gradually tolerate more ambiguous situations. Mike will feel secure that his father understands him and also be able to learn what it is he needs to make himself feel more at ease in ambiguous situations.

In Ferhana's case, it was imperative that she felt what it was like to be experientially in the moment for 20 or so minutes, so that she could have a chance to get in touch with the feelings of why it is so uncomfortable for her to trust, and her fear of getting hurt. It takes about 20 minutes to really get the full effect of being in the experiential, limbic zone in one's brain. If the practitioner had cut in and out of that zone by asking cognitive questions, it likely would not have afforded Ferhana the opportunity to have the deep insight into her discomfort as she did.

In Josh's case, illustrating two contrasting ways to play an activity and asking him to reflect on how it felt for him and how it might feel for his son develops the parent reflective function or mentalization process. Parent reflective function is the ability for a parent to see the child's beliefs, motivations and perspectives as their child experiences the world and to see those experiences as separate from their own and as legitimate expressions. By having contrasting experiences within a Theraplay game, a parent can become aware of their own responses. They can begin to distinguish their experience from that of their child. They can begin to appreciate that just as they have their experience of these games, so their child might have their own, entirely different, feelings about an event.

When actually doing the work, we usually find ourselves moving back and forth between experiential and didactic approaches rather than staying at one end of the continuum. As illustrated in the example above, in order to be able to mentalize and see your child's perspective, you have to be able to identify and examine your own, which implies the need for the more experiential focus on the parent's attachment history. However, it is helpful when preparing your parent demonstration session to be able to conceptualize these two dichotomies so as to be able to define your focus and goals.

Summary

Just as in the Theraplay session with the child, no matter how certain you feel about the type of approach a parent needs in the parent feedback and demonstration session, it is crucial to remain attuned and flexible while in the session. You may think that a parent is defensive and closed off and then come to find that she is deeply engaged and responding with enthusiasm and openness. The opposite is also true. A parent who seemed secure in herself and open to a more experiential or exploratory process may "clam up" and you need to pause and check in with how she is feeling. In other words, the slide or the lever between experiential and didactic is fluid and may keep moving within a session. In all situations, you will gather a great deal of insight and new information about the parent, the child and their relationship with one another over the process of analyzing and feeding back the MIM and preparing the parent for the work.

Chapter 5

Theraplay® Sessions

Getting Prepared

CHAPTER PLAN

This chapter will discuss the following areas:

Room set-up

- The importance of the room set-up
- Session preparation and clarifying expectations of the parent
- Being near the floor

Materials

- Specific issues about materials
- Clothing

Videoing

- What is videoing used for?
- Why is it important to video?
- Choosing not to video

Choosing Theraplay® activities

- Developmental perspective
- Therapeutic purpose
- Practical considerations

Two different approaches to planning a session

- Practitioner A plan
- Practitioner B plan

Summary

When preparing for a Theraplay session there are some immediate practical issues to think through and prepare for. These include setting up the room, ensuring you have the right materials, setting up the video equipment, and choosing which activities you are going to use and in what sequence.

Room set-up
The importance of the room set-up

In order to focus on the relationship between people, the set-up and planning are very important. If the parent or child is physically uncomfortable then this will impact their level of engagement. If materials are disorganized, then the practitioner will take their focus away from the child in order to manage the materials and this will break the connection. The importance of these organizational issues can be understood within the Structure dimension. The adult provides a clear and comfortable setting to allow the child and parent to feel safe. As an example, having one's back well supported is similar to a baby being held well by a parent—you can relax, confident that a safe adult has anticipated and provided the support you need.

The connection and back and forth communication between the individuals must be center stage. Materials and distractions are therefore kept to a minimum. The room should be clean and plain, not filled with toys or other distractions, and should have a safe, contained feeling. You should make sure that the child and parent are comfortable and well supported, even when they play on the floor. Your exact layout will depend very much on the setting and the comfort level of the parent. You may, for instance, be in a family home, a clinic, a community hall or a residential meeting room and each venue presents different challenges. Each parent and child will also have different needs.

The typical room set up for a session includes a comfortable sitting area on the floor where the child and parent can sit with their backs supported (e.g. large cushions up against a wall, a room corner or a couch). It helps to have a rug demarking the play area. A couple of smaller cushions and a blanket to create comfort complete the core requirements. Some parents and children may not be able to sit directly on the floor due to physical limitations and you may need to build a small seat (e.g. a flat, firm cushion) or in some cases work from a chair. Theraplay can easily be adapted for people with physical and cognitive disabilities and you can select and adjust activities to ensure they are manageable for the specific situation.

Other room considerations include privacy (it will be hard for everyone to relax if there is a risk of people watching from outside, walking through the room or making a lot of noise), space and videoing. Theraplay can be successful in a wide range of rooms, and because the practitioner can bring all materials needed, it is possible to be very creative. Young children usually benefit from a smaller space, with enough room to engage in some standing and moving activities, although the space does not need to be very large. Older children typically need more space.

We recommend that you have the materials organized in a simple container with a cover (e.g. a basket or a bag with a zipper) which allows easy access and also makes it clear to the child that the materials are distributed by the practitioner. The aim is to keep things simple and clear.

EXAMPLE: Saleh is 8 years old. I have set up the room with a range of colorful scatter cushions in the center of the room and my materials are in a basket. I have my list of activities in mind and feel ready. My plan is to come in with Saleh and his father as a train and this seems to go well. I ask them to sit down on the cushions. The father and I sit, but Saleh remains standing and restlessly begins to rearrange the cushions. I decide to try to engage him with some measuring, to see if this might help him focus. I get some crepe paper from my basket, but Saleh, who is still standing, rushes behind me and begins to take the materials from the basket. I don't want to criticize Saleh because that is not the Theraplay way, but I have a feeling of rising chaos and embattlement. I try diverting him with another activity but he now begins to throw the cushions with mounting excitement. Help!

Let's think about how the practitioner might have set things up differently to give them the best chance that the session would go well. Saleh entered the room enthusiastically but was left standing when the adults sat. From this point, he became more restless, and each attempt the practitioner made to capture Saleh's focus created a new set of issues. Let's consider the basics. There were many scatter cushions on the floor. Perhaps it was not clear to him what was expected or exactly where he should sit. Even if he had sat down he might not have felt contained or settled sitting in the middle of the room with space all around him. In Theraplay, we try to build in success wherever possible. Would there have been a way of supporting Saleh so that he could more successfully sit down and begin to calmly engage with the practitioner? Here is a more successful alternative.

EXAMPLE: I try again, this time organizing the room a bit differently. I have two large firm cushions leaning up against the wall in the corner, with my materials to the right-hand side where I will sit (facing Saleh). My basket of materials is covered with a blanket so that the materials are not obviously on show. The exact place where I want Saleh to sit is obvious (a large green cushion), with similar clarity for his father. I have planned a check-in activity that does not require any materials so that I will not need to turn away from Saleh to get props in this early settling part of the session. Again, I plan for us to come in as a train. I am at the front, then Saleh, then the father. I say the train is taking us to the green cushion, and as we approach, I take Saleh's hands and help him sit down. I immediately move into the check-up activity, looking at his hands, which I am already holding. This time Saleh sits down and engages. He does not throw cushions or grab items from my materials basket. Being provided with this high level of structure and clear expectations, Saleh is able to play and relate. He is feeling more settled and at ease, just like a young child in a confident parent's arms.

What is interesting in this example is how the practitioner's interpretation of Saleh's behavior might go in a number of different directions, mainly as a result of the session set-up and atmosphere. In the first example, Saleh could potentially be described as controlling and oppositional. It is easy to envisage an escalating level of difficult to manage behavior as the session progressed. The practitioner is likely to experience mounting anxiety and to try a succession of different activities to entice Saleh, which runs the risk of becoming overstimulating for him, causing him to become more dysregulated. Practitioners in this situation often describe themselves as trying to maintain calm on the surface (like a swan gliding along) while their feet are desperately paddling below. This scenario often ends with a descent into chaos or perhaps with the parent or practitioner becoming firm in an unhelpful way (parent: "Come on, stop messing around, you've got to do what the lady says"). Our mantra "be a confident leader" can quickly turn on its head so that the idea of a safe and clear leader becomes instead an adult-child battle of wills.

In the second example, we see how the practitioner provided a simple and very clear set-up and expectation, and this allowed Saleh to relax. The practitioner supported him to manage the transition into the room (which is often a difficult moment) and he remained in an open and engaged state so that he could connect with her. The careful preparation of the setting and sequence has allowed Saleh every opportunity for success. The result is that we see a young child who is eager to engage in reciprocal play. This is an example of how Theraplay views structure. The practitioner sets up a clear and manageable context within which the child knows what is expected and is supported to be able to make the most of it.

Session preparation and clarifying expectations of the parent
As we have said, the room set-up and preparation can have a very significant impact on how well the work will progress. Feedback from our own experience,

as well as from parents, is that clarity in expectations about the practical elements of the work, including where to sit and what role the parent is expected to take, is very reassuring. Parents are not usually familiar with being centrally involved in a therapeutic intervention. Parents who have had prior experience of therapy commonly report that they were uncertain about what an intervention might have been about, what the practitioner might have been thinking or hoping for and what their specific role was. This uncertainty can create anxiety. Within the Theraplay model, we try to be as clear with parents as we are with the child and will spend considerable time preparing, practicing and reviewing sessions directly with parents. Using this direct approach, we attempt to communicate in as transparent a way as possible with parents. The aim is to help the parent feel clear and comfortable about the purpose and method of the intervention and most crucially to feel safe.

There are parallels here in what we commonly observe in groups (of adults or children) where there is a capable and kind leader and a mutually agreed purpose. The group will be settled, focused and calm. They will enjoy being led and will relax into this safe structure. Some practitioners new to Theraplay may find the shift towards a higher level of organization, predictability and transparency something new. They may not feel comfortable with, for instance, directly asking a parent to do something, feeling that this is too "bossy" or directive. They might prefer to be tentative, questioning and to leave pauses to allow the child and parent to express themselves. We are all more able to connect and relate when we know what is happening. Both parent and child therefore can experience an increased sense of safety within the structured framework that Theraplay provides.

Being near the floor

Children naturally play on the floor and there are many advantages of setting up the work in this way. If everyone is comfortable, there is often a feeling of immediate connection when playing at a child's natural level on the floor. Being lower down also allows the child more opportunity for fuller body contact with the ground, which is helpful for regulation. Most sessions will include a variety of quieter and livelier interactions and so there will usually be a combination of quieter seated activity and more physically active games. You will therefore need some clear space in which to move about and will need to move any furniture to create some space.

You may need to make adaptations to the room set-up depending on what is most appropriate to meet the individual need of the parent and child. For example, if the parent is unable to sit on the floor, seat the parent on an armchair and place the child in an armchair of matching height so they can be eye to eye. The main consideration is to provide a setting that is comfortable, both physically and emotionally, for the parent and child. There may be personal, physical, cultural and contextural issues that will need to be taken into account. In any adaptations, it is important to hold the Theraplay framework in mind, rather than focusing too much on the rules. It is much more important for a child and parent to feel comfortable, relaxed and safe than to insist on a set way of organizing things.

Materials

The materials and props used in Theraplay are simple and inexpensive. Some materials are used routinely and need replacing and others you will only buy once.

- Materials that need routine replacement: snacks and drink, foil, straws, newspaper, black paper, crepe paper strips, balloons, stickers, cotton balls, feathers, powder, lotion.

- Materials that need occasional replacement or washing: pillow covers, throw blankets, scarves.

Practice question:

- Can I bring additional toys and materials into sessions?

EXAMPLE: Isaac is 10 and has been coming to Theraplay sessions for a few weeks. This is session seven and I am making my session plan. So far, Isaac has taken part in most of the activities to some extent but prefers to fiddle with the props rather than to really engage. I am running out of ideas and his parents have told me he really likes puzzles. I know that puzzles are not part of Theraplay but I think perhaps a puzzle will help us connect more easily, so I decide to bring one into the session and I choose something that I think will catch his interest. Isaac and his father arrive and Isaac immediately notices the puzzle box and his eyes light up. His interest in the new toy is clear and I feel pleased that I have found something that will capture his interest. I begin the check-up by doing some measuring and quickly realize that Isaac will need to play with the puzzle first as he is now preoccupied with it, so we unpack the puzzle and Isaac begins to put it together. He becomes very absorbed and settled while making the puzzle, the most relaxed and capable I have seen him. I try to make small comments and to help him with it, but he ignores me and pushes my hand away. When he has finished the puzzle, he admires it, briefly shows it to his father and then decides to take it apart and make it again. Any attempts I make to involve myself in the play are ignored and the only way either his father or I are able to become part of the play is to follow his instructions. The session continues in this way until I state that we need to put the puzzle away and move on to something else. Isaac complies with a sense of frustration and his level of engagement in the remainder of the session is low. After the session, I am troubled and am unsure how to move forward. Isaac is clearly more comfortable with the puzzle and doesn't much enjoy the Theraplay activities. I had introduced the puzzle in the hope that this would aid our engagement but it seems to have had the opposite effect. I am wondering whether Theraplay is the right approach for him but can equally see that providing the self-absorbing activities he likes will not help make therapeutic gains.

In the example above, the practitioner was struggling to find a satisfying way to elicit reciprocal interaction with Isaac. She had obviously been thinking hard about what Isaac would like and made efforts to provide him with an attractive alternative, the puzzle. If reciprocal social interaction is generally difficult for Isaac (as seems to be the case), it is not surprising that he finds the puzzle more comfortable. He doesn't have to look at anyone and can stay in his own world, doing something he feels good at. It is likely that he will prefer the puzzle over anything else. A puzzle may be a useful way to help Isaac keep purposefully occupied and calm in a parenting or school context but it is not part of the Theraplay approach. Within a different kind of therapeutic context, activities such as drawing, coloring, doing puzzles, playing board games and using toys designed for symbolic play are useful tools. Theraplay, however, is focused on the direct intersubjective impact of interactions between the people present, and the purpose of the simple props is to facilitate this process rather than divert from or replace it. The only exception to this would be a simple rhyming book which can sometimes be helpful because it provides a break from intensity but has the rhythmic effect of a song.

The task with Isaac is to deepen our understanding about what is activating him and to adjust the way we engage with him within the Theraplay to make it more manageable. This might involve playing side by side, deliberately averting our eye contact and focusing on the kinds of engagement he finds easier, for instance exciting play rather than intimacy. There are times when you might decide the child is not yet ready for the emotional intensity required in Theraplay and may begin the work in a different way.

The question of bringing alternative resources into Theraplay sessions links to a broader question about integrating other approaches into the Theraplay. Many practitioners have training and experience in other aspects of therapeutic work and may want to consider introducing other approaches into sessions. These can include, among others, dyadic developmental psychotherapy (DDP), eye movement desensitization therapy (EMDR), life story work, play therapy and working alongside occupational therapists.

Experienced practitioners naturally develop ways in which the approaches can be helpfully integrated but we would express caution about bringing in these different approaches prematurely. Theraplay as an approach is most effective when used as a stand-alone intervention and often the addition of other approaches reduces rather than increases its impact. This is usually because the practitioner, and hence also the child and parent, become confused about what it is they are trying to achieve. The work often becomes a loosely structured integration of techniques, with the practitioner falling back on their most comfortable mode of working, which is usually to talk. It is much more advisable to learn and practice utilizing Theraplay as a pure model before attempting to include other approaches. It can be challenging for new practitioners to "stick with" the non-verbal approach within Theraplay when they are more familiar with verbal and cognitively driven approaches. Similarly, practitioners who are trained in child-led symbolic play-based approaches may find the closing down of some communication difficult (e.g. if the child begins to play symbolically or introduces conversation). It is important therefore to appreciate the possible benefits of keeping the focus on the Theraplay.

Practice question:

- What happens if the child brings a toy into the session or uses the materials to start pretend play?

EXAMPLE: Valentina is 8 years old and has a history of abuse and neglect in her early years. She is coming to Theraplay sessions with her main carer, her grandmother. Valentina arrives clutching a doll and bag and is reluctant to put them down. I decide that it is better to have a smooth beginning and to allow Valentina the comfort of her toys than to make a fuss about this, so we come in together and I start the check-ups. I am putting lotion dots onto Valentina's hand and arm and joining up her freckles. Valentina says her doll has freckles too, and so once I have done Valentina's lotion I do the same for her doll. I am now wondering what direction this session will go in. Will Valentina want her doll to be involved in all the activities, and is this okay and potentially helpful within a Theraplay approach? At this point, I feel it is better to involve Valentina's doll in parallel to Valentina as she seems to be finding this helpful. As we play Bean Bag Drop (the doll now on Valentina's lap), Valentina then suddenly announces that her doll needs to change and she begins unpacking her bag, which it turns out is full of different dolls clothes, and Valentina begins to sort through the clothes and to talk to her doll. "I know, you want to wear your blue trousers, they will look good, let's get changed" and she glances at me to join her in this play with the doll. I have a decision to make now. Do I continue to keep Valentina's engagement by joining her in her play with the doll, do I ask her to put the doll away or try to direct the play involving the doll towards more Theraplay-focused interaction? I can see that Valentina would much prefer me to simply join in with her dressing the doll game but I decide that if I continue then the session will become entirely focused on this pretend play, so I say, "I can see you really want dolly to join in today. This session is just for you. Let's put dolly to sit on the couch and you can play with her later." Valentina looks surprised and disappointed and clutches her doll more tightly and I decide it is important to show Valentina that I have noticed how much she needs her doll, while at the same time trying to redirect the session towards Theraplay. "Oh, you really love your doll, I think you are disappointed that she can't join in today. I'm sure we can still find some fun things to play together."

I move back into the Theraplay and after a brief reluctance I manage to re-engage Valentina. Over the course of the sessions it becomes very clear that Valentina lacks confidence in interpersonal play and connection and if left to her own devices she would always have chosen play at one removed using dolls (and with little flexibility to let others join in). As she realizes that I keep returning to the Theraplay she begins to relax and we have increasing moments of delight and connection.

You can see in the example above that it would have been easy to continue the play with the doll but progress would not have been made in terms of her ability to connect in an intersubjective way. Having redirected the child to the interpersonal play between her and the practitioner, she gradually relaxes and becomes more comfortable.

Specific issues about materials

You will have been provided with a standard list of Theraplay materials, which are portable and inexpensive. This section will focus on some specific features of some of the materials that can impact on the work. The materials that tend to be standardized (e.g. foil, cotton balls) don't require any explanation, whereas for others (e.g. cushions, lotion, stickers) the choice of materials has a bigger impact and a few examples are discussed below.

- Blanket: The blanket needs to be both soft and strong. In order to lift a child and swing them, it is better to have a woven blanket than a stretchy fleece blanket. Some people prefer a thick brushed cotton sheet for covering and lifting children. You will also need softness for the nurture activities, and a texture that is comforting.

- Cushions and seating: Finding the best cushion arrangement is important. We recommend a combination of cushions: large cushions to provide a clearly defined and comfortable place for the child and parent to sit, and smaller cushions to be used for activities. Many people use the seat cushions from their couch to form the support for the child and parent to lean against and this works well. If you are working in someone's home, however, you must make sure that this is acceptable to them. If not, you need to find another solution. Bean bags can be useful as long as they provide adequate support (e.g. the chair-style bean bag rather than a huge flat one). If you do use a bean bag, you need to arrange for the parent to sit beside the child. It is useful to have two bean bag chairs side by side, so that they can lean against each other.

- Lotion: This can have different connotations for different children and needs some consideration. The scent and texture are important. The best choice is usually a hypoallergenic and odorless lotion with a consistency that is not greasy. Check with parents during your consent process.

- Scarf: Choose a thin scarf which has some translucency so it can be seen through. You can then play Peek-a-Boo without the child feeling completely blocked out (especially important for children who have experienced trauma).

- Newspaper: This is used for various activities including newspaper punch and flick. Not all newspapers are suitable. You need a large traditional newspaper (not glossy) without staples. It takes some practice to ensure that you hold the newspaper correctly, so try it out so that you are confident before including it in sessions. The knack is to hold the newspaper taut across the middle—don't dig your fingernails into the paper or it will rip—and hold it away from your body (so the child doesn't accidentally hit you).

- Powder and lotion handprint: You need black paper (other colors are not as good), and again this activity needs a bit of practice so that you get the right quantities of lotion and powder (you don't need much powder—just tap the paper to spread it around). Use the blowing of the powder as a shared activity (e.g. sit beside the child and blow together). This also prevents you blowing powder into the child's face or having to turn away from them to do it. Some people can't tolerate powder and others have responses to the smell, so you can get odorless talcum powder if needed.

- Bubbles: It's important to have high-quality bubbles that reliably work and a container and wand that are easy to negotiate without looking so that you can remain engaged with the child. Bubbles can be a challenging prop and it is really worth mastering the structuring use of bubbles; when you blow a bubble, put one on the wand and ask the child to pop it with a part of their body, such as a finger or foot. Once you are confident in this technique then you will know you have a way to introduce regulating structure if the child becomes over-excited. It can also be helpful to have a second wand available if you know the child will want to grab the bubble pot so that you can give them something to have in their hand (e.g. you blow the bubble, they try to catch it).

- Stickers: It is common to see stickers as a prop become counterproductive because they are too small or complicated. For older children and teenagers, of course, there may be good reasons to choose something more appealing. Avoid stickers with evaluative messages (good job, etc.). Stickers are used in sticker matching and need to be large and plain. There is a wide array of choice in stickers. It is best to keep to simple ones, since adding the complicated picture stickers increases the cognitive load of the task. The child will try to match color or image as well as place, or will start a conversation about the picture on the stickers. If we consider the aim of the sticker-matching Theraplay activity, we are trying to connect with the child via a simple physical mirroring by using the stickers. It is a non-verbal and sensory experience and can be very regulating. Simple, large, plain stickers are the best (e.g. plain round circles). The stickers need to be easy to peel off (i.e. not too small and fiddly) so that you can locate and peel the sticker off without needing to look at it. You may also want to be able to tear the sticker paper in some situations so that you can give the child some stickers.

Clothing

Theraplay is active and involves different movements, getting up and down and crawling. You need to wear comfortable clothes and be very aware of clothing that is exposing (e.g. of your cleavage and bottom). Many new practitioners review their videos and are alarmed at what they have on show. High-necked tunics work very well, low-cut jeans, cropped tops and skirts don't. Care around clothing also applies to the families we work with. Let families know that they need to wear comfortable clothing, and in situations where a child is repeatedly brought to sessions in a school dress, then remind parents to bring leggings or have a spare outfit available.

Videoing

We strongly recommend that you video your Theraplay intervention and this requires preparation, appropriate permissions and equipment. Different countries and organizations have different regulations around videoing, consents and storage and you will need to work within your local parameters. Videoing sessions can raise different issues and people can have concerns about:

- being seen (self-consciousness about being exposed in some way)

- their agency support ("My boss won't let me," "It takes too much time," "It's too expensive")

- potential legal vulnerability after the session.

The legal regulations around video use vary across countries and you will need to refer to and adhere to your local guidelines. Consent and storage issues need to be agreed in advance of any work undertaken. Videoing is being successfully used across the world in many different contexts, and with some preparation and thought it is almost always achievable.

What is videoing used for?

The purpose of videoing in Theraplay is to improve the effectiveness of the intervention. In other words, the purpose is therapeutic, rather than evaluative. The videoing is not intended to be used as a way to collect evidence of poor parenting or to focus on practitioner mistakes. The aim is to be strengths based: we use the video to support our work with the parent. You will need to feel confident about the clear purpose and ethics of videoing and to be able to communicate this clearly with those involved.

The process of actually using the video material is that you (and at times your supervisor and close colleagues) will review the video after the assessment or session. You should look in detail at specific sequences and patterns and may rewind the video to review moment-to-moment interactions. This can significantly improve your quality of understanding about strengths and challenges and improve the quality of feedback you are able to give the parent. Parent review sessions are built into the Theraplay process and it is usual practice to show illustrative video clips to the parent to aid discussion and understanding. There will be a lot of variation in what you might decide to focus on, depending on the perceived benefit to the parent.

Why is it important to video?

🖐️ **EXAMPLE**: Sharon is facing multiple difficulties in parenting Keely, her 7-year-old daughter, and is feeling desperate. Sharon feels rejected by Keely and thinks she doesn't have the skills to make the changes needed to help her daughter. She has agreed to undertake a Theraplay MIM assessment but does not feel hopeful that a Theraplay approach can help her. Sharon and Keely attend the MIM assessment and agree to be videoed. Sharon does her best to complete the sequence of activities in the MIM but, as she had predicted, Keely is oppositional and refuses to undertake most tasks. Sharon tries to keep going but by the end of the assessment she appears low in mood. She explains that she feels defeated and is obviously anxious about my perception of her. I assure Sharon that I am not looking for faults but at ways I might be able to help her, and I book a feedback session in quickly so she doesn't have to wait long. I review the MIM video and can see areas of obvious struggle but I also find some brief positive moments. My priority in the feedback session is to begin to build a supportive relationship with Sharon so that we have a context in which I may be able to be of help. Rather than showing video which highlights the difficulties between Sharon and Keely, I show Sharon the brief moments when Keely is looking up at her mother with a warm expression. I tell her that I can see that Keely really wants to find a way to be closer to her mother. Sharon sees this clearly in the video. Sharon is surprised and very moved. She talks through her tears about how she had thought Keely hated her and about how incompetent she feels as a mother. I empathize with her about how hard it is to feel Keely's warmth. We look together at a still image of Keely looking at her mother and agree that both Keely and her mother appear to want the same thing, to be closer. This video feedback has given us a clear shared focus for beginning work together and Sharon agrees to meet again.

When we review any video, we are always surprised at how much detail we see that was not obvious at the time. The video is an incredibly rich resource which, when used well, can significantly impact parents' perception and experience of their child. Like all interventions, the most important factor is the skill and sensitivity of the practitioner, who must be able to interpret what might be going on and decide what will be helpful to share with the parent. The decisions about this are often complex. It may, for instance, be quite clear that a range of difficulties are apparent in the video recording but you might decide that sharing these issues immediately would not be helpful. As we said above, in order to be of most help to parents and children, the adults involved need to develop a sense of trust and safety between them, so developing this trusting relationship with parents is the initial priority. Feedback from many parents and practitioners is that, while initially anxious, they find the video feedback to be an extremely valuable tool that clarifies many issues and brings hope.

Choosing not to video

Practice question:

- Are there times when you would not video?

There are some situations in which the use of video becomes an obstacle to the work and evokes significant anxiety in the parent, child or young person. An example is given below. In these cases, you will need to decide how to sensitively address the issue. There are various options, for instance in the MIM the practitioner can observe quietly and write notes as an alternative. The well-being of the child or parent is of course the central priority.

EXAMPLE: Daniel is 10 years old and has experienced neglect and abuse in his early years. He is now living with his long-term foster carers. Daniel and his carers agreed to undertake the MIM assessment, consented to the use of video, and are ready to begin a series of Theraplay sessions. During the MIM, Daniel completed all the activities and tried hard to please. He appeared to miscue a lot, smiling when he did not seem comfortable. During the first Theraplay session Daniel seems anxious, and while he goes along with all of the activities he is not relaxed. I review the video after the session and notice that Daniel glances frequently at the video camera and I begin to question the impact of the presence of the video on Daniel. I reflect on his early history, and after discussion with his foster carers, I feel it is possible that he may have had prior experience of being videoed as part of abuse. Whatever the context of his anxiety, Daniel is unlikely to express his distress directly and it is my responsibility to interpret his non-verbal signals. I therefore decide to present the consent issue regarding video more directly to Daniel. At the start of the next session I say that I wasn't sure he was comfortable with the videoing and tell him that it is fine if he prefers not to be videoed. When put to him this way, Daniel says he would prefer not to be videoed. I therefore remove the video camera and we continue the work without use of video. Daniel is markedly more comfortable, and his experience of me having noted and addressed his discomfort deepens his trust in my ability to help him.

In this case, the practitioner had to weigh up the ethical issue of using the video when the child's consent was unclear, with the disadvantage of having no video material to review and feed back. Had the practitioner not presented "no videoing" as a concrete and acceptable option to Daniel, he may have continued to participate, but his discomfort might well have negated any potential benefits of the work.

Choosing Theraplay® activities

When planning your Theraplay sessions, you have to choose a sequence of activities and there are many choices. Your choice should be based on your understanding of what the child needs at the moment and on the underlying purpose or effect of the activity. The activities that have become part of the recognized repertoire of Theraplay are those which have been found to be impactful from a relationship and therapeutic perspective. The simpler the activity, the better, and if props or materials are used, it is important that the relationship purpose is kept central.

There are very many Theraplay activities that have been tried and tested and are listed in various publications, as well as at the back of this book. The repertoire is constantly developing. Some of these activities are based on well-known relationship-focused play (e.g. knee bouncing, Peek-a-Boo, traditional action songs) and others have been invented specifically for Theraplay.

You will be trying to select activities that will suit the child:

- from a developmental perspective
- for a specific therapeutic purpose
- taking into account practical considerations.

Developmental perspective

The activities differ in terms of the kinds of cognitive and practical skills that are needed to participate in them. Additionally, some are clearly more suited to a very young emotional age and others more appealing to older children. You will be pitching the activities at the child's emotional age rather than their cognitive age and will need to get to know the child well in order to ensure that the child is capable of engaging with them. The first couple of Theraplay sessions can usefully be considered as part of an extended assessment process, as a great deal of new information and understanding is usually gained in these early sessions.

Therapeutic purpose

The activities vary in terms of what elements they draw on. Some activities are specifically focused on a particular dimension, such as Nurture. Others are more exciting and stimulating or highly structured and regulating. The activities also vary in terms of the relational intensity that they evoke (for instance, Mirroring is more relationally intense than La La Magnets) and you will make a judgment about what will be most useful with the family you are supporting. Your therapeutic choice of activities and objectives for the session leads directly from the MIM assessment and feedback process and your developing understanding of the child and family.

Practical considerations

There are some practical considerations when choosing activities. If, for instance, the child or parent has a particular limitation, strong preference or cultural sensitivity, then you will need to take this into account.

Two different approaches to planning a session

The following session plans are for a 4-year-old child. It will be the child's first Theraplay session. These plans have been made by two different practitioners, who were asked to share their plans with their supervisor before the session as a learning exercise. Both practitioners are new to Theraplay and have put a lot of effort into constructing their session plans, but practitioner B clearly has a better grasp of what is required than practitioner A. Here are the two session plans.

 PRACTITIONER A PLAN
    Crawling in as kittens
    Measuring with crepe paper
    Bubbles
    Foil print
    Balloon in the blanket
    Kicking the balloon with legs lying on back
    Squeaky pigs
    Draw around hand
    Blanket swing
    Snack and song
    Hold balloons between bodies to walk out

🖐 PRACTITIONER B PLAN

Hold hands and do big steps in
Song (tommy thumb/hello song)
Bean bag drop
Peek-a-boo
Cotton ball hide
Cotton ball throw and pick up
Circle song (ring a roses)
Snack and song
Hold hands and gently swing child out (1, 2, 3 wheeeee)

These two plans look very different and yet they are for the same aged child. The supervisor discusses the plan with each practitioner and here is a summary of her thoughts.

Practitioner A plan

From a practical point of view there are many activities in this sequence that require different props and materials. This will create practical difficulties for the practitioner within the session as they will need to manage the various materials, using crepe paper for measuring, moving on to bubbles, foil and a balloon within the first few activities. Using a lot of props also usually means that the practitioner will need to turn towards the basket to organize the materials and this creates a break in the connection with the child during transitions between activities. When you watch the video of a session in which the practitioner has to shift focus to manage the many materials, the impact on the child becomes very clear. Many children cannot manage it and will try to move away. Using multiple props like this is often a mistake made by those new to Theraplay. Props can feel attractive as they give you something to focus on (rather than each other) and reduce the level of intimacy in an activity, which might provide you with a sense of security. As always, it is important to think about whose needs are being met by the activity, the practitioner's or the child's?

The mindful use of props can, of course, be very helpful when you are using them for a specific therapeutic purpose, for instance you might introduce a prop deliberately to reduce eye contact and take the level of intensity down if a child is finding this difficult.

A different reflection on the plan is that this practitioner also includes the squeaky pigs from the MIM assessment. His explanation is that the child liked playing with the toys. This indicates a misunderstanding about the difference between the MIM assessment which uses a variety of play materials (such as the squeaky toys) and a Theraplay session that uses only simple props to aid the relational play.

Practitioner B plan

This plan is simpler and shorter, using few props, and the activities chosen feel clearly appropriate to the young developmental age of the child. Peek-a-boo, Cotton Ball hide and Ring a roses are all activities that 4-year-olds will typically delight in and do not have high cognitive demand. Practitioner B has also chosen a straightforward entrance and exit that do not require the child to do much (i.e. they don't have to understand symbolic play as in the first example, and can just be led by the adults in and out of the room). Two simple songs have been included, in addition to the song in the snack section, and this will provide natural rhythm and structure. There is a nice mix of quieter and livelier activities.

You can see in these two short examples that the planning and thinking behind a Theraplay session depends on the practitioner's understanding of what lies behind the activities. As you develop your understanding of the guiding principles behind Theraplay, your sessions will become more purposeful and based on your understanding about what the child needs. Further examples of session plans for different contexts and different aged children can be found in Chapter 19.

Summary

Being prepared, organized and thoughtful about the practical aspects of Theraplay sessions makes a big difference to how the work will proceed. The parent and child will feel your confidence and care when expectations are clear and you will gain a much more accurate understanding of what the underlying issues are for both parents and children.

Chapter 6

Theraplay® Sessions with Children

CHAPTER PLAN

This chapter will discuss the following areas:

When Theraplay® sessions go well

Early sessions: Common issues

- The child doesn't respond as expected
- The importance of being in touch with your feelings and emotional response to an interaction
- Significant changes in the child's behavior over the first few sessions

Leading a Theraplay® session

Supporting an out-of-control child

- What might be underlying the out-of-control behavior?
- What adaptations are made around safety?
- What are the key strategies that can help the Theraplay® practitioner keep control while remaining playful?
- Plan your session carefully

Supporting a child who appears over-compliant

Supporting a child who appears very anxious or frightened

Supporting a child who is very controlling

Supporting a child who appears defensive

When Theraplay® sessions go well

By the time you begin the sessions, you will have undertaken the intake, MIM, feedback and parent preparation and will have a clear sense of what your goals are. You then begin the sequence of Theraplay sessions involving the child.

A typical example session would be as follows:

Entrance: clear entrance activity.

Check-up: show deep interest in the child and help the child to settle.

Goal-directed activities: with focus on the dimensions and areas agreed
    following MIM—sequence of quieter and livelier activities.

Nurture sequence: snack, song.

Exit: clear exit activity, with the child leaving well regulated.

What we are aiming for when embarking on sessions is that we will make a positive initial connection with the child and that this will establish a context of safety within which we can develop the relationship. The first couple of sessions often form an extension of the assessment process in that you are getting to know the child and how things feel in the room and you begin to feel clearer about what your objectives might be. You familiarize the child (and parent) with the structure and pattern of the session and hope to see a deepening of the child's capacity to remain regulated and to connect. We often use cycles of up- and down-regulating activities to create a flow—where you start with a quieter check-up and seated activity, move towards livelier and more exciting play and then into a quiet and nurturing sequence towards the end.

As the sessions progress, you will get to know the child very well and can see how he manages when you introduce the parent more into the interactions. This is often a sensitive judgment as you want the parent to feel confident and the interactions you facilitate to go well. You will involve the parent more and more as the sessions develop, often doing games in a circle, one direction then the other, or you and the child doing an activity in a pair and then swapping so that child and parent do it together. In this stepped way, you can ensure that there is a manageable pace. We often experience a delightful and moving connection between the parent and child as they increase in security with each other. Towards the end of the sessions, you will facilitate the parent to lead much of the session and in effect you become more of an observer, facilitating the child and parent from the side. Throughout this whole process you will, of course, have been regularly meeting with the parent for review sessions and discussing and illustrating issues through the use of video feedback. There is a countdown to the last session, so that all are prepared, and this last session usually includes some marker of the ending, such as a special cake or a celebratory activity like Decorate the Child. We would typically provide a follow-up session some months on to hear how the family are getting on.

Once you actually begin Theraplay sessions then different issues will be revealed, some you may have predicted and others not. This next section discusses some common issues that arise within early sessions. The remainder of the chapter looks in more depth at common Theraplay session scenarios.

Early sessions: Common issues
The child doesn't respond as expected

By the time you begin the first Theraplay session, you will already have gathered a lot of information about the child and family. You will have discussed the child in detail with the parents and formed some hypotheses about what some of the underlying issues may be and this will have informed your goals and plan for the first session. This preparation is very important but it is essential to hold your hypotheses lightly. Just as the parent feedback session following the MIM often changes how we interpret what we have seen, so the actual experience of being with the child, feeling what it is like to interact and connect with them, always deepens our understanding. The child may not respond in the way you have anticipated and you may need to adapt your plan significantly in the initial sessions.

The importance of being in touch with your feelings and emotional response to an interaction

Practice questions:

- What do you do when a child doesn't respond as expected?

- How can we make sense of our emotional and physiological response to a child?

EXAMPLE: Changi is 6 years old and has been living with his adopted parents since he was 2 years old, following a period of neglect while living with his birth family. His parents describe him as "delightful" but they are troubled by his recent increase in aggression. In our initial discussion, his parents say that Changi gets upset when told a simple "no" and has always been reluctant to let them help him, even when very small. Although Changi appears somewhat subdued and is reluctant to accept help from his parents during the MIM, the overall picture is of a young boy who is well regulated and engaged, with very capable and warm parents. I feel confident with my session plan and am looking forward to starting the Theraplay sessions.

Our first session seems to start well. Changi smiles and holds his hands out to jump into the room with me. We move through the initial check-up and then stand up to play La La Magnets. Changi joins in, smiling broadly, in retrospect maybe too much so. I am starting to feel uncomfortable and can't work out what is going wrong. Each activity in itself is going to plan. The father is quietly sitting and watching with a smile but Changi's body language is a little stiff and I feel emotionally cold and as if we are just "going through the motions." Soon it becomes more intense than that, and I feel that something unpleasant is happening, even though everything on the surface seems fine. The father is still smiling and looks supportive and I take comfort from that. Perhaps it is just me and that this is going okay after all. I decide Changi needs some higher level of engagement and I try to bring more excitement and animation into the session to see if this will help. We toss a ball on a blanket between us and I call out excitedly when it flips up, with an animated expression trying to encourage some genuine excitement. Changi joins in, his facial expression and level of energy appearing to match my own, but I feel increasingly confused and uncomfortable. Something is not right. The session continues in this manner. On paper, it looks like a model session and both the parent and child are behaving superficially in ways that appear consistent with expectations.

When the session is over I reflect on what just happened. The experience I felt in the room leaves me confused and anxious. I don't understand what was so difficult about it but am left with a rather distressed feeling and realize that I would rather not see them again.

It is impossible to fully articulate the felt experience of being with a child. Even when a session is videoed, the video footage often fails to capture the visceral felt sense of being together. We must always take account of how it feels to be with the child in the room and not just how it looks from the outside, or the video. This experiential feedback, what it is actually like to try and "be with" the child, can hold very important meaning. In the example above, the practitioner hadn't predicted that Changi would leave her feeling this way, and while the session was in progress she became confused and anxious. Changi's way of responding on the surface seemed to be indicating that all was well, but the felt experience of trying to genuinely connect with him didn't. When the practitioner tried to seek some feedback from the father's expression, he too was signaling non-verbally that things were fine, which only deepened her sense of confusion. What was she missing?

One of the main goals of the Theraplay approach is to form a connection with the child on a non-verbal, sensory and direct level. This kind of primary intersubjective connection is based on the very early patterns of relational connection between infants and their parents. The infant coos and you coo back, the infant is upset and you match their energy in a quick rhythmic jiggle to connect and then calm them by slowing the rhythm. The to and fro of these basic interactions produces a feedback loop so that each partner feels good (and this feedback loop includes associated "feelgood" physiological changes in terms of hormone and chemical changes in the brain). With Changi, what seemed to be happening was that the practitioner was trying to connect with him in this very direct and connected way and in contrast he responded in a way that was not genuinely reciprocal. The practitioner was therefore feeling increasingly alone in the interaction, an unpleasant experience. She continued to try and provide inviting and warm interactions (as is the Theraplay way) but the lack of feedback she was receiving left her feeling uncomfortable. The fact that Changi (and his father) looked to be engaged added to her sense of confusion. It is worth saying at this point that none of this sequence of interaction would have been a conscious effort from Changi's side. Changi was clearly trying very hard to join in and to respond to the practitioner and was giving all the superficial facial and behavioral signals to indicate that he was engaged, but when the practitioner looked back at the video she noticed stiffness in Changi's body. It was as though part of Changi was genuinely trying to cooperate but another part was hesitant.

This is a classic example of "miscuing," where a person shows one set of responses while actually feeling another. In Changi's case, he expressed friendly engagement, smiling and joining in when actually the experience felt disconnected. It is hard to know at this point what Changi was experiencing. It could for instance be anxiety or just shut down and numbness. The practitioner's focus now must be to try to understand what he was feeling so she can help him. She knew from his history that as an infant it is very likely that Changi missed out on some fundamental early relating and simply does not know how to relate in this primary intersubjective way. She must find a way to provide Changi with the support within the sessions which will allow them to discover ways in which he can be more genuine and emotionally present in his interactions. This first session really took the practitioner by surprise. Due to her lack of experience, she had not picked up on the more subtle signs of Changi's miscuing during the MIM. Since his parents were also interpreting his responses as accurate signals (rather than miscues), her conversations with them had not highlighted this issue so far. If she could go back and rewrite her MIM report in light of her new insights, it would read quite differently. The practitioner now realizes that her interpretations of the MIM, the parents' views and her hypotheses based on the history were all subjective and depended on her own experiences, sensitivity and knowledge. This first session brought a new perspective and understanding because she has been able to reflect carefully on it. She will now direct her attention to be more attuned to Changi's fear of closeness and will proceed with a higher level of awareness of Changi's compliance and miscuing.

This new understanding has also reduced the practitioner's level of discomfort and brought a feeling of openness to Changi, which in turn will help her find new ways to connect with him.

Many professionals and parents now understand the basic idea of miscuing from a theoretical point of view, but how it shows itself and actually feels in the minutiae of everyday interaction is often less well understood. When Theraplay is undertaken with skill and supervision, these more subtle yet profoundly important issues often come to the fore very quickly. The directness of the approach really amplifies the difficulties the child may be experiencing with primary intersubjective connection. This is a major strength of the Theraplay model when facilitated skillfully. It is important to hold in mind that a child who has spent many years miscuing as a way to manage may be hard to read, for parents and practitioners alike, and that having a high level of awareness of your own responses, triggers and issues is essential.

Significant changes in the child's behavior over the first few sessions

A frequent experience when beginning Theraplay is that the interactions with the child in the first couple of sessions may seem clear and smooth and then, around session three or four, something changes and it feels harder to connect. This pattern has been experienced so routinely that experienced practitioners will refer to "session three" with raised eyebrows! Obviously, there are many occasions when the work develops in a different way, but this experience is sufficiently frequent to warrant some thought.

Practice questions:

- Why might the child initially engage well and then become more difficult?

- How can we anticipate this and form a useful shared understanding with parents?

EXAMPLE: Kesri is 9 years old and has come to sessions with her foster mother. In the first two sessions she appears engaged and playful and there are some moments of clear enjoyment and intimacy with me. During the snack and song, Kesri sits close to her foster mother and appears to really enjoy the contact between them. She gives me warm eye contact and there are some moments of spontaneity and delight. Her foster mother is surprised at how cooperative Kesri has been and is feeling more hopeful.

Kesri arrives for her third session and immediately announces that the sessions are "boring" and that she doesn't want to be treated like a baby. She refuses to enter the room playfully and flops down on a couch in the room and asks how long she has to stay at the session. Her manner is reminiscent of a surly adolescent and I am struggling to think of a way to engage with her that will not be rejected. Her foster mother looks disheartened and tired. I make a few attempts to involve Kesri and each time she gives me a look of disdain! I can feel the energy drain out of me and feel rather humiliated. At this point, I would rather end the session or begin talking to Kesri's foster mother than face further put downs from Kesri. I try to reorient myself to the new situation by remembering what has brought Kesri into my office in the first place. I know that she is routinely hostile to her foster mother, rarely accepts support, has experienced several placement moves and has no sustained friendships. Kesri is clearly an unhappy and lonely child and I decide that I will gather my energy and continue in my attempts to connect with her. I tell myself that even if she does reject all my efforts, it will have been important to keep giving her the message that I want to be here with her.

I try to engage Kesri with a blanket and ball throwing game and try to lighten the atmosphere with funny walks, but my attempts to draw her in appear futile. I decide to sit down and make a foil sculpture of my foot (I predict that she will refuse to let me do hers) and I can see I have caught her interest. I try not to make a big thing of her glances and continue making my foot mold, working hard to keep a warm, non-verbal presence, and when finished I hand her the mold. She looks at it for a moment and I decide to make another of my other foot and at the same time I pull off a piece of foil and hand it to her. We are both now fiddling with the foil in parallel—I am making a foot mold, she is tearing her foil into little pieces. I realize that if I look at her she will retreat and so I accept this low intensity parallel activity as the most she can manage today. I am excited that she is doing anything with me but I realize that I must not show her my pleasure too directly because this will be too hard for her. I would like to create a nurturing sense for her, but I know that she will not be able to relax into having the snack alongside anyone. I tell her that I have a snack for her and simply hand it to her. While she opens it, I collect a bin and place it at a distance from both of us and I begin throwing pieces of foil into this bin. I am making concerted efforts not to look at her too directly and am actively trying to find low intensity ways of helping her stay connected. She joins me in throwing foil pieces into the bin. Our session ends soon afterwards and as we get up to go Kesri looks at me briefly with a warm and open gaze. I realize in that moment that she is glad I have persisted in my attempts to be with her and that the work is really beginning.

For many children and their parents, beginning a sequence of Theraplay sessions will be a new and unfamiliar experience. If they have accessed professional support before, they are likely to have engaged in talk or in play of a less direct nature. Parents might not have been included in the work at all and the expectation from everyone is usually that the work is focused on addressing difficulties of one kind or another. When a child initially responds warmly, one explanation is that the direct level of engagement from the practitioner is disarming for the child and they are not responding in their habitual manner. You may see them engage and respond in a delightful young manner, which may not reflect their usual day-to-day functioning (for instance, if they are generally uncooperative and the family is in a conflictual pattern). The practitioner and parent may feel relief and a premature sense of excitement that the sessions are going so well. Another explanation is that the child may be choosing to go with your directives outwardly, while holding you at arm's length. This way, they have time to decipher your intentions without calling too much attention to themselves.

As the sessions continue and the child becomes more able to predict what the practitioner is doing (both with respect to the pattern of activities and also the practitioner's warm and unconditional style), we often see a change in the child's willingness to engage. The child's habitual self-protective responses come back to the fore and the previously "friendly and engaged" child shifts abruptly into oppositional responses. The child seems to be intentionally disrupting sequences of engaged interaction that previously had gone well. It is helpful to be prepared for this possible change and to forewarn parents so that the adults do not show disappointment in the child. This change can in fact be seen as a positive sign—the work has begun! The child is now bringing their vulnerabilities directly into the sessions to be addressed. From the parents' perspective, this change can be a mixed experience. On the one hand, there is a sense of relief that the child is behaving in the difficult ways that the parent has been experiencing at home ("At last a professional can see what I'm trying to deal with"; "It's not just me"). On the other hand, many parents feel embarrassed and responsible for their child's behavior and may find it hard not to correct or intervene in some way. They may also fear that the practitioner's warmth in the face of the child's difficult behavior may make things worse.

From an attachment perspective, we know that as children feel emotionally safe, they may show more of their internal confusion and distress. Common expressions such as "they take it out on the people they love the most" ring true in a therapeutic context as well as in families. A helpful message to parents is that the child will find intimacy with the parent harder because the "parent is the most important person to them." This will often provide much-needed reassurance to a parent that it is not that they are a bad parent but that their child is frightened of intimacy, and that closeness with them, the parents, may be even more difficult because they are so essential to the child. From this perspective, it is a positive sign when the child shows more challenging behavior in the session.

There are many different ways children find to manage uncomfortable experiences. One common way of expressing discomfort is by becoming uncooperative. Parental statements such as "he always spoils games so we don't play anymore" are typical. The child may then get used to activities ending "because of their behavior."

When we see an increase in uncooperative or difficult behavior in sessions it is often a sign that the work is beginning—we need to value it and patiently work with it. Theraplay as an approach disrupts the child's usual ways of managing when they are emotionally uncomfortable by providing a response that is different from what the child may be predicting. Within the initial Theraplay sessions, the child may be so surprised by the practitioner's warmth, and the feeling that someone seems to be genuinely enjoying being with them, that they allow themselves to be swept up and they join in delightful sequences of much longed-for interaction and closeness. These are experiences they desperately need and have missed and you may see a dramatic change in the child's appearance (they may look much younger) as they allow themselves to relax. This feeling of connection and closeness is, however, unfamiliar and brings a strong feeling of vulnerability with it. There will often be a tension between connection and disconnection that becomes increasingly obvious as you get to know the child. The child both desperately wants moments of connection and also finds them overwhelming.

As the routine of sessions becomes more familiar, the practitioner may find that the child becomes harder to entice into play. The child may become engaged for a moment, then "come to" as if becoming aware of the connection that is occurring and they will then actively retreat in a range of ways. This can be experienced by everyone as a backwards step—the child is becoming "resistant" or oppositional. It can be more helpful to think of this response as a natural stage of the process whereby the child is showing you the things that are so difficult for them. Your task then becomes to find the ways in which you can help the child feel more comfortable; in other words, you are trying to gently and persistently widen their window of tolerance for connected experiences. This may take time and patience but it only really begins once we see the child responding in their habitual self-protective manner. Therefore, this difficult moment (which can arise specifically in early sessions or may be present throughout) can be reframed for all as something important and positive.

Leading a Theraplay® session

One decision to be made is about to how much to lead and how much to follow. Theraplay is described as "adult led" in the sense that the practitioner plans and leads the overall structure of the session. This differentiates the approach from many other play-based approaches (such as child-centered play therapy or child psychotherapy) where the interaction is led by the child who initiates some play or dialogue and the practitioner follows and perhaps joins in or comments on it.

It is worth thinking more about what "adult led" means in Theraplay because it is not as simple as it may sound. The practitioner plans the sequence of activities for a session and endeavors to maintain a sense of pace and movement through the session (in this sense it is adult led). At the same time, the practitioner must be sensitive to the child's responses and the impact of any activity or way of interacting and adapt spontaneously in order to help make the most of the sequence. This might mean changing the plan many times as the session unfolds and making minor adaptations in response to the child from moment to moment. In this sense, there is a great deal of following from the child's cues and feedback.

The aim overall is that the practitioner leads so that the child has a "safe experience of being led." For some children, this will be a new experience, and because it might feel strange, they may do a range of things to try and make this unfamiliar experience more manageable, such as trying to change the game or take the lead, or withdrawing from the person attempting to engage with them. It is important to understand why persevering with this idea of leading is important. After all, it may well feel easier (for everyone involved) in the short term to simply follow the child's ideas.

Practice question:

- Why might it be helpful for the child to have an experience of being led?

Here is an example of the dilemma a Theraplay practitioner might face.

EXAMPLE: Bella is 6 years old and has had to become self-sufficient because she did not receive early safe adult care. She is competent and very independent. Bella has been playing happily with toys downstairs while waiting. It is time to come upstairs for her first Theraplay session. I organize a playful way to come into the room, walking sideways holding hands. As soon as Bella realizes this is the plan she pulls my arms roughly and walks forwards, with an angry look on her face. I start to sing a silly hello song and Bella looks directly at me and says with scorn, "That's not a nice shirt." It is less than a minute into the session and I am already having doubts about this approach! Her negative response to me appears to be triggered by any attempts I make to lead. We are quickly embarking on what feels like a battle of wills; surely things will develop more therapeutically if I allow more flexibility and follow her?

Bella had been managing very well when she was playing downstairs (with toys and in play led by her). She was well regulated and calm. As soon as I attempted to take the lead and draw her into an interaction between us, Bella became defiant and unhappy and I began to feel disliked, a bit mean, and my confidence wavered. In order to persevere, I need to be convinced that this is the best approach. Why might it be helpful for Bella to have an experience of being led? She is competent, self-sufficient and clearly not enjoying this new experience.

I persevere in this instance because I think Bella does not know how nice it is to be led by a safe adult. She has adapted to an unsafe situation and has missed out on essential early experiences of safety and dependence. Her competence and self-sufficiency have developed from necessity and are quite forced. She doesn't feel safe enough to move between emotional states of relaxation and following to confidently leading. She only feels safe when she is leading and in control. With this in mind, I feel it will help Bella to be able to relax while being led, clearly an experience that is new and may be difficult. So, I decide to persevere, focusing on basic Theraplay principles. I try to finish each activity sequence (even if it has to be done quickly with a lot of humor, or with a background of objections and distractions). I choose activities that might be very engaging to draw her in momentarily and organize the transitions between activities so that they are fast and seamless. It is quite clear that if I pause, Bella will interrupt and try to take charge. I still want us to have a positive experience, of course, and I work hard to find ways of playing that seem to be easier for her. The kinds of games which allow standing side by side, for example funny ways to cross the room, work better than face-to-face games. Activities where we make a very loud noise and then play with the modulation of the sound work well; she enjoys the excitement of doing something she is often told off about. She is also drawn towards more cognitive activities, and I presume this is because it gives her more of a feeling of familiar competence (we hold the edges of a blanket and I say, "If you are wearing socks then run under the blanket"), and I intersperse these with the more intimate activities which are difficult for her to accept. What emerges is that these quite high-energy, engaging activities help Bella to have fun with me while I provide a confident and enthusiastic lead. The message I'm conveying is "look how we can play together, you are fun to be with and I'm going to organize things so that they work out well."

Bella becomes increasingly relaxed and less oppositional, and I decide she might manage sitting quietly with her mother. I arrange for us all to sit down (side by side, with the mother snuggled close to Bella) and I sing a rhyme while she eats a snack. As I sing, the rhythmic repetition, the warmth and stability of the mother leaning against her and the snack allow her to relax further and she molds into her mother's body. We sit in this way for over five minutes and it feels close and profound. This is the first time that Bella has allowed her new mother to sit close in this way and her mother is quietly crying. I try to extend this new experience for the mother and Bella as long as I can (adding an extra humming verse once the story has finished). As soon as it is clear we have reached the end of the song, Bella leaps up and rushes to the other side of the room calling out what the next game will be and abruptly leaps onto her mother, hurting her in the process. The closeness and moment of reliance on her new mother has obviously left Bella feeling vulnerable and her response is overactive, poorly regulated and difficult to manage. She is now leaping around on the back of the couch. I try to keep calm, check that her mother is okay first and then, following my original plan, I move towards the end of the session. It seems very important to complete the sequence. Bella is strong and physical and it would not be possible to pick her up, so I try to entice her back with a game of crawling; she re-engages and we all leave the room crawling together.

In this example the practitioner decided to continue with her attempts to keep the overall lead, to draw Bella in as far as she was able and to ignore many of her interruptions and ideas. This was based on the practitioner's knowledge of her history and the way in which she related generally, and the practitioner interpreted her interruptions and opposition as attempts to avoid warm intersubjective connection. Had the practitioner engaged in what felt like constant invitations to argue with her about what they were doing, she would have been comfortable with this familiar combative interaction, so typical of her interactions with the world, which often led to aggressive escalations. The session felt quite difficult (probably for all parties) but overall the practitioner kept a feeling of leadership and high warmth. The practitioner's sense was that the period of quiet intimacy at the end of the session was only possible because of what went before and that Bella was then able to allow herself temporarily to be cared for and to let softness in. It is worth noting that the practitioner didn't in any way attempt to feed Bella, to hold the packet of the snack or direct her towards anything more demanding during this phase and focused only on creating some extension of a feeling of closeness.

Supporting an out-of-control child

This section covers the following different practice questions:

- What might be underlying the out-of-control behavior?

- What adaptations are made around safety?

- What are the key strategies that can help the Theraplay practitioner keep control while remaining playful?

For most parents, teachers and therapeutic practitioners, the challenge of trying to engage and manage a very out-of-control child feels daunting. How we manage the problem varies greatly depending on the age and size of the child as well as on our expectations of their developmental level. We do not expect infants or toddlers, for instance, to be able to respond to our instructions, but as a child matures, our expectations of them increase. We may find the screaming, tantrums and oppositional behavior of a toddler highly stressful but we are usually able to accept, tolerate and manage it as part of the process of raising a young child. Once the child is aged 4 and above, in most situations we assume that they will respond to some extent to our senior adult status! We expect them to listen to us to some extent, to be relatively calm and to do what we ask them to do within reason, especially if we are not the parent.

When a child of 6 or 14 is displaying out-of-control behavior, not only is it physically challenging but it also challenges our expectations about what "should" be happening. An 8-year-old "should" be able to follow instructions without screaming, and most 8-year-olds can. When we are faced with an 8-year-old child who shouts in our face, seems deliberately to do the opposite of anything we ask, flails around and flies into a rage or high distress without warning, it is unsurprising that we, ourselves, enter a state of stress. Adults respond differently to this stress. Some may become forceful and determined that the child will comply, others may attempt to tackle the situation via persuasion and support—and in either situation, if the child doesn't respond the adult will continue to feel stressed and ineffective and may respond with anger or growing resignation. In either scenario, we face a significant problem in that the child is in an emotionally unstable state (and may be hitting, throwing things or charging around) and we as the adults are at a loss as to what to do.

Children who experience intense states of being out of control of themselves are likely to come to the attention of a range of adults outside the family, from schools to specialist providers. In practice, even so-called "experts" can find it very hard to know what to do when a child is creating havoc.

The Theraplay perspective provides a combination of a direct approach with a solid underlying theoretical understanding, and this is often helpful.

What might be underlying the out-of-control behavior?

In order to find an approach that is helpful to a family it is essential to understand as clearly as possible what might be underlying the child's behavior. This can be hard to unpick and children's behavior can be confusing. Sadness, anxiety and tiredness, for instance, may be expressed as overactivity or irritability. The child may be overstimulated or the context (environmental or emotional) may be outside their window of tolerance. Behaviors can look similar with very different causes and the most appropriate response will therefore also vary considerably. The issues that can lead to out-of-control behavior in children often include:

- tiredness, hunger, physical discomfort

- acute distress about something that has happened

- anxiety, sadness, anger, frustration

- general difficulties in regulation

- sensory sensitivity

- trauma history and triggers

- difficulties in the family functioning around the four dimensions of Structure, Engagement, Nurture and Challenge.

As the practitioner, your role is to work together with the parents and other adults involved to try and deepen your understanding of what might be going on. You will glean a lot of information from the intake and MIM process and will begin to form hypotheses about the various factors that may be contributing to the behavior. Maintaining an open and curious attitude to this exploration is very important, and in many ways this process of trying to formulate an understanding of underlying issues continues throughout any piece of therapeutic work.

It is very helpful to keep returning to this question of what might be underlying the behavior. When we are faced with out-of-control or challenging behavior from children it is surprising how quickly we can move towards blaming or adopting overly simplistic behavioral explanations. This is understandable because the child's behavior is very stressful for those around them.

EXAMPLE: Jake, aged 8, is engaged and calmly doing the Hand Stack activity with me and his father. I decide to move to a livelier activity and set up a seated tug of war using a blanket, with the father and Jake on one side and me on the other. I playfully start the game with some animated encouragement: "That's it...pull...see if you can pull me to the other side...oh no...you're so strong." I am shuffling towards Jake, and his father and I are both being quite loud and enthusiastic. Jake suddenly let's go of the blanket and lashes out at his father who is taken completely by surprise. What just happened?

In this example, I think something has triggered Jake into a fight-flight response. He suddenly felt unsafe—perhaps the volume and animation of our energy overwhelmed him. He couldn't run from the situation as he was wedged close to his father and so he lashed out and caught his father's face with his arm. This kind of situation could easily be misinterpreted as "Jake being aggressive," whereas I think we had inadvertently created a situation in which Jake felt unsafe and lashing out was the only way he could manage.

I immediately stop the activity and put my efforts into trying to help Jake calm. I say that maybe our loud voices frightened Jake and I reassure him that he isn't in trouble as he is clearly anticipating that the play won't continue following his outburst. I express to his father that I think I made a mistake in organizing such a loud game, as a way to communicate to the father what I think has happened and also that I am taking responsibility for the incident. I suggest that the father and I sit quietly and wait until Jake is ready to sit down again and have a snack with us and that I will be more careful not to scare him again. Jake takes a few moments and comes back to sit close to his father. I follow up with the father after the session.

Part of our contribution, as Theraplay practitioners, is to offer new hypotheses that can direct the adults towards warmer and more empathic ways of supporting the child. We also need to be very sensitive to our own triggers, the impact the child may be having on us, and to seek guidance and support from our own supervision.

What adaptations are made around safety?

When a child's behavior in the room becomes potentially dangerous there are some important adaptations to be made.

First, you need to have confidence that you will be able to manage the situation. If you know a child is volatile you should undertake a risk assessment before sessions begin—about whether your room and premises are suitable (could the child run out into the road, for instance?), and about what you and the parent will do if the child becomes explosive. Such risk assessments are usually routine practice when working with unpredictable children. In high-risk situations all potential hazards will need to be assessed (the child running off, trying to enter kitchen or office facilities, climbing out of windows, throwing objects or needing to be held in some way to keep them safe) and you will need to ensure that you feel adequately prepared and qualified in working with this kind of scenario. It is better to be over-prepared as this will help you all feel safer. You also need to make sure that your relationship with the parents is on solid ground and that you have agreed an approach should an incident arise. These kinds of discussions and agreements should be built into their consent process.

Once you are actually in a volatile situation there is little time for discussion and you and the parents may need to act decisively and in tandem to help manage the situation.

You will usually have a good sense of what the likely risks may be from the history, the MIM and parent preparation and can make environmental adaptations, such as removing heavy objects that could be thrown (like a table lamp), or checking that the outside door has a high lock for instance, to ensure the safest possible context. Child safety is obviously paramount, and if the child behaves in a dangerous manner then you and the parent will take actions to prevent harm. During the session itself, if there is an incident, for instance the child pokes the adult too hard, then the "no hurts" rule applies. You will immediately stop the activity (while not becoming angry), check that everyone is okay and if possible find a way to successfully "re-do" the activity so that it can be achieved in a safe way. This principle applies to both physical and emotional "hurts" and it is your responsibility as the practitioner to find ways to redirect and repair without shaming.

 EXAMPLE: Keiron is 9 and is aiming frequent derogatory comments towards his mother during the session. He tells her she is stupid and scowls at her when she offers some warmth. He begins to deliberately bump into her when sitting next to her and I can see that she is uncertain how to respond. I had been trying to keep going with the activities and remain upbeat (and so had she) but now I am feeling uncomfortable. Should I carry on playing or do something that could potentially spoil the atmosphere? It's hard to know. There isn't really time to think but I decide I can't keep allowing Keiron to be hostile to her and that this situation could escalate. Hostility to his mother is one of the reasons the family have come for help. I remember the "no hurts" rule and try to find a way to use this idea that doesn't inflame things. I say, "You're looking really fed up, Keiron. You know, I think maybe I haven't set this up right, it's too hard for you to sit so close to your mom. (I move to sit between them.) I'm sorry I hadn't thought this through properly, let's change this about a bit so we can play and it can feel okay." I stop talking and don't enter into discussion; instead I focus on engaging Keiron in a new regulating activity of stickers. He looks relieved and joins in the activity. I can feel the tension from him reduce as soon as I have created this physical distance between them. Once we are settled I turn to the mother and say, "I hope that feels okay for you, it's important no one gets hurt and I had made it too hard." The mother nods and I continue with the session.

On reflection afterwards, the practitioner felt that she had increased the intensity between the mother and Keiron too quickly. Keiron was obviously not coping well and needed more support from the practitioner to manage the distance between them. He had given many signals that he was finding it hard and the practitioner had reacted rather slowly, hoping that distraction on its own would work. The practitioner had given him too much responsibility. Once she realized that he couldn't manage the responsibility, and she provided a way in which he could engage without hurting his mother, Keiron relaxed. This dynamic presented dilemmas for the practitioner because she wanted to increase the closeness between Kieron and his mother (this had been one of her main aims) but realized that she had moved too quickly towards that goal. She realized that she would need to organize the joint activities in a much more gradual and supported way. After this session, the practitioner reflected on what had happened and could see that had she not reduced the level of her expectations, the situation could easily have escalated and the intervention would have been very unhelpful.

When a child is persistently hostile or aggressive towards their parent, it is your responsibility as the practitioner to address this. The Theraplay approach tries not to criticize the child but rather to try to understand what might be triggering or leading to the fight behavior. In the session itself, we redirect the play and find ways to adapt the situation so that the child can manage more effectively. Because it is not helpful to allow aggression to continue, you need to tackle the issue in a clear, direct way, one that increases, or at least maintains, the connection between the parties involved. The child's aggressive manner conveys the clear message that "This is too hard for me, I don't feel safe, I can't be with this person at the moment without being mean." You need to consider what you have done to contribute to this dynamic. Perhaps you have involved the parent too quickly or without sufficient preparation, or at the moment the level of responsibility given to the child is too high. You might need to seat the parent at a distance in an observer role (and potentially provide a second worker to support them) while you build a relationship with the child. Alternatively, it may be that the activity was too stimulating and caused the child to feel out of control.

Sometimes saying a few words to name what is happening can be very useful. Within a Theraplay context these words would usually be kept brief and would be used to provide regulation and clarity for the child and parent: "Oh, that didn't feel quite right, let's do it this way." You would not be inviting any extended discussion. There are some specific situations in which it might be useful or important to talk—see Chapter 20 on using reflective dialogue in Theraplay.

Other adaptations with respect to safety include the careful choice of activities, choosing those that are more likely to regulate, and avoiding use of materials that could become hazards (e.g. removing props and objects in the room that might be thrown, leaving shoes outside the room, checking that the room is safe, reducing the quantity of material in your basket).

What are the key strategies that can help the Theraplay® practitioner keep control while remaining playful?

As described above, before you can know what strategies might be effective, you first need to understand as much as you can about what is underlying the behavior. Close and detailed observation of the child, what they do and how it impacts them, brings a lot of helpful insight.

What does the child gravitate towards? What activities or responses seem to help them feel calmer or more engaged and what seems to make things worse? Very often you will need to think on your feet, try out activities and approaches and use your initial couple of sessions as an extension of the assessment process until you begin to understand the child more clearly.

With a child who can easily tip into an out-of-control state, regulation is key. Your role is to try and provide co-regulation as far as possible and to set up a context in which the child is most likely to be able to remain regulated. Children differ greatly with respect to their sensory systems and also in the kinds of responses or activities that help them regulate. You will need to assess the individual child in detail.

EXAMPLE: Chanel, aged 7, has arrived for her session. Her mother looks rather upset. They have had problems in the car on the way to the session (Chanel kicking and shouting). I greet them and move to go towards the session room. Chanel leaps up and tries to barge past me to get into the room. I have anticipated this and stand in front of the entrance and say in a confident and playful voice that we will go in as a wheelbarrow (I have chosen this activity because I think it may help regulate her and it will also slow her down). Chanel refuses and tries to push past me shouting "move out of the way." I have to think fast. I decide it's too hard for her to cooperate with me, so I change plan and state that we will all walk in together, while I take hold of her hand and guide her towards her usual cushion on the floor. I do this quickly as I know that she will begin to drag me if I'm too slow. As soon as she is seated I provide a snack and blanket and I begin measuring her hand. The combination of sensations seems to calm her slightly and I have a moment to think and re-plan my session as it is now clear that what I had in mind will not work.

Chanel is clearly too stressed to manage activities that give her a lot of responsibility; she may well become aggressive and destructive if her arousal state goes back up. I can see that she won't be able to sit for long, so I move towards some structured physical activities that are not too intimate—La La Magnets goes well followed by Funny Ways to Cross the Room. We hold hands in both of these activities and this helps me feel how she is coping. We sit down again and she picks cotton balls out of my basket and I immediately regret having left them in there. At this point I wish I had no materials! Rather than fight about the cotton balls, I decide to turn her actions into a game. I cup my hand around hers and say "squeeze," while pushing our hands together. I predict that Chanel will not want to give up the cotton balls, so I quickly direct a game of "how many can you pick up with your hand?" I place several balls in front of her while holding her hand and say, "Ready, steady, go," letting go of her hand on the "go," and Chanel gets the idea and picks up the balls in her hand. I quickly cup my hand around hers and say, "Ready, steady, throw," letting go as she releases the balls. I have my arm around her tummy to stop her dashing off after the balls and set up a crawling race to collect them: "Ready, steady, go." This activity works well. Chanel is now engaged. The activity allows stopping and starting and a level of anticipation and excitement that she can manage, and we play several rounds.

The session continues in this vein. I am having to think quickly to stay one step ahead and I feel as though I'm on a knife edge, trying to engage Chanel sufficiently to keep things on track but trying not to over-excite her or trigger aggression.

Chanel struggles significantly with nurture and I decide to keep the nurture light and short. I provide her with a second snack, which I do not attempt to feed to her, and I read a short rhyming book before ending. I have barely had a moment to check how Chanel's mother is managing. The session is short and exhausting but we have managed to get through it without an explosion and Chanel is clearly more regulated as the session ends.

After the 30-minute session I am sweating, with adrenaline coursing through my body. I feel relieved she has gone, and that I survived, and am filled with empathy for Chanel's parents. Living with a child this volatile must be utterly exhausting and it is easy to see how parents have to develop strategies to manage—becoming resigned to not being able to influence their child or becoming angry and punitive.

Plan your session carefully

Careful thought is needed when planning your session. The impact of particular activities and approaches depends on the child and also the kind of activity. Some examples are given below.

Activities that support regulation include:

- those with high inherent pattern and rhythm
- those that involve stop and start

- those that give the child low levels of responsibility; in other words, avoiding rule-based to and fro activities and gravitating towards activities that can continue without the child's full cooperation. This allows the session to have a sense of form and organization, which will be reassuring for everyone.

Things to be mindful of:

- Avoid baskets full of interesting objects that can be emptied and spread across the room.

- Plan a session that takes the child's volatility into consideration. Your aim is to help the child engage while staying regulated. Avoid activities that might overstimulate the child, such as Push Me Over, Row, Row, Row Your Boat, Crawling Race and Hide and Seek.

- Avoid activities that create unpredictable movement and excitement. Bubbles, balloons, feathers and balls can lead to escalating excitement, which can tip into aggression.

- Physical activity involving large muscles and movement (i.e. high levels of proprioceptive input) tends to be regulating but great care needs to be taken around spinning, chaotic movement (as created when playing football, for instance) or movement that doesn't include breaks. This area links to specialist knowledge around sensory integration, and if the child you are supporting has significant issues related to sensory and occupational therapy you may need to seek specialist guidance (further information in Chapter 18).

- When children find close intersubjective connection, nurture and touch difficult, they may only be able to sustain these kinds of activities for very brief periods before needing a big shift in focus and energy to keep them regulated. Sessions may therefore work better when you move from episodes of more intense connection to high physical regulating activity and back again.

When issues of regulation are a primary issue with a child you may need to rearrange the usual session sequence and the session flow may feel quite different from a typical session (more information about this is available in Chapter 18). Children who find close touch and nurture hard to accept, for instance, will not respond well to a close check-up right at the start. Instead, you should focus purely on regulating input. Starting the session with a snack and a structured game using a prop (to reduce intimacy) will work better than going immediately into a close check-up. Similarly, during the session you may find you need to add high-energy activities after quiet nurturing ones in order to help the child reorganize themselves.

There may be a fine balance between energetic and physical activities (which might help engage a reluctant child and provide potentially regulating proprioceptive input) and calming activities to help bring excitement levels down. You will need to remain open to the unique sensitivities of the particular child—what one child will like or find helpful may be a trigger for another.

When considering any activity, it is useful to ask yourself, "If he goes up, how am I going to bring him back down?" There are many small ways that you can provide co-regulation to help bring a child down in their excitement level:

- Match their energy and then organize the play so it becomes quieter (e.g. join/match the child in shouting "we are great," then when you have their engagement, playfully bring the volume and intensity down).

- Practice going up and down in levels of excitement within a safer activity before you experiment with something more risky (e.g. have the child lie down with feet in the air and balance pillows on his feet before stacking pillows and having him balance on top and jump off).

- Focus on the transitions between activities and limit the amount of "loose" time (e.g. use high adult support and structure to help the child sit down, move across the room and shift from one activity to the next).

- Plan a short and focused session using few props (e.g. choose one prop and plan a sequence of activities using this prop. This allows you to be fully engaged with the child and means you do not need to break contact with them to manage your materials).

All students learning Theraplay will say that the first couple of dysregulated children they work with provide a very steep learning curve! If you are supervised well during these early Theraplay sessions, you can learn a great deal from these children and apply your learning to many similar situations. When you observe a very volatile child in the hands of an experienced practitioner, you will be amazed at the level of engagement and organization that can be achieved. With experience, your confidence and range of adaptations will grow.

We will now change focus to think about children who appear quite different in their behavior.

Supporting a child who appears over-compliant

Children who are over-compliant can present parents and practitioners with dilemmas and in many ways they can be some of the most challenging clients to work with.

Over-compliance describes a situation in which a person follows the directions of another person to a degree that may be deemed unhealthy. This can be a subjective and culturally specific notion but there are some typical patterns that cause concern. For instance, a child who does what they are told to the point that they will put themselves into harmful situations is clearly vulnerable.

Children who are described as over-compliant often appear passive and lacking in emotion. They may superficially "behave well" and be "easy" to manage because they follow instructions but also they may not express opinions, may not engage in spontaneous play and may show little delight and joy. For parents, this sense of a lack of genuine engagement and energy from the child can, over time, feel very exhausting: "You don't get much back," "It's as if they aren't really there." This group of children are unlikely to come to the attention of teachers or other services because their behavior is not typically challenging. Their levels of distress or unmet need can easily be missed. In addition, some very compliant children can have sudden and out-of-character explosions when overwhelmed that take everyone by surprise.

Over-compliance can develop in different ways and in this discussion we are thinking about something more than individual temperament and family and cultural differences. The over-compliance that we are concerned about is usually underpinned by experience of fear in the early years. The child has learned that the best way to keep safe is to remain passive, to do what they are told and to merge into the background.

Our approach to helping an over-compliant child is likely to be very different from helping a child with very poor regulation.

Practice questions:

- How can we tell if a child is being over-compliant rather than just well behaved?

- What can the practitioner do to help the child feel more relaxed?

EXAMPLE: Fadi, aged 10, is polite and quiet. He arrives with his foster father and smiles at me as I introduce myself. I explain the set-up of the sessions and he takes his foster father's hand as we enter the room. During the early part of the session, Fadi appears happy to participate in all of the activities and from a superficial standpoint the session is going really smoothly. It is quickly becoming apparent that Fadi will do whatever I ask of him and his warm and appropriate facial expressions give an appearance of some level of enjoyment. I have, however, a growing sense of unease. The feeling is almost as though Fadi is not present. He smiles and joins in and yet I don't feel a visceral sense of engagement or delight. I try to be more enthusiastic and bigger in my own expressiveness to see if this will increase the feeling of energy, but this seems to have the impact of making Fadi seem more passive rather than more engaged and I decide to become quieter. The session continues in this seemingly easy but rather flat way and there are only a few moments during which I get a mild sense of delight. This happens when we are playing slippy slip and I catch a brief giggle as I surprise him by falling backwards.

I leave the session with an unsatisfactory sense of not really having got to know Fadi in spite of my efforts. He smiles as he leaves and asks his foster father when he will be back again.

The main consideration around compliance is to try to ascertain whether the child is genuinely relaxed or whether they appear frozen in their response, or as though they are "going through the motions" in terms of their relating. When a child gives warm facial responses, as Fadi does, this distinction can be very subtle.

I decide to review the video of the session quickly in order to understand more about Fadi. Watching carefully, I can see that his smile and warm expression are quite fixed throughout, showing little variation. His smile appears to reflect the adult expressions rather than to emanate from him. The video review also allows a more detailed observation of the rest of his body. While Fadi was smiling at me and participating in the activity, there was a stillness in his body which became particularly noticeable during the more intimate nurture sequence. It becomes clearer to me that Fadi was not finding the lotion or song pleasant at all. In fact, he looks uncomfortable, pulling his body slightly away from both me and his foster father, while holding his hands out smiling. This wasn't as obvious when I was in the room with him and I could easily have missed it had I not been looking for the signs. Reviewing the video has helped me see the discrepancy between his non-verbal facial and bodily behaviors. His warm looks were accompanied by a slight bracing in his body and I realize that the situation with Fadi is much more complex than I had thought.

I need to think about how I might help Fadi feel more comfortable in our next session. I decide to have a parent session with the foster parents to look through the video together and to reflect on their perceptions of Fadi. I think I will need to take things more slowly, to focus more acutely on his bodily non-verbal feedback and to try to find ways to help him feel safe enough to relax.

When you are working with a child who seems to be compliant but you have a gut feeling of unease, it is essential to review your video of the session. Your "gut sense" is often wiser and can help you pick up the discrepancies in the child's behavior that may not be obvious. It is very helpful to focus on discrepancies between facial and other bodily non-verbal communication. When you view the video, you may see that the child is looking you in the eye and is cooperative and polite but his body is stiff, his movements not fluid and his smile looks plastered on, without much change. With over-compliant children there is a real possibility that you may be adding to their distress if you miss these cues and you need to pay particular attention to ensuring that they are feeling okay, by noticing, commenting and repairing. As an example, you are playing a sticker match game and playfully put a sticker on a child's nose. She subtly flinches and then smiles. This child is not finding the experience pleasant—quite the opposite—and she is tolerating something unpleasant that you were hoping would be therapeutic. A helpful response would be to notice immediately, comment on it (so that she knows you have noticed), make the situation more manageable, find a way to show the child that you take responsibility for it and hope that she is okay, and hold on to this understanding for the future. As an example, you notice the slight flinch: "Oh! I don't think you liked that sticker on your nose (take it off). I thought it would be fun but I can see it didn't feel nice for you; let's put it somewhere else (put on a safe place like a sleeve)." Continue with the activity (if the child seems relaxed enough) and be more watchful, checking with the child whether things feel comfortable or not (and noticing if her body gives a different message). If this pattern continues in a habitual way (e.g. the child always expresses that she is fine when you think she is not), then this pattern is worth commenting on: "Oh goodness, it's really hard to know when things feel okay and when they don't. Dad and I will keep checking together. It's important that the games feel okay when you come here and it's fine not to carry on if it doesn't feel right."

Supporting a child who appears very anxious or frightened

Children may be highly anxious about coming to sessions for a range of reasons, and the initial task is to try to make some sense of their anxiety—they might be worried that they are going to be in trouble or will get things wrong, they might be anxious about having to play or there might be home-based issues that are holding the child back. In all of these scenarios, you must be sensitive to the child's state and show them in the way that you interact with them that you have picked up these signs of anxiety. This usually entails taking sessions slowly and sensitively, giving the child time and opportunities to express preferences, observing responses very closely and picking up on signals that the child is not managing. These are similar observations as those discussed when supporting over-compliant children (who are highly anxious under their compliant presentation), but the experience in the room with a child who is frightened can feel quite different. They may be very quiet and withdrawn, unable to make eye contact or to participate and you can feel the anxiety viscerally and feel anxious yourself that you may be making things worse by trying to engage them.

If a child appears frightened then your only focus is to help them feel safer. This often means taking a step back, providing them with a safe place (e.g. soft cushions in a corner) where they can sit quietly, perhaps providing a snack or blanket and withdrawing all demands. Do not try to entice them into play at this time or expect them to be able to manage intimacy. They may need to hide. They need time to calm, and many children prefer to be alone in a cosy corner, under a blanket, behind a couch, although sometimes they may be able to accept comfort from the adults.

Practice questions:

- What approaches help you engage with a child in a high state of anxiety?

- Are there times when you might decide to use a different therapeutic approach?

EXAMPLE: Diego is 10 and is brought to his first session by his mother. They have previously completed the MIM (in a different building) and Diego appeared very wary and withdrawn. He stands quietly by his mother's side looking down. Diego appears highly anxious and I wonder how best to begin the session. As I move slightly towards him to greet him, Diego stiffens and I realize I can't begin any play at this point as he is obviously frightened. I decide to pause and give Diego some time to orient himself to the room. I say to his mother, "You haven't been here before and it can be hard coming to a new place, let's have a look around so you can see where everything is." Without making any demands on Diego, I point to different things in the room, show him where the toilets are and open cupboards and doors so that he can see where they lead. I describe what is going to happen in a simple way: "In a minute we're going to go into the next room to play some games together." Diego immediately glances anxiously at his mother and it seems that just the idea of "some games" has added to his worry.

I wonder aloud whether it would help to know in advance what we will be doing and go to collect my list of activities and show it to Diego. "This is what I was thinking of trying today. I've written a short list. We can try some of the activities and see what you think." Diego glances at the list and then at his mother and begins to look a little reassured. I say, "We can always stop if you don't like what we are doing." I decide then that it would be helpful to go into the therapy room. "I tell you what, Diego, let's stand at the door and see how many steps it takes to get over to those cushions. We three stand side by side here (I decide not to link arms with Diego at this point as it feels as though this would be too much for him and I focus only on supporting him to enter the room) and let's walk together." I begin to count as we walk towards the cushions. The mother helpfully follows me and Diego comes quietly in next to her. He is tense and scanning the room but at least we are now in a more enclosed and comfortable space where there is more potential for him to calm. I quickly feel that I need to find a way to engage Diego that feels safe and predictable and that anything demanding (including touch) will heighten his anxiety. I also think he will benefit from some explanation about how the session will run to reduce his hypervigilance. The session progresses in a slow and careful way. I talk more than I would usually do and demonstrate each activity with his mother first so he can see what is required. Gradually, Diego begins to relax a bit and seems to appreciate that I will not force him or criticize him in any way.

After 15 sessions with Diego, I find that his trust in me and in the process has deepened and he has opened up immeasurably. There are moments of delight and spontaneity and times when he is beginning to assert himself. Looking back, the key was to be highly sensitive to what he could manage and to give him time to absorb what was being expected of him. This meant many repetitions of the same activity, done in the same way, combined with a constant awareness of his emotional state.

A highly anxious child will need many safety cues in order to begin to relax. The kinds of cues that can be helpful include:

- keeping the pace calm and predictable

- explaining what will happen next

- demonstrating on yourself or the other adult before expecting the child to participate

- ensuring that your vocal tone and facial expressions are relaxed, warm and not overly dramatic

- providing reassurance that the child does not need to continue if it feels too much and checking in with them regularly

- picking up on their non-verbal cues (positive and negative) and making these explicit (this helps the child to feel that you are noticing their messages).

As in all therapeutic interventions, you will be continually reflecting on what it is you are providing and whether it is helpful for the child. When working with any child who is highly anxious or frightened, it is essential that you do not become overly focused on the activities you had planned. This can be a particularly difficult challenge if you are a student learning the Theraplay model, as your focus may be on learning the structure and sticking to the expected protocol. This is one of the reasons we strongly recommend beginning your practice with more straightforward families rather than highly traumatized children who may need a lot of adaptations to the usual protocol.

When children are highly anxious and frightened, you will be focusing only on helping them feel safer and this will mean using the adaptations we have described above. Often this gentler, slower and more reassuring Theraplay approach will be sufficient. There are times, however, when you might feel that the child is so alarmed they need a less emotionally demanding therapeutic approach before they are ready for Theraplay. You might, for instance, focus initially on working with the parents to help them develop therapeutic parenting and find ways to provide calm, predictability and regulation in the day-to-day environment. This bedrock of environmental safety in the home setting is needed to help stabilize the child before moving on. You might find a less relational approach is more manageable to begin with (e.g. non-directive play or focusing on physiological regulation via occupational therapy). For children with complex difficulties, there is not a single approach that will resolve all issues and you will want to seek advice and guidance from colleagues. Taking a neuro-developmental approach to thinking through what is manageable for the child at different points in their development is a powerful and useful way of reviewing your work (Perry, 2001).

Supporting a child who is very controlling

Many parents and practitioners use the term "controlling" to describe the way a child might behave, for instance when they will not follow instructions, or they resist our attempts to influence them and will only participate in interactions or activities (sometimes across all areas of everyday life) on their own terms. In other words, they seem to want to be in control of everything. The lived experience of parenting or trying to engage with a child who behaves in this way is exhausting and can be extremely frustrating. Many people use the word "controlling" in a pejorative manner—"The child just wants control, they want to dominate me, they do it on purpose to wind me up"—and this illustrates how hard it is for the adults to maintain a state of warmth and openness when faced with this kind of behavior. Before looking at examples it is worth unpicking what this kind of behavior represents.

Practice questions:

- How can we understand controlling behavior in a way that is not pejorative?

- What approaches are helpful?

In an ordinary healthy relationship, there is reciprocity and "give and take" in the way communication takes place. "I influence you, you influence me, we influence each other." There is a natural to and fro that develops its own understanding and rhythm; my delight amplifies your delight and, vice versa, you can feel my sadness and I can tell that you can feel it. This is a genuinely reciprocal relationship in which both parties are open and engaged and genuinely connected to one another, developing the ability to mind read and the capacity for mutual empathy.

Babies are born with the capacity for reciprocity. How the process unfolds depends on the sensitivity of the relational context around them. Infants and young children with safe, sensitive and interested parents will naturally enjoy and develop reciprocal ways of relating. This process begins in utero (movements and sensations being impacted in the maternal environment, sounds, rhythms, hormonal changes, etc.). At birth, the infant and parent gaze at and mirror one another and this interaction rapidly develops into a highly sophisticated synchronized "dance" between the two which includes timing, prosody, movement and facial expression (Stern, 2000; Brazelton, 2013). Children who have not experienced this quality of responsiveness in their early years miss out on the fundamental "primary intersubjective" experience that is the building block for future relationships. This is a profound loss and impacts all spheres of development. Theraplay focuses on creating intersubjective relating. (For further discussion on reciprocity and the social engagement system see Chapter 1.)

One way that babies and children cope with a lack of safe reciprocal care is to resist the influence of others (as they have experienced that it is unsafe and deeply painful). We may see a pattern develop whereby the child tries to influence others but tries not to be influenced by others. This is obviously a one-sided kind of relating, and while it can help the child to feel some level of safety, it has the cumulative impact of blocking out the other person. When people say in frustration that a child is "controlling," there is often an unspoken message that the child is doing it deliberately. In most situations, this is not the case—the child simply does not know any other way to be. They don't know how, or don't feel safe enough, to relate in a relaxed reciprocal manner and as a consequence are missing out on a wide range of experiences and learning.

This becomes one key focus in our Theraplay intervention. Can we help the child to experience connection and play with us for a few moments in a way that feels genuine, enjoyable and manageable? This is, of course, harder than it sounds. A child who has survived by becoming self-sufficient and has found habitual ways to protect themselves from the influence of others will find it very hard to play in a way that feels straightforward. For the child, it is as though maintaining control is as important as breathing. It is helpful to remember that from the child's perspective the overriding drive to maintain this way of relating is based on survival.

When thinking about how you can best help this child you need to hold in mind that they may not know another way to be. Keep reminding yourself of this. The impact of very controlling behavior on those around can be difficult to cope with and may have strong impacts on you personally (countertransference responses) that you may need support to understand. It is essential that you seek appropriate supervision if you feel yourself being triggered into negative or blaming responses. Your role is to provide the possibility of (likely very brief) reciprocal experiences that will be new for the child, and the Theraplay approach is an ideal vehicle from which to provide this support.

EXAMPLE: Bobby is 4 and arrives with his adoptive father. We have had a few sessions now and the father is well prepared and feeling confident about how we will work together. Bobby is like a hurricane, charging about the room and immediately pulling any objects he sees from the shelf in the entrance lobby. He flits from one thing to another and needs a high level of adult supervision.

I have talked with his father previously about how we need to avoid talking and negotiating and to have a focused session in which he and I work as a team to provide some clear adult structure around the play. The father has agreed that Bobby will sit on his lap and that one of us will have physical contact with Bobby throughout, either holding his tummy or his hand. We each hold one of Bobby's hands and do "1, 2, 3 Weeee!" to get him into the room and to his cushion. I start with a quick hello song while counting Bobby's fingers and then we move through a sequence of organized activities which have inherent structure but not too many rules. In Bean Bag Drop, I place a bean bag on his head. With my mouth and eyes open wide in excitement, I say "Here it comes" as he drops it (using a count down would be too hard for him). Each time I repeat this pattern, with the bean bag on his head, he tries to find a way to alter the game, dropping the bean bag to the side, behind him or trying to grab and throw it. I am quick and adapt to make the activity work out, ignoring his lack of cooperation and instead catching the bean bag and having another go. Trying a different approach, I put the bean bag on my head to drop it into his and the father's hands, but he deliberately removes his hands so as not to catch it, and so a similar problem arises. Whatever I do, Bobby tries to alter it in some way that breaks the cooperation and moment of connection. This seems to be the constant issue for Bobby. He wants to engage and is very playful and animated but can only do this on his terms. He is finding it very hard to relax and accept my adult lead.

The father and I have discussed this underlying pattern and have found that if we ignore much of his controlling behavior and find ways to keep a sequence and pattern going, Bobby will rejoin the game. So, I put the bean bag on my head, get ready to drop it into his hands, and when he removes his hands I just drop it into his father's hands, say, "Yeah, we did it!" and begin again. As we progress through the session we have more moments of spontaneous delight but they are still very short lived. It is as if as soon as he realizes he is connected in the here and now he then redoubles his efforts to disconnect. Our hope is that with many repeats Bobby will start to realize that he can rely on us to organize the games so that they go well. The father tells me that he has learned something from observing the way I keep going in a positive manner and he is integrating this approach to good effect at home.

It is very hard for a child like Bobby to relax while being led and yet he is only 4 years old. It is obvious that he cannot meet all his own needs and that he needs the support of the adults around him. With an older child, it may be less obvious but often the core issue is the same. Bobby does not know that it is safe to connect with anyone else and cannot relax into and enjoy intersubjective play. Although he is so young, Bobby is relying on himself and does what he can to retain influence and control over interactions. This is a very sad situation and one that needs addressing as early as possible.

Here are some approaches that are usually helpful:

- Underpin the sessions with clear structure, organization and sequencing.

- Facilitate the activities so that they work out well, whatever the child does. This will give them a sense of being fun to be with while being led. One implication of this is that you will avoid activities that are destined to fail. Rule-based activities (e.g. Red Light, Green Light, Mother, May I?, Eye Signals game, Mirroring) that require a child to wait to take their turn and to do something specific will often go badly because you have given the child too much responsibility. It works better to select activities that can be played even without a child's cooperation (like blowing a feather and seeing where it lands, making foil prints, drawing shapes on the child's back) and if they join in it is a bonus. This allows you to keep a sense of flow and order and also protects both you and the parents from becoming frustrated with an uncooperative child.

- Watch the transitions between activities and in particular pay attention if the child ends every activity. If this is the case then it means you need to organize the transitions differently. You may need to pre-empt endings and find ways to take ownership of new ideas so that there is still a sense of adult leadership.

- Be very clear about what you want the child to do. We often hear people say that a child is being "controlling" and then a close look at the session reveals that the activity has not been set up clearly enough for the child to know exactly what is expected.

- Acknowledge to the parents how hard this pattern of behavior is for them and spend time thinking this through with them. When parents are desperate to tackle controlling behavior it can sometimes be hard for them to appreciate how the playfulness of Theraplay might help. Time spent reviewing video footage and noticing how the child can be redirected or how sequences can be extended can be very helpful.

The examples above are relevant for many children who do not know how good it feels to experience a safe adult leading them, and with some work this group of children often do well with a Theraplay approach.

There are, however, some children with more severe difficulties for whom Theraplay within the usual protocol is just too demanding. This group may need significant adaptations and a more flexible approach. We do not recommend that you undertake work with children with severe difficulties in the early stages of your learning because it is important to learn the standard protocol and to experience what Theraplay can offer before making adaptations. As someone new to Theraplay it will be hard to unravel what issues are arising because of your own lack of experience and what may have to do with the particular child or adaptations needed with the model. If you do find yourself working with a child with whom nothing seems to work then you should seek supervision and guidance.

Supporting a child who appears defensive

There are many parallels when thinking about patterns of behavior that are described as "controlling" and those often described as "defensive."

Most people would describe defensive behavior in a child as including the following:

- refusing to participate

- making derogatory comments ("that's boring, you're rubbish")

- deliberately trying to provoke you.

Faced with someone who behaves like this towards us, we often are hurt and feel like withdrawing. This is obviously the opposite to our aim within Theraplay, which is to connect and engage.

When considering how to make sense of defensive behavior, as with controlling behavior, it is important to think about what might be underlying it. Children who have not had a positive experience of relating with others (for whatever reason) will understandably become distrustful of others. Being ignored, demeaned or scared as an infant or young child is an overwhelming experience and the child will try to protect themselves as far as they can. It can help to think about defensive behaviors as "self-protective."

Practice questions:

- What is the child trying to protect themselves against?

- How can you/should you persist in trying to connect when the child doesn't like it?

- Are there particular strategies that can help a defensive child engage?

The most typical reason that a child is defensive in Theraplay is that they may be trying to protect themselves from a feeling of closeness which is associated with pain from their earlier experience. An experience of connection can overwhelm the child. It exposes them to their own vulnerability, to their (often hidden) deep need of others, to their inner sense of worthlessness and to their loneliness. Yet they desperately need to connect with others and may be caught in a crippling state of tension. They may seek some kind of contact (this could be via provocative behavior) and at the same time reject your attempts to make contact with them. In this "push-pull" kind of situation it can often feel simplest just to withdraw, but this will leave the child on their own. Although they may seem to want you to withdraw, it is important that you don't, as it will leave them in their usual lonely and isolated position.

EXAMPLE: Jamie (aged 13) sits slumped in the corner of the room and his expression turns to a scowl as I approach him. "Hi Jamie," I say in a friendly tone and he doesn't respond. I'm already feeling nervous. This is our second session and in the previous one he had glared at me through most of the session, muttering, "This is stupid, I'm not a baby, why don't you have any proper things to do here?" His foster carer and I had managed to get through the session somehow but it had felt like a battle and I am worried now that he will simply refuse to come into the room at all. I have spoken with my supervisor and she suggested focusing on challenge activities and skipping the check-up or anything too intense at the start, so I have planned my session with this in mind. I start laying down pieces of newspaper in a line with gaps between them leading to the session room and say, "I'm not sure whether this is too hard but let's see if you can go from one to the other without touching the floor." "Easy," he huffs and gets up to try. He can do it without support and he has now come into the room, so I decide to stick with this idea and try to make it more appealing. "Okay, you're good at this, so I'm going to make it harder," and I spread the sheets out around the room with a big gap between them. Jamie rolls his eyes but begins to try and as the gaps get bigger I stand by him in case he wants to lean on me. He is determined to manage it on his own but I can feel a shift in his state; he is now more engaged and determined, and less dismissive about being here with us. I follow on with more challenge activities—cotton ball blow football and then jump across the river—and I can feel Jamie becoming increasingly relaxed. There are moments when he appears to be genuinely enjoying being with us. The session is going much better than I had anticipated and I am starting to feel more drawn towards Jamie. His vulnerability feels clearer to me and I'm no longer feeling that he hates me and the sessions. In particular, he likes to be watched while he succeeds and I realize that I can't pretend, I need to stick with activities with genuine challenge in them and to find a tone of voice that is humorous but not patronizing. We begin to make up creative celebrations together and I can glimpse his delight at being our positive focus.

As we progress over the weeks, I become better able to find a tone that will help Jamie engage in the initial part of the session (which he finds hard) and by using a range of challenge and some high-energy-based activities he gradually relaxes and feels safer. Now, eight sessions in, Jamie has stopped saying he doesn't want to come, says the sessions are "alright" and we are having many moments of connection and lightness. His foster carer tells me that Jamie is allowing more expressions of interest and affection from her at home. As I end my session with a complicated personalized handshake with Jamie, I reflect on how easy it would have been to assume that Jamie wouldn't have been able to benefit from this approach.

It is always hard when you are faced with a child who is being rude and rejecting. Our usual instinct is to withdraw or become angry. We may be tempted not to persist, both for our own self-interest (because persisting can trigger more rejection) but also because we might question what is helpful for the child. Most of us are steeped in the idea of the importance of listening to the child, allowing them to express what they do and don't like and showing respect for their wishes. When a child or young person clearly expresses that they don't like us, the activity or the session, it can take a lot of confidence to persist in trying to connect. Theraplay provides a wide variety of approaches for engaging a reluctant child or young person and has had many years' experience of the benefits of doing so. Many children begin to soften once they genuinely feel that you like them and want to be with them, and this change can feel profound and extremely helpful for parents to witness and be part of. It is as if you disarm the child's usual defensive responses—they forget for a moment to be hostile and find themselves enjoying the connection. Once you have survived a few sessions with a child in a hostile state and have experienced this shift in practice, then it becomes easier to maintain an upbeat and persistent manner.

Here are some points on strategies that tend to be most effective:

- Focus initially only on activities that you think will be manageable—you need to find some way for the child to engage with you.

- Choose activities involving some level of challenge to draw the child in.

- Use caution around nurture or close check-ups—keep these playful and light.

- Use humor without being self-deprecating.

- Take care with your tone of voice—you need to be confident and warm but may need to use a less sing songy tone (which could be interpreted as patronizing).

- Seek support and supervision (this kind of work can be demoralizing and dent your confidence).

- Support the parent so that they take the child's rejection less personally. Share your understanding with the parent that their child's response is their way of protecting themselves and keeping a distance rather than because they don't like the parent. It can be very reassuring for the parent to understand what underlies the difficult behavior.

Chapter 7

Working with Parents

CHAPTER PLAN

This chapter will discuss the following areas:

Including the parents

- – Ideal or hoped-for sequence
- – Understanding the parent's position
- – Challenges for the practitioner
- – Basic assumptions about working with parents in Theraplay®

Organizing your work with parents

- – Reasons for shifting to triadic work or including more family members

Strategies for making a parent feel included in the session

Strategies to avoid making the parent feel rejected when their child cooperates with you

Strategies for working with parents who have limited caregiving capacities

Utilizing the monthly parent-only sessions

- – Using video feedback and role play in session with parents
- – Using video feedback to develop parent reflective function capacities
- – Helping an insecure parent become more confident
- – Using role play to teach a parent to be more structured with a dysregulated child

Addressing persistent and unhelpful parent behaviors

Strategies for coping with a chronically resentful, burned-out parent

Summary

Including the parents

This chapter will discuss the range of issues that arise when including parents in the Theraplay intervention. Many practitioners have had little experience of including parents in their sessions with children and are unfamiliar and sometimes uncomfortable with the special dynamics that are created by their presence. The child is our main focus but we are also responsible for creating a context in which we are aware of the parents' needs and can help them succeed. If we only focus on the child's needs (and this will be the most frequent bias), then we can often miss important cues from the parents. In any work involving children and parents, the parent element is often the most important aspect and yet usually receives less of our attention.

Ideal or hoped-for sequence

When including parents in the work we hope that we have an enthusiastic and open response from them from the outset. Many parents are eager to be involved in the work. It makes intuitive sense to them that they would be included and they feel valued. Although most parents have some anxiety about the MIM process (as they feel worried about getting things wrong), once we move into the feedback and they can see that we are taking a strengths-based and sensitive approach to their role, many parents become excited about gaining some new understanding about their child and hopeful about changes that may be possible. When the parent is personally robust and is open to the Theraplay approach then we expect to follow quite a predictable sequence in terms of their involvement. We carry out the parent preparation session as described in the intake chapter and set up a system for parent reviews. This is typically one session in four, and many practitioners also have contact before and after sessions (either by email or by having a quick conversation) so that parents can let them know anything significant that has happened before sessions and have a check-in afterwards. This informal feedback can be very important.

In early sessions, we give the parent more of an observer role, asking them to sit to one side, or have the child on their lap, but to let us lead and we let the parent know that we will be very clear in any expectations we have of them. As the sessions progress, we involve them more and more, carefully choosing the right moments to ensure it goes well until we reach a stage where the parent is able to lead many of the activities themselves. We expect at this stage that there has been a generalization of the Theraplay approach into the home setting and we are usually working towards an end of the sessions. In order for this process to go well, we obviously need to develop a trusting and positive relationship with the parent and they need to feel confident and competent in their role. This is a complex process, impacted by many different variables, which are discussed in the rest of this chapter. When the parent role goes well you will feel as though you are working together as a seamless team.

Understanding the parent's position

Parents are in a vulnerable position. They are only seeking therapeutic support because things are not going well at home with their child. This means that parents often feel insecure and negatively evaluated, even when we work hard to focus on strengths. Unresolved issues from their own experiences may additionally come to the fore when they are in the session itself. Seeing their child respond warmly to the practitioner's nurturing care may trigger anxiety. Perhaps the parent never received such warmth when they were young, perhaps they feel "left out" in that moment or perhaps they feel embarrassed by their child's behavior.

Challenges for the practitioner

The position of the parent within sessions can be challenging for the practitioner for many different reasons. The parent may want to intervene or correct their child; they may be too competitive or be too excitable and rile up their child. They may look subdued, distracted or dismayed, which causes the child to feel worried about their parent rather than being able to enjoy the here and now.

For many practitioners who have specialized in work with children, remaining open and supportive with parents when they are doing something unhelpful can be the most difficult aspect of the therapeutic role. We easily slip into criticism of parents at the expense of our empathy for them because we have been drawn to the work by our interest in supporting and protecting children. However, we must extend our empathy to the parents as well or we risk significantly undermining the therapeutic work.

This is a major issue because if parents don't feel supported then they can't make the changes that are needed and may resent the practitioner and withdraw from the work. Within the Theraplay model, it is vital to maintain a supportive stance towards parents, get alongside them and find ways to facilitate positive development in their relationship with their child. It is therefore essential for Theraplay practitioners to develop a high level of self-awareness and personal insight on this issue. It can be helpful to think about the stance we take towards children. We try to see their perspective even when things are difficult and we work hard to find ways to help them manage. This is exactly what we need to do with parents. This does not mean that we cannot be direct, nor does it change the safeguarding responsibilities all professionals hold in work with children, but it means that we take as much care in our work with the parents as we do with their child.

A note about how we refer to parents within sessions: during a session we usually refer to the caregiver by their parenting role name rather than their personal name (exceptions would include foster carers, relatives and residential social workers). This is because we are focusing on deepening the relationship between the caregiver and child and want to use every opportunity to promote this connection. You might say, "Oh Mom, look at your boy's amazing hands," for instance. This does not mean that we are not interested in the unique adult and her range of experiences, some of which will be explored within the adult sessions. Parenting is only one aspect of an individual's role, and often our most vulnerable. Outside the child's session, it is essential to give time and attention to getting to know the adult as an individual and to call them by their name.

Basic assumptions about working with parents in Theraplay®

Here are some basic assumptions that we hold about the work with parents:

- Parents want to and can learn how to interact with their children in a more helpful way.

- We may need to use a variety of creative modalities to impact change, such as: modeling, frequent parent meetings, role-playing, use of video feedback and the use of an empathic, compassionate relationship with the practitioner.

- If a parent does not make the adjustments we are suggesting and does not seem to benefit from our guidance or modeling, we do not assume that the parent is resistant or not capable of change. Instead, we assume that we do not understand them deeply enough and try to find new avenues to be more empathic with them.

- We believe that any improvement in the parent-child relationship, however small, is valuable for the child and therefore worth our time and effort.

- We assume that if all else fails, the power of radical empathy and humble conversation about the obstacles both parent and practitioner are facing in their work can go a long way towards building parents' trust and cooperation.

- Only when we have tried everything we can to assist parents in improving their relationship and behaviors with the child do we move on to consider that the parent and child should receive therapeutic support separately.

- Theraplay is a potent, intense modality that commonly brings up countertransference issues between practitioner and parents. Practitioners must make a serious commitment to using reflective supervision or peer consultation to examine any negative feelings towards parents.

Organizing your work with parents

The Theraplay model focuses first on one parent-child dyad before going on to triads. This is because the attachment relationship is a dyadic process.

- A child has an attachment style that is unique and specific to each individual parent. In other words, a child can be securely attached with one parent and insecurely attached with the other parent.

- In Theraplay, we regard the parent to be our client as much as the child and we tailor our interventions precisely to meet the needs of both in the room.

- We are trying to build on our relationship in every session; therefore having consecutive, uninterrupted sessions with the same participants is crucial.

- We are attempting to attune to the non-verbal communications of our clients on the minutest level. When we have three clients (not to mention four if trying to work with two children and two parents), we are no longer able to observe and respond to the majority of non-verbal communications and needs of the individuals with whom we are working. We simply do not have enough eyes, ears and attention to register everything that is occurring and are forced to become focused on the overall structure and flow of the group. This focus could have utility for a family system but it is not the default mode to start the intervention.

- When both parents are together in the session, the partners' relationship with one another, as well as the child's responses to being in a triad, with all the potential triangulations that can occur, will be a significant influence on the feel and direction of the session.

Practice questions:

- When it's time to start the Theraplay sessions, which parent should you work with first?

- How do you keep the other parent involved?

The ideal situation would be to start with one parent and do a sequence of weekly Theraplay sessions and then after three sessions conduct a fourth, parent-only, session where both parents attend. In the majority of cases, it would take several cycles of this pattern to produce enough progress with the first parent to warrant switching to the second parent. So you would repeat the pattern of three sessions with the first parent and every fourth session a parent session where both parents attend, until you and the parents determine that sufficient progress has occurred with the child and first parent and that it is time to work with the child and second parent. The typical length of time with one parent is 12–16 sessions (including the parent-only sessions).

Sometimes it can be helpful for the second parent to observe the Theraplay sessions. Observation by the second parent can take place from a one-way mirror or a video connected in a separate room. It is not ideal for the observing parent to be within the room watching. This creates a dynamic where the child may be reacting to or reverberating from the feelings that he is sensing from the other parent's non-verbal communication. The child may also feel confused as to why he is not engaging with the observing parent. Also, the active parent may act differently when the co-parent is present. Our goal at the beginning is to isolate the dyadic relationship between each parent and the child rather than bringing three people's dynamics into the mix. We do not alternate parents from week to week or leave it to the parents to decide each time which parent will come so that we are surprised as to who walks in through the door.

Often the question of "which parent goes first?" or "which parent to work with?" is very simple—it's the parent who has the time to attend. At other times, it is the parent who feels a sense of urgency with their child's difficulties or the one who is more distressed about the child's behaviors. Alternatively, one parent may be too resentful of the child to start the work, or resistant to Theraplay in general. That said, we place great value on working with both parents at some point in the intervention. If a family meets you for the first time and one parent states that the other parent is not on board with seeking help, is too busy to attend, doesn't think there is a problem and so on, you should still make every effort to engage the uninvolved parent. You could specifically invite them to the parent sessions, include them in communications and periodically contact them by phone to get their feedback and impressions. The best way to increase the likelihood that the parent will change their minds about being involved is to persist in trying to involve them. Frequently, the parent that is uninvolved feels unheard or undervalued in some way and is therefore critical or dismissive of the process. If you make an effort to pursue them despite their initial bluster or seeming indifference, they may feel more inclined to get involved.

Reasons for shifting to triadic work or including more family members

It may be that certain family issues stem from interactions when the family is all together and what they need most is to learn to work better as a triad (or more if the problems also involve other children or family members). In those cases, you would move to working in a triad having had a sequence of several (at least three) parent-child sessions with each parent and the child, and then bring both parents together with the child in a Theraplay session.

The default goal of Theraplay is to discern the needs and provide intervention to the child and parent on a dyadic level, because that is the first level of parent-child interaction at birth. It is the relationship where the baby first learns about themselves, their value, their attributes and what it is like to be in a relationship. It is not that we are uninterested in the larger dynamic of the family system. We will sequence the intervention so that more members can come and benefit from the experience. However, we first want to root our understanding very firmly in the primary needs of the child within the more intimate parent-child dyad.

Strategies for making a parent feel included in the session

Practitioners new to Theraplay inevitably find it difficult to be focused on so many things at once in sessions: you have to remember how to do the activities, to keep one step ahead of the child so he doesn't grab your supplies, think of a quick adaptation to a game if the child is resisting your structure, notice the child's non-verbal communications so that you don't overstimulate or trigger him, stop yourself from saying "well done!" all the time, while hoping that you have remembered to operate the camera correctly! You are worried that your voice sounds too high pitched or too monotonous, your activities are too challenging or not challenging enough and your pillows are too floppy to stay upright to form the child's chair. How on earth, then, are you expected to consider the parent's needs, make them feel comfortable, included and successful—especially when the parent lets you know in the feedback session that they are skeptical that playing can possibly make a difference?

Even if you feel you don't have the bandwidth to keep their needs in mind for the entire session, there are many ways to make a parent feel included.

Before the session begins:

- Create a special seat for the parent that is as comfortable as the one for the child.

At the beginning of the session:

- Greet the parent by looking them warmly in the eye and calling them by name so they feel as if you really see them as a person.

- Include them in the entrance activity. For example, "Joey, you, Mom and I are going to put these beanies on our heads and see if we can balance them all the way inside to your special chair."

- Have the parent sit right next to their child, or you can arrange the child on the parent's lap. Either way, tell them explicitly where you want them to sit.

- When you help the child take their shoes off, indicate to the parents that they can take their shoes off too in order to get comfortable.

During the session:

- When you do your initial check-up, you can comment on a particular feature that they have in common or bring the parent into the picture, "Wow, your boy's eyes are particularly blue with that shirt on!" and have the parent look and remark.

- If you have decided that you rather than the parent should do the lotion activity, you can still include them by glancing at their hands. If they are particularly dry or have an obvious scratch or bruise, you can say, "Oh, I see Mommy needs a little lotion too" and give her hand a quick rub.

- Any game where you take turns playing with the child (first you model the game, and then the parent plays) is by nature including the parent. So, for example, in the La La Magnets game, first you would demonstrate, then have the parent switch positions with you so they are facing their child and calling out the body parts. If, however, you don't want the parent responsible for the structure, you can include them by having the child sit on their lap and they can hold the child's hands so they are doing the activity together as they face you.

- When you use the format of modeling the activity first with the child and then having the parent take a turn, make sure to arrange the parent in a way that facilitates the activity going successfully. For example, if you are doing slippery slip, begin facing the child while the parent is sitting at the child's side watching, then when it's the parent's turn, signal to the parent that they should get up and switch places with you to sit directly face to face rather than attempting to do slippery slip from a side angle.

- When doing any activity involving the mention of the child's favorite things, ask the parent to name the favorite item. For example, if you are doing paper toss, ask the parent, "Dad, what is your girl's favorite food for dinner? What is your girl's favorite sport to play? What is your girl's favorite animal?"

- Say encouraging things to the parent, such as "Wow! Your dad knows you so well!" or "Dad is good at playing bubble tennis! Have you played this before?" or "Dad is giving it his all!"

- When you are playing a game like a crawling race and the parent is not directly participating, direct them to be the one to say "Ready, steady, go!" or, if you are playing balloon pass, ask the parent to count how many passes you and the child make until it drops.

- Play games that require three people. For example, the aluminum foil guessing game, where the parent closes their eyes and you make prints of three different parts of the child's body, then the parent opens their eyes and has to guess. You can do the same with cotton ball hide and a range of other activities (see Chapter 23).

- Place the parent and child in a pair during a game, for example play hide and seek and have the parent hide with the child under the blanket and you go searching for them both.

Other general guidelines include:

- If the parent accidently gets hurt, make sure they are okay and take care of them as you would the child—apply the "no hurts" rule to all.

- Just as you do with the child, make sure that all activities can be carried out safely. For example, if a child is in a mummy wrap and is about to bust out of the paper, tell the parent to stand back so they don't accidentally get hurt.

- If you notice that the parent has some kind of need, make an effort to accommodate them. For example, if they have a cold, bring the tissue box close to them; if they look cold, offer them a blanket; if they have a sore back, ensure that the seat you have prepared for them is comfortable and ask how you can change it to make it better.

Strategies to avoid making the parent feel rejected when their child cooperates with you

Children with attachment issues often develop adaptive skills that can feel manipulative to the parents. It is very common for such children to be overly friendly, cooperative and appealing to strangers. They may act as if they are helpless in order to get attention. They may report incidents of simple limit setting from the parent as mean or even abusive to outside parties, while at home they can be uncooperative, angry and sometimes aggressive. The result is that parents often feel rejected, ineffectual, isolated and angry. In this context, the enticing, engaging manner of the Theraplay practitioner can unintentionally exacerbate these problems.

If you have gathered from the assessment that these dynamics and feelings could be at play, then consider the following modifications in your approach:

- Increase the parent's face-to-face engagement with the child and reduce your own. In other words, don't spend any more time than is minimally necessary playing games such as Peek-a-Boo, Patty Cake, La La Magnets or Push Me Over with the child yourself. You need to do just enough to be able to model for the parent and also get a feel for what the child is like in those interactions, but no more.

- Reduce the use of your own social engagement system. Be more matter of fact in tone, smile and react a little less, and reduce your fun, silly approach so that you do not seem more appealing than the parent.

- Refer to the parent as the authority, the one who knows best and is most familiar with what their child needs. This can be done by relying on the parent to call out the child's favorite things, for them to be the caller in Mother, May I?, or for them to decide what body parts to match in La La Magnets. Reinforce the parent's claiming of the child, using statements like "Your mom knows you well" or "This is a job for your mom to do."

- Reduce the amount of touch you provide to a child to the minimum necessary to keep the structure. Let the parent do the nurturing touch whenever possible.

- Provide a strong structuring presence in the room so that the parent does not feel they have to be the disciplinarian.

- Have the parent and child be a team against the practitioner, in games such as cotton ball war and tug of war.

- Use games that reinforce their similarities such as parent-child handprints, special handshakes, feather decorate, sticker match, mirroring games.

- Be aware of the parent's affect and body language during sessions and check in with them frequently (before and after sessions) to find out how they are feeling.

Strategies for working with parents who have limited caregiving capacities

If you have tried in every way possible to guide a parent to be the adult, to provide structure, to be attuned and have failed, you should lower your expectations of the parent. This may mean that rather than asking the parent to suppress their needs and focus on the child, you should focus on providing nurturing, structuring and engaging regard for the child and parent alike. This allows the parent to be "off the hook" for a responsibility they cannot currently meet and will allow them to relax and open up to the experience of connecting with their child.

 EXAMPLE: Eena is a 24-year-old mother to 5-year-old Darla. As a child, Eena suffered abuse and neglect at the hands of her parents, who were alcoholics. She witnessed chronic domestic violence between her parents. Eena ran away from home at age 15 and spent time in foster care. At age 18, Eena became pregnant with the child of a much older man, with whom she lived for three years until she took Darla and fled the relationship due to emotional abuse by her partner. Eena is now living in sheltered housing for young families and is enrolled in a work-study program.

In the MIM, Eena provides no structure for Darla. Eena does not read the directions out loud and takes a long time to get out the materials. Darla, talking to herself, wanders around the room. Eena calls Darla over several times, but Darla begins playing with a toy she has discovered in the corner and does not answer. Rather than move towards Darla, Eena begins to re-do the braids in her own hair. After several minutes, Darla approaches her mother and they began the squeaky animal task. Several times, Eena playfully puts her pig up to Darla's face as she squeaks the pig loudly. Darla mimics her mother's motion but unintentionally bops Eena on the cheek. Eena yelps "Hey! Don't!" and a quick look of disapproval flashes across her face. Darla then drops her pig and spends several seconds crawling underneath the table to retrieve it. The MIM proceeds in this chaotic way. During the nurture activities, Darla seems uncomfortable with her mother. For example, during the lotion activity, when Eena puts lotion on Darla's arm, Darla squeaks "Ick Ick" and slips her arm out, while at the same time emitting a high-pitched, nervous giggle. Eena then spends several moments massaging the lotion into both of Darla's arms while talking about how pale her skin is and that she looks like a ghost. Darla looks disengaged and then grabs the bag for the next activity. During the feeding activity, Eena teases Darla by pretending to put the biscuit into Darla's mouth but then popping it into her own mouth at the last minute.

I plan to focus on the dimensions of Structure and Engagement followed by Nurture. I know that the activities I choose have to be developmentally young, not only because of Darla's age but also because Eena can get unfocused and dysregulated if she is not fully drawn into the "here and now" moment. The goal-related activities I choose are: La La Magnets, Sticker Match, Cotton Ball Blow and Push Me Over. In the parent session, I model the La La Magnets activity and other activities and practice them with Eena. Once we are in the session with Darla, I take turns with Eena suggesting body parts to join. When it is Eena's turn to pick the body parts, Darla begins jumping in with suggestions and corrections. Eena is thrown off and is frustrated and the other activities continue in a similar way. During the sticker match, Eena whines jokingly that she wants a different color and admonishes Darla when she doesn't put the sticker where she had put it on Darla. In the cotton ball game, several times Eena blows too hard so that Darla can't catch it. Darla does the same, mirroring her mother's dysregulation and Eena gets annoyed. I struggle through the session to calm Eena and redirect her criticism. When the session is over, I feel exhausted and unsettled.

After a good night's sleep and time to settle down, I review the video of the session and notice that Eena is behaving the way a child in need of attention behaves. It is as if Eena is calling out "See me!" She is not yet ready to have the responsibility I am giving her.

I decide to switch my tactics in the following session so that Eena can feel as seen and cared for as Darla. I choose activities that require little self-regulation and where Eena can relax. I choose Manicure, Powder Prints—walking on a roll of dark paper, aluminum Foil Prints, Bubble Pop and Weather Report. In each activity, I provide all of the structuring and caregiving for both Darla and Eena. I make a foil print of Darla's foot, then one of Eena's foot, a foil print of Darla's elbow and then one of Eena's elbow. During the Weather Report activity, I arrange both daughter and mother sitting side by side and put one hand on each of their backs as I describe the weather. Rather than have Eena feed Darla, I give them their biscuits at the same time and they have a "crunching race." Throughout, Eena looks pleased and relaxed and Darla looks delighted with the joint activities. Both mother and daughter feel open and connected. The best of Eena comes out: a playful, sweet, warm person rather than a needy, immature and lost parent. The secondary benefit is that Darla, who is often parentified, sees her mother being taken care of so she can temporarily relinquish her need to be in control.

By helping the parent and child enjoy each other's presence without the parent having to struggle or feel like a failure, you make it possible for the child to experience the joy of being with a parent who for this brief period is totally present and available. Sometimes the only realistic goal for intervention is to allow the parent and child to feel connected, relaxed and joyful together in the safety of the practitioner's guiding and structuring presence. For some families, this is all you can hope for. For others, this is the first step to something more. If there is hope for the parent to be able to evolve into a more available and responsive caregiver, this kind of experience is likely to be the best avenue to work towards that goal. Why is that? It's for the same reason that you would start at a developmentally younger level with a child who is struggling to meet the demands that his chronological age is asking of him. When you support the younger developmental needs, the person becomes available to grow and to open up to new experiences. In the case of an immature or preoccupied parent, the possibility of feeling nurtured and protected by the practitioner allows the parent to begin to really see and feel their child, which may lead to new insights and skills that can be built on and developed.

Utilizing the monthly parent-only sessions

The recommended sequence for Theraplay intervention is that you do three parent-child Theraplay sessions (generally once a week) and then have a parent-only session every fourth session. This parent-only session is your opportunity to work with the caregiver to work towards the following important goals:

- To connect with the parents and hear from them about their experience of the Theraplay sessions on a personal level.

- To answer their questions about why you do what you do and why you respond the way you do.

- To determine if there have been any changes in their relationship with their child or their child's behaviors.

- To help them reflect on an interaction by observing pre-selected clips of a previous Theraplay session.

- To show them how to do an activity by demonstrating it with them.

- To role-play them being themselves and you being the child or you being yourself and them being the child.

- To explore less helpful interactions in order to understand the parent's motives better and problem solve with them about more helpful ways to respond.

- To give guidance on discipline issues at home that fit within the developmental framework of Theraplay.

- To discuss how parents can use Theraplay at home in their everyday life.

You will not be able to cover all of these topics in one parent session; therefore it's useful to have a plan of what you would like to cover. At the same time, you need to be open to the possibility that the parent will come in with their own list of significant and urgent topics that they want to cover.

Using video feedback and role play in session with parents

Reviewing a video segment of the Theraplay sessions is one of the most potent tools for helping parents make therapeutic gains. One two-minute clip of an interaction can open up a treasure trove of self-reflection that can produce more progress than ten sessions with just talking. Why is that? Because watching themselves on video provides the parent with the opportunity to go back in time and remember what they were feeling in a particular moment. They have the advantage of pressing the "pause" button to reflect on the meaning of the situation with the benefit of what they know in the present moment. This opportunity for integration is extremely effective for developing a parent's reflective function capacities.

Role-playing during the parent-only meetings allows the parent to learn and practice what it is that you are asking them to do, on an experiential level. Adding the experiential learning piece to your discussion and video review will allow the parent the opportunity to apply and integrate the behavior that they are attempting to master. For example, if talking about a regulation issue during a handstack game where you want the parent to count more rhythmically, then, in addition to showing the video clip example and discussing the concept, you could practice the same activity in several ways. The first way would be you assuming the role of the practitioner while the parent acts as their child would, using more dysregulating, fast movements. After this, you would take a turn as the practitioner using a steadier, rhythmic voice and firm touch. Finally, ask the parent to be themselves while you act as their child and have the parent practice being a more regulating leader.

The next few examples illustrate different ways of supporting parents using video feedback and role-play practice.

Using video feedback to develop parent reflective function capacities

🖐 **EXAMPLE**: An example of helpful use of video feedback comes from Alex and his mother, Janet. Alex was adopted from a foreign orphanage at the age of 5. Before his adoption, Alex endured abuse and neglect at the hands of both his birth parents and then the orphanage workers. He becomes anxious and often dissociated when he feels stress of any kind. However, he is receptive to caregiving from his adoptive parents, which indicates that perhaps he had had one secondary attachment figure in his past who allowed him to be open to caregiving. For example, when he is scared of going to bed alone, he will ask his parents to sit with him, and their presence calms him so that he can fall asleep. Another example is when Alex felt scared of a boy on the school bus, he told his parents and was grateful when they intervened with the school bus monitor.

Unfortunately, Alex's parents, particularly his mother, are ambivalent about closeness and intimacy. Janet can be engaging and playful in the more up-regulating activities, but when it comes to quiet, nurturing games like Feeding, Caring for Hurts and Weather Report, Janet makes small rejecting comments or teasing remarks that detract from the intimacy of the moment. Alex then responds in turn and matches her negative messages and then the purpose of the activity is spoiled. For example, when doing the powder print on Alex's feet, Janet says "Yuck" and "Pee yew!" as if his feet smell, even though his feet do not have any odor. Another example is during feeding, when Alex has his legs on her lap, Janet holds his legs but occasionally tickles his leg, which makes Alex squirm.

I had wondered about these behaviors in the first parent session; Janet responds that that is her way of teasing and connecting, but she understands and will try to refrain from these behaviors. However, they do not stop even though I gently remind and redirect her during the session. So, for the second parent session, I cue up a segment that happened two sessions earlier. In that session, Alex was balancing on pillows, and because I didn't steady them properly, the pillows slid out from under him and he fell. Alex was physically fine but he curled up in a ball and looked like a sad little baby. Janet reached her arms out to hold him. Alex leaned towards her and Janet wrapped her arms around him. However, as soon as Alex rested his head on her shoulder, Janet started rubbing Alex's head hard in a quick rhythm that tousled his hair and made it go into his face. Alex said "Ow!" in a whiny way.

I cue up the video and play only the first 20 seconds when Alex looks like a sad baby and Janet reaches her arms out. I ask Janet to try to put herself back in that moment and remember what she was feeling. Janet responds, "I felt bad that he fell but also a little baffled that he is so sensitive. He's 12 years old!"

"But something made you reach out to hold him. Do you remember what you felt?"

"I wanted to make him feel better."

I then play the rest of the segment. After watching, Janet says, "He wanted to get away, he doesn't like when I hug him." "Let's look at it again," I respond. I cue up just the moment when Alex's hair was in his face and Janet started squeezing. We watch it and I pause. "Put yourself back in that moment. Do you know what you were feeling?" Janet responds, "I can't really tell, I just know he wanted me to let go." "So, would you say you felt a little uncomfortable with that situation?" "Yes," Janet responds. "Neither one of us is a very cuddly person so it's just kind of awkward." "I hear a lot of mixed feelings about this close situation. Let's watch the video one last time." After watching it the third time, Janet is able to say, "He doesn't look very comfortable. I was rubbing his head too hard." "Perhaps that is part of it, but my guess is that Alex senses your hesitation and both of you find a way to shut off the intimate moment. Because it seemed like the head rubbing and hair tussle was not that comfortable for him." "Are you saying it's coming from me?" Janet responds, looking worried and a little hurt. "I think it may be coming from both of you and you've created this pattern without realizing it. But for a child with Alex's history of poor caregiving, for a while it's up to the adult to be mindful so as to create new patterns."

Reviewing this segment of video brought Janet one step closer to becoming aware of and able to choose new responses to her feelings. In the next session during the feeding, Janet rests her arm on Alex's leg and does not rub, poke or tickle. I give her messages of "Great, I see that you are making an effort!" with my eyes and she smiles and nods a little towards me. Alex does not jump up from the couch as he has done in previous sessions. This intervention does not provide a quick fix for Janet's discomfort with closeness and intimacy: some of these same themes continue throughout the work. However, watching the video did allow her to break down the pattern of behavior and associated feelings and consider from a new perspective what her contribution was to the "dance" she was sharing with her son.

Helping an insecure parent become more confident

EXAMPLE: Ivana, mother of 6-year-old Lucy, comes for Theraplay intervention. Ivana has very low self-esteem as a parent. Her experience of trauma leads her to lose her temper, threaten Lucy with severe punishments and sometimes resort to physical force. Ivana and Lucy's father had gone through a contentious divorce the previous year and Lucy blames her mother for the chaos and the disruption that ensued. During the MIM, Ivana provides very little structure. Ivana tries to direct Lucy but can't make it work because she keeps asking Lucy for permission to do everything. Her hesitant manner and her many questions leave Lucy feeling tense and frustrated. By the end, Lucy rejects all of her mother's bids for engagement. The two cannot sustain cooperative interaction for more than a few seconds.

Even after a lengthy discussion during the MIM feedback, particularly focusing on reducing the number of questions, and presenting ideas confidently, Ivana is hesitant and apologetic when interacting with Lucy in the first three Theraplay sessions. For example, during the basket toss game, when I ask Ivana what her daughter's favorite food is for dinner, she looks worried as she stammers, "I think it's spaghetti. Am I right Lucy?" Instinctively, Lucy snarls, "No! It's pizza!" "Oh, I'm sorry. It's pizza." Ivana responds meekly. Additionally, during the third session when I ask Ivana to look for hurts on Lucy's hand and put lotion on them, Ivana keeps asking, "Can I put some lotion here? Can I take care of this one?" Lucy is tense and arbitrarily says yes and no to her mother's pleas. I notice this but worry that if I remind Ivana not to ask questions, she will feel even worse. I also know that Lucy's father had criticized Ivana's parenting in front of Lucy, so do I not want to replicate that dynamic.

The first issue that I have to deal with is my own feeling of stuckness with Ivana. In peer supervision with a trusted colleague, I reflect on my feeling that Ivana is too fragile to be guided in session. The colleague hypothesizes that Ivana's apologetic and hesitant inferior manner is an unconscious way of defending against change. I reflect that I might be hesitant to "correct" Ivana in session because my own father was rather domineering and I perceived my mother as powerless and in need of protection. This makes me feel a little "stuck" myself. It is important for me to examine my feelings regarding this dynamic in the therapeutic triad before moving on to planning the parent session. After examining my feelings about Ivana and my role in the triad, I am able to reflect on the best strategy for the parent session with Ivana.

I focus on two goals: 1) Show Ivana the lotion activity and ask her to put herself back in that moment. 2) Do a role play in two ways: a) I demonstrate on Ivana the way to do lotion without hesitancy and questions; b) I play Lucy and Ivana plays herself so she can practice.

When Ivana looks at the segment, she states that she feels as if Lucy is somehow an angry animal that you need to approach with caution. I suggest that Lucy really wants to have the shared experience, but is afraid that it won't go well. I explain that that is a "miscue." We had talked about this idea during the MIM feedback, but this time, with the example of the lotion, the message that Lucy is actually scared more than angry made emotional sense to Ivana. After this conversation, I role-play the lotion activity with Ivana. I tell her to react as she thinks Lucy would. Ivana plays Lucy well, intermittently pouting, pulling her hand away, showing me her elbow and then pulling it away. All the while, I carry out the activity in a soothing, rhythmic way, examining both the back and the inside of Ivana's hand. When I rub the lotion, I provide firm, soothing touches rather than light dabs. I acknowledge and accept Ivana's skittishness and hesitancy but show no worry or hesitancy on my own face. I just continue to look intently and confidently at what I notice on Ivana's hand.

When the role play is over, I ask Ivana how she feels. Ivana marvels at how much effort it took her to keep her guard up. Ivana says, "It must be very tiring for Lucy to have to be on guard all the time." She also notes that, after a while, my persistence in continuing the activity without showing any feelings of rejection felt like a surprise and relief to her. "By the end of the activity, I could feel myself forgetting that I was supposed to act like Lucy did."

Then it is Ivana's turn to play herself while I play Lucy. Now Ivana is able to mirror my reassuring and confident energy as she looks at my hands. Even though there is a little nervous wavering in Ivana's voice, she proceeds without showing any sign of hurt or rejection when I protest and say, "No, not there." I stop Ivana at one point to encourage her to hold my hand with firm warmth rather than the delicate touch she is providing. Ivana accepts the suggestion and provides more pressure and contact. It is clear that Ivana understands the difference and is able to translate it into action.

When the session is over, Ivana has a much more energetic demeanor than at the beginning. It is as if Ivana has internalized my reassuring confidence and energy. Ivana agrees that, in the next session with Lucy, she will repeat the lotion activity and try applying what she has learned.

The following week, while Lucy is playing with toys in the nearby playroom, I take three minutes at the beginning of the session to remind Ivana of the interventions we learned the previous week. I remind Ivana to hold Lucy's hand with a full, warm grasp, to move smoothly and rhythmically when rubbing in the lotion, to not ask permission for caring for the hurts (while still calmly accepting it if Lucy objects to a particular spot), and to confidently move on from looking at one part of her hand to another without showing hesitancy. I even hold Ivana's hand with the same reassuring grasp that we practiced the previous week.

When it's time to do the checking for hurts and lotion, Ivana takes command and starts examining Lucy's hand without hesitation. She looks carefully and confidently, and when she notices a small red spot, she declares, "Oh, you have a hurt right there, I'm going to take care of it for you." Lucy is markedly quieter and more settled this time compared to the previous session, and protests far less to her mother's nurture.

Even though this intervention is a success, Ivana needs this type of help for most of the other activities as well. Because of her anxiety, it is hard for Ivana to apply what she has learned from the lotion activity to another context. For example, when we play the pizza game, Ivana becomes hesitant again. Ivana says, "Let's put mushrooms on this pizza," and Lucy responds, "I don't like mushrooms" (even though she had ordered mushrooms on her pizza the previous evening!). Ivana says in a surprised and hurt tone, "Oh, I'm sorry. I thought you liked mushrooms." I buoyantly intervene: "That's okay, Mom, what else does she like?" Ivana responds, "Parmesan sprinkles!" and I exclaim, "Great! Parmesan!" and help Ivana put the next pillow on top of the pizza.

Using role play to teach a parent to be more structured with a dysregulated child

EXAMPLE: Another example that uses role playing in a helpful way is with Monica, mother of Connor, age 5, who has moderate autism. From a young age, Connor was hyperactive, chaotic and could be aggressive towards Monica when dysregulated. Monica stayed at home with Connor until he started school because his behaviors were too difficult to be handled in a preschool setting. Monica comes in to the session with scratches, bruises and welts up and down her arm from trying to care for Connor.

During the MIM, Monica looks exhausted. As Connor runs around the room and climbs on furniture, Monica passively calls Connor to come back to the table. She tries to entice him with the pigs and lotion but her meek affect is no match for Connor's frenetic energy. I actually have to end the MIM after four tasks because Connor keeps running out of the room, and when Monica tries to guide him back inside, Connor kicks her.

In the MIM feedback, Monica and I spend all of our time talking about immediate strategies for protecting Monica from Connor's wild aggression. During our conversation, Monica becomes aware of the fact that Connor's aggressive behavior has been happening for so long that she has become accustomed to his unsafe behaviors and has accepted his aggression as par for the course. I explain to Monica and her husband, Tim, that they will have to "press the reset button" at home and look at restructuring their home environment, their daily schedule and their attitude towards Connor. First, I told Monica that she will have to relearn her own physical and emotional boundaries and find the strength to confidently manage Connor's physicality in a way that keeps her safe. But before she can do that, they will have to put some temporary safety measures in place. They will have to work out a way for Monica not to be alone with Connor. Monica needs another adult around to relieve her when Connor is being wild and when she feels she does not have the strength to manage him. Second, Monica needs to find time immediately to do some restorative and restful activities for her body and mind, such as taking a day off for herself, getting a massage and getting a health check-up she has long been neglecting. We agree on two weeks for Tim and Monica to work on these plans.

After two weeks, Monica and Tim come to another parent meeting to discuss their progress and next steps. Fortunately, Tim is able to leave for work later in the morning so that he can help with the morning routine and getting Connor on the bus. For the afternoons, they arrange for their 17-year-old teenage cousin, who is tall and energetic, to play with Connor. Monica had also taken the previous Saturday as a "girls' day" with some girlfriends and had attended two tai chi classes, which had been one of her favorite activities before Connor's challenges took over her life. At this point, I feel we are ready to start Theraplay sessions.

In the sessions, with the proper structure and matched energy, Connor is able to calm down and become organized rather quickly. Within three to five sessions, he is no longer attempting to run out of the room, kick or hit. I match his energy and get on "the same wavelength"— what Daniel Stern refers to as matching his "vitality affect" (Stern, 2000). I have to be active and hands-on with Connor, but in a confident way that prevents him from being chaotic and hurting anyone. Monica was happy to see Connor calm down enough to enjoy the reciprocal activities but she finds it hard to rise to the active level of energy that Connor needs in order to really feel her structuring presence. Therefore, Monica and I spend several sessions role-playing the different ways in which Monica can physically use her body, her posture and her voice tone to transmit confidence and energy.

One game we play is the Push Me Over game. In the Theraplay sessions, when it was her turn to play with Connor, Monica did not firmly hold Connor's feet in her palms and so he felt he had nothing to push against. He started pushing before her signal and she got thrown off balance and said, "No, wait, don't." She slowed down her pacing to regain control but by then Connor had rolled on his side and she had lost him. In the role play, I have Monica play Connor and I demonstrate the Push Me Over in two ways. The first is where I have little energy in my arms and have a light grip on her feet and a thin voice as I count. My posture is less erect. We play the game that way several times. Then I switch to having a confident, erect posture, strong, extended arms, a firm grip on her feet, a focused, energetic look in my eyes, and I count crisply, "One, two, three!" When we contrast these two ways of carrying out the activity, Monica is profoundly struck by how different the two versions feel and how much better, more grounding and more pleasurable the second variation is. We talk about how, in order to capture his physiologic attention, she will have to match her son's wavelength and then guide him towards the calmer direction she wants him to go in. Monica, being an academic with experience in the sciences, is very captured by the image of matching amplitudes and wavelengths and seems really to catch on to what I am saying.

When it is her turn to practice providing the structure, she understands better how to use her own energy and body to give counterbalance on my feet, and I feel her presence.

Addressing persistent and unhelpful parent behaviors

There are times when, despite your best efforts to guide a parent towards more adaptive and attuned responses, the parent keeps repeating unhelpful behaviors in the sessions. These are behaviors such as bringing up outside events, asking too many questions, insisting on increasing the challenge level, being sarcastic, being competitive, getting silly and tickling the child during quiet, nurturing moments—the list goes on! There is a common element under these behaviors, which is that the parent has an underlying worry, need or motivation that they are trying to express and which we have not yet met. To understand how to address this significant task, let's take a look at one manifestation of this phenomenon: a parent who is critical of their child in a session.

Before starting a Theraplay intervention, you will have described the Theraplay process to the parent, including their specific role. This should include letting them know that you will take charge of the discipline and redirection in the sessions. Parents need to be reassured that you do not expect their child to behave in a "polite" manner. They also need to understand that you will want to invite the child's most natural behaviors so that you can make sense of their responses and respond in ways that help the child. Nevertheless, all parents will feel uncomfortable if their child screams "No!" to your overtures to play, runs away from the place you've told him to sit, or tells you your games are stupid. At first, a parent may not be able to refrain from showing their displeasure or making a corrective comment. When they do, you can reassuringly look at them and say, "That's okay, Mom, I'm fine with hearing your son's strong opinions," or "He's just showing us how active his body feels."

The first few times you meet, you may have to remind the parent that they don't have to worry. You may also have to bring it up as a subject in your first monthly parent meeting. The parent may ask why it is okay for their child to call you stupid or not listen to an adult's directive when those are the exact behaviors they came to get help with! This is your opportunity to explain to the parents that your aim is to surprise their child by not reacting to him as he has come to expect so that you can move past these behaviors and see what lies underneath them. You may need to go back and forth in explaining the Theraplay tenets that lead you to work with their child in this way. The goal is that by the end of the parent session, the parent is willing to try to refrain from making critical or sarcastic comments. If it is helpful to them, you and the parent can agree on a special signal that you can give them when they slip up and make a critical comment.

If, after several rounds of sessions and parent talks, the parent is still correcting the child or sarcastically teasing him, it is time to talk to them about what other beliefs, feelings, motives or wishes lie underneath their unhelpful comments. You can start the conversation by saying, "I notice that it is hard for you to refrain from making sarcastic or critical comments in session. We've worked on it for some time now and yet it is still happening. I wonder if you have any thoughts on why this pattern keeps on happening?" Initially, the parent may become defensive and repeat the same reasons and the same questions they asked during your first parent meeting. For example, the parent might say, "I think he's doing all these shenanigans just to get attention. He's perfectly capable of behaving himself when he wants to. How can letting him get away with it help make him behave better?" At this point, resist the urge to restate your excellent explanations rooted in sound developmental theory and research. This will only get you into a back and forth discussion where you are speaking past each other. Instead, you can say, "You have expressed those same concerns before and I have given my reasons for why I believe this approach is valuable, but my fear is that repeating those reasons won't get us any further." Your best bet is to leave your agenda for the session behind and go back to the parent's concern. Become curious about it and ask the parent to explain it further. Listen with true curiosity and attentiveness to what the parent is trying to say beneath their words. Some common feelings the parent might be experiencing are fear, shame, despair, helplessness or rage. Here is a partial list of possible underlying reasons why parents might criticize their children (even if they can see that their own behavior is detrimental to the child):

- They were brought up with critical parents and they now feel ashamed that they are behaving in a way they vowed they would not.

- They feel that their child is disrespecting them, which brings up feelings of rage or humiliation they felt when they felt powerless and small.

- They feel resentful that their lives have been ruined by the child's behaviors.

- It makes them feel better to believe that the child actually acted bad on purpose because it means that it could get better.

- They feel powerless because important people (spouses, grandparents, teachers, police officers, coaches) expect them to be able to control their child.

- They worry that the child will never mature and will be dependent on them forever.

No matter what the reason might be, your objectives at this point in the therapeutic process are to 1) develop an understanding of their underlying motives, 2) develop compassion for the parent and 3) deepen the therapeutic alliance. One way of achieving these objectives is by using the attitude of "acceptance, curiosity and empathy" (ACE), a dialogue format which is a component of dyadic developmental psychotherapy (Hughes, 2011a). This approach works well for parent behaviors that intrude into the Theraplay session, such as a parent who talks too much, asks too many questions, tries to trick the child, is sarcastic, is overly competitive, or gets silly and tickles the child during quiet, nurturing moments. Here are examples of the ACE attitude to a parent who says, "Why should I let him keep disrespecting the adults in the session? You're only reinforcing his bad behavior!"

- Accepting statements: "Thank you for telling me what's on your mind. I could tell that was important for you to say."

- Curious questions: "Do you sometimes feel that his disrespect means you are not important to him? I wonder whether you worry that letting him disrespect you will lead him to get into bigger trouble when he grows older?"

- Empathic statements: "I can see why you would be so stern if you thought that his behavior might get him into trouble with the law. You really care about him deeply and want the best for him. If that's how you are feeling, no wonder it's hard for you to tolerate disobedient behavior."

For a list of common parent defensive statements, what may underlie them and some possible responses, see Chapter 21.

Only after you have appreciated the parent's perspective and you feel that they trust you can you go on to discuss your concerns about any potential negative effects and unintended consequences of their behavior. In this more open position they may be able to weigh up the pros and cons and adjust their behavior.

Strategies for coping with a chronically resentful, burned-out parent

Even with all of these interventions, the parent may still feel so bad that they display only defensiveness, hopelessness, apathy or rage. The extent to which the parent feels hurt and resentful may become alarmingly clear to both the parent and the practitioner in parent sessions as the parent starts to express these same angry feelings towards you, the practitioner. Faced with these negative feelings, you are likely to feel taken aback and defensive, perhaps even a little ashamed.

But remember the following: if a parent appears angry and resentful and shows a lack of compassion towards the child, it is likely to be due to the accumulated effect of years of feeling that they are failing to meet their child's needs, without real support or understanding from anyone.

When a parent presents in this manner, the parent is likely to be in a state called blocked care (Baylin and Hughes, 2016). This is a parent state that occurs when working with particularly attachment-averse children who, due to their early experiences of not being able to trust others, are chronically rejecting of a parent's caregiving overtures. The parental brain is wired to seek proximity and provide caregiving because it receives intrinsic reward from seeing the child satisfied and responsive. These feelings produce relational hormones that reward and reinforce the caregiving behavior. If, however, a healthy parent, whose brain is capable of registering and reading a child's need for caregiving, tries to meet the need and is constantly rejected or their efforts are returned with mixed signals, the parental brain becomes flooded with stress hormones. Over time, the pain of extending themselves and being rejected can cause the natural parental mechanisms of nurturing and connection to shut down, and the parent starts to feel that they have "lost that loving feeling" towards their child. They then operate strictly from the rational part of their brain that tells them that they should provide for the child because it's their role and obligation. However, their behavior is distant and mechanical. This then triggers feelings of self-reproach and self-doubt about why this has happened to them and whether it is their fault. They can become pervasively resentful and depressed and have feelings of helplessness and hopelessness.

It is important to identify this phenomenon in parents early in order to bring it into awareness and help parents understand that it is a normal human reaction to feeling rejected and as though they are a failure as a parent. There is great relief that can come by articulating and putting these feelings into context. The next step is to provide radical empathy for the parent's experience and help them bolster their self-care and their support system.

If you encounter a parent in this state, here are some suggestions about what to do (or what not to do):

- Don't say or do anything before you take a few deep breaths and let the initial wave of intense feelings wash over you. You may feel a need to defend the child or yourself or you may be intimidated and feel like running away. You might hear alarm bells in your head as the idea pops into your mind that the child is not safe with this parent. These are normal feelings—let them move through you and pass. If you need to say anything, you can say, "Wow, I hear your really strong feelings and I am taking a moment to reflect on what you said. I want to process and listen to these important feelings."

- Do not jump to conclusions and do not judge. Remind yourself that there is a good likelihood that this parent is able to be a compassionate, understanding person with the ability to self-reflect. Perhaps it is the feelings of isolation, despair and chronic shame that have led them to respond in this way.

- Once you have regained your composure, do not provide psycho-education or try to convince the parent that what they are saying is inaccurate. Let go of the "agenda" you planned for the session. Instead, tell them you are grateful that they shared what are obviously very difficult feelings and that you want to understand them better.

- Take an active listening stance as you ask the parents to tell you more about their difficulties in caring for their child. Provide empathy for everything they are saying. Use all of your social engagement system to show that you are resonating with the level of their intensity and understanding their point of view.

- Once you feel the intensity of the parent's negative affect decrease, consider declaring that you are going to fetch both yourself and the parent some water. Don't do this if it feels disruptive or disrespectful, but sometimes the 30-second break where you have your back turned or you stepped away allows the parent a pause from the intensity and helps them to collect themselves. Additionally, this small act of caregiving can feel soothing, as can the act of drinking. Finally, a drink provides a small reprieve from the back and forth demands of conversation and may make the parent feel more in control.

- Towards the end of the session, take a deep breath and attempt to "zoom out" and summarize the important process that occurred in the session, mainly that there was a deepening in the relationship because the parent helped you understand the situation better. You are reframing the event of the parent's showing you their intense negative feelings, which they undoubtedly have felt ashamed of, into positive progress.

- Finally, tell them that you would like to continue the conversation to explore further what you learned about the family during this session and ask the parent to come back without the child for the next session.

Summary

We see the parent as our client as much as we do the child in a Theraplay intervention. From the moment we meet them at the intake meeting, our goal is to make them feel that they are an individual with wants, needs, dreams, desires and histories of their own. Our aim is to help make them feel heard, cared for and attuned to. We start with the basic premise that a parent has the best intentions for their child and that they are doing the best they can. Our main premise is that it is the parent who is the most important person in the child's life and, therefore, is the one who should lead the healing in their child's life. That is why we include parents in the intervention from the beginning and invest our energies in connecting with them and making them feel important.

Complex Parents

There are some situations in which, despite attempting various interventions to help a parent be successful within a Theraplay session, you find that the unhelpful attitudes and behaviors of the parent persist and you cannot continue working with the parent directly within the session.

At this point, you have to decide which plan of action to take among several options:

1. Work with the child yourself and have the parent in a different part of the room. Ask the parent to focus on noting times when the child reacts in a certain way, for example getting hyperactive and what came just before that, or challenging the rules and how you handle the situation. This choice is based on the premise that when the parent is afforded the opportunity to observe their child from a distance, they will gain insight

into the child's underlying motivations and feelings in a way they could not when they are in the moment interacting with the child.

2. Work with the child yourself and add a second practitioner to the team who could be with the parent, guiding, interpreting and supporting them as they observe the session.

3. Work with the other parent and involve the first parent in the monthly parent meetings only.

4. Work with the parent alone for several sessions.

Alternatives for continuing with the parent in Theraplay® sessions

Option one may be useful for a parent who is moderately hesitant or wary and wants to observe and understand things first before trying them or could benefit from seeing their child from a different, more childlike perspective. This option is not as good for a parent who feels very isolated or like a failure. The risk is that if your interaction with the child goes well, it will reinforce the idea that other people can be successful and that they alone cannot. Also, since the parent already feels very alone and unsupported, it is not good to have her sit by herself. It would only increase the parent's self blame and feelings of inadequacy.

Option two of adding a second practitioner to support the parent as they observe the work with their child is often the ideal option for a parent who is suffering from extreme feelings of failure and isolation. This scenario provides the parent with the support of someone dedicated uniquely to their viewpoint and experience while also able to guide the observation of their child and help the parent gain insight and perspective. Once the parent practitioner has assessed that the parent feels more supported and is ready to engage with their child in the Theraplay session, the parent practitioner accompanies the parent into the Theraplay session and provides moment-by-moment support and guidance. For example, the parent practitioner could decide to join in for the last three activities of matching up foil prints to the child's body parts, sharing a snack and creating a special handshake. Then, depending on how successful the interaction is with the parent involved, the parent practitioner could decide to extend the length of time they spend within the next Theraplay session. Unfortunately, in most settings there are not enough resources to dedicate two workers to one family, but we encourage you to find creative ways to facilitate this type of arrangement in your setting if it is clinically indicated for the family. It is possible that once the parent has had the support of the parent practitioner for several sessions (e.g. six to eight sessions), they will come to feel sufficiently secure to participate in the full Theraplay sessions without the parent practitioner present.

Option three, working with the other parent rather than with the parent originally selected to go first, has some advantages but also some distinct disadvantages. This option may be good for situations where even though one parent is with the child most of the time and has more problems with the child, that parent is too burned out to be the one to do the Theraplay work. However, the following conditions would need to be met: 1) the child's behavior issues are similar with both parents, 2) the parents must feel minimally supportive of each other (not blaming one another's weaknesses for the child's behavior), and 3) there should not be a pattern of playing good guy, bad guy between the parents. If these conditions are met, then switching to the other parent to do a segment of work could be your best option. It gives the first parent a break from the very hard work of confronting the child's difficult behaviors in sessions, as well as the accompanying hard work that the parent must do for themselves. The parent can also take comfort in knowing that the child is getting his needs met and there is progress and hope. If the first parent is the one who has typically had to cope with the majority of the child's issues, they may also find relief in the knowledge that their partner is having to confront and cope with the child's issues directly. Concurrently, through the work with the other parent, the child's behavior issues may improve, which may hasten the first parent's readiness to participate in the intervention.

The risk of this scenario is similar to the risks of option one, only more extreme. Deciding to work with the second parent after the first parent has exhibited difficulty working directly with their child could be interpreted by the first parent as a painful rejection: they may feel that they have failed the test of worthiness as a parent. They may agree on the surface that this is the best course, but inside may feel tremendous hurt that they showed their vulnerability and were then rejected, confirming their worst fears. The best way to gauge the risk of this is to openly acknowledge these possible feelings with the first parent. It is best not to try to simply reassure the first parent. Rather, spend time exploring whether the first parent has even some small part that feels rejected or as if they have failed. You could phrase the exploration in the following way: "By shifting to working with your partner and your child, a part of you could feel rejected, as if you have failed, or that you are not important or that things are hopeless. That would be a normal response to our decision. Does any part of you feel that way?" If the parent acknowledges these feelings, accept and empathize with those sentiments and tell them that you appreciate their ability to be self-reflective. Reassure them that one of the biggest factors in a good outcome is the ability to be aware of these painful feelings. Let them know that you will be checking in with them about these feelings during the monthly parent sessions and invite them to let you know at any time if they are struggling.

Option four is for situations where the first goal must be to support the parent in their very painful and difficult feelings so that they can begin to have a more open perspective towards their child. You may decide that this option is necessary at any point during the Theraplay intervention process. As an example, a parent may be able to move along well until a particular aspect of the work comes more to the fore (e.g. the intimacy of nurturing their child). You may try various interventions, like psycho-education, modeling, guiding and practicing by role-playing, but find that nothing seems to help. This kind of situation can bring up strong feelings. You may feel that the parent is resistant, does not comply with your advice, is angry at you or is passive-aggressive. You may feel that the parent is blaming you and expects you to be the one to come up with magic solutions to the child's behavior problems. If you feel this way, your first step before making any other clinical decisions is to get supervision or consultation from a trusted colleague. You may be having countertransference responses, which you must become aware of and deal with before taking any clinical steps. Once you have made some sense of your own feelings, and as long as you feel that adult work is within your role and capability, you could propose doing several sessions (perhaps four to seven to begin with) of individual work together before moving on to the next phase of the intervention.

In order to avoid triggering feelings of shame and defensiveness in the parent, it is best to frame the individual work within circumscribed goals. The goals should focus on exploring limited aspects of the parent's history and state of mind as it relates to parenting this particular child. You can explain that this is the ordinary way an intervention is set up. One way to explain your approach to the parents might be to say that perhaps pieces of their own building blocks are shaped in such a way that they are not compatible with the child's building blocks and that you want to find a way to structure or mold their building blocks so that they fit a little better to the child's internal structure.

At this juncture, practitioners who have not had a lot of experience, skill or training in working one-on-one in adult psychotherapy may feel inclined to "refer a parent for their own work." However, we would advise you not to jump to that conclusion too quickly, for the following reasons: 1) since you are well along in the intervention process you have gained the parent's trust, which is a crucial factor in the work; 2) by referring a parent to an adult psychotherapist, you run the risk of losing the focus on the issues that have surfaced in your Theraplay intervention as they relate directly to the specific child. In other words, a parent may be struggling to overcome feelings of fear towards their child because the child reminds them of their angry father, but the adult psychotherapist may guide the parent towards an exploration of their attitude towards authority in general, issues of self-esteem, confrontations at work with superiors and so on. And while this type of exploration could be useful and necessary, it is not focused enough and you lose control of the progress with the parent-child relationship. If you decide that you must refer the parent to an adult therapist, that therapist should be someone whose work you know well and who can stay focused and supportive of the primary goal, which is to improve the child-parent relationship. It is also important that the adult therapist subscribes to a similar theoretical framework; otherwise, you run the risk of the parent receiving mixed messages from you and the adult therapist.

Our strongest recommendation would be that, if at all possible, you do the individual work with the parent yourself. That way you capitalize on the foundation of your already built-up trust and you can remain focused on the issues as they relate to that particular child, whose issues you already know.

What is needed to do the parent work?

This leads practitioners to the next question: How is a practitioner supposed to structure individual sessions with the parent if they are not deeply trained in attachment-focused adult work?

In order to be able to provide therapeutic support to adults, you need training and supervision in this type of work. The best training framework for this work is provided by the DDP (dyadic developmental psychotherapy/ practice) training focused on parents. This process involves providing PACE (playfulness, acceptance, curiosity and empathy) for the parent while exploring attachment-related themes from their own childhood.[1]

 EXAMPLE: Ilan is 8 years old and lives with his parents, Sarah and Mike. Ilan was adopted at age 4 from foster care and from the beginning of his adoptive placement has displayed challenging behaviors typical of children with attachment trauma. One of the main features of Ilan's troublesome behavior is to target his mother in an indirect manner, for example he will give her dirty looks, pretend he doesn't hear her requests, damage her belongings and make belittling comments about her appearance. Despite their indirect nature, these behaviors are nonetheless corrosive to the relationship. The effect has been cumulative rather than acute, but Sarah feels worn down, rejected and angry.

1   There is a webinar on doing individual work with parents as part of the Theraplay intervention process by the authors to help illustrate the process. This video can be found at www.theraplay. org/thepractitionersguide. For more information on accessing DDP training, go to https:// ddpnetwork.org. Another excellent resource for learning about attachment-focused work with adults can be found in the accelerated experiential dynamic psychotherapy (AEDP) method (https://aedpinstitute.org).

Ilan's father works long hours as an owner of a construction company and is not available to help with the daily parenting. Mike is more available at the weekends and takes Ilan on fun outings such as playing sports and going to the swimming pool. Mike does not experience Ilan's negative attributes as his wife does. This difference in experiences causes tension and strife between the parents. Mike feels that Sarah is too sensitive and not empathetic enough to Ilan's underlying trauma and Sarah feels that Mike does not show a unified front when she thinks that Ilan needs disciplining.

After the parent demonstration session, Sarah looks tired and defeated as she contemplates the expectation that she will be asked to be joyful and open towards her son as I had been in the role playing with her and her husband. "I'll try but I don't know if I can do this. I have bent over backwards trying to accommodate this kid, and I have to tell you, I have very little generosity left to give."

Hearing Sarah's ambivalence, I am not sure how to deal with her hesitation and how to proceed with the intervention. It is clear that she is the one who needs the most help untangling her relationship with her son. Also, Mike is not available to come to sessions. I know that the parents' conflict about Ilan's behavior will have to be addressed but I feel that it will be a long road. I sense that it will be a while before I gain the parents' trust to be able to delve into their relationship. I decide to do the first Theraplay session with Ilan and his mother.

As I plan my first Theraplay session for Sarah and Ilan, I try to think of activities that are structured by me (so that Ilan will not challenge his mother's leadership), and are immediately appealing (such as Newspaper Punch and Basket Toss, balancing pillows on feet and kicking them off, Foil Prints, and Powder Prints of Ilan's hands). I make sure that I am the one directly interacting with Ilan, but I involve Sarah the whole time. For example, I ask her what her son's favorite items are, to be used for cue words for paper toss, have her count how many pillows he has piled, and at the end ask her to compare his hand with the powder print to see if she can see her son's unique fingerprints. Ilan cooperates and seems genuinely intrigued and engaged during the whole session. Sarah's body looks stiff and she alternates between having an artificial-looking smile on her face and looking distant. The session lasts only 35 minutes and I want to check in with Sarah to hear how she feels about the session. Sarah agrees that Ilan can spend 25 minutes in the adjacent playroom, either drawing or playing games on her phone. I show Ilan where his mother and I will be chatting and settle him on some pillows on the floor with a small table and coloring supplies.

When I go back to Sarah, she looks frozen like a deer in headlights. I ask her how the session was for her and she responds that she felt extremely uncomfortable. She says that it is a terrible effort for her even to be neutral on the outside while on the inside she feels anger and resentment towards her son. Sarah expresses resentment that Ilan is cooperative with me but is so awful to her at home. She reproaches herself for having such feelings towards her son and seems a little hostile towards me. She also reveals that when I asked her to engage in the powder print game, she felt as if I was forcing her to pretend to care when she had already told me that she felt too angry to provide nurture to her son.

It is clear that Sarah is hesitant to engage in the intimate work with her son which is implied in the Theraplay. Throughout the assessment phase, I had been aware that she was reserved and, at times, defensive and tired. Yet at the same time, she kept herself together and made enough insightful and cooperative comments during the MIM feedback and the parent demonstration session to make me think that the Theraplay protocol with this family could proceed in the standard format.

But it took the first actual Theraplay session for Sarah's real, unadulterated discomfort with the process to come out. This is often the case when a parent is ambivalent about whether they can engage in Theraplay. Because you learn so much from this first session, if you are unsure about whether the parent can participate, plan a brief Theraplay session that involves the parent in the engagement games but does not require them to provide the direct structure (e.g. do not put the parent in the position of being the "caller" in the Mother, May I? game). After the first session, you may feel a lot clearer about the best way forward.

I am happy that Sarah and I had the experience of the Theraplay session with Ilan because it gave a much truer picture of Sarah's feelings in relation to her son. Their relationship is much more difficult than she had let on during the assessment phase and she feels terrible and despondent about herself as a mother.

One of the most telltale signs that Sarah was not ready to engage in Theraplay was revealed in my countertransferential reaction to what she told me. When she said I was forcing her to do the powder print, she said it in a hostile way, as if I had harmed or violated her. I felt a wave of shame wash over my body. It sounded to me as if Sarah was saying that I didn't know what I was doing, or that I had violated her boundaries. I felt the impulse to defend myself or to apologize. Instead, I got "intellectual" (distanced myself) and launched into an explanation of why nurture was important.

When you feel these powerful, confusing surges of raw, conflicting emotion and a desire to strike back or withdraw, that is your signal that you are encountering a countertransference reaction. The most important thing to do in this instance is to pause, take a deep breath and ground yourself. Grounding yourself means allowing 30 seconds to require nothing of yourself, where you look around the room, feel your body in your chair, notice the tension in your shoulders, stomach or chest and accept those feelings. You can say to the parent, "Hold on one moment while I take time to reflect on what you are saying." You are likely to be experiencing sensations similar to those the parent is feeling about their own inadequacies. Once you take the moment to recognize these feelings in your body, you can take a deep breath and provide a more empathic, curious response. Consciously set your shoulders back, unfurrow your brow and put animation in your facial muscles. You can say something like: "Thank you for sharing your thoughts and feelings with me. It helps me understand the situation better." Showing gratitude that you discovered these difficult feelings will reduce both the parent's defensiveness and your own. Resist the urge to find solutions or provide explanations for the problems the parent is presenting you.

What the practitioner could have said to Sarah after taking a moment to notice her defensive feelings was: "Oh, thank you for telling me how uncomfortable that was for you. Now I understand just how unpleasant it was. You are also saying that you felt I was forcing you. Can you tell me more about that?" If the practitioner had given Sarah the opportunity to say more about her experience of being forced, the practitioner might have got a better understanding of what the specific dynamic was between them that had troubled her.

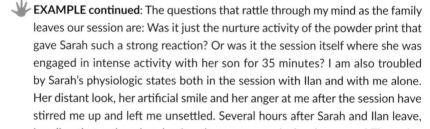 **EXAMPLE continued:** The questions that rattle through my mind as the family leaves our session are: Was it just the nurture activity of the powder print that gave Sarah such a strong reaction? Or was it the session itself where she was engaged in intense activity with her son for 35 minutes? I am also troubled by Sarah's physiologic states both in the session with Ilan and with me alone. Her distant look, her artificial smile and her anger at me after the session have stirred me up and left me unsettled. Several hours after Sarah and Ilan leave, I realize that rather than having them come again for the second Theraplay session, it would be best to invite Sarah to come alone for the next session so that we can continue to talk about her experience.

Fortunately, Sarah is able to arrange to come by herself for the next session. I ask her to tell me more about what it had been like for her in the session and she describes that it was as if I had asked her to expose herself to something toxic by opening herself up to Ilan. She had spent so much of her time guarding herself against his dagger-like looks, his rejections of her authority and his moodiness that she could not let her guard down in the session. I realize then just how unsafe and threatened she feels in her own home. I empathize with Sarah about how hard and tiring that must be. I validate that it's no wonder she felt so stressed in the session with him and tell her it was courageous that she showed up and powered through in the first place. This seems to shift Sarah's defensiveness a bit, as she senses that I am not judging her attitude or behavior. I become aware that Sarah is so vulnerable and feels so ineffective that she is unable to have compassion for Ilan's underlying feelings and motivations related to his trauma history.

Deciding which plan of action to take

Let's review the practitioner's options:

1. Work with the child by herself and have Sarah watch. This would not have been constructive for Sarah, since she felt so discouraged and misunderstood. If the practitioner interacted with her son and it went well, it would reinforce that other people (like her husband) could be successful and that she could not. Also, since she seemed so alone in her situation, leaving her by herself to observe would only strengthen her sense of being lost and alone with her struggles.

2. Work with the child by herself and add a second practitioner who could be with the parent, guiding, interpreting and supporting her as she observes the session. This would have been the ideal option for Sarah. It would have provided both the support of someone being dedicated uniquely to her viewpoint and experience while also being able to observe Ilan from a distance and possibly gain some insight and perspective. Unfortunately, the practitioner did not have the option of adding another practitioner for Sarah.

3. Have the other parent work with the child in Theraplay. This would not have been helpful in this case, since the major themes of Ilan's attachment issues surfaced in the context of the relationship with his mother. It was also where the main source of pain and struggle was generated for the entire family. The crucial issue in Ilan's family was that Ilan did not exhibit behavior problems with his father and, also, there was a strong phenomenon of changing between good guy and bad guy with the parents. Had those features not been so prominent in Ilan's case, the practitioner might have switched to working with Ilan's father first.

4. Provide therapeutic support to the parent alone for several sessions. The practitioner chose this option because she sensed that the most important and first goal to be addressed was to support Sarah in her very painful and difficult situation so that she could begin to have a more open perspective towards her son and learn new skills. They spent seven

sessions doing individual work together before moving on to the next phase of the intervention.

EXAMPLE continued: My individual work with Sarah has three parts. The first is for Sarah and me to establish a deep connection and sense of trust. This work is accomplished by me first suspending (at least temporarily) any effort to keep Ilan's perspective and needs in mind. I have to put aside my child-focused hat and live in Sarah's mind and heart for some time. This starts by Sarah talking about her experience of becoming a mother to Ilan, what she went through, what she wished for and what it meant to her to adopt him. I am careful to listen to the "underlying music" of the hopes, dreams and wishes she had when starting out on this journey. While exploring her story, I listen intently in order to give her a sense that I am very invested in her point of view. I am focused on having a direct gaze, an open, alert body posture and indicating through facial expressions and nodding that I am following the minute aspects and fluxes of her story. This intentional use of the social engagement system, as outlined by Stephen Porges's polyvagal theory (2011), is especially important because I know how judged and defensive Sarah feels and that her brain and mind are scanning for any sign that I think she is to blame for the situation with Ilan at home.

The second part is to deepen Sarah's understanding of her conflicts as a normal reaction to her circumstances and not a consequence of her being a fundamentally damaged human being. I use the theory of blocked care as outlined by Baylin and Hughes (2016). This theory is helpful because it normalizes the shut-down feelings parents experience when trying to parent a child who rejects them over a long period of time. I explain that this rejection is so painful that all of the caring and loving aspects of her brain have been shut off to protect herself and that is why she feels nothing but contempt for her son. I highlight that it is normal to be troubled and to feel ashamed of her own uncaring attitude and to be hard on herself about it. What a destructive cycle that becomes. So the second part of our work together is to accept and normalize her current state.

Once Sarah feels supported and able to understand her responses, it is possible to begin to focus on understanding Ilan's behaviors (my understanding and empathy of her experience has allowed her to become more curious about Ilan). I want to help Sarah to understand that Ilan's behaviors stem from his non-conscious wish to confirm his negative beliefs about himself. Using video, we look at discrete annoying behaviors and think about what Ilan might be expressing through them. We compare Sarah's new understanding with her previous reactions of alarm, fear and rejection. For example, we examine Ilan's tendency to demand more stuff, and activity. Sarah can understand that Ilan's frenzy to be stimulated and to consume things (like food, toys, etc.) is his attempt to avoid the emptiness or sadness he feels when he is not distracting himself. As Sarah begins to realize that Ilan is not being ungrateful for all she is doing for him, she is able to feel more empathy for him when he displays these behaviors.

There are other behaviors, however, that Sarah reacts to with anger and defensiveness despite our discussions about Ilan's underlying trauma. For example, Sarah feels that she cannot control her extreme sense of betrayal when Ilan changes from being irritable and contrary with her to being upbeat and affectionate when his father comes home. Sarah feels that her husband won't believe her version of the truth and she feels she cannot trust the validity of her own experience. I offer ideas like chatting with her husband on the phone during his journey home so that she can tell him how things have gone with Ilan that afternoon and feel more connection with him when he returns. Sarah does not resonate with my suggestions. I ask Sarah whether there have been other times in her life when she has felt that people did not believe her and that she could not trust her version of the truth. On further exploration, Sarah reveals (with a great deal of pain) that she had been bullied through elementary school for being overweight and she feels that her teachers and even her parents minimized her experiences. She had felt very alone then and this experience reminds her of those younger experiences. I enthusiastically commend Sarah for showing courage to make this connection and examine her own mind and attitudes as they relate to Ilan. It is the beginning of a process that allows Sarah to differentiate between what is going on at home currently and how lonely and unsupported she felt as a child. For the next session, I arrange to come in on a Saturday to meet with both Sarah and Mike so that we can talk about Ilan's transitions home and how to support Sarah. After seven sessions focusing on supporting her, Sarah feels ready to engage in Theraplay sessions with her son.

The Theraplay sessions went well because Sarah was able to trust the practitioner enough to let her guide her and take risks. When they interacted together, Sarah felt that the practitioner was as much on her side as she was on Ilan's as she tried to help him. The practitioner's work with Sarah also reminded her not to make herself the focus of the engagement and fun with Ilan so that she could avoid reinforcing her sense that other people could be successful with him but she could not. The practitioner provided structure and facilitated the interactions with Sarah and Ilan but minimized her face-to-face engagement with him.

Contraindications for Theraplay®

To do Theraplay, you have to establish that there is a basic safety within the relationship with the parent and child. What this means is that Theraplay is not an appropriate intervention for parents who:

- have serious mental illness or addictions and who are not actively seeking their own treatment or are not complying with their own treatment plan (skipping therapy appointments, not taking medications)

- are involved in a current, ongoing domestic violence relationship where the parent is constantly afraid at home and is not able to keep themselves and their child safe

- have severe personality disorders which significantly detract from their capacity to be aware of how their actions negatively affect their child. If the parent is so self-centered, emotionally labile or expresses such extreme anger that their child is constantly on guard and cannot afford to let their guard down, then they will not be able to benefit from the Theraplay intervention you are offering.

In reality, rarely is the situation clear cut, especially with parents who have personality disorders, that you can determine just by the intake session whether or not Theraplay is appropriate. It may take the intake plus conducting the MIM, the MIM feedback, talking to other intervention providers involved in the case and possibly doing a few "diagnostic" Theraplay sessions to determine whether the family is appropriate for Theraplay.

Below is a detailed example of a highly complex case where it was unclear whether Theraplay might be possible.

Using the assessment process and first few Theraplay® sessions as part of the decision process

 EXAMPLE: Margaret requests therapy for her 10-year-old son Taylor, due to panic attacks and some aggressive behaviors at home such as throwing books when angry. Taylor's parents are divorced and Taylor spends every weekend with his father, Jim. Margaret describes the relationship between herself and her ex-husband as strained.

Before the divorce, Jim had a gambling addiction that caused him to be belligerent, controlling and unpredictable towards both Margaret and Taylor. Additionally, Jim had been arrested several times for getting into physical fights with friends at their home in front of Taylor. The neighbors heard shouting and lamps crashing to the floor. Child protection services got involved. It was at that point that Taylor's parents separated and divorced. Taylor told the child protection worker that although his father did not hit him or his mother, he was scared of his father's temper and had stomach aches when he was around his father. The child protection worker determined that Taylor would not have any visits with Jim until Jim received therapy for gambling addiction and anger issues.

Eight months later, Jim has been attending individual therapy plus an addictions support group and has stopped gambling. Because of his progress, the social worker recently decided that Taylor should visit his father every weekend. The first two visits went well. However, on the third visit, Jim got into a verbal fight with a family friend. The friend left the house before a physical altercation occurred. At the time of the incident, Taylor did not react. However, when Margaret picked Taylor up from his father's, Taylor was particularly subdued and seemed shaken.

Margaret sensed that something had gone wrong. Taylor then told Margaret that Jim shouted and made threatening gestures at the family friend and that he was scared that his father would hit the friend. Taylor's panic attacks started in anticipation of his fourth weekend visit with his father. Margaret says that she does not want to have joint parent sessions with Jim but that Jim knows about her enquiry for therapy services and is willing to participate.

In my intake meeting with Jim, the three most important goals are to determine whether Jim 1) has self-awareness about his temper, 2) can accept responsibility for his behavior and 3) is prepared to apologize to his son. I also have to determine whether or not I sense that Taylor is actually emotionally and physically safe with his father. To help my understanding of the situation I decide to do a MIM and MIM feedback with Jim, speak to Jim's individual therapist as well as addictions group leader about his progress and also have an individual session with Taylor to ask him about how he feels at the visits with his father.

During our intake meeting, Jim seems articulate, thoughtful and caring towards his son. However, when I ask specifically about how the argument with his friend several weeks prior has affected Taylor, Jim says that Taylor hasn't actually experienced any fear and that it is Margaret who is making up Taylor's negative reaction. Jim says that Margaret is anxious, overprotective and always makes situations worse by being over-dramatic. When I ask about the previous incidents of violence Jim has displayed in the home before getting therapy intervention, Jim minimizes the incidents, saying that he has "made his amends to all the necessary parties and that it was all in the past." Jim also says that Taylor was never the witness of his anger outbursts. When I confront him that this contradicts the child protection report, Jim responds that that incident is the only one where Taylor was present and that Taylor was playing video games at the time and couldn't even hear the lamp crash. I leave the meeting feeling quite certain that he does not have enough insight to start the Theraplay work. Jim has agreed for me to speak to his counselor and addictions group leader, so I give a call to each of them. To my surprise, both say that Jim is following his intervention plan to abstain from gambling, is a productive group member and is making good progress in therapy. They both say that Jim takes responsibility for his behavior and they are quite certain that Jim will be open to repairing the relationship with his son. Since Jim receives positive reports from his therapy team, I think it would be helpful to observe the parent-child interaction. I conduct a MIM with each parent and Taylor on separate days.

In the MIM with his mother, Margaret lets Taylor take the lead in most activities by asking many questions and giving lots of choices. At times, it seems that Margaret is overly encouraging and not aware that her energy seems a bit overwhelming to Taylor. Overall though, there are many moments of warmth, laughter and comfort between them. Taylor especially likes the lotion activity. Margaret provides rhythmic, firm touch on Taylor's wrist and hands and Taylor sighs and says, "I'm about to take a nap."

In the MIM with his father, overall it seems that Taylor is more tuned in to his father than his father is to him. Taylor looks a little on edge, with his shoulders stiff and sitting forward in his chair. Taylor and Jim have some fun moments in playing a familiar game, which involves making all sorts of whistling sounds together. At times, Jim has a rather unattuned way of interacting with Taylor, especially in the structure/challenge activity "Adult draws a quick picture and encourages child to copy." Jim draws a very detailed picture and, when he is done, slides the paper over to Taylor's side definitively but without any words. Jim remains quiet and stiff while Taylor labors over his drawing. Taylor concentrates mightily and, at times, asks whether he is doing it right. Jim doesn't answer, and at one point says, "You can figure it out." For the familiar game, Jim and Taylor come up with Thumb Wrestling. They play four rounds. The first two times, Jim wins and Taylor lets out an "aaaw" that sounds disappointed but also looks as if he is having fun. When they play the third round, Jim moves his elbow to get leverage and says, "Hey, no cheating." Jim wins the third round and Taylor looks dejected. In the fourth round, Jim is about to pin Taylor's thumb again and then Taylor uses his thumbnail to dig into Jim's thumb. "Hey! Oww!" Jim yelps and starts wiggling his whole arm until he gets free from Taylor's grip. He then pins Taylor's thumb for the fourth and final time. They begin to argue, with Jim saying Taylor tried to take an unfair advantage by digging his fingernail, and Taylor arguing back, "But your thumb is twice as big as mine!" Jim cackles but Taylor, while smiling, also looks hurt.

As Jim turns to get the next card, Taylor holds his own thumb and says quietly, "It's not fair."

In the MIM feedback with Jim, I first show him a segment of the teach task, where they both enjoyed whistling. I commend Jim for choosing something that captures Taylor's attention. I highlight how apparent it is that Taylor admires him. Jim smiles with pride and says his own father was a master whistler. I then show the copy task and why Jim did not respond to Taylor when he asked for reassurance. Jim responds, "Taylor is a smart guy. He can do all sorts of stuff like code computers. He could totally do that drawing. He just sometimes acts like he can't so that I'll bail him out. But I just tell him 'You can do it.' And see? He did." "So what do you think is underneath Taylor's need for confirmation or reassurance?" I ask. "Basically, to see what he can get away with. See, his mother babies him so much, he's learned that all he has to do is give one of these 'woe is me' looks and I'll give in. He's checking to see if I think he's as weak as his mother thinks he is. So I'm just like 'nope, not going to work.'" When I cue up the thumb wrestling game, Jim laughs as he watches and says, "He doesn't like to lose." I ask, "What you do think Taylor was feeling as the game progressed?" Jim responds, "I told you, he's always trying to get away with stuff. He's smart and he beats me at chess half the time, but he can't be whining when he loses fair and square." I respond, "Okay, but help me out. This is just a game for fun, and your thumb is twice his thumb's size. Do you think it's important who wins in this instance?" Jim responds, "No, it's okay for him to win sometimes but it has to be fair. I was going to let him win the last one but he dug his nail into me so hard, I thought 'I'm gonna show him!'" "Is it possible he might have done that because he felt helpless that he didn't have a chance to win the first three times?" "He's not helpless! That's exactly what I'm trying to teach him! He can win if he doesn't cry if things don't go his way."

At this point I am thinking to myself that Jim hasn't shown any empathy for the underlying experiences his son has had. My mind is racing with thoughts about the possible reasons why Jim is so uncomfortable with Taylor having feelings of vulnerability. As a young child, did Jim experience humiliation when he cried? Did an adult overpower Jim physically to "teach him a lesson?" Does he feel worried or guilty about something he did to Taylor that he feels defensive about? These aren't necessarily coherent thoughts in the moment, more a sense in my gut that there is danger lurking behind this subject for Jim and I should tread carefully and slowly, lest I lose him. But I am wondering whether Jim has the minimum amount of reflective function to be able to participate in Theraplay. So, I try two additional angles to see if we can get beyond Jim's negative and blaming attitude about his son. First, I replay the video again and then pause it just after Taylor says, "But your thumb is twice as big as mine!" Taylor's mouth is smiling but his eyebrows are wrinkled inward and his eyes look sad. I ask Jim, "What does that face look like to you?" Jim looks for a moment and then says, "He looks like he's mad at me." "Mad at you? I see him looking a little rejected." "Yeah, I could see that. I remember being that small once and it was frustrating not being able to do what I want and always be bossed around." Now I'm thinking to myself that this is progress! Because if Jim can reflect on his own feelings of powerlessness as a child, perhaps he can begin to develop the reflective function necessary to separate his own feelings from those of his son's and be able to support his son with his struggles.

"Oh, so Jim, when you were a kid, did you also feel like the big adults had all the power but wouldn't help you?" Jim cracks a wry smile. "I know what you're doing. You're trying to get me to talk about my own childhood. I have a therapist. Didn't you talk to her already?" "Yes, I did, but I would like to be able to talk to you directly about it because how we were raised has a big influence on how we parent our children." Jim's looks pensive for a moment and then frowns. "You know what, this is supposed to be about Taylor. And anyway, I am not the one who even asked for this therapy. Margaret did. I'm just here to help out my son and be involved in his upbringing."

"Okay, fair enough Jim. I'm just thinking out loud here about how I'm going to be able to help you and Taylor. Part of what we do in Theraplay is play a bunch of funny, silly games, just for fun. Just for the sake of being together and feeling connected. Most of the games are cooperative so there is no winner or loser, but if there were a game like Thumb Wrestling, would you be willing to let Taylor win two out of three rounds?" "Look Miss, like I told you before, Taylor beats me fair and square at checkers or a 50-yard race. You're the professional and I'm sure you know what you're doing, but I'm not going to lie just because you said."

"Oh, I'm so sorry, I apologize if it sounded like I was asking you to lie. I didn't mean you should do that. I think I didn't explain my reason why I would sometimes ask you to allow him to beat you in a game that's just for fun. You see, when kids are little, they really do feel small, powerless and afraid, so being able to 'beat' your father at a silly game when the stakes are low allows a child to get a little sense of courage and strength that they need when they go out into the world, like school or like on the football field." "Okay," Jim says, but he looks distant. I sense a feeling of unease, as if Jim is suspicious of my motives and maybe he feels that I'm trying to trick him. Jim's distrust of me is based on numerous reasons that I can only guess at. His ex-wife is the one who initiated the work with me, he feels resentful that he is doing so much to change by participating in other therapies, he feels as if I'm blaming his childhood, but is it more than that, possibly something that makes Taylor feel truly unsafe with his father? I make a decision that I will need to meet with him at least one more time to see if we can explore these feelings more deeply.

I say to Jim, "I don't think we're quite seeing eye to eye yet. Maybe I didn't explain the reasons why I think this approach might help you and Taylor." "Help me and Taylor?" Jim exclaims. "Taylor and I don't need the help. Taylor is actually fine and so am I. It's really his mother who is stressing Taylor out by making a big deal out of everything. That's what I told you from the beginning." "Fair enough, but since you are Taylor's father, it's going to be important for you to find a way to support him with that. I'd like to invite you to come next week by yourself again so I can hear more about how you think we can do that." Jim responds, "I will come with Taylor if you want me to, but I'm not coming just for you and me to talk. The information sheet you sent me by email said that the parent comes here once to go over the video or whatever. I've done that."

I feel put on the spot because the session is over, our time is up and Jim has drawn a line in the sand. He won't come by himself an additional time. I feel ill-at-ease about the way the session is ending and a bit like I've done something wrong. I feel pressured to make a decision. I tell Jim that I'll work with Taylor and his mother for the first eight sessions and then will work with him and Taylor for another round of eight sessions.

What I wish I had told him was that I would have to think some more about the best way to proceed and that I would send him an email with my follow-up thoughts. What I need is time to reflect and to consult with a trusted colleague or supervisor about these mixed-up feelings I am having. I feel uneasy about my work with Jim thus far, not just the MIM but also how the feedback went. I'm worried that Taylor doesn't feel safe with his father. But I'm also confused about whether Jim's challenge to my authority by saying "No, I won't come again to talk alone with you" is provoking an overly angry response from me based on my own issues of feeling helpless.

My assumption is that I will definitely work with Taylor and his mother on building Taylor's resilience and helping Margaret to contain her anxiety so as to be more emotionally available to support Taylor. Regarding Jim, here are my options and the benefits and risks:

Option	Benefit	Risk
Do a standard course of Theraplay intervention where two parents are divorced or have contentious relationship of eight (or more) sessions with the mother and then eight sessions with the father.	Involves the father, who is a major factor in the child's problems. The father might learn to trust the process once the relationship with the practitioner deepens.	Makes the child vulnerable with the parent, who may be unsafe. May destabilize the child's current useful and necessary defensive coping skills with the father.

cont.

Option	Benefit	Risk
Do not work with the father in Theraplay directly but provide occasional meetings to update the father on the child's progress.	Keeps the father involved while not directly exposing the child to the father's negative responses in Theraplay. May help the father to develop trust with the practitioner over time.	Missed opportunity to work on issues directly with the father and the child. The father may feel left out and could sabotage the process.
Do not work with the father at all.	Does not expose the child to the father's negative responses in Theraplay. Focus on work entirely with the mother is less complicated for the practitioner. Possibly makes work with the mother and the child more focused and potent.	Major missed opportunity to help the father in any way or assess his abilities. The father at bigger risk to feel left out of process.
Do a modified form of Theraplay with the father— what we call "diagnostic Theraplay sessions," focusing on Engagement, not Nurture or Challenge, and keep Structure firmly in the practitioner's control.	Provides opportunities for relational improvements without challenging the father's rigid thinking. Opportunities to further assess the father's skills and ability to receive guidance. Builds trust between the practitioner and parent.	Relies on the practitioner being strong in leading the structure. Requires the practitioner to have time and opportunity to consult with trusted colleague to assess interactions. Requires videoing and time to review.

 EXAMPLE continued—developing a plan. I choose the last option because of the clear benefits versus risks. What is so powerful about Theraplay is the ability to involve the parent in a way that might circumvent some of their defenses and allow the parent to discover and show other relational or parenting strengths that come with the structured play of Theraplay. So, after working for a series of eight sessions (two months) with Margaret, I invite Jim to come and do three Theraplay sessions with Taylor. I get help from a colleague to think of activities that will be connecting for both Jim and Taylor and that do not focus on Jim as the structuring or authority figure. I avoid games like Mother, May I?, Simon Says, Mirroring and Peanut Butter and Jelly. I also avoid games with direct competition and high challenge or games that evoke physical dysregulation like Cotton Ball Hockey, Crawling Race and Balloon Pass. Instead, I focus on easy, cooperative games or mild nurture games, like having both Taylor and his father pop bubbles together simultaneously (I blow the bubbles) (see the list of activities for different kinds of clients in Chapter 23).

Quite a few positive interactions happen in these sessions. It is obvious that Taylor is really seeking out and enjoying face-to-face interaction with his father, as long as it is highly structured by me. For example, when we play the musical body parts game (Beep and Honk adapted for the older child), Jim and Taylor show an incredible ability to make up a mutual tune on their body parts together that has a strong, reciprocal beat and that brings out Taylor's surprising talent and charisma. Jim seems to really enjoy his son's creativity and the two of them have real "moments of meeting." However, the situation feels fragile because when Taylor and Jim press on each other's face (nose, chin, ear), they both get agitated as each of them seems to think the other is pressing too hard. I see Taylor flinch a few times, so I make a rule that no face parts will be included as a musical instrument. Instead they use knee, elbow, toes, shoulder, wrist and so on.

Several times, however, I see worrisome behavior that I want to talk to Jim about in the parent-only session. One example occurs during the pillow sandwich game. At first, Taylor seems keen to do the activity. He readily lies on top of the first pillow as I ask what he liked on his sandwich. I have Jim call out the favorite items as we pile the pillows. As a joke, Jim calls out, "Mayo!" Taylor says, "No I don't!" Jim repeats "Mayo!" louder and Taylor again says no. Jim has the next pillow ready and puts it on top of Taylor's face for a second, as if to drown out Taylor's voice. "Hey!" Taylor whines in protest. I feel a jolt of energy run through my body. I feel caught off guard and angry. "Let's not do that!" I say and remove the pillow from Taylor's face. I try to finish the game but Taylor looks upset and he sits up, knocking off the pillows. "Why'd you do that? The sandwich got all over! Guess we can't eat it!" Jim tries to joke. "I don't think he liked that you put the pillow on his face," I say. "Aww, it was just a joke and he knows it. There was even a space between the pillow and the floor, I made sure!" Taylor turns away from us, as if to gather himself, and grabs a stray feather from under the couch. He blows it towards his father in what feels like an effort to distract from the discomfort of the situation. "That's a good idea," I say, going along with Taylor's distraction. I note to myself that I need to talk to Jim about the pillow in the face before the next Theraplay session.

The following week, I ask Jim if we could have a quick conversation while Taylor waits in the waiting room. I remind Jim about the incident with the pillow from the previous week and share my observation that Taylor was uncomfortable with the interaction and maybe even a little scared. I tell him that, while his intentions might be friendly, his son is sensitive to that type of play and I ask him not to do it again. Jim seems to barely remember the incident. He responds that he certainly was not trying to scare Taylor and was indeed trying to be humorous but that he would not do something like that again. I go over the activities that I have planned for our Theraplay session. I remind Jim that the games are just for fun. I also ask Jim to try to notice if Taylor flinches at all, like in the musical body parts game, and if so, to adjust to make him more comfortable. Jim agrees.

The session goes fairly well on the surface but I feel that I need to be vigilant to control the activities so that Jim doesn't do anything surprising that will make Taylor uncomfortable. During the Paper Toss game, things go awry. At first I am in charge of saying the cue word for Taylor to throw the paper ball into his father's arm basket. Jim tries moving the basket so that Taylor misses, so I remind Jim that this is just for fun and to hold the basket steady. When it is Jim's turn to say the cue word of "elephant," he tries to trick Taylor by saying many E words like eggplant, empanada and exaggerate. Taylor's body language shows he is getting worked up because he hunches his shoulders and starts to giggle in a high pitch. When Jim finally says "elephant," Taylor throws the paper ball right at Jim's face. Jim yells "Hey!" in an indignant but playful tone, then immediately takes the paper ball and throws it right back at Taylor's face. This all happens in less than a second.

"Wait a minute you two!" I say. "Remember guys, this is just for fun. No one needs to get stressed from playing this game. Dad, why don't you just say 'one two three throw!' so Taylor will be ready to throw." "Oh, that's no fun!" Jim exclaims, but then says "Okay" and cooperates. The session ends fairly quickly after that but I feel dysregulated. I realize that Jim can escalate and catch me off guard very quickly and that I'm not in control. Luckily my next session is a parent-only session (as is written in the parent handout that Jim clung to when he said he wouldn't come to two parent sessions in a row because that wasn't what was written in the guidelines).

In the parent-only session, I cue up the part of the video to where the paper toss escalated to throwing balls at each other's faces. First, I ask Jim what he sees without any input about my thoughts. Jim says that Taylor gets aggressive at times and needs to work on his impulses. I ask Jim, "If you think Taylor got impulsive or aggressive, why do you think he felt that way?" Jim responds that Taylor is sometimes immature for his age and needs to learn to control himself. I then rewind to show the sequence to Jim of how he had made the game harder by moving his arms and then saying many tricky cue words. "Let's watch your son's body language as you try to make the game more challenging. What do you think his body is telling us?" We watch again. "I think Taylor might think this is too easy so I'm trying to make it more fun. Otherwise he can start acting out." "I see," I say. "So you think this was too easy for Taylor and you're trying to keep him engaged by making it more challenging?" "Yeah," Jim responds. "So why do you think Taylor hit you in the face with the paper ball?" "Well, that's what always seems to happen. He gets bored or thinks he can't do it and then he ruins the game." "That's just it, Jim," I say excitedly. "I do think the game goes awry because he's worried he can't do it, but I think the reason he feels that way is because he senses you're trying to make him fail or you're testing him in some way." "That's just the way I am, I make it challenging to make it fun and

Taylor has to learn to follow the rules." "Can I ask you, Jim, how did you feel when Taylor threw the paper at your face?" "He's a little rascal," Jim responds. "He was just testing me, so I gave it right back to him so he can see how it feels." "Were you feeling a little stressed yourself by the situation? Maybe you feel like you have to prove yourself here with me?" "No, I'm not stressed," Jim dismisses with a chuckle. I continue, "I don't think he was testing you. I think Taylor threw the paper at you impulsively, yes, but almost as a way of reacting to the stress of not being able to meet your challenge." "No," Jim says. "Taylor knows I'm just playing." "Okay," I say, feeling defeated. "Let me restate what I'm trying to say: I think your behavior of increasing the challenge or playfully teasing is the cause of the stress. Your manner of interacting is contributing to Taylor's overall stress and maybe contributing to his anxiety in other parts of his life. My worry is that if you can't change these patterns of interacting with your son, it will get in the way of you developing a secure relationship with him."

"Well, that's your professional opinion, and I'm sure you know what you're doing, but I know who I am as a parent and that focusing on me is rather messed up. I will take what you said under consideration. But I think you're looking at the wrong person in terms of who is responsible for Taylor's anxiety. You worked with Taylor and his mother for two months before working with me and him. Did you see how she acts with him? She's constantly telling him there's something wrong with him! It's the same as she did with me for all these years and that's why we're in this situation today." We end the session with me trying to repair with Jim and refocus on our goals to help Taylor. But clearly my stating my worry about Jim's behavior has upset him so that he is defensive beyond the point of having a constructive dialogue. Back to my trusted supervisor I go!

In reflecting on the situation with my supervisor, I decide to discontinue the work with Jim. I have to accept that Jim doesn't see the issues as I do. Perhaps I should leave the door open for meetings with him to check on how Taylor is doing when with him?

I have a phone conversation with Jim about this decision. I emphasize that he is very important to Taylor and I see him as an important part of his life. I tell Jim that I understand that he wants Taylor to become strong and self-confident, not anxious. I clarify that in order for the work to take place, Jim would need to recognize and take responsibility for some of the stress that he is contributing to in Taylor's life. Jim responds to this phone call with understandable defensiveness, saying he disagrees with my conclusion. I tell him that I would be open for meetings with him in the future to check on how Taylor was doing when with him. Jim thanks me and we end the conversation.

In the meantime, Taylor has to go back and forth between the two parents. Since I cannot work on helping Taylor feel safer with his father directly, I focus on increasing his security and self-confidence with his mother. I proceed to do a regular Theraplay intervention with Taylor and Margaret, and this important work does make a difference in helping Taylor speak up for himself and feel more resilient. I also help Margaret to develop supportive strategies to use for when Taylor feels undermined after visits with his father.

In principle, work with both parents is very important when a child has anxiety and is having to go back and forth between two parents. It took the practitioner several months and many encounters with Jim before she came to the conclusion that she would not be able to do Theraplay with him and Taylor. Ultimately, the essential reason that she did not feel that Theraplay was appropriate was that the aggression Jim displayed was deep and represented a more significant issue of lack of safety. The likelihood is that this was due to some unresolved trauma in Jim's past that lay unconscious. But when Jim was not able to show any self-reflection about how he could be causing or contributing to his son's stress, the practitioner decided that doing such intimate work as Theraplay directly between him and his son would not be indicated. This is because children who feel fundamentally unsafe with their parents at home will act out in the session or will not be able to open up to engage, despite your best efforts. Furthermore, it may destabilize a child, whose justified coping strategies of keeping their parent at a distance are crucial to their safety.

Working with a child alone when there is no parent available

Usual practice in Theraplay is to centrally include a parent figure, but there are some situations in which we might consider other options. There are some settings where the parent is not accessible because they live too far away (e.g. residential group home), or in a school or other setting where the parent is not readily available. In those settings, it might make sense to do Theraplay work if the setting supports this type of work as part of the child's overall intervention plan. You would adapt the kind of work and typically include a secondary attachment figure in sessions. It is obviously imperative that the parents consent to a practitioner working with their child in Theraplay and every effort should be made to assign a consistent adult who serves as an attachment figure (like a classroom assistant or residential child care worker) to participate in the Theraplay intervention.

There are other circumstances where a practitioner may deem it appropriate to work one to one with a child in Theraplay for a period:

- A foster child awaiting another placement where the practitioner is the most constant person in the child's life, or an older adolescent without involved caregivers.

- The parent is willing to be involved but we see that they have a negative impact on the session. For them, a second practitioner, observation only, extra practicing, video viewing and their own therapeutic support would be useful.

- The parent is unwilling to participate but wants the child "to be fixed." Perhaps a period of the child getting what they need in Theraplay with the practitioner would lead to behavior change that might make the parent's life easier and that might help them then get involved.

- The parent is unable to participate due to illness or some other responsibility and there is no one else to step in. Perhaps there could be a trial of child-only sessions until the parent can become involved.

- A foster parent or some other kind of guardian doesn't see involvement as their responsibility. We might help the child until another caregiver is identified who, it is hoped, will step into the parent role.

In all of these examples we are still focusing on the relationship between the child and their parent figure, even if they are not present. You are holding the relationship in mind and focusing on how to deepen it or how to keep them connected, like forming a bridge for the child while working towards reintroducing the parent figure.

Beyond the above-mentioned groups, however, there is a subset of children who do not have a parent or attachment figure who is willing and able to do the work with the child. In community mental health, there are many instances where the parent is unwilling or unable to come to sessions. Often these are biological parents who are marginally functioning and very preoccupied. They are inconsistent in their attendance (if they attend at all) and aren't able to follow through on recommendations for helping the child. It is often the case that this group of parents have chronic problems and may be resistant to change no matter how much the community invests in them. So, the reality is, a practitioner could be working in a setting where the child is dropped off by a driver, case worker or a caregiver who promptly disappears.

Different child therapy providers work individually with a child in such a situation, but with an attachment-focused intervention like Theraplay that places so much emphasis on the importance of the parent, it is a big step to consider proceeding with work without the parent present. From a Theraplay perspective, we have to consider the various risks of providing such an intervention. We might, for instance, potentially undermine the parent, the network might take a step back, thinking that the child is now receiving help, or our energies may be more helpfully directed towards involving safe adult figures in the child's life in some way. Alternatively, when a child does not have a responsive caregiver and there is little potential for that situation to change, we need to consider the ethics of leaving them without a Theraplay provision if we feel they might benefit from it. This is a group of very vulnerable children and the issue of effective provision in the absence of available parents needs further consideration by the mental health community.

It is our position that if no one else can provide the attuned and responsive caregiving and joyful, reciprocal interaction to a child, then the Theraplay practitioner could consider providing some work. You would need to proceed with caution and give particular consideration to the length of intervention and how you would link in with the child's network. This scenario is obviously a last resort and you would be making efforts all the way through to be linked with any potential attachment figures from the child's network who could take the attachment figure role. Within this thoughtful context, some Theraplay provision may give the child a positive experience of an adult, some support around their regulation, and experiences of engaging in reciprocal relationships, which may enable them to be more likely to seek out other adults in the future who have similar attributes.

Before embarking on Theraplay alone with the child, there are some particular cautions to bear in mind:

- Verify that indeed the parent is not able or willing to come by making real and repeated attempts to invite and support the parent into the process, including helping them overcome obstacles such as transport.

- Attempt to educate the parent about the importance of their presence.

- Verify that the parent is not dangerous, threatening or the kind of parent who makes allegations against providers as a matter of course.

- Have the parent at least come in to do a MIM and feedback.

- Explain Theraplay to the parent and have them sign consent for the Theraplay intervention.

- Have the support of the organization administrators for doing Theraplay alone with the child.

- Video the sessions and seek supervision from a Theraplay supervisor.

Issues to bear in mind if you are working with a child alone:

- Do not do the more overt nurturing activities such as placing a child in your lap, rocking a child or feeding them (just share a snack with the child in a more playful or matter-of-fact way). But all the other things, including the Weather Report, taking care of hurts and manicure, are certainly worth considering, depending on the presenting problems and all the other clinical considerations you would have covered in your assessment. Many of the Engagement, Structure and Challenge games that promote connection, reciprocity, regulation and self-esteem are very much warranted.

- This should not be the new Theraplay practitioner's first case.

We are mindful that raising this discussion about the possibility of using Theraplay with a child alone brings to the surface mixed views and questions. We know that Theraplay can be impactful across a wide range of contexts and advocate that this issue about how to proceed with a child who has no safe attachment figure warrants further exploration.

Summary

This chapter has discussed a range of complex parent issues that require significant modification of the standard Theraplay protocol. There are guidelines for when not to use Theraplay with particularly troubled parents. However, there are also many parents with complex issues where the answer of whether or not to use Theraplay is not clear cut. There is a lot of room within the Theraplay model to modify the intervention in order to assess and develop the parents' capacities as well as provide a helpful intervention for the child. One of Theraplay's strengths is that it can be helpful to families even where the parent doesn't really understand how it works, and this means that it can be a useful intervention for families for whom other talking-based therapies are not accessible. As long as we are able to form a good enough relationship with the parent so that they can follow our guidance to some extent, then working together becomes possible. Even when this is not possible, we advocate that it is worth considering adapting the Theraplay intervention to allow very vulnerable children to be provided with the benefits of some Theraplay work. In all situations, the child's safety is, of course, paramount.

Chapter 9

Theraplay® Outtakes and Bloopers—What No One Ever Told You

Facilitating Theraplay sessions can be many things—exciting, rewarding, hard work and, at times, challenging. Sessions are also often unpredictable and can be hilarious. Children have a knack of surprising us and taking things in a direction we may not have anticipated. No Theraplay handbook would be complete without some examples of the kinds of ridiculous situations you may get yourself into. Here are some memorable stories and what we learned.

These examples are from various practitioners who have shared their experiences. When it is not the two authors' individual experiences, you will see the name of the practitioner who contributed the anecdote.

Polystyrene balls

I was working with a very volatile boy, Tommy aged 9, and had been feeling quite anxious and out of control. His parents didn't know how to respond when he became dysregulated and they tended to freeze, leaving me faced with a hurricane-like situation. The venue we were in was tricky as it was shared with other community groups and at the end of the last session he had shouted inappropriately at a group of elderly women arriving for their Christmas party! I didn't feel I could manage alone. So, I decided to call on the help of a colleague and moved to a more suitable venue. This time I had the support of my colleague (who sat with the father in an adjacent room) and I was feeling confident. I had my session plan ready to go. This session would be better. We did our entrance and I sat Tommy down on a large bean bag. Within a matter of seconds, however, he had discovered the zip on the bean bag and began to pull out minute polystyrene balls from the bean bag's filling. My stomach sank as I noticed what he was doing. Who knew that the bean bag (which must have contained many thousands of these balls) did not have an inner cover? I had to think quickly. I managed to keep a confident and upbeat voice as I oriented Tommy towards the pile of polystyrene balls and began a counting game. Tommy's father and my colleague had been watching in disbelief and amusement at the unfolding scene. Unbelievably, Tommy engaged with my random counting game and I managed to divert him away from the idea of emptying the whole thing. A near miss! I survived the session and had dreams about the room filled with thousands of static polystyrene balls clinging to the furniture.

What I learned:

- Avoid venues shared by vulnerable groups.

- Check that your bean bag has a childproof cover!

- It is easier to think when you have a colleague to support you.

- Just because your experienced colleague is there, don't assume disaster will not strike.

Big red nipples

I was working with a 15-year-old young man called Josh and his very playful foster carer. Josh enjoyed many young Theraplay activities and behaved emotionally and cognitively more like a typical 8-year-old. He loved the sessions. We were playing Sticker Match. My stickers were large, round and red. In the middle of the game he playfully placed a sticker on his foster carer's breast. She looked at herself, then burst out laughing and put one on his. They both sat giggling with their matching red nipples. I wasn't sure what to do but decided to take this as playful exuberance of an emotionally young child. So I left the nipples where they were and redirected the rest of the play to ensure no other inappropriate stickers were placed and the session continued in a warm atmosphere.

What I learned:

- When you find yourself in an unexpected situation you just have to find a sensible way through it.

- I reflected afterwards in my supervision that it would have been better to have responded to him in that moment as a 15-year-old young man, to have removed the sticker from his foster carer's breast and to state that we don't put stickers on private parts. Although he was emotionally young, he was still a pubescent young man who needed clear messages around boundaries.

- It's easy to get carried away when a spontaneous situation is very funny. Sometimes you need a reminder about whose needs you are meeting.

- But not too often—hilarity in a session can be wonderful.

Shredding my stuff

I was having my first session with Jasmine, a lively 5-year-old, and was worried about having sufficient games to keep her engaged because she couldn't sustain attention well. I had a wide range of options in my basket. She immediately pulled items out and began rapidly shredding my crepe paper, spreading it around the room. Any attempts I made to engage her were fruitless (she was very happily occupied!), and as I attempted to tidy up she then grabbed the bubbles and emptied them over her parent. The situation continued in a state of chaos and I was one step behind Jasmine the entire time. After they left I sat sweating and exhausted in my demolished room.

What I learned:

- Don't have much in your basket. It's better to have one or two basic props (e.g. in your pocket as a last resort) and think of several activities that use one prop rather than having to manage lots of materials.

- Cover your basket (e.g. with a blanket) or have a lid so it's clear to the child that this is not for them.

- Managing bubbles (or balloons for that matter) is not for the faint-hearted.

- If a child needs your full attention, you need to give it to them.

- Make good use of the parent who can help by being a bean bag and hold the child on their lap.

- Negotiation doesn't work.

How dare you pierce my juice box!

Ahmed was a bubbly and friendly boy. He tended to be quite rigid and self-sufficient but liked to play and I had found a way of moving through a sequence of activities that seemed helpful. We came to the snack and I picked up his juice box and pierced the lid with a straw (getting it ready for him—I hadn't done this before but things had been going well). Ahmed went into an instant and dramatic meltdown about the straw, crying, calling me "naughty" and desperately searching for another drink. He remained upset with me for the rest of the session. I tried everything I could think of to divert and regulate him but nothing worked. I felt powerless and embarrassed and the session ended with me handing his mother his shoes and jacket as she carried him (still wailing) from the room. I felt very poor at my job. I emailed his mother afterwards and was very surprised to receive a delighted response—she was so relieved that "at last someone has seen him how he is with us!" This began a new openness in our dialogue and I was reminded of his trauma around feeding (severe reflux) which may have explained his distress around the drink. The mother and I agreed a plan for the next session. I would provide a drink already pierced right at the start so that he wasn't waiting for the next drink incident for the whole session. She was very clear that it would be unhelpful to avoid piercing the box again and it seemed most important to follow her guidance. I was nervous about the next session but it went well, we were back on track and we had shared an important experience of rupture and repair of our relationship.

What I learned:

- Sometimes something very innocent you do can have a big impact.

- Parents are often delighted if you fail to manage their child as it makes them feel less incompetent.

- You may make mistakes and children are quite forgiving.

My great new ideas

Polly was 8, very creative and she liked throwing things. I had been thinking about fun things we could do for our next session and I thought skittles would be perfect (all children like skittles!). I spent the week collecting empty water bottles and arrived full of enthusiasm to our session. Polly was excited and immediately engaged in throwing bean bags at the skittles. They were, however, very noisy and echoey and began flying around the room. Polly quickly became overstimulated and I had my work cut out trying to find a way to calm her down and get rid of the bottles.

What I learned:

- Just because a child will love an activity doesn't mean it's a good idea.

- Stick to the tried and tested Theraplay ideas while you're learning. There is probably a good reason why some "fun" activities aren't on the list.

- Work out how you are going to get rid of or tidy up exciting props before you bring them out (a big binliner is a handy thing to have in your pocket).

Bad socks and pants

I had been in a rush for work and wasn't focusing on what I was wearing. I got into the session with Winston and his mother, took off my shoes (as I always do) and noticed huge holes in my socks. There was no point disguising them and we all laughed about them. As we got going in the session, I then realized that my top was riding up my back and that a gap had appeared. My self-consciousness increased when I remembered that Crawling Race had been one of my planned activities, so I began frantically replanning my session based on minimal exposure. Things got worse through the various activities, and by the time I got to the Blanket Swing, and couldn't use one hand to keep pulling down my top, I had to give up and accept that the video would be an embarrassment. I knew exactly what my supervisor would say!

What I learned:

- Wear tunics and decent socks.

- If you're not comfortable, you can't focus on the family's needs.

- You see things from a whole different angle when you review your video!

Piggy-back ride (Annie Keimaier)

I was working with a lovely foster mother and her 4-year-old son who had experienced severe trauma. Theraplay sessions were intense and difficult. He would often become dysregulated, try to distance himself from his mother and me, and also try to control us. One day he became quite agitated and withdrew from us. I asked his mother if I could give him a piggy-back ride down the hall and back in order to stay connected with him, but in a playful way, and give him some rhythmic proprioceptive input to help him down-regulate. I put him on my back and galloped steadily down the hallway chanting, "This is the way the gentleman rides…" I could hear him laughing and feel him bouncing up and down on my back as I held his legs with my arms. We turned at the end of the hall and headed back to my therapy room. Unfortunately, I tripped and fell to the floor, landing on my shoulder. He rolled off my back and ran to his foster mother with his arms outstretched and hugged her. Even as I was in pain, I noticed, "It's *so* good to see him seek his foster mother out for comfort and reassurance."

What I learned:

- Accidents can happen anywhere, any time. I genuinely don't think the piggy-back ride was a poor choice. The fall was a random accident.

- Sometimes what seems like a big incident can have positive consequences. The fall actually helped the boy strengthen his attachment relationship with his foster mother and begin to develop some empathy for others' "hurts." When I saw him at the next session, the boy, his mother and I discussed what happened.

Bad language

I worked at a large agency that had a child clinic but also several other offices, including program administrators, bookkeepers and technology people. My client Charlie, aged 7, had an annoying habit of using foul language and calling people mean names at home. It made his father very angry. My supervisor told me to play the Peanut Butter and Jelly game but use naughty words instead. We started off with stupid, dummy, butthead and idiot, but then it got more serious. Charlie screamed "DUMB-ASS!" at the top of his lungs about 15 times and I matched him each time. Eventually, I got him to say it in a whisper, say it like a little granny, say it like an opera singer. We had a grand old time and even the father, who started out looking tense, got into it. The session was over, and I walked Charlie and his father to the door and said goodbye. When I turned around to walk to my office, two administrators were standing there staring at me. Beyond them I could see the accountant peering through her office window with alarm. They asked whether I was okay and let me know that things sounded so violent in my session with Charlie that they had considered whether to call the police!

What I learned:

- You should have a meeting or write a memo to your entire office, letting them know types of behaviors they might be witnessing so they can figure out what's within the scope of the work and what should in fact cause them alarm.

- So that your colleagues don't have to worry about you, develop an SOS code like doing a certain "knock knock" rhythm on the office wall next door, for when you do indeed need help.

The gopher

I was new at Theraplay when I started working with Olivia, aged 6. Olivia was totally wild in our first session—she managed to jump off the couch, throw my cushions around the room and open my cabinets as I ran after her from place to place. When I turned my back to close the cabinet door, she bolted from the room and down the hall! Olivia's foster mother was a like a deer in headlights and didn't move. I ran after Olivia. Luckily it was 4:30pm and some of my colleagues had gone home already. I found Olivia burrowed deeply behind my colleague Chrisy's desk. Olivia had used Chrisy's gym bags to barricade herself even further. I tried being playful by offering to play This Little Pig with her socked foot and Olivia kicked me! I tried playing peek with the smelly t-shirt she had pulled over her head and Olivia snarled at me and hid herself even deeper. I felt so stupid because my Theraplay trainers had told us to be in charge and here I was, absolutely helpless to extract this child from underneath the desk. It was 35 minutes after the session was officially supposed to be over before Olivia agreed to emerge from her burrow, and that was because her mother finally offered to buy her a milkshake at McDonald's.

What I learned:

- With a child who is apt to try and escape, guard the door! Sit closer to the door than the child (or have the parent do so) and try not to turn your back on her.

- I needed supervision because I had no idea what to do. My supervisor told me that if a child has burrowed and is hiding, it is likely to mean that she feels scared, threatened or exposed. The approach to take is a calming, reassuring and supportive tone rather than playful. Offer the child a blanket to reinforce their need to hide, slip in a drink with a straw for them to sip (don't try to hold it for them), keep 2–3 feet away but stay close enough and use a reassuring tone to say that you understand the child's need for a break, that things got too intense in the session, and that you're glad she is showing you what she needs.

- Only after she starts talking or peeking out should you offer a more interactive activity like measuring her foot with licorice or a foil print.

Poop time (Nicole Charney)

I had a 5-year-old girl who was anxious and needed to control everything. One problem she had was that she would never poop anywhere else except her house. She wanted to poop in school but she could not do it and it led to problems with constipation. We started doing Theraplay in the regular way, with a fun entrance, noticing what she brought with her, then Caring for Hurts. She loved it, so I extended the activity and sang the "oh lotion" song while massaging her hand. At that point, the girl told her mother, "I need to go to the bathroom." Her mother said okay and went with her. It took a long time. From the other side of the door, I asked if everything was okay. The mother responded that the girl was pooping! I said, "Wooooow, that's great." After that, during the middle of every session, the girl would announce with pride "I'm going to the bathroom." And every time, her mother and I would respond, "We said we love your poop. It's so brown, we love the smell!" From then on, her fear of pooping outside the home disappeared. She took our sessions as her place to liberate herself by always pooping in my office. Theraplay was her diaper.

What I learned:

- Theraplay can provide a child with such safety that they are liberated emotionally and physically.

Part 3

Becoming a Theraplay® Practitioner

Chapter 10

Developmental Phases in Becoming a Theraplay® Practitioner

─────── CHAPTER PLAN ───────

This chapter will discuss the following areas:

Maintaining a reflective approach

Stages in Theraplay® student practitioner development

- Development of the practitioner summary

Stage 1: Introduction to the model—what is this all about?

- Practitioner and Theraplay® student

Stage 2: How does it actually work? Is that it? Simplicity and depth combined

- Practitioner and Theraplay® student
- Parent perspective

Stage 3: The practicalities of getting started and early sessions

- Practitioner and Theraplay® student
- Parent perspective

Stage 4: Excitement and doubts—I'm not sure about this

- Practitioner and Theraplay® student
- Parent perspective

Stage 5: This is hard work

- Practitioner and Theraplay® student

- Parent perspective

Stage 6: Developing deeper practice
- Practitioner and Theraplay® student
- Parent perspective

Summary

As trainers and supervisors (as well as practitioners) we have supported many student practitioners new to Theraplay and have observed and delighted in their development. Just as children move through predictable stages of development, so someone new to Theraplay (whether a parent, child or student) also typically moves through predictable stages. This chapter will focus on the process of absorbing the Theraplay approach from the student practitioner perspective. While Theraplay may look simple, there are many complex layers that make up effective practice, and the actual delivery of Theraplay, as in all interventions, depends on the training, experience and personal qualities of the person delivering it. When considering practitioner development therefore, some individuals will progress more quickly and to a deeper level than others.

This chapter has relevance for Theraplay students (those in the supervision practicum) as well as practitioners more generally as they gain experience. We have therefore used the terms student and practitioner interchangeably throughout the chapter.

As we consider the developmental process, it is useful to separate out the wider Theraplay framework (the core theoretical principles, values and perspectives) from the "method" (i.e. how to administer the MIM and how to set up the actual play activities). Many people new to Theraplay confuse the method with the more subtle and essential underpinnings of the Theraplay approach which guide the interpretation and delivery of effective Theraplay. In the following, we will think broadly about Theraplay from the perspective of a developing student practitioner. We begin by discussing why a reflective approach is essential and move on to explore six broad stages of development.

Maintaining a reflective approach

Although Theraplay has many practical elements, in order to do it well you need to reflect deeply on your work. When working with a client in Theraplay, we try to keep as many ways of engaging and relating together as open as possible so that we can emotionally connect. We then try to find ways to sustain this connection so that the relating becomes more coherent. This is a complex process. As we develop a relationship with a child who struggles, we may experience moments of connection but also many challenges and times of disconnect or impermanence. There can be a feeling of shifting perspectives and angles, where the sense of connection can come and go, and it may be difficult to have a sense of the whole. It is our reflective practice that helps us make sense of these dynamics.

Theraplay is fundamentally about human connection, and a Theraplay intervention is designed to facilitate a transformational experience principally using a non-verbal modality. In order to experience the visceral connection inherent in Theraplay, both the client and the practitioner need to have an "open heart." This means that both need to feel sufficiently safe in order to experience connection. There is a great deal of clinical research and thinking about this fundamental process and we have made reference to it throughout this book.

As practitioners, our primary concern is how we can effectively facilitate a safe relational experience for the person we are trying to support. What do we need to do, how do we need to be, what works or doesn't work, how can we find our way through difficult situations within the process? It can be difficult to retain our own sense of openness when the other person cannot. Self-knowledge and an understanding about how people relate are required in order to be able to facilitate this process. Theraplay combines a range of practical skills with detailed observation and reflection. While the approach may superficially appear simple, this ongoing self-reflective and questioning approach is needed in order for students and practitioners to develop and deepen their practice.

Stages in Theraplay® student practitioner development

There are some recognizable stages in the development of a student practitioner, and the rest of this chapter will explore those.

People new to Theraplay usually come into the training (Level One and MIM or Group Theraplay) with experience in other therapeutic modalities. Initial questions are usually about understanding what the Theraplay approach is and how it may fit with their prior experience and expectations. During the training, participants are provided with a great deal of information, both theoretical and practical, and participants are typically struck with the accessibility of the approach and its apparent simplicity. This is both extremely attractive and also raises questions about how such simple play activities might facilitate profound change.

As people begin to embark on implementing the MIM and initial sessions, they become preoccupied with practical considerations as they familiarize themselves with what we would describe as the method (the basic routines, tools, activities of implementation). Gaining a grasp of the practical aspects takes practice. What frequently happens when students then embark on actual sessions is that they realize that facilitating sessions can be extremely challenging and is much harder than it looks. Some sessions may generate a great deal of excitement in the student and others a great deal of doubt. People sometimes lose confidence at this stage—in themselves or in Theraplay itself—and may question the approach.

As students begin to bring their work to supervision, there is a marked shift in the way in which they begin to understand the model and process of Theraplay. When things go well, we see a deepening of practice, with students becoming increasingly skilled at being attuned and responsive to the child and parent moment to moment. Students may also begin to express a greater awareness of what they don't know. This deeper level of practice requires a high level of reflection and self-awareness in the student, as well as practical skill, and is the stage at which Theraplay intervention has the potential to become profoundly impactful. This is a long learning process and is far removed from "just playing games." We see parallel processes in the experience of children and parents.

These broad stages can be summarized as follows:

Stage 1: Introduction to the model—what is this all about?

Stage 2: How does it actually work? Is that it? Simplicity and depth combined

Stage 3: The practicalities of getting started and early sessions

Stage 4: Excitement and doubts—I'm not sure about this

Stage 5: This is hard work

Stage 6: Developing deeper practice

Development of the practitioner summary

1. Introduction to the model	2. How does it actually work? Is that it?	3. The practicalities of getting started and early sessions	4. Excitement and doubts	5. This is hard work	6. Developing deeper practice
What is Theraplay? How does it fit with what I have learned before? It feels different, is it too personal/ too tactile?	How can these simple games work? It all seems so obvious.	What do I actually do, when and how? How do I explain the approach to parents?	This is great, I can't believe how much he likes the games. This feels really awkward and I don't feel comfortable.	I'm so tired after sessions. It looked so straightforward on the videos.	So much is going on. Now I am beginning to see the detail, to pick up more subtle observations and to remain attuned and flexible. I'm aware of how much I'm missing.

This chapter will now focus on these various stages of development.

Stage 1: Introduction to the model—what is this all about?

Practitioner	Parent	Child
The practitioner attends training, is presented with a great deal of information and has direct and often surprising and quite challenging experiences.	The parent comes across Theraplay via different means, hears accounts, may access reading and agrees to give it a try.	The child is told about Theraplay by their parent, usually along the lines of "We're going to see someone who can help us by playing together."

Practitioner and Theraplay® student
Theraplay® as an approach challenges some prior assumptions about therapy

Theraplay training (specifically in this instance the Level One four- or five-day Theraplay training) is often a student's first experience of the Theraplay model in any detail. Participants attending this training will already be working with children and families in some kind of professional context. It is an intense and tiring training which many participants describe as one of the best they have ever attended. One of the features of the training is that the participants move between didactic learning (covering theory and the foundations of the

Theraplay model), observing video examples of Theraplay practice and having hands-on experience of Theraplay (via involvement in a wide range of group and dyadic play activities). The training is designed to provide participants with a learning experience which is modeled on the Theraplay dimensions of Structure, Engagement, Nurture and Challenge and the core principles of relational connection and exploration within a context of safety. The aim is that the participant will begin to experience Theraplay in a felt sense through engaging in it, rather than just understanding it from a theoretical perspective. This *combination of reflection and felt experience* forms the beginning of absorbing the Theraplay model that the individual practitioner may then apply.

It is very interesting to observe how different participants experience this core training. Some people are filled with relief and excitement. Some find that Theraplay is not a good fit for them, and for others it raises some quite searching questions that they are keen to explore. The most common questions raised are about how direct and personal Theraplay is. The activities may involve close proximity, touch and genuine moment-to-moment connection, and participants experience for themselves the intimacy of the to and fro nature of this kind of relationally based play. Many are reminded of their early years experiences or their experiences of parenting (both positive and negative). The challenge within the model is not usually related to the theoretical underpinnings or rationale, which most people will be well versed in, but to the nature of the intervention, and specifically how personal it feels.

Questions are frequently raised about:

- the direct and personal nature of the intervention

- the use of touch

- the central involvement of the parent throughout

- the extent of the adult lead.

We will look at each of these in turn.

THE DIRECT AND PERSONAL NATURE OF THE INTERVENTION
Across a wide range of helping professions (including Theraplay), practitioners are taught about the importance of maintaining appropriate boundaries for a range of good reasons:

- The practitioner needs to have sufficient distance to be able to observe the difficulties the client is facing and to provide appropriate support, without becoming overwhelmed or too involved.

- While theoretical models vary considerably, most focus on the need to create a safe space in which the client can express themselves, and this requires the practitioner to hold back in different ways from sharing their own experiences.

- A further, often unstated, rule is that practitioners do not touch their clients and there are many anxieties about risks of allegations, which are a dominant narrative within the current climate. Many practitioners are trained to avoid physical contact and this reflects the predominant culture.

Theraplay concurs with the first two points but differs from other modalities in its use of safe touch.

Although there are good reasons for these widely held principles, there is also a tension at the heart of much therapeutic support work about how close the practitioner becomes to the client: I want them to feel me alongside them (i.e. "they feel I get it") without it becoming too much (for either of us). Theraplay is modeled on the infant-parent relationship in which being personal, tactile and genuinely intersubjectively connected is at the heart of the relationship.

What is so interesting within a Theraplay context is that a simple-seeming activity, like playing a mirroring game, very quickly brings this experience into the room—"It feels so intense, like it's just me and you in the room." And this is exactly the point, and the power inherent in the approach. Primary intersubjective experience is personal, it is about you and me, here and now being connected. The wider therapeutic considerations continue to have relevance in the way in which the work is undertaken, but a big shift often begins for practitioners when they begin Theraplay training, a shift towards a more genuine and transparent relationship and a questioning of some of the previous assumptions they may have been bringing into their work.

THE USE OF TOUCH

Theraplay is very clear about the use of touch and how this links to healthy parent-child development. Videos are shown throughout the training showing close physical proximity and contact. Within sessions, touch is used in different ways, aligned to the Theraplay dimensions.

Structuring touch is used to provide organization (e.g. holding hands) and safety (e.g. scooping a child onto their parent's lap). Engaging touch is used to show delight (e.g. this little piggy) and deep personal interest. Nurturing touch is used to soothe (e.g. rocking) and show care (e.g. lotion on hand). Challenging touch is used to provide support to children when they are stretching themselves (e.g. support when balancing). During the training, participants often have many questions about the use of touch in sessions as this differs from most other models. Cultural, family and personal differences often become apparent around this topic. During training, participants understandably ask questions about touch, and these questions are discussed.

The training covers the fundamental importance of touch in the development of human relationships and we often see a significant shift in people's perspectives towards more acceptance and appreciation of the idea. There are, of course, individual differences in levels of comfort. These differences may relate to our unique sensory systems and attachment history as well as our own cultural experiences. These issues are explored in an experiential way via involvement in the range of pair and group activities, and participants begin reflecting on their own experiences of giving and receiving support and comfort. Participants are often surprised by the strength of feeling elicited by being in physical contact with another person and what a fundamental and profound experience it is. By the end of the training the majority of participants experience the pleasure inherent in receiving comforting and organizing touch and describe feeling "held" and noticed even though they may wonder about how they might integrate this shift into their work with clients.

THE CENTRAL INVOLVEMENT OF THE PARENT THROUGHOUT
A further element integral to the Theraplay approach is the centrality of parents within the work. The main attachment figures are seen as critical, and the fundamental goal of the Theraplay intervention is to deepen the relationship between the child and their parents. This has many implications in terms of how the work is set up and undertaken and how the practitioner approaches the parent. Many practitioners will not have previously included parents so centrally and this brings with it a lot of complexity. One of the challenges for those new to Theraplay is that the parent is present throughout. This may be the first time parents will be directly observing themselves within a session with their child. The routine use of video can also heighten this sense of exposure for the new practitioner (as well as for the parents and child). Detailed discussion about work with parents is given in Chapter 7.

THE EXTENT OF THE ADULT LEAD
Therapeutic interventions range from highly structured to very non-directive or child/client led. Theraplay is modeled on healthy adult-child relationships. Children in a healthy relationship experience a fundamental sense of safety provided by the confident and caring presence of an adult who takes overall charge. Theraplay describes this adult lead within the Structure dimension as someone who provides the organization and reliable scaffolding needed for things to go well.

The Theraplay practitioner takes this guiding role within sessions. In practice, this means planning and leading sessions and taking responsibility for maintaining a sense of structure, organization and purpose throughout the session. The session will have a clear beginning, middle and end and a recognized flow. Those looking in would quickly recognize what is going on as Theraplay. For many people (practitioner, parent and child), this planned adult lead role creates a satisfying framework for organizing sessions. It gives a feeling of "knowing what you are supposed to do," and many new to the Theraplay approach find this reassuring. Like all things, however, it is easy to oversimplify what "adult led" actually entails, and there is more discussion of this throughout the book.

Stage 2: How does it actually work? Is that it? Simplicity and depth combined

Practitioner	Parent	Child
The practitioner reflects on how different the approach is and wonders how such a seemingly straightforward approach (that makes sense) might work with complex difficulties.	The parent wants to know what will be involved in terms of their own role. They may feel excited to be involved and also exposed and anxious about how they should be. They may wonder how a bunch of silly games can help their child.	The child is told they are going to play some games with someone. They may be curious as well as anxious.

Practitioner and Theraplay® student

Anyone embarking on understanding more about a therapeutic approach will be interested in whether it is effective and, if so, how it works. The Theraplay approach makes intuitive sense in the way it replicates many of the typical ways in which adults will play with and care for young children. We have fun with them, laugh together, gently tease, have to and fro interactions, provide excitement and calming and we nurture them and soothe them when they are upset. Theraplay has formalized these kinds of developmentally crucial interactions into a model of intervention which can then be applied in a systematic way for children who need support in various ways. Most people new to Theraplay can quickly see these links and often feel a sense of immediate understanding: "Of course, it's so obvious that that would be helpful." This sense of clarity is often quickly followed by the question "Is that it? You just play these simple games and somehow something changes?" Many participants in training and students in early work ask questions about how the approach applies to specific children with complex difficulties.

The seemingly simple and accessible method (leading a sequence of relational play activities) and a basic explanation for it (filling in the gaps your child needs support with) make the approach very appealing to a wide range of practitioners working with children, as well as to parents. It is an approach that people feel they understand easily and this brings many advantages. The Theraplay approach, for instance, can be used across a very wide range of contexts by practitioners with differing levels of training and role and by parents directly. The non-verbal nature of the intervention means that it is highly accessible for young children and those with learning difficulties, including vulnerable parents (for discussion of applications see Lindaman and Hong, 2020).

The apparent simplicity of the approach, however, can mask the depth of skill and reflection needed to facilitate the work well. During their training, students in Theraplay will be presented with the model alongside video footage of Theraplay in practice. The work, when done skillfully, often appears to flow and to look quite straightforward, and the level of structure inherent in the model (both in the administration of the MIM assessment and in the structuring of sessions) can create a false and attractive impression of ease. It is extremely common for practitioners to feed back, a few months into their actual Theraplay practice, that "this is so much harder than I thought it would be. It doesn't feel like I expected it to."

Don't confuse the method with the methodology or reflective framework

Some people focus exclusively on the methods involved in Theraplay (the practical activities and structure) and lose sight of the more subtle reflective framework. This can result in delivery of work that is overly simplistic. Theraplay as an intervention can be vulnerable to this misinterpretation due to its very accessibility, which means that some people adopt the practical aspects of the Theraplay method within their practice (e.g. using the activities) and then may go on to describe this as Theraplay. This is usually done in situations where individuals have attended Level One training (or even a workshop run by a peer) and have not undertaken any supervision. Most learning about how Theraplay can be undertaken therapeutically is learned via supervision. There is nothing wrong with using the Theraplay ideas per se, but it is important to differentiate the use of a few activities from the in-depth and sensitive intervention that Theraplay can be. We would not describe the use of some activities as "Theraplay," but rather as using some Theraplay-based ideas. More information about this can be found on the Theraplay website.[1]

Parent perspective

Parents who seek help hope that the intervention being offered will have a positive impact on their child. With a Theraplay approach, there are some elements that are initially very appealing to parents and other aspects that they may find harder to understand.

---

1   www.theraplay.org

On the positive side, when parents first learn about the approach they tend to be relieved that they will be kept centrally involved. It makes pragmatic sense to parents that they remain involved since they know their child best and are around most in the child's day-to-day life. From the outset, the Theraplay approach places the parent centrally, keeping them in the room throughout and explicitly describing the core aim as being to deepen the relationship between them and their child (rather than the child and the practitioner).

Theraplay also sounds appealing and parents can quickly see that their child will enjoy it. It is often harder, however, for them to see how "a bunch of silly games" will be of sufficient impact when the issues they are facing are likely to be distressing and stressful. In some cases, initial interest can shift to some skepticism about how the Theraplay will impact, and in others the level of distress in the family may mean that significant adult support is required first.

Detailed discussion of work with parents is given in Chapters 7 and 8.

Parents are likely to feel anxious about the MIM and may feel worried about being negatively evaluated. Similarly, they may feel anxious about their role and performance within initial sessions. They are likely to have many questions and it is essential that the practitioner gives them time to discuss these and focuses on developing a sense of trust.

Stage 3: The practicalities of getting started and early sessions

Practitioner	Parent	Child
Practitioners become preoccupied with practical questions as they try to absorb their new learning: How do I explain the approach to parents? How do I explain the MIM assessment, carry it out, analyze and feed back? What does parent preparation actually comprise? What do I do if the parent is skeptical or I don't think they are ready to be in the room? How do I get video consent issues organized? What activities shall I choose? How do I remember which to do? How do I set up the room? How do I lead? How do I stop asking questions? What do I do if the child doesn't do what I ask or they don't like the activity? What do I expect of the parent and how do I organize this?	Parents will have different opportunities to discuss the model and prepare. They will have attended an initial intake meeting, and through the process of undertaking the MIM, discussion feedback and participating in a parent preparation session they will begin to get a clearer sense of what the approach entails. They are likely to have many questions.	Many children immediately engage with both the MIM and the first session because the activities presented are novel and interesting. They may be surprised by the kinds of activities involved and are usually relieved that their parents are in the room with them and that they are not in trouble or under pressure to talk. In early sessions, children typically engage in quite a compliant manner.

Practitioner and Theraplay® student

Following the initial training, most participants will be feeling excited and nervous in equal measure and will be trying to absorb the model and the many practicalities that are involved in the MIM assessment and the organization of sessions. There is a significant volume of material to take in during the early stages and it is therefore understandable that most focus in the initial weeks is on mastering the practical aspects involved. This includes practicing the activities so that they become fluent as well as the details around set-up, completion and interpretation of the MIM assessment.

Students new to Theraplay are typically swamped with many questions about the practicalities of how it all actually works. Early supervision sessions also focus initially on basic technical corrections of practice, in the way the MIM is organized, the sequence of a session, appropriateness of activities and misunderstanding about various aspects. Practice is needed for these elements to become embedded. The level of new learning required in the early stages makes it much harder for practitioners to stay closely attuned to their clients and it can be easy to lose sight of the underlying purpose. It can be very helpful to revisit the theoretical and reflective framework in order to stay in touch with the deeper purpose of the work.

Theraplay is all about the process of connecting and deepening relationships. Initially, the connection will be with the parents, via the first adult meeting and MIM process. Once sessions begin you will be focused on both the child and the parent. As the practitioner, you are looking for connecting opportunities throughout (to both parent and child, as well as facilitating the relationship between them) and it is very helpful to keep coming back to this core principle.

In addition to the practical challenges and new learning, once the work is under way it is easy to become pulled in different directions, for instance to feel protective of the child and overly critical of the parent or vice versa. Many interventions that helping professionals make with good intention can be experienced by the client as blaming or unsupportive. Theraplay makes great efforts to appreciate these dynamics, and students may need support to develop their ability to guide and support their clients without blame.

Finding a way to form a relationship with parents that feels secure and comfortable and gains their confidence is key, and without it no effective Theraplay work will be possible. The initial task is to meet with parents and explain the Theraplay approach as you begin to get to know each other. There may be differences between services—some will have a formal referral intake process which may involve questionnaires and other assessments alongside the Theraplay. Services may also have differing roles which may have an impact, for instance some may be integrated into a setting so that clients are expected routinely to access the Theraplay, and for others it will be an active choice following research and battling for funding.

Involving parents

Supporting and connecting with the parent is crucial to the success of the work. The parent review sessions will usually combine some reflection and discussion with reviewing some video clips to deepen understanding. However, many parents need more ongoing support than this and practitioners may follow up via phone or email before and after sessions and have additional adult-only sessions as discussed in Chapters 7 and 8.

Parents often have an array of issues that they wish to discuss, from practical parenting dilemmas and school problems, to personal anxiety, marital issues and concerns about the way they may be feeling about their child. Responding in a sensitive way requires experience and training that may fall outside a specific Theraplay model. We know that practitioners bring a wide range of prior experience to their work. Whatever your background and experience, the support of the parents is critically important. It is not enough to focus only on the child element of Theraplay. All practitioners need a broad understanding of child development, trauma and adult issues and to have a clear appreciation about the limits of their own understanding and role. For some, the parent support element of the role will be unfamiliar and create most uncertainty.

There are myriad practical questions, such as choice of activity and what to do when a child doesn't respond, and these will continue throughout the practitioner's development. Although these practical questions are obviously a key focus at the start, what becomes apparent with experience is that the practitioner faces these decisions throughout, about how to undertake an activity or which direction to go in. These moment-to-moment decisions become increasingly fine tuned with experience.

Parent perspective

Parents are likely to feel anxious about the MIM and may feel worried about being negatively evaluated. Similarly, they may feel anxious about their role and performance within initial sessions. They are likely to have many questions and it is essential that the practitioner gives them time to discuss these and focuses on developing a sense of trust.

Stage 4: Excitement and doubts—I'm not sure about this

Practitioner	Parent	Child
The practitioner throws their energy into the early sessions, with a focus on developing their understanding of the child and parent. There is a level of unpredictability in these early sessions as everyone gets to know each other. Early experience within sessions can lead to excitement and doubt.	Parents are often surprised by what happens in the room and the way in which their child responds. They may quickly feel excited and build confidence that the intervention will have an impact or conversely be flooded with doubts and uncomfortable self-consciousness.	The child may be anxious about what is going to happen, but is typically drawn into the spirit of the play and may be unusually responsive with the practitioner. As they become more familiar with the format then they usually begin to find sessions more difficult.

Practitioner and Theraplay® student

The students' experience in early sessions can have a big impact on how they feel about the work. A piece of work may go well and fill them with excitement, or conversely they may face difficult issues from either parent or child, or both. The supervision support the practitioner receives over these early sessions can be very important. A feature of Theraplay is that you become immersed in the particular session that you are involved in and there can be quite intense peaks and troughs in terms of how you feel about your work. If you have a successful piece of work early on then this can give you confidence in the model and help embed your learning. We recommend that students initially focus on families where the difficulties are not complex and severe.

Parent perspective

Similarly, for parents, the experience of Theraplay in the early stages can be variable. It often begins with a sense of excitement and hope. There can be huge relief that the family can have some positive experiences together. However, there may be a serious realization of the complexity of the task that often becomes more apparent over time and can feel very daunting.

Stage 5: This is hard work

Practitioner	Parent	Child
The practitioner facilitates more sessions and faces unexpected challenges for the first time. Sessions may not go to plan and they may find sessions very hard work. They may be surprised by the impact some of the sessions are having on them (physically and personally).	The work feels more difficult. They may feel uncomfortable observing their child interacting with the practitioner. The child's behavior may become more directly challenging in the sessions, towards both the practitioner and parent, and they feel the burden of their parenting task.	Now that the practitioner and parent are consistently trying to connect with them, the child's fear of closeness and connection may really come to the fore and show itself in a range of behaviors.

Practitioner and Theraplay® student

As practitioners have more experience using Theraplay, they often are surprised about how exhausted they feel after sessions. They find that practicing Theraplay is much harder than they anticipated. Carrying out a sequence of activities and managing a session with children with significant difficulties is a challenge, regardless of the tools you have at your disposal. We often provide Theraplay for children for whom other interventions have been ineffective and so have an over-representation of complex issues to address. In addition, the effort of trying to find ways to genuinely connect on an intersubjective level with a client who finds this very hard is in itself completely exhausting. Theraplay demands a lot from everyone involved. It is energetic and emotionally intense and can have a visceral impact on the practitioner. For this reason, very close attention needs to be given to self-reflection and issues such as transference and countertransference.

It is well known in Theraplay circles that the work can become markedly more difficult at about the third or fourth session. This is the point at which the child now understands more about what the sessions will comprise and how the practitioner will behave. The child often begins to express themselves in a more spontaneous and less compliant manner. This is frequently described as a "resistance phase," when the child tests out the boundaries of the sessions and may become more oppositional. We prefer to think of this as "the work." The child now feels confident enough to demonstrate the key issues that may be causing concerns, and this trickier presentation is therefore a good sign that the child is feeling safer.

It is very important that practitioners are aware of how they may be activated by a child who is non-compliant. It is easy to start using descriptors like "oppositional, controlling and defensive" about children who behave in this way. It is more helpful to couch one's understanding in terms of "self-protection"— in other words, there is something about the way you are interacting with the child that is causing them some discomfort and they don't know another way to respond. When you, as the practitioner, feel irritated and begin to take rejections personally, then you too are more likely to behave in a self-protective manner (e.g. to emotionally withdraw in some way). Before you know it, you may become drawn into the exact negative interaction that is so familiar to the child. These dynamics are present in all relationships and therapeutic interventions, but our experience in Theraplay is that the impact of the child on the practitioner and vice versa can be particularly direct and intense. You might, for instance, not want to be close to a particular child or find yourself getting irritated when they behave in certain ways. The practitioner's self-awareness, understanding of transference and countertransference and access to high-quality supervision are paramount.

Parent perspective

Parents may similarly begin to find the work more difficult. They may feel awkward about the child's behavior and we often see parents begin to intervene and correct their child within a session. Another response may be distress because the child seems more amenable to you than to them, or a feeling of being a failure if, for instance, their child clearly rejects them whenever they try to join in an interaction. These issues present difficult dilemmas for the practitioner, who is trying to meet the needs of both child and parent within sessions. It is common at this stage for practitioners to decide they need a higher ratio of parent sessions in order to have some of these conversations.

What we frequently see is that the child connects for a moment when they are surprised or disarmed in some way (through the sensitive, playful efforts of the practitioner) and then abruptly does something to create distance.

This "see-saw" type pattern can be disorienting for the practitioner. Even more disconcerting can be the child who gives repeated verbal and non-verbal messages that they do not like the interactions of the practitioner. It is very interesting how often children give these messages non-verbally through their play and then do not want to leave sessions and are delighted to return. One of the most powerful messages Theraplay practitioners give to children is that they find the child enjoyable to be with and want to find ways to be closer to them, whatever the child's behavior. This can understandably make the child feel confused and vulnerable (because others have not responded to them in this way) but is at the same time compelling as all children (and people) want to feel connected to others. Over our years of supervision, we have heard many students say "but I was convinced he hated me" and express astonishment when parents report the child talking warmly about them and being impatient to return to sessions.

This issue gets to the heart of Theraplay. When a child does not know how to be intersubjectively connected with another person, then playing and interacting via Theraplay will feel difficult, at times unpleasant and not mutually enjoyable. The practitioner persistently tries to find ways to keep connecting, and though it may not feel mutual, the child in fact may have experienced more connection (in small doses) within the session than they have before and will know on some level that this is vitally important to them.

There are, of course, situations in which this intense level of connection is simply too hard for the child (or parent) and many adaptations (or a different approach) will need to be made in order for it to be more manageable. It can be difficult as the practitioner when you find yourself in this situation, especially if you are new to Theraplay.

Stage 6: Developing deeper practice

Practitioner	Parent	Child
Practitioners develop a much higher level of observational skills and awareness of what is happening in the here and now. This is initially expressed as a realization about the detail they may not be noticing, a stage of "conscious incompetence."	When parents are able to understand and appreciate the subtle layers underpinning Theraplay, they can become highly skilled and effective "co-therapists" in the sessions. They also begin to integrate Theraplay into every day. They develop a deep understanding about why relating may be so hard for their child and this has deep impacts across all of their parenting.	The child begins to believe that both the practitioner and their parent can help them and that they genuinely do want to be with them. The child gradually takes more risks in becoming vulnerable and allowing themselves to feel close.

Practitioner and Theraplay® student

Once students have had the opportunity to deliver a range of sessions, they feel more at ease with the practical aspects and are able to have more capacity for moment-to-moment attunement and responsiveness within sessions. This level of understanding of the model develops through supervision. Theraplay supervision is quite specific. Sessions need to be video recorded and the superiors will spend one hour looking at one session with the student. The supervisor will spend as much time as possible actually looking at the video recording, observing and discussing the details of different aspects of the session with the student. For many students, this may be the first time they have received detailed supervision in this way, and some may not previously have watched themselves on video. It is a very rich process and the learning curve in the initial sessions is steep.

Most particularly, once students have grasped the basics, there is a deeper level of observation about the child's non-verbal behaviors and small sequences of interaction can be tracked and analyzed. Often multiple viewing of a short sequence is needed to unpick what may be happening. Through this process, the student develops much keener observational skills and begins to be able to become more attuned to the child's state moment to moment in the sessions. The same applies to the students' appreciation of the parents' state. Alongside this deepening awareness, students practice and fine-tune the ways in which they can support the child or adult and the ways in which they can helpfully influence interactions that are as manageable as possible for all. Students vary a great deal in their capacity to develop and balance the practical and reflective elements of Theraplay practice. The differences between students usually relate to personal attributes, experience and attitude rather than to professional background.

Typically, students will go through a period of growing awareness about what they don't know—"I know I am missing so much but I can't see it yet"—as they develop this deeper level of sensitivity. This process has been described as a period of "conscious incompetence" (Curtiss and Warren, 1993) which is a precursor to becoming more able to perceive interactions in a more detailed way. Students often express this growing awareness when they attend Level Two training and have experienced some supervision.

With ongoing experience and supervision, the practitioner develops the ability to observe and interpret cues in increasingly subtle ways and can remain attuned and responsive in the moment. This is the stage where the practitioner can finally feel that they are actually *doing* Theraplay. It's a transformational moment where the practitioner can see the magic of tying all of the elements together and really being in the flow of the experience.

Parent perspective

The parent perspective varies depending on a number of factors, including how skilled the Theraplay practitioner is and how well they include and develop the relationship with the parent, alongside the parent's own well-being, level of understanding and ability to absorb the subtleties of Theraplay. When the different aspects of Theraplay with the parent go well, then the impact on the child can be profound. Not only does the practitioner have an effective co-therapist in the room but the parent integrates Theraplay into their everyday lives in a multitude of ways. This impact on the parent is the major therapeutic factor. It is fascinating and humbling to observe the changes in parents' levels of awareness and sensitivity to their child's behavior and communication over this process and to witness the way this impacts their whole parenting approach and the child.

Summary

The process of learning about Theraplay and developing your therapeutic practice can usefully be viewed as a developmental process that goes through some quite predictable stages. There is often a parallel process going on for the parents and children involved too. When you are going through this learning process there may be times when you feel confident and competent and other times when you are all at sea. It is notable that as you become more experienced and skilled you will often feel as though you know less, as you become aware of the infinite levels of detail and possibility within any particular interaction. It is this combination of apparent simplicity and underlying complexity that makes the process of becoming a Theraplay practitioner so fascinating.

Chapter 11

Overcoming Common Barriers

CHAPTER PLAN

This chapter will discuss the following areas:

Questions and answers about common logistical barriers to Theraplay®

- I'm not allowed to video

- Theraplay® takes twice as long to plan—I can't fit in (or charge for) the extra time I spend

- I'm exhausted after I do one session

- I can't meet with parents alone because they don't have a babysitter and I have nowhere to put them in my office

- I can't meet with just one child because the parent has to bring all her other children

- I can't charge if I am seeing the parent only/my agency doesn't support adult-only work

- I can't touch the client because: my agency has a policy against it/ my client was sexually abused/I am a man working with girls (or vice versa)…

- My agency doesn't allow food

Summary

Questions and answers about common logistical barriers to Theraplay®

This chapter looks at the common barriers you might experience when trying to begin Theraplay practice. We list some typical issues and respond to them.

I'm not allowed to video

Videoing your sessions is the single most potent tool you can use to exponentially grow in your Theraplay practice. The energetic, non-verbal interactions you have with the client go beyond what any person can detect in the moment. The micro-communications that we are asking you to become aware of are nearly impossible to detect at first. Your videoing of the sessions and rewatching of them will allow you to develop the awareness necessary to really attune to your client. So, what we are saying is: the motivation to be able to video your sessions goes way beyond the need to receive supervision from a Theraplay supervisor. Videoing your session will allow you to be your own supervisor as you study your actions and reactions with the client. You can also share your video with a trusted colleague so they can provide you with feedback.

Videoing your sessions is also crucial for being able to maximize the therapeutic gains in your parent sessions. When you cue up a short segment of a Theraplay interaction to show a parent, they can see and reflect on their own contribution to the dynamics with the child in a way that they could not while in the heat of the moment. They can also see the changes and the progress they have made.

The reason we are emphasizing the importance of videoing is to motivate you to make every effort to overcome obstacles that lie before you when it comes to videoing.

The barriers to videoing include the following:

- *The clients are in foster care and the child welfare system will not allow videoing.* This has not been our experience. It may take a special meeting with the child's legal guardian within the child welfare system to explain the therapeutic importance of the video as a tool for showing the caregivers and for registering the significance of behaviors of children who often use their behavior rather than words to display their feelings. If legal worries of lawsuits or exploitation are reasons for not videoing, present the counter-argument that legal worries should not be put out as barriers to exploited or vulnerable children receiving a state-of-the-art intervention that gets to the heart of their attachment trauma difficulties. A related argument is that the videos might not be able to be secured properly and may be transferred into the wrong hands of people who might exploit vulnerable children. However, there are ways to safeguard sensitive information such as multiple electronic barriers and limited storage times. It may take consultation by a trained IT professional to provide you with the proper safeguards and you will have to abide by strict protocols for securing the videos, but this is no different from other confidential records such as case notes and assessments. This is simply a part of a professional practice that needs to be implemented as part of an organization's larger responsibility to keep client records confidential.

- *The client has a negative association with being videoed from being previously exploited by untrustworthy adults.* This is a serious issue that needs to be explored by the current, safe caregiver as well as the child. Any child should be asked whether they are okay with being videoed, whether there is a legal obligation due to their age or not. One possibility for overcoming their fears is to acknowledge and have empathy for their worries that they will be teased or get in trouble for what they do. You can reassure them that the video will be kept solely to help the adults find the best way to help them. You can offer to show them bits of the video at the end of the session through the viewfinder so that they can feel in control. Typically, if the caregiver feels safe with the idea of videoing, the child's stress will recede as the engagement and liveliness of the sessions take over and the trust between practitioner and child increases. If the child or caregiver is still uncomfortable, then it is wise not to video in this case. However, videoing other families who do feel comfortable will help you gain self-awareness for any of your other cases where videoing is not possible. If you absolutely cannot video any of your usual clients, we recommend finding a parent-child dyad outside your workplace that would volunteer to do Theraplay sessions and give permission to video. You do not need to have a "clinical" family to do Theraplay—you can recruit someone from your neighborhood, from church or from friends. The idea, however, is that you have to have some experience analyzing your own behavior in a session.

- *Those involved do not want to see themselves on video because of feeling ashamed of their body (this is often an unspoken objection).* This applies to parents as well. Often a parent's first reaction during the MIM feedback is about their body: "Oh gosh, I look so fat." While this is totally understandable, confronting these feelings (especially for the practitioner) can be a huge gift. After all, it takes a tremendous amount of acceptance of one's own self and an integration between one's body and mind in order to really be present for a client in a Theraplay session.

You have to be able to feel with your whole body in order to be receptive to the child's bodily feelings.

- *The practitioner is afraid of being scrutinized by an authority figure (this is often an unspoken objection).* Some practitioners have experienced being openly criticized and even humiliated in educational situations. It can leave them permanently scarred and is not the way Theraplay approaches supervision. Every Theraplay supervisor has been in the position of being on video and having their actions minutely analyzed. However, the basic tenets of Theraplay are safety and connection. Each Theraplay supervisor has been carefully cultivated over years of supervision to refine this skill of being able to give constructive feedback while remaining empathic and supportive.

Theraplay® takes twice as long to plan—I can't fit in (or charge for) the extra time I spend

This is a truth that we can't seem to get around. Our modern-day demands have forced us to think of our time as valuable if we can monetize it. Or we are so busy that we don't have the time it takes to cultivate new skills. We have a few remedies for improving this stressful problem, but the bottom line and unavoidable truth is that a Theraplay intervention takes a long time to implement.

Here is a breakdown of the time needed for administering a MIM:

MIM set up	30 minutes
MIM takedown	10
Technology time (downloading video from camera, etc.)	10
Analyzing the MIM (verbal/non-verbal communication, answering questions by dimensions), summarizing by dimensions	60

Assuming that a parent-child dyad takes 45 minutes to complete their MIM, you have to dedicate almost two additional hours to setting up, taking down, analyzing and summarizing it. So, you should plan for two extra hours just for the MIM itself.

Then, on to the next step: preparing for the MIM feedback, which involves formulating intervention goals, formulating messages to parents and selecting segments to show parents. We recommend scheduling 90 minutes for one parent for a MIM feedback and two hours for two parents because the process is so rich and evocative. The preparation for the feedback session should flow quite smoothly from your analysis and summary.

Time to prepare for MIM feedback:

Setting provisional goals, formulating messages to parents and selecting segments to show parents	45–60 minutes

For Theraplay sessions (excluding the session itself):

Planning session, setting up the room, camera, assembling supplies	20 minutes
Cleaning up all the powder, shredded crepe paper, newspaper balls and biscuit crumbs	10
Downloading and reviewing the video, writing the session supervision form	60

When you are just starting out and if you are in supervision, you should allow an additional hour and a half. This is a significant amount of time that with experience can be shaved by 20 minutes or so but can't be eliminated completely. That is why it is best to have a conversation with your supervisor or organization about the investment it takes to do proper Theraplay work. Your organization needs to support your Theraplay work in terms of the extra time it takes. The benefit to the organization is producing effective, high-quality work that will make a true impact for clients. It can also have the benefit of building your organization's clinical reputation.

The best option for those who cannot spend a great deal of time is to work only with one Theraplay client. That way you can spend the extra hours on only one case but still get the tremendous benefit of learning the Theraplay method, albeit at a slower pace.

I'm exhausted after I do one session

That is normal at the beginning.

There are different kinds of Theraplay-related exhaustion:

- Physical exhaustion, where a young, hyperactive child needs so much activity that you sweat like a dog and feel like you just did an aerobic workout! It might put you in touch with the fact that your physical strength or stamina is not what it should be. Or you might have physical limitations like knee or back problems that make it too challenging to get up and down from the floor so many times.

- Emotional exhaustion, where the child (or parent) is sullen, lethargic or passive and you feel drained from trying to entice them and keeping up the energy.

- Physical, emotional and spiritual exhaustion, where the child is running around, flailing their limbs, opposing your every initiative, and possibly being aggressive.

It is undeniable that Theraplay sessions take more physical effort, but the essential reason why new Theraplay practitioners feel exhausted is because of the intensity of the demand to be "on," to be so present, so attentive, so much anticipating the child's (and parent's) need. The level of focus and concentration is much higher than usual sessions, where you have the luxury to keep a bit of distance and be in your own head for some moments. In a Theraplay session, you do not. We liken this exhaustion to learning to meditate: at first entering the process seems daunting because it is too much to ask to constantly be aware and so engaged. Our whole mind resists letting go of all the thoughts and preoccupations that we are normally so reliant on as points of reference for who we are. Our body resists going into a session like a dog being dragged into the dreaded bathtub.

But as you may have also noted, the flipside of feeling exhausted is the sense that you gave it your all, that there was richness and connection, that things were really happening in the session. In short, it's a feeling of satisfaction that you engaged in something meaningful.

So, feeling exhausted is normal and it's worth it. The intensity of the effort also dissipates over time, once your mind gets trained on all the details and you find yourself being able to enjoy the session without feeling the toll as much. In fact, a Theraplay session can be an experience from which you emerge invigorated and your spirits lifted.

I can't meet with parents alone because they don't have a babysitter and I have nowhere to put them in my office

Some solutions: bring something for the child to use with headphones (e.g. so they can watch a video) and let them sit in the room with you; arrange for a volunteer to babysit; organize a session through a secure conferencing program like *Zoom*. A web-based conferencing service is great because it allows you to share your screen and show the parents segments of the video as if they were with you in your office. If none of that is possible, schedule a time for a phone session.

I can't meet with just one child because the parent has to bring all her other children

It is worthwhile to be as creative as possible to enable a parent to focus on one child for a period of time. However, if there is absolutely no possibility of this, you can do Theraplay with two or multiple children, whereby you do the activities simultaneously in tandem (i.e. you play Patty-Cake face to face with one child, and the parent plays with the other child, then you switch children and repeat) or do circle games (basically group Theraplay).

I can't charge if I am seeing the parent only/ my agency doesn't support adult-only work

This is usually a limitation imposed by agencies who do not understand the critical importance of working with parents, and can also be imposed by insurance companies. It goes against all therapeutic rationale because the value of work with the parent, on whom the child's well-being is so wholly dependent, is obvious. If it is possible to have the child in the room watching videos and wearing headphones while you work with the parent, then this is one option. The best option, however, is to be an advocate and change the system so that it allows you to legitimately work with the parent and have it recognized as part of the therapeutic process.

I can't touch the client because: my agency has a policy against it/my client was sexually abused/I am a man working with girls (or vice versa)...

We will not go into all of the reasons why touch is crucial to healthy child development and healing here. We leave you to refer to the copious amount of research provided in your Level One training handouts. There is a lot to unearth that is non-conscious about the prohibition of touch. Perhaps it is an agency policy, in which case it would be worthwhile reviewing it with organization administrators and examining the rationale underneath. You can still do many nurturing Theraplay activities without touching the client directly. If a hug is not okay, is a special handshake okay? If a special handshake is not okay, then do a mutual cheer that has four steps where each person takes a turn at adding a movement (like a hip shake or hop) that you can do together. If you cannot do the Weather Report directly on the child's back, can you do it if you drape a blanket over them? If you can't cradle them, can you swing them in a blanket? Even without any touch, you can be attentive and nurturing by providing them with a dab of lotion and having them rub it in themselves, offering them a blanket if they are cold, tissues if their nose is runny, food or drink if they are hungry or thirsty. All (that's right, we said all!) Structure, Engagement and Challenge games can be modified to eliminate the touch and still have therapeutic effect.

Think to yourself, what is the purpose of this game? What effect am I trying to achieve? Then answer the next question: How can I modify the direct touch part of the activity and still meet the goal?

If nothing else, you always have your melodic, rhythmic, resonant voice. When you use your voice as if you're telling a story or singing a song, it has a calming, organizing and reassuring effect, much like touch does.

This leaves us with the more essential question: how comfortable are *you* giving and receiving touch? Once again, we cannot overstate how significant our own sense of bodily self affects our Theraplay practice. There are many non-conscious reasons why you may not feel comfortable with providing touch as part of therapy. These reasons need to be unearthed and examined with a trusted colleague, supervisor (not necessarily Theraplay supervisor) or therapist. If you do have major hesitations with providing structuring, engaging or nurturing touch, you can rest assured that they will come out as part of your Theraplay supervision process. Your supervisor will likely identify a pattern that highlights a certain type of barrier and gently enquire about it.

My agency doesn't allow food

The idea of providing some type of pleasurable nourishment experience is crucial because of its significance in parent-child relationship and healthy child development and that is why we incorporate it. Perhaps the policy can be modified for therapeutic purposes? If there is a strict prohibition against food, is providing a drink (even plain water) through a straw allowed (sucking and swallowing is the most basic form of self-soothing)? If not, then skip the feeding. There are many other ways to nurture a client and the therapeutic utility will not be compromised. Ensure that you have a discussion with parents around food preferences and allergies and include this within your consent form. Parents are understandably unhappy with us if we provide sweet foods or treats to their child without their agreement.

Summary

This chapter has summarized and explored some of the most common barriers that practitioners face as they try to set up and begin to undertake Theraplay interventions. There are some hurdles to overcome but across the world practitioners in a wide variety of settings are finding ways to successfully provide Theraplay interventions.

Chapter 12

The Theraplay®
Supervision Process

A Journey of a Lifetime

CHAPTER PLAN

This chapter will discuss the following areas:

Embarking on supervision

– Outline of a supervision session

The different stages of the supervision practicum

The Foundational Theraplay® Practicum

– What constitutes a Theraplay® session?

– Context

– Use of self

Potential questions to ask/discussions

Towards Intermediate

The personal process

Towards being a fully certified Theraplay® practitioner

Summary

It is not possible to learn how to provide Theraplay as an intervention without receiving high-quality Theraplay-specific supervision. We would consider the Level One training as just the starting point and that the process of really understanding and developing your skills in the model comes via the supervisory process.

The Theraplay supervision process is embarked on with the same attitude and philosophy as Theraplay intervention with the family. Your supervisor will work hard to create a context of safety and trust (a secure base) and will be checking in with you to gain feedback about how you are finding the process. They will try to pick up when you may be feeling anxious or if there is tension and will make efforts to repair (the cycle of rupture, repair and reflect). The aim is for you to have a rich and positive learning experience.

Theraplay supervision is quite specific and the experience of receiving it can feel very new for some people. You will, for instance, be showing a video recording of yourself while you facilitate a session. Your supervisor will go through the video with you in detail, highlighting areas that go well or in which you struggle, and will provide detailed feedback about how you might adapt your approach in order to support the child and parent most effectively. Like all learning processes, the experience of being supervised and of developing your skills builds over time and there can be times when the process is challenging and others when it is a delight. There are some recognizable developmental phases that most students experience and this chapter will summarize some typical themes.

We acknowledge the contribution made by the Worcester supervision group in developing this chapter.

Embarking on supervision

The standard supervision intake process is:

- You register with The Theraplay Institute and send the documents needed (curriculum vitae, indemnity insurance, professional body) and fee. You are then matched with a supervisor.

- You set a date for your first supervision where you will show a MIM. In most of the world, supervision is done virtually by a secure video-conferencing site. There is no need for you to send your video electronically, you simply share your screen.

- Ideally, your supervisor will be able to provide supervision on the MIM before parent feedback is given and you can receive support in planning your MIM feedback and the first session.

- Once you have completed your first Theraplay supervision session with this client then you are formally accepted onto the supervision practicum (i.e. you have done two of the initial eight supervision sessions).

Outline of a supervision session
One hour, one case, one session.

- Before the supervision session, review your video and complete the session supervision form or MIM form (all of the forms are available on The Theraplay Institute's website and a completed example of each form is available in Chapters 13–16). For UK students, there are UK-specific forms.[1] These forms help you to think through what the session was like and to start to appreciate what Theraplay as a model is focusing on.

- Send your supervision form and MIM analysis in advance to your supervisor—do this in plenty of time so that your supervisor has time to read it (e.g. 48 hours before the supervision session).

- At the start of the supervision session you have a few minutes to provide brief context and history, although it's not usually necessary for the supervisor to know too much detail. As much time as possible is spent analyzing the video. The focus is particularly on you and what you are doing.

- You and your supervisor watch the video together from the beginning and will look at the entrance activity and check-ups as well as the room set-up and the exit too. Your supervisor will want to see that you have understood the basic structure of a session. After that, your supervisor and you decide together what you will view. You can learn so much from any section but you may also have some particular questions that you want some help with. Your supervisor might decide to watch a particular short section a few times so that you can track the sequence. Similarly, they might want to watch some video without sound so you can concentrate on the child's non-verbal communication.

- You discuss the various issues together, and the content of this discussion varies a great deal depending on where you are in your learning. Towards the start of the supervision process, there tends to be a lot of practical discussion around what activities to try or how to adjust what you are doing. As you become more experienced, the conversation usually becomes more reflective and increasingly detailed.

---

1   UK-specific forms are available at www.wp.theraplay.org/uk

- Together you agree some concrete learning goals for the next session. You and your supervisor should note these down.

- Write some reflective notes after the supervision about what you found helpful or less helpful and how your practice has been impacted.

Here is an example of some goals at the end of a supervision session. This is for a practicum student who needs to incorporate more structure in her sessions with a boy who is very dysregulated. You can see here how concrete the suggestions are.

1. When you walk in with the entrance activity, make sure to get the child settled into the sitting area (pillow, bean bag, etc.) as the last part of that activity. Don't leave him standing or arranging his own seat. Hold his hands, count to three and sit down with him simultaneously.

2. Initiate (without hesitating) taking off his shoes for him or at least help him.

3. When doing an activity like paper bust out, have the child positioned facing the parent so the parent can see, make eye contact and be involved (say, for example, "1, 2, 3, rip!").

4. Squeeze newspaper pieces up with him (hand over hand) rather than letting him do it himself.

5. Put a rhythmic chant into the hand stack game, like counting rather than having to say "slow down, wait."

6. If he jumps on the couch and you can't get up quickly enough to redirect him, join his activity but hold his hands while he's on the couch and prescribe that he jumps five times and then off the couch with your help.

7. If he makes growling or yelping noises, he is getting overstimulated. Instead of saying "Are you being silly?" say "Oh, that was very exciting" in a calming, quieter voice and offer him something soothing to do like have a sip of a drink or do pillow sandwich.

8. Talk to his mother after the session and discuss with her that when her son is escalating it is important for her not to laugh. Her nervous laughter may serve to overstimulate him more and it's confusing.

The different stages of the supervision practicum

Once you have joined the supervision practicum there are three stages of qualification:

- Foundational (this requires a minimum of eight supervision sessions)

- Intermediate (this requires a minimum of eight supervision sessions)

- Certified (this requires a minimum of eight supervision sessions).

A second supervisor reviews your work at the Intermediate and Certified stages.

More information about what these stages entail and what title you can then use in your practice is available on The Theraplay Institute's website.

The Foundational stage of the supervision process takes you from the very start, having completed Level One training, to a position when you should understand the basics about how to undertake the MIM-based assessment and facilitate Theraplay-based sessions. This is often a steep learning curve as you experience the reality of trying to use Theraplay activities with a child in the room.

Reaching Foundational status is an important milestone and we would consider it the minimum requirement if you are going to be providing Theraplay-based interventions to families. It is important that to incorporate the basic Theraplay protocol into your clinical practice you have access to suitable clients. These are families and children where there is no significant relational trauma and parents who are non-complex in presentation. The idea is that you are able to develop your Foundational Theraplay skills without having to make adaptations for trauma. This can be challenging to achieve in some work contexts.

The Foundational Theraplay® practicum
What constitutes a Theraplay® session?
As you progress through the first few supervision sessions you would be expected to have developed the understanding of the following areas.

Setting the environment
You choose an appropriate setting and set up the room so that child and parent are comfortable and supported, everyone has a clear place to sit, there is a boundary to the space if the room is big, the camera is placed so that it can capture most of the action without being intrusive, props are prepared and contained in a basket or bag that is easily accessed, and a blanket and cushions are available. You have considered the boundaries of working in the home, office or school so that it is clear when and where a session takes place. You have considered whether the time of day and length of session are suitable for this child.

Sequencing a session

You understand and can use the sequence of a standard Theraplay session— entrance, check-up, five to six activities, nurture element, exit. You purposefully choose activities that are developmentally appropriate, have a flow of lively versus quiet ones, and use only activities that are within the list of Theraplay activities. You can integrate simple rhythmic songs familiar to the family.

Involvement of parent(s)

You have prepared the parents for the sessions. It is clear to you and to the parent what the role of the parent is—typically the parent starts mainly observing with any participation organized and well supported by you. You have considered whether to have the child sit on the parent's lap or next to the child.

Context
Safety

You understand the limits of your skills and training. You work with cases that are within your working boundaries and are supported by management and clinical supervision.

Adaptations

You accept cases that are appropriate for the standard Theraplay model without adaptation and without blending with other modalities such as DDP within the sessions. We acknowledge that many of your client groups may be trauma-based cases and may need some adaptation, but it is important when learning how to facilitate Theraplay sessions that you find more straightforward families to work with, otherwise there is a risk that you will not learn the standard model and what it has to offer.

Touch and intimacy

You are clear about the use of safe touch within a context of relationship and an activity. Use of intimacy and touch is explicit, agreed and transparent. (There is a whole section on this in the Level One training handout, and the issue of touch can also be brought to supervision.)

Use of self
Use of supervision feedback

You make use of the feedback and apply the supervisor's recommendations to the next session and this learning to your other cases. Some issues will take several supervisions to be embedded. You can't expect to change everything at once or take everything in. Agreeing and recording learning goals for supervision and providing reflection on your supervision may be appropriate.

Attunement

You can begin to see things from the child or parent's point of view. Your observation and reflection skills and attunement to the child improve over time. You begin to develop a sense of the intersubjectivity being played out in the session. This can be hard at the start because you are focusing on the practicalities of facilitating the session. In early sessions, your focus is often on what activity you will do next and how to manage the situation in front of you. It can be hard to really observe and notice the child's responses when your mind is taken up with your own thoughts. You often see a lot more when you review the video, so don't be discouraged when you see what you have missed—this is the value in being able to look at the session again later, and the more you do this, the better you will become at noticing and responding to signals in the moment.

Awareness of self in the room

You build an awareness of yourself in the room and begin to develop a personal style. You consider your positioning, clothing, voice tone, energy level, attitude to touch and style of leadership. You consider how comfortable you are with each of the four dimensions and with different elements of the Theraplay approach, such as leading, closeness and touch, and reducing questioning, choices and talking. The work is intense and interpersonal and activates your own attachment systems, so an awareness of this is important.

Potential questions to ask/discussions

Supervision questions and feedback can be direct and challenging but are always delivered within the philosophy and attitude of Theraplay. Our expectation of students is that they have internalized enough of their own secure base that feedback can be received with an open and non-defensive stance. If issues arise, your supervisor will work collaboratively with you to find useful ways forward.

The practicum is primarily a skills training and is different from clinical or management supervision. It is worth considering the differences in the kinds of supervision you may wish to seek. Most practitioners are required by their regulatory bodies to be accessing clinical supervision, and this covers a wide range of clinical issues relevant to the role and entails the supervisor holding some clinical responsibility for the clients a person is working with. Managerial supervision involves caseload management and management of other work-related issues. In contrast, Theraplay supervision focuses specifically on the Theraplay work you may be undertaking with the aim of promoting skills development within this modality. It can best be described as a training supervision. Your Theraplay supervisor does not hold clinical responsibility for the work you undertake. Most practitioners will therefore be receiving different kinds of supervision, and if your caseload is complex it will be essential to be receiving clinical supervision in addition to Theraplay-specific supervision.

If you have been practicing independently for a long time without supervision, you may find it de-skilling to receive feedback that perhaps suggests you were not applying the Theraplay model in the standard way. Don't worry. This is a natural part of the learning process. When you become more aware of what it is you don't know (this learning stage is often described as "conscious incompetence"), then this indicates that you are truly embarking on the learning journey and the making of mistakes is integral to this learning. There is a lot of room for interpretation in the Level One training and in the absence of supervision many people go off on tangents. For example, you hear that you have to be structured and be a leader in the session, but at the same time you are told that you have to make modifications for trauma like providing choices. You are told you should try to use physical contact whenever you can to provide structure, connection and regulation and yet one trauma modification is to keep more distance. Your supervisor will help you to make sense of some of these dilemmas. They will both provide you with the reassurance you need and help build up your confidence and guide you.

Potential questions your supervisor might ask you:

- What's your main question for this session?

- What's your goal? What is the purpose (of this sequence, activity, overall intervention)?

- Can you explain why you're doing this activity?

- Why do you think that did/didn't go well?

- Did you notice that…?

- What dimensions were the focus?

- How would you do this differently?

- What do you think the child/adult is experiencing/feeling/telling you?

- How did it feel in the room?

- How did you feel at the end of the session?

- What is your plan for the next session?

Towards Intermediate

Around the time that you finish your Foundational level, you will find that there are certain cases or certain sessions where you feel triumphant and on top of the world. You may feel as if you are a brilliant professional and feel highly satisfied with your work. The next day, though, you will have a Theraplay session where you feel totally out of sorts, as if you have missed the mark completely with the child and parent and that all you did was make a messy situation even messier. This is normal and is part of the process of deepening your Theraplay work and is in line with the rupture and repair cycle of attachment. One of the strengths of the Theraplay model is that there is strong congruence between the processes experienced by everyone in the therapy setting, the supervisory setting and the theoretical underpinnings of the model. Rupture leads to reflection, reflection to repair, repair to resilience.

A true milestone in your practicum is when you realize how tailored Theraplay needs to be to each client's individual circumstances and that there are no actual rules and that every Theraplay dictum can be modified. It can feel scary, as if you are starting all over again without having any scaffolding, but actually it's just that you are about to embark on building even deeper Theraplay infrastructure within yourself, based on experience and integration, on being truly in the moment and on pure attunement. This is the period where you will be much more acutely aware of the following dialectical dilemmas:

- Being structured but at the same time flexible and spontaneous.

- Sticking to your session plan and abandoning everything on the list and just going with what the client signals.

- Responding playfully to an upset child or not playing because it feels like dismissing the child's feelings.

- Being attuned yet not verbally responding to all of the child's questions and demands.

- Feeling lovingly towards one child and only anger or disgust or dread with another.

- Attuning to the child and parent at the same time.

There are many similar questions, the answers to which may seem inherently contradictory. Students have described the experience as becoming much more aware of what you don't know. You are beginning to appreciate that while Theraplay may seem logical and straightforward as an approach, it is in fact deeply complex and subtle.

As you gain this deeper awareness, your supervisor may in turn begin to challenge you on more of the detail of the sessions. There may also be material that needs to be addressed outside the supervision session. Reading or further training may be recommended by your supervisor. You may also be encouraged to engage with self-exploration or even to seek your own personal therapy if there seems to be material that is rattled by the deeper therapeutic process as you progress to Intermediate level. We are all creatures of attachment, and as we work at a deeper level with the unsettled attachments of our clients this can, and maybe should, be deepening our sensitivity through empathetic engagement. This, in turn, means we will often be engaged in deep self-reflexivity, which can be unsettling.

These are all legitimate feelings and you are developmentally on target for the stage in your practicum. If you are feeling wobbly and criticized, then we would hope that your supervisor will be attuned enough to realize and discuss this with you. Common issues that arise during this stage of supervision are that you may feel your supervisor is overly focused on errors or things you didn't do, you feel as if your personality should shine through more, or there are context-specific issues (around your culture or work context) that need further exploration. Please raise any concerns for discussion within your supervision. This discussion may take 20 minutes of your supervision.

All of this is okay and you should expect a containing, empathic and attuned response from your supervisor. You should leave the conversation feeling understood and also with a specific action plan for fine-tuning the communication between you to make you feel more comfortable.

The Theraplay supervision practicum, however, is an evaluative process as well as a learning one and there are certain lines that delineate that which is Theraplay and that which is not Theraplay, that which is adequate skill and that which is skill that requires remediation. In order for you to progress towards the Theraplay qualification levels (Foundational, Intermediate and Certified), your supervisor will need to ascertain that you have reached an appropriate level of skill and these discussions will therefore come into supervision at key stages. In fact, the reason why we have an intermediate and final supervision session done by a secondary supervisor is to help ensure the universality of the content of the Theraplay session and the skill of the practitioner.

As you confront the dilemmas above and work through them with guidance from your supervisor, there will emerge a sense that you are able to grapple and hold these dilemmas within yourself in the session while still being able to be present and attuned with the client.

The personal process

There is no way to go through the Theraplay practicum without running into and butting up against personal issues that underlie your personality. These issues come up as recurring themes in sessions and in supervision. You may become aware of them yourself while reviewing the session videos, with a trusted colleague, or in your Theraplay supervision sessions. The table below shows some examples of common personal themes that practicum students encounter.

Common issue (that your supervisor pointed out)	Your explanation	Possible non-conscious themes to explore
You are relying too much on words or giving the child too many choices.	Your other training taught you to do this and you feel scared that you will re-traumatize the child if you don't get verbal consent, explain and give choices.	You are relying on a framework which is comfortable to you on a personal level and transferring that as a rationale for intervention.
You increase the challenge level too much.	The child or parent is high achieving and you are afraid you will lose their interest if your games are too simple. You are uncomfortable with treating a child in a manner not congruent with their chronological age.	You have been taught that you need to prove yourself. You are afraid that someone will judge you. You are afraid of being criticized that you are letting the child off the hook, or about your own dependency needs.
Your affect is too buoyant, you're too loud.	That's what Theraplay work is supposed to be. I'm resonating with the child.	You fear you are too much. You are anxious about some aspect of the work.
You need to use touch more.	I'm not a touchy person. Touch is not part of our culture.	Can you provide enough to meet the child's needs? Do you fear getting in trouble? Do you feel loveable enough on a physical level?
You need to be more directive with the parent.	That will undermine the parent and make them feel de-skilled. The parent is not my identified client. If they feel criticized, they will stop coming. If I criticize the parent in front of the child, it will undermine their authority.	You need approval from authority figures. You have pressure to earn an income and can't afford to lose clients. You don't feel safe.

All of the above issues and more can helpfully be brought into supervision and discussed. Everyone has their own specific issues to consider and engaging in Theraplay work requires a high level of understanding of yourself and your own sensitivities. This is the case for all of us and links to the developmental model of attachment. The very directness of Theraplay can mean that your own issues can be activated within the work.

Towards being a fully certified Theraplay® practitioner

All of these processes will be taking place simultaneously with your actual Theraplay work and supervision. Most students do finish their entire practicum to certification within the standard 24 supervision sessions, though 24 supervision sessions is the minimum and there is nothing wrong in taking more time. You can choose to do your supervision every one to two weeks, but the shortest time it ever takes students is two years. The typical length is more like two-and-a-half to three years. The reason for this is not because the supervisor or student didn't have time to meet more than once a month. It is more likely because the process of integrating the Theraplay method is not necessarily linear. It depends on how many Theraplay sessions you do between supervisions, how much support and time you have to review your videos and to fill out the session supervision forms and generally how many other demands there are in your life. It also depends on how much you practice your Theraplay skills outside your other work. Theraplay is such a useful life skill with all humans in general. The more you use it in your daily interactions with co-workers, your family and even out in the community, the faster you will integrate the Theraplay way.

People come into Theraplay supervision from a wide array of backgrounds and experience. You may already be an experienced clinician or you may have done limited direct work or may come from a profession that involved little supervision. If you need more development, here are things that may be suggested by your supervisor:

- Source recommended readings, resources, webinars.

- Take a course—neurosequential, family systems, trauma.

- Access additional management supervision—organizational skills, paperwork, IT.

- Seek additional clinical supervision—working with difficult families, domestic violence.

- Access your own therapy.

There will still be times that you are preparing to go into a Theraplay session and you may feel a kind of dread because you don't have the energy to give to this child and parent today. Theraplay is hard work. You are tired, you are preoccupied and you have a million other things to do. However, the magic of a Theraplay session is that once you are in the "flow," once you actually cross the threshold of your session and begin, you are so fully immersed in the attunement and interaction with the child, you're so focused on noticing and responding, that your fatigue and preoccupations leave. There is simply no room for them when you are "in the moment." When the session is over, you often feel lighter and more energized, or more settled and less burdened because you actually did something deep and meaningful. You practiced the craft of really being with and attuning to the uniqueness of this particular child or dyad and it simply feels good (even when the session was hard). At this final stage of the practicum, when you show your supervisor the session, you will already be aware of what she is going to say. You understand what was going on with you and can give yourself feedback for what to work on next time. Your supervisor responds to you with admiration and as a colleague rather than as a teacher to a student. You feel grounded and satisfied. You have arrived.

Summary

Engaging in the Theraplay practicum is a commitment on a practical and emotional level. It requires openness to being observed and to observing your own practice in a lot of detail. There is no doubt that supervision is the most effective way to develop high-level skills. The Theraplay supervision process is facilitated with the same level of care, sensitivity and directness as our work with families, and those who embark on the journey describe a steep and rich learning curve that is both challenging and exhilarating.

As in all therapeutic interventions, we continue to develop and face new challenges even after qualification and there is an expectation that clinical supervision will continue in line with your accrediting body's expectations for supervision. If you are undertaking ongoing Theraplay work then it is good practice to check that you can access specialist Theraplay consultation in addition to any generic clinical supervision to ensure ongoing high-quality practice. The deeper your practice becomes, the more likely you are to have times of uncertainty and reflection as you are now more aware of what it is you don't know. You might begin to integrate other approaches into your Theraplay work and will refine your skills in a continuing reflective process.

Part 4

Examples of Completed Supervision Forms

Part 4 includes four different forms. The first three are completed anonymized examples of three kinds of supervision form so that you can see what a completed form includes. The forms relate to one family so that you can follow the story of the sessions. The family comprises Dom (aged 6 years) and his adoptive parents. Names have been changed for confidentiality purposes and the family and practitioner have consented to inclusion of their material in the book. The three forms are:

1. Marschak Interaction Method (MIM)-Based Assessment Form Example

2. Theraplay® Dyadic Session Supervision Form Example

3. Theraplay® Final Evaluation Supervision Form Example

You will see that there is a high level of detail and reflection involved in completing the forms, which involves looking at the video of the sessions, often repeatedly. During the practicum, a student will fill in multiple forms of this nature and will become increasingly able to recognize sequences and to unpick the minutiae of interactions. The fourth form is one that a student will fill in when they are reaching foundational level and is included here so that you can see the range of skills that are expected.

4. Foundational Self-Description by Dimension (Session 8) Form Example

Chapter 13

Marschak Interaction Method (MIM)-Based Assessment Form Example

This form is completed by students when they have undertaken a MIM-based assessment and are taking the MIM for supervision. This particular anonymized form relates to 6-year-old Dom and his adoptive parents and has been completed by a Theraplay student who, at the time of completing this, was mid-way through the Theraplay practicum. Where numbers appear in the text, this indicates the exact time on the video. This is very useful as a reference if you are actually reviewing a video in a supervision.

Marschak Interaction Method (MIM)-Based Assessment Form—UK (anonymized example completed by student)

Where the practitioner administering the tasks has not yet completed the practicum, the form is to be called Marschak Interaction Method (MIM)-Based Assessment. Only a certified Theraplay practitioner is qualified to administer and analyze a MIM assessment. Both types of MIM protocol must be followed by a parent feedback.

"Parent" has been used throughout, meaning "parental figure" or "caregiver" for the child. Edit as appropriate.

Practitioner administering MIM			
Child's name or initials	Dom, male	Child's age at MIM	6 years, 2 months

Child's developmental issues affecting MIM (if any)
Currently being assessed for autism spectrum disorder

Parent 1: relationship to child, name or initials, date of MIM
Adoptive mother (M), DDMMYY

Parent 2: relationship to child, name or initials, date of MIM
Adoptive father (F), DDMMYY

Brief context for MIM: family history, reason for referral, setting, any special circumstances
Dom is a 6-year-old boy who was adopted by M and F when he was 16 months old. Birth mother had severe depression and led a chaotic lifestyle that included misuse of drugs. Dom was removed from her care at 4 months following reports of neglect and placed briefly with a foster family for emergency care before moving to a single foster carer for just over a year before being adopted. He is reported to have made strong attachments there and to develop healthily.
As Dom progressed through his first year at school (aged 4 years), he was known to stash objects, overeat, take on the role of teacher, organize other children and become anxious during transitions. Through the referral meetings and school observations, it quickly became apparent that Dom was not relaxed and settled either at home or school. He didn't like to be alone, was increasingly controlling, insisted on keeping to certain routines, gorged on food when it was left out, needed to hide objects, sang and talked loudly when distressed, and couldn't express his emotions verbally. School have engaged the support of other professionals and are investigating autism as a possible explanation for some of Dom's behaviors. A MIM-based assessment was carried out to observe the relationship between Dom and his parents and to consider Theraplay sessions as a possible intervention.

List of tasks administered
There was a misunderstanding about who was coming to do the MIM. I had thought only the father was coming on that day but both parents came together. I had little time to rearrange the tasks into the two-parent MIM and this made the MIM much longer than anticipated.

With parent 1 (mother)

Time		Task* (examples given for nursery and school age)	Dimension
01:00	1	Take a squeaky toy each and have the two animals play together	E
03:00	2	Take eight blocks and give eight blocks to your child. Build a stack or pattern. Say to your child, "Build one just like mine with your blocks"	S, C
08:35	3	Put lotion on each other	N
12:10	4	Tell your child about "When you came to live with us"	N
15:10	5	Teach your child something he doesn't already know	C
17:35	6	Leave the room for one minute without your child	N, E
20:15	7	Play a game that is familiar to you and your child	E
25:03	8	Tell your child to give dolly a drink	S, N
28:00	9	Feed each other	N

With parent 2 (father)

Time		Task*	Dimension
00:30 (toilet visit) 05:30	1	Take a squeaky toy each and have the two animals play together	E
09:40	2	Each take paper and pencil—draw a quick picture and encourage your child to "Draw a picture just like mine"	S, C
13:45	3b	Take a plaster out of the box and put it on your child	N
18:15	4	Tell your child about "When you came to live with us"	N
21:20	5	Leave the room for one minute without your child	N, E
25:50	6	Engage your child in three rounds of thumb wrestling	E, C??

With both parents (if two MIMs done back to back)

Time		Task*	Dimension
00:35	7	Make a stack of hands together	S, E
03:55	8	Sing a song together ("Comb each other's hair" was also in the envelope by accident)	E, N
07:05	9	Feed each other	N

* Note about making substitutions to the recommended task list: With some families, you may decide that it would be appropriate to substitute a task. Alternatives for prenatal, toddler and adolescent age groups are listed in the Theraplay third edition book (Booth and Jernberg, 2010), in your Level One handout and in Salo and Booth (2019). Ensure that the alternative you choose corresponds to the dimension of the original task on the list. As with all of your practice, be mindful of the many trans-culture, developmental and situational issues that inform how you relate to the families in your care and discuss potential stressors with parents at your initial referral meetings. For example, you may be aware of a child's sensory needs that could make the lotion task stressful and unpleasant (talc could be a good alternative); the early stages of adoption may make "Leave the room" traumatic for the child (the toddler task in which the parent remains in the room could be more appropriate); the parent may be bald or wearing a headscarf, so "Comb each other's hair" would not be possible and could be substituted by "Tell each other's fortunes." In all substitution decisions, the principle is for the child and parent to feel emotionally and physically safe, and for the tasks to be developmentally appropriate. If you are unsure, consult with your Theraplay supervisor, or send an enquiry to The Theraplay Institute for guidance.

STRUCTURE DIMENSION

1. Parent provides structure/directions.
2. Child accepts structure/directions or is child defiant, insisting on doing things his/her own way.
3. Parent's efforts to structure and organize help regulate the child.
4. What role does the parent take?
   - parent in peer or child role
   - parent unable to set limits
   - parent turns authority over to child
   - parent in teacher role (pedantic, rigid, focused only on task at hand).

Observations of verbal and non-verbal interactions that support conclusions about:

Child and Structure:

Dom is wanting to control most situations. He seems to enjoy structure and has a set way of doing things (e.g. putting the envelopes back to one side after each game) and, when he is leading, can structure his play, for example in Blocks and Hide and Seek. He often objects to someone else creating the structure for him and his habitual response seems to try to be in charge and to fill any gaps or pauses with talking and busy activity.

Mother and Structure:

The mother attempts to structure the activities but Dom doesn't often allow this. She asks questions ("Shall we…?"; "Would you like to…?") rather than gives statements. She lets me know after the session that she decided to follow Dom in the MIM whereas she would usually be more directive. Structure seems to be a high priority for the family. Even when Dom takes over the directorship, he does so in a structured way, for example tidying tasks away and putting them in order. The building blocks task becomes tower building, each with a random set of blocks rather than having a mirror set to create identical towers. There are mini-battles for control when the mother tries to lead Dom. In Feed the Dolly, she shows him how he was fed as a baby, which he accepts (although he is standing up a lot—how relaxed was he? I notice he puts water in his mouth when perhaps he's stressed).

Father and Structure:

The father is trying to structure all the interactions and often succeeds in saying, "No, Dom, uh uh no, we're going to do it *this* way." As he becomes firmer, Dom backs down. He does this kindly and often goes into a lighter voice once Dom has acquiesced. I think structure is very important to both parents and they feel safe within rules and "doing the right thing." The father seems able to adjust and be flexible with bending the rules and to help regain the relationship with Dom if there has been a short moment of conflict.

ENGAGEMENT DIMENSION

1. Parent able to engage the child and how.
2. Child's response to parent's attempts to engage.
3. Parent responds empathically to the child.
4. Parent and child are physically and affectively in tune with each other.
5. Parent matches level of stimulation to child's ability to tolerate it.
6. The two (three) are having fun together.

Observations of verbal and non-verbal interactions that support conclusions about:

Child and Engagement:

Dom sometimes seems wrapped in his own tasks and ways of doing things. He walks away, moves the table, goes out of the door, gets more and more water (there's a water fountain at the entrance to the space), has water in his mouth and is over at the camera but comes back quickly when called or a parent comes to guide him back. There is fairly constant dialogue with all members of the family. They are learning focused, chat about the tasks, have mini-verbal battles for control. I wonder about Dom's anxiety levels—are they quite raised? His body looks hot and he needs the toilet urgently in the second MIM. Dom's response to his parents' attempts to engage is to join in with the activity described but on *his* terms with *his* rules. I wonder how frustrating this is for mother and father. I see that he is wanting to engage but it rarely looks a relaxed and pleasant "moment of meeting." When all three are together, this seems more possible. Interestingly, the more physical activities such as Hand Stack, Hide and Seek and Thumb Wrestling, where there is no object, seem more fun. Activities that are talking based are the ones where it seems most difficult to engage Dom.

Parent 1 and Engagement:

The mother is attentive to Dom all the time. She seems eager to "get it right" and to succeed in this project. They engage in the activities with enthusiasm and seem to want to be physically near one another, although rarely touch. There is a lot of verbal communication, including many small questions from the mother: "Shall I go first? Was that fun for you? Do you want to do that next? What do you want me to do?" It seems that Dom can respond with less resistance when his mother gives a statement: "You go first." Dom is up and about a lot of the time. Both the squeaky toy and familiar game involve hide and seek games. This must be a safe option for them both which they are used to playing and both seem to be enjoying the interaction. Solid structure to the game allows it to go very well.

Parent 2 and Engagement:

The father is engaged with Dom, focused on him throughout, although sometimes looks despondent when Dom is rejecting or unresponsive. He never gives up and keeps trying to engage his boy. There are lovely moments of connection where they are both engaged in the sillier activities such as Thumb Wrestling or some spontaneous tickling (the father says they are used to doing more rough-and-tumble play). I notice there is little direct eye contact but they may be connecting in other ways. It is as though they keep missing each other, dancing around one another with the father quite static and Dom moving all the time. The father doesn't tease or overwhelm Dom, playfully letting him win games. Their emotional levels seem out of sync, with Dom's energy level being higher than his father's, which at times is much lower, perhaps trying to bring Dom down from his hyperarousal. Throughout (with both parents) there is no mention of emotional states.

NURTURE DIMENSION

1. Parent provides nurturing contact (touch, physical contact, caregiving).
2. Child accepts nurturing contact.
3. Parent asks child to take care of him/her.
4. Parent recognizes and acts on child's need for help in calming/having stress reduced.
5. Child accepts parent's help for calming/stress reduction.
6. Child is able to soothe self.

Leave the room task

1. Parent prepares child for separation. Note: describe child's behavior during separation and at reunion.

Tell about when a baby came to live with us task

1. Nature of story.

2. Reflection about parent/child feelings.

3. Child's response.

4. Parent attunement to child's response.

Observations of verbal and non-verbal interactions that support conclusions about:

Child and Nurture:

Does Dom become very active and task orientated when he is under stress? The focus on filling up cups and his mouth with water happens when he seems uncomfortable with the task. Often this is when nurture or babyhood are mentioned. When his mother reads the card about leaving the room, he looks quite shocked (17:35) and is quiet and not protesting. When his mother goes, he looks towards her and after a few seconds follows her to the door: "Just checking where you are." Dom is still near the door when she comes back in. The greeting is off camera, but I don't think there is any physical reunion and verbal acknowledgement that he may have found this difficult. When his mother asks if he enjoyed it and what he did, he simply responds with, "I checked where you were," which is a factual response.

In this same task with his father, Dom busies himself with sorting out the plasters while his father is away. He doesn't look up when his father returns, and he draws his father into his sorting activity. In Feed the Dolly, Dom fills his mouth with water (a stress reducer?) while his mother tells him about feeding him as a baby. In the lotion task, Dom begins by offering his own arm but then will only put lotion on his mother and not have her touch him. In "When you first came," Dom looks puzzled. Was he wanting to hear the story but feeling quite stressed? I see he's moving the table around the room (needing to be stretched and get some sensory input?) and going up to the camera often. He does come back when his mother asks him to and is able to listen to a few minutes of talking.

Parent 1 and Nurture:

In "Leave the room," the mother doesn't prepare Dom and leaves quite abruptly. She tells him where she is going and makes light of the separation, perhaps to help him not be too distressed. On her return she gives a cheery "Hello" and says, "I liked that. Did you like that one? What did you do when Mommy was away?" She seems to miss any potential distress in Dom, which I think Dom is maybe covering by becoming busy with the water. With the lotion task, Dom creams his mother's arms, face and neck, and she seems to be really enjoying this. She tries to return the nurturing to Dom by asking, "Shall I do it to you now?" but he doesn't want that. (Afterwards, she said she does put lotion on him at home with no issue, which is useful to know.) In "When you first came," the mother is quite factual and asks, "What do you remember?" There is nothing about Dom's feeling states or his mother and father's. Dom is sitting some distance away, pushing the table back and forth (again, sensory needs being met, in distress?) as his mother narrates the tale with enthusiasm and a sense that this was a happy time.

Parent 2 and Nurture:

Plaster—Dom wants to choose his own plaster and get his father to put it on in just the right way. He attempts to put one on his father first but his father says, "No, that's not the game." Dom wants his father to do it in the same way that his mother did. He has a mini-tantrum (15:13) when he gets frustrated over the exact way to do the task. There doesn't seem to be an easy flow between them. In the task "Tell your child about 'When you came to live with us,'" the father doesn't read out the card but weaves the start of his narrative into the interaction: "I was just thinking about when you were a baby." The father chooses to talk about a rocking toy that Dom used to enjoy playing on and, like the mother, asks, "Do you remember…?" With Dom standing and his father sitting, they get into a discussion about how small Dom was and what a big boy he is now. "Leave the room"—again, the father chooses to not read the card out loud and doesn't prepare Dom for what is happening. He just says he needs to leave. I notice that Dom rarely sits down throughout the sessions. He seems to sit down briefly when asked to by a parent but quickly gets up, going to get the next envelope or taking the card from them. I wonder what this is like day by day for his parents, and what Dom's stress levels are. How attuned to this emotional aspect of him can the parents be considering how active and talkative he is? There are fleeting periods of restfulness, relieving of tension, recovery or direct nurture, but he could be hard to nurture because he is so rarely still.

CHALLENGE DIMENSION

1. Activities chosen by the parent are developmentally appropriate.
2. Child responds to the task.
3. Parent makes mastery appealing.
4. Child is able to focus and concentrate.
5. Child is able to handle frustration.
6. Parent helps child handle frustration.

Observations of verbal and non-verbal interactions that support conclusions about:

Child and Challenge:

Does he challenge himself beyond his capabilities? Not often. Actually, I wonder if he is more anxious about failing and so doesn't stretch himself too far. He chooses to play Hide and Seek with each parent which is a simple, non-challenging game when played in this room. Dom seems frustrated and irritated much of the time and tries to gain control. I wonder if he is anxious about not being able to achieve highly or meet his parents' expectations. Is he aware of any expectations at all? He perseveres in the block task and builds several big towers for his mother to copy. In this task, he focuses and concentrates for long periods. With some tasks, such as "Tell your child about…" he ends the tasks quickly by walking away or sitting down in silence, perhaps through too low-level challenge or not having his ideas followed by the grown-ups.

Parent 1 and Challenge:

My experience of the mother before the MIM (I have known the family for nearly a year) is that she is very keen for Dom to achieve highly in academic activities and sets up tasks for them to do at home that have an outcome or product that can be evaluated. It is interesting in the MIM that she seems less driven in this way and sits back to see what Dom decides to do (had I perceived her view on challenge aspects wrongly?). In the blocks task, she follows Dom's tower building and doesn't set him any challenge to copy. In "Teach your child," she leads them back to a conversation about the planets that they were having on the journey here. This seems a high level of scientific understanding for a 6-year-old (although Dom kept up really well!), but I wonder if she misses the younger, emotional elements of Dom when she celebrates his cognitive achievements. When both parents are together, the mother playfully accepts when the Stack of Hands activity falls apart and she introduces a new challenge game with the father. Her level of challenge seems to be lowered and more playful when the father is present.

Parent 2 and Challenge:

In picture copying, the father makes this manageable for Dom. I notice that mastery is very appealing in this family—achieving high levels in any learning is celebrated. The father makes sure that Dom's efforts are also acknowledged. Much praise is given and Dom is encouraged to participate. The father keeps the tasks at a level Dom can manage and doesn't overwhelm him or impose his adult mastery, for example in Thumb Wrestling where he challenges and stretches Dom but allows him to win each round. The father seems well tuned to Dom's capabilities while also stretching him a little further.

GENERAL REFLECTIONS

Once you have considered the questions relating to each dimension, it is useful to ask yourself some general questions in order to gain understanding and empathy for both parent and child:

- What would it be like to live 24 hours a day with the child?

  It would take a lot of energy and may often be unsatisfying and frustrating. There would be few moments of relaxation and just enjoying being together, especially when being playful and "silly." I would feel frustrated that he so often says, "No, no, no…I want to do it this way… No, I'll do it… But I don't want to…" I would know that Dom can be distracted and enticed into other activities quite quickly (which is what his father does a lot at home, I think) but generally doing anything together could seem like a mild battle. I would feel that I wanted a closer connection to him but he just isn't still long enough to cuddle or be calm with. I might feel pleased with his high levels of cognition but also exhausted by his relentless activity and talk.

- Would living with the child make you feel good about yourself?

  Yes and no. I might feel delighted to be his parent and pleased with how well I can understand him and keep our relationship going at times. At other times, I might feel a bit helpless, at a loss, as though I'm failing as we can't get out of the house without Dom's rituals and rules.

- What would it be like to live 24 hours a day with the parent?

  (notes written from the perspective of being the child) I like to be busy and productive, which is quite like my mom. She asks a lot of questions and sometimes I don't know how to answer, especially when she asks how I'm feeling. I don't really understand then. Mom likes me to do well at school and get lots of certificates and stickers and I feel I have pleased her when I get these. She worries quite a bit and is always in a rush to move me on to the next thing. With dad, there are moments of fun and playfulness, especially when he lifts me and throws me. Dad is interesting to me, teaches me new things and is a source of praise, which I relish. Dad may seem busy and tired sometimes and not so available. He isn't sarcastic or judgmental, but we often have frustrating battles over who is in control. I want to be like him and think I know more than him sometimes.

- Would living with the parent/child make you feel good about yourself?

  I feel safe with Mom and want to be near her but it doesn't always feel good on my body to be cuddled, which I think makes her sad. I feel an interesting person with both of my parents. I am able to get Dad's attention easily but I might also pick up that I irritate him sometimes. I feel safe near him and want his attention all the time.

PARENT FEEDBACK

- List specific positive observations about child and parent.

  There are many strengths especially in Structure and Challenge dimensions: everyone's keenness to be engaged with one another, the focused attention that they give to Dom throughout, the ability to sustain tasks for a long time (the mother—blocks; the father—plaster), the appropriate challenge that both parents give so that Dom is not stretched too far (the father—picture copy; the mother—hide and seek familiar game). When all three are together the pleasure of interacting increases (sing a song). They clearly all want to be together and there is a lot of energy in this family.

- What overall messages do you plan to share with the parent about their interaction with their child?

  First, acknowledge that this was a very long MIM and not as planned. More difficult moments seemed to be with direct physical contact (the mother—Lotion; the father—Thumb Wrestling, although this became more fun when the father persevered) and talking about memories ("When you first came"). All of these are part of the Nurture dimension. When a toy or object is involved and when there is a pattern to the activity, the family seem much more confident and at ease than when these are not present.

- What questions do you have for the parent based on your observations?

  Directly after the MIM, the father explained that he had tried to "battle on" to keep Dom on task and keep going with the structure. Normally, at home, the father would be led by Dom when he objects or "isn't listening'" and then comes back to the focus task sometime later. In contrast, the mother said in the MIM that she tried to follow Dom's lead and let him do things the ways he wanted but at home she would normally persist and lead more herself.

  I want to get a clearer picture of how "normal" the interactions shown in the MIM are. How true a picture of Dom did I get? When did they last really enjoy Dom? What helps to soothe him? How does he show he is sad or angry? What was he like when he came to them? Was he able to accept holding, rocking, feeding? Could he drop off to sleep easily? What were the games they played in those early months?

  I also want to explore the upcoming autism assessment as many of Dom's patterns of behavior and responses to his parents may indeed be indicative of autism spectrum disorder but it is important to also consider Dom's trauma history and sensory needs. When is the assessment date? Would it be helpful for me to meet with the assessor and share my MIM observations?

- Which tasks do you plan to show the parent during the feedback session?

  Strengths/positive interactions:

    The father: end of Thumb Wrestle activity, draw picture

    The mother: section of squeaky toy, middle of familiar game (Hide and Seek)

    Both: end of Hand Stack activity, middle of sing/comb hair

  Areas to consider and work on (mini battles for control, holding water in his mouth, avoiding intimacy):

    The father: "Leave the room" whole, when you first came

    The mother: start of blocks, when you first came (water), middle of lotion tasks

    Both: getting settled into the first task

  If feedback has already taken place, note the above information as well as the parent's response.

INTERVENTION PLANNING

Based on your analysis of the MIM and the information gathered at the feedback:

- What do the child and the parent need?

  This family need to regain a sense of fun and pleasure in one another (parents have said they used to be much more silly and playful). Dom is more likely to be able to relax and let go of his need to be in control if his parents could be less focused on achieving an end result and relax themselves into the moment. There is a noticeable absence of any acknowledgement of feeling states. Most of the interaction is busy and talkative with mini-conflicts and each trying to establishing control. (What would happen if the parents acknowledged how Dom may be feeling and voice that? Discuss in later review session?)

- Which dimensions will be the primary focus of the intervention to meet those needs?

  Primary focus will be on Engagement and Nurture dimensions. Focus on reducing the amount of verbal communication and increasing the non-verbal interactions. Parent staying firmly but kindly in charge, moving towards nurturing activities and feeling states even if Dom may initially object. Finishing sequences of activities even if Dom interrupts. Building in much more physical contact that is nurturing and fun.

Engagement: There seems to be tension in their engagements as though trying very hard to engage but not quite meeting one another in a relaxed, joyful way. Activities where the challenge level is low but involves direct engagement without objects as a distraction: Blanket Tunnel, Hand Stack, Row, Row, Row Your Boat, Feeding, Blanket Swing, Popcorn Toes, Preparing Pizza.

Nurture: Parents' attempts to nurture are not always rejected. There are times when Dom accepts it but generally when it is being reciprocated. He gives a lot of help and nurturing, especially to his mother (with the lotion and water). Activities that help him to relax and receive: feeding, singing, non-verbal games, story books that have a rhythm so there is no space for interruptions, lotion accompanied by a song.

In addition to these dimensions, I would also consider the other dimensions to a lesser degree.

Structure: All the family relish rules and structure. This is an important part of family functioning. Dom often tries to gain the control of structure (for safety?; out of habit?). Some activities may allow his parents to be in charge of structure in a way that Dom can accept in a relaxed, trusting way. This could reduce his anxiety and need to interrupt. Also, *less* structure may benefit them— being daft and silly together with fewer rules and challenges and no learning involved. Build this in gradually so that they begin from a familiar place. Activities—Bean Bag Drop, Cotton Ball Throw, Cushion Jump.

Challenge: He is generally high enough challenged and he doesn't set his own challenges too high. He's curious, adventurous and wants to learn. Achieving and being task oriented is important to this family. Activities with *lower* levels of challenge could be helpful: Cup (Russian doll) Stack, Cushion Jump, building up number of cushions from two to five.

Outline for first session and what to practice at the parent demonstration session:

First session preparation with the father

(Shoes off)

Entrance—down the ramp together (funny walk)

Check-ups—brief, little talk

Lotion—using flat hands

Measures—not how big/tall Dom is, not lots of talk

Row, Row, Row Your Boat—hold by elbows rather than hands

Blow Me Over—the father okay to lift Dom over his head?

Blanket Swing/Tunnel—Horsey Horsey song, which the father already sings

Snack—with a little rhyme (not mutual feeding this time)

Story—with a rhythm pattern

Cushion Jump—into the father's arms

Exit—decide on the day, attuned to Dom's state.

Chapter 14

Theraplay® Dyadic Session Supervision Form Example

This form is a standard session supervision form which the student completes in preparation for supervision. The notes are written about a single session and this session is then reviewed during supervision. This example is again about Dom (the same child as featured in the MIM form). The student has completed the form as her final supervision session which will be reviewed by an external supervisor.

Theraplay
INSTITUTE

Student/Practitioner		Supervisor	
Child/adult name and relationship	Dom, boy Mother, adoptive parent	Setting for session	Office
Child's age	6 years, 8 months	Session# and date	10

If this is your first supervision session for this family, please provide your supervisor with the following information:

Background information on child and family (use initials only) including child's age, school setting, family constellation, reason for referral and, if fostered or adopted, brief reasons for removal from birth family and placement history.

- Video of MIM-based session, along with the MIM-Based Analysis Form.
- Evidence of consent given by the parents/caregivers (and local authority, if applicable) to video record and to share the video and information about the family with your supervisor. Please do not send consent form directly.

A. SPECIFIC GOALS FOR THIS SESSION

From previous sessions, and in discussion with the mother, I want to:

- have a quicker pace and to make transitions shorter and physical so that Dom feels more able to stay connected
- notice his cues for what he needs more quickly before he has to indicate it by wriggling off or fetching what he wants
- add more rhythm and bounce to some of the activities, i.e. get Dom's body into a more regulated state first so that he can accept physical nurture and tolerate intimacy
- reduce the talking, questioning and discussing between adults and child so that there is direct communication through the body and non-verbal signals.

B. SESSION ACTIVITIES

List of activities as planned	Time on video	As actually happened in the session*
Entrance: Wheelbarrow	04:15	Entrance: Wheelbarrow
Feather Blow	05:05	Feather Blow
Check-ups and Lotion	06:20	Slippery Slip *As soon as Dom saw the lotion he grabbed the bottle and lotioned his arms to play Slippery Slip. I chose to go with this, partly to use up excess lotion and partly to respond to his body wanting to have firm input. We did Check-ups straight afterwards as a more nurturing activity with the lotion once he was calmer.*
Slippery Slip	09:30	Check-ups
Cushion Jump	11:45	Cushion Jump
Row the Boat	14:10	Roll over Ball/Pizza/Balloon Catch *After Cushion Jump, Dom was too highly activated to sit down and seemed too sensitive to be touched for Row the Boat, so I shifted to rolling him over the gym ball in a rhythm, with his mother and me pressing his back to make a pizza. Sang a song too. This helped bring down his hyperaroused state.*
Bubbles	20:45	Bubbles
Snack with story	27:35	Snack with story. *We've found that reading a rhythmic story while he is being fed allows Dom to linger in a relaxed state with his mother.*
Blanket Swing	36:15	Blanket Swing
Feather Blow	37:00	Feather Blow
Exit—crawl	39:00	Exit—crawl with ball on back

* Please briefly describe why you made the decision to change from the planned activity/activities.

C. YOUR ASSESSMENT OF YOUR WORK IN THE FOLLOWING AREAS (GIVE SPECIFIC EXAMPLES BY ACTIVITY)

1. Your efforts to keep child optimally regulated:

In previous sessions, Dom has run away from the space, climbed over the armchairs and pulled away from touch, especially during transitions. I want to help him to remain regulated enough to participate and to move from one activity to the next without the need to break away. I had prepared his mother for this in the review and said that we can make transitions smoother by weaving in a patterned "1, 2, 3" or singing a short song and trying to keep hold of his body most of the time. I asked her to help with this body scaffolding if it didn't seem to activate him negatively. For the beginning activities, this seems quite successful. I know that Dom's body is calmer when he has done some stretching or lifting, hence the Slippery Slip at the start, and, for Cushion Jump, I ask his help to lay out the cushions (11:45). These are big, heavy ones and, unusually, he is then ready to engage in the activity without running around the couches first. At the end of the activity though, his mother and I let go physical contact with him for a few seconds and immediately Dom climbs onto the chairs, grabs the camera and is very restless and seems hot (13:30). To calm him again, I have him lie tummy down over the gym ball and we rock him to and fro (14:40) rather than moving into Row, Row, Row Your Boat as his body clearly isn't ready for this lighter touch or direct eye contact yet.

It can be difficult for his mother and me to sustain this level of physical focus while also building "moments of meeting" between her and Dom. I can see that Dom still needs times to run off and come back to reset/reconnect.

2. Your pacing of activities:

In previous sessions, I had been quite slow and relaxed in the pace to try and give the family an experience of something less frantic. However, too slow a pace means Dom frequently interrupts and breaks the connections, and so in this session I quicken the pace again, especially during transitions so that the whole session flows more. It still doesn't feel a comfortable pace as I am always aware of Dom's sudden need to break off and his mother's felt rejection when he chooses to move away. With Dom, I have learned to prolong some activities if he is in a regulated state so that he can begin to experience calmness while emotionally and physically connected to his mother. I am surprised that he tolerates being swung in the blanket for so long (for Dom three minutes is long!) as previously he has shifted around, talked and hung his legs out (36:30).

3. Variety and sequence of activities (balance between nurture/structure, quiet/boisterous, faster/calmer):

I plan the session to be moving towards the snack to try and optimize the opportunity to bring Dom down into a relaxed, trusting state where he isn't controlling the interaction. I know that he will be initially compliant and will need high levels of structure to feel comfortable, so we always start and end with the Feather Blow. The more boisterous activities (Cushion Jump, Balloon Catching) are in the first section so that Dom's body can be stretched, and he can have the experience of challenge and engagement with me and his mother. The bubbles activity has become less and less boisterous over the weeks and Dom now lets go much of his previous need to control and allows his mother and me to structure his popping (25:35). This means that he is tired when he sits down for the snack and story which happens in a quiet atmosphere, although that calm state is suddenly broken by Dom at the end of the story. He starts to wriggle out of his mother's lap because he wants to get some water. I say I will get the water and I make a playful comment about his toes. Unusually, he accepts this and he waits for me to return. He needs to break off from his mother and sit higher than her on the couch but then has several minutes of quiet sucking at the cup (35:00). Here I need to decide what to move on to next. I feel the shift to Blanket Swing may be too stimulating but decide to go with this as a small challenge. For the first time, we are able to sustain the calm state. We even stop singing and just swing him and then wrap him up as a parcel, which seems to take him, and his mother, into a much quieter relationship.

4. Your overall use of engagement (use of surprise, "moments of meeting," etc.):

I try to maintain physical contact with Dom as much as possible in order to keep the engagement more constant. In previous sessions, we have moved suddenly in and out of connection. Today, there are many spontaneous "moments of meeting" when we all laugh and Dom makes eye contact, briefly, with me or his mother, for example slurping his yoghurt (32:25), slipping back (10:10), and Dom catches a bubble on the wand (26:45). I add in some surprises when Dom is about to break off, for example I move into a brief This Little Pig at 10:15, which re-engages him, and I turn him on to his tummy to do a brief pizza massage using the gym ball on his back. (Previously he hasn't tolerated any touch directly on his back for this.) I try to keep the transitions playful and physical and at the end of the pizza activity I roll him back to the cushion on the ball (20:20).

5. Your attention to child's non-verbal signals:

The whole family use verbal communication, including lots of questions as a prime way of relating (02:45). Much of what we have been doing over the weeks has been to reduce the amount of talking so that we can notice Dom's non-verbal signals and also to respond non-verbally so that he has the experience of his needs being taken care of before having to ask. There are still times when I miss his intentions, for example when he needs water at 34:45. Some of his cues are clear—he rolls down his sleeves to indicate no more lotion and waves his arms around to indicate "again, again!" Dom's body can get very hot and his breathing and heart rate quicken when he is experiencing stress or is unsure about what is happening. This can be in seemingly calm activities such as reading the story. I have begun to remark on some of these physical cues out loud (03:00, 24:20) so that Dom and his mother are attentive to his body states too. By watching the video with the sound off, I am aware of the signals that I am missing in the room and so I know that I need to become more attuned to what he is showing his mother and me. Many of these non-verbal signals seem to be of a much younger child and I can learn to read them more accurately if I remember that his emotional development is lower than his cognitive ability.

6. Your modifications for trauma history:

Dom was adopted at 16 months and lived in two foster placements having been with his birth parents for the first four months. While there is no known history of domestic abuse or alcohol addiction in his birth family, physical and emotional neglect was part of his early experience. I am learning that Dom's experience in the womb may have also caused trauma due to his mother's misuse of drugs, her depression and her chaotic lifestyle. She says he didn't enjoy physical holding as a toddler and would prefer to be on the ground on his own. I wonder about a deprivation of sensory input pre-birth and an over-sensitive system that finds relaxing into another's body stressful. Dom becomes very obsessed with doing things in the same routine at home and at school. It seems both to reduce anxiety and create more to have these rigid routines and so I am aiming to gently challenge him with some unpredictability and a more flexible approach. I can see that he is gradually less fearful and is more resilient to newness. There is a strong possibility that Dom may have a neurological condition such as autism and is due to be assessed for this.

In this session, I modify some activities to maintain physical contact with Dom and closer proximity of his mother without activating his body so much that he needs to break off. In our version of Slippery Slip (08:55), we move away from it being primarily a nurturing activity to an engagement one. I move from his arms to his feet when he shows me that his arms have become too sensitive. His mother sits behind him and gently strokes his hair and cheek, something I have not seen him allow before. I am able to use deep pressure with his feet and pattern the slipping so he knows when to expect it. There is a lovely moment at 09:29 when he leans back against the couch with his mother holding his body between her legs. It is rare for him to flop like this.

I know that in other settings Dom will grab food, hoard it and gorge, sometimes until he is sick. I have provided thick yoghurt to suck through a straw (to slow him down) and reduced any talking so that he begins to experience eating in a slower, more attentive way. His mother and I create little songs to comment on his slurping or crunching, again to focus him on the tastes and textures he has in his mouth. This is beginning to have the effect of reducing Dom's need to grab food as soon as he comes in, and to chatter. The next stage will be to help him accept being fed by his mother as a relaxing, nurturing, pleasurable activity.

7. Would you work differently with this child in the future? If so, how?

Generally, reducing the verbal stimulation and volume will help Dom to relax and gradually accept more direct intimacy with his mother. I notice he and his mother can be calmer and more available for connection when the father is also present in sessions. I would try and get the father there more often as he seems to regulate the others so that the whole family engage much more directly, often in a physical way.

D. COMMENTS ON THE CHILD'S BEHAVIOR

In this session, I notice that Dom is less anxious, talkative and controlling than in previous ones. His body movements seem to be those of a much younger child and this is particularly clear when he is rocking on the ball. He holds the yoghurt cup and climbs up on the couch in a very toddler-like way. Dom moves away from his mother often and sometimes his body seems to be so sensitive that he can't tolerate touch. He is very eager to engage and is easily enticed back to an activity if this is done in a playful rather than shaming way. For now, most of his interaction is with me, with his mother being the companion and observer, although today he flops against her many times and allows her to stroke his hair while he is engaged in an activity.

E. PARENT INVOLVEMENT

1. Your efforts to provide structure for the parent (e.g. did the parent have a comfortable place to sit? Did the parent know what was expected/how to do the activities? Did you provide enough direct coaching/guidance to parent?):

The mother and I had had a long review session and so she knew that we were trying something different today (see goals). She sits on the cushions next to Dom, which seems comfortable for her, although I'm aware it didn't allow her to see Dom's face. I asked her to try and be physically closer to Dom today, as in previous sessions she would sit on a different seat when Dom directed her to move away from him. She does sit closer and is even right up against his body (33:25) in several activities which Dom is able to tolerate and, I sense, get some pleasure from. She is able to go along with new plans as they emerge, for example in rolling the ball on top of Dom with deep pressure. Within the session, I give her non-verbal coaching, for example in the Blanket Swing when we stop singing but keep swinging. When I give verbal direction, she wants to follow too precisely at times, so I've learned to show it in my actions rather than coach out loud.

2. Your facilitation of parent-child engagement:

In previous sessions, I have had the mother lead some of the activities or take turns with me but we have found this doesn't yet bring a pleasurable interaction between her and Dom. He still cuts off at random, which means we can't sustain the connection. Dom will tolerate more intimacy from me than with his mother (because I don't mean so much to him?), and I hope that in practicing accepting this nurture from one adult he will then accept and enjoy it from his parents. The mother's nurturing movements in, for example, lotioning can be jerky and tentative (am I creating that nervousness? Do previous rejections from Dom make her a bit hesitant?), so we are working on a firmer, more nurturing touch (07:05) with flat hands. I am building in more activities that involve physical contact between them with the mother often in a "support" role so that Dom can have an experience of feeling body contact without being task or question oriented. For example, when Dom leans back into his mother in the slipping game (08:30) and when we are rolling the ball over his tummy, his mother sneaks in some caresses and strokes as he comes out of the lying position (18:10). Often, the mother will mimic what I am doing without the need for verbal communication and she is much more spontaneous in these physical gestures now and Dom is accepting lovely touch such as stroking his hair, tapping his knee and holding hands. The wheelbarrow entrance (down a ramp) is a way of the mother and Dom engaging without face-to-face contact and has become a challenging and fun activity for them both. He has got a strong upper body! In jumping along the cushions (12:50), the mother and I hold Dom's body between us and pattern the leaps from one cushion to another so that he is engaging in a cooperative, synchronized movement with his mother rather than battling against her or running off.

For now, these are ways to have the parent-child relationship develop without either needing to break off, but the goal is to have Dom and his mother having prolonged, direct face-to-face contact that feels relaxed and pleasurable for them both.

3. Parent's reaction to child:

I am aware that the mother's confidence in parenting can be quite fragile as she wonders if his difficulties are somehow her and the father's "fault." I sense these sessions can wobble her belief in being a good mother at times.

We have talked about the mother observing Dom as he plays with me, to notice some of his very young behaviors and what helps to soothe/relax him. She is deeply committed to parenting him but sometimes her eagerness can lead to a stressful battle between them. The family have let me know that they are doing many of the games at home now, and I have provided them with a list of all the ones we have done. However, I want to ensure that this doesn't lead back into task-orientated play, so I encourage them to focus on the calmer, nurturing ones and to lessen any talk or overt need for approval. Also, integrating the "feel" of the Theraplay activities into everyday life is the long-term aim.

In the session, I can see that the mother sometimes moves away from Dom, especially if he has rejected her advance, which is understandable. However, there are also many times now when she gives (and Dom seems happy to receive) caresses and tussles of his hair and she can laugh with him rather than mildly reprimand him as happened in the first few sessions. Overall, I believe she's enjoying him far more.

F. TRANSFERENCE/COUNTERTRANSFERENCE ISSUES

Unusually, I feel very sad after this session. I wonder if I am picking up the mother's feelings related to external work-related factors. I find it harder to engage with them that day or to feel a positive enthusiasm because in the review the parents had alluded to being skeptical about the benefits of Theraplay. I am perhaps feeling hurt by this and less positive towards the family, feeding into my issues around not being good enough or approved of. I also sense that Dom is puzzled by the quicker-paced session with fewer opportunities to control the transitions and I am nervous about changing too many activities at once. In addition, the sessions are held in the later afternoon and that day all of us seem very tired and wanting the session to be over.

G. PLAN FOR THE NEXT SESSION

I plan a similar session to this one but with a longer period of quiet, nurturing activities in the second half (Blanket Swing, lying over the ball for pizza massage, rocking while being read to). I think Dom is now ready to tolerate more intimacy, especially if his body has been stretched and activated by more rigorous activities first. I need to think about where the mother sits so that Dom and she can be more physically attuned and build in some opportunities for eye contact. I aim to have the mother be the primary object of relation more, so that her confidence is built, and Dom has more low-challenge/non-verbal experiences of his mother that involve physical intimacy.

H. QUESTIONS FOR YOUR SUPERVISOR

I am looking at the positioning, as the mother is still often to the side and some way apart from Dom. She can't see his face. Is there a way I can rearrange the seating to facilitate much more connection?

What function is the snack having? As yet, it isn't a nurturing activity and often sets Dom and his mother up in conflict as he pushes away her advances to feed him. How can I provide them with a calm, nurturing activity around food that enhances their intimacy?

What activities might I add in that will build the mother's confidence and give maximum opportunity for Dom and her to engage in a joyful way without a nervousness that the connection is going to be suddenly disrupted?

Chapter 15

Theraplay® Final Evaluation Supervision Form Example

This form represents the written feedback given to the student by the external supervisor, in this instance Phyllis Booth. Phyllis reviewed the student's notes of the MIM and of the specific session and then reviewed each video providing the written feedback below. Routine supervision usually happens verbally as a conversation between supervisor and supervisee. In this case, the student had submitted the forms as part of her final exam.

Theraplay
INSTITUTE

Student/Practitioner	Student	Supervisor	Phyllis Booth
Child/adult name and relationship	Dom, boy Mother, adoptive parent	Session#	10
Date	DDMMYY		

MIM: PHYLLIS'S FEEDBACK

I wanted to check in on the MIMs a bit.

MIM with mother

The mother says, "I'm in charge." Did you say this to her or does this come spontaneously? It is best not to say something like that, since we want to see how the parent manages this without our prompting. Also, I would recommend that you not ask the child to wait while you announce for the camera what is taking place. The MIM is a rather strange set-up for families. It is best not to add to the "on stage" element by making this announcement.

You mention that the MIM was very long. Did you have a reason for making it so long? Also, how did you choose the various activities? We generally recommend staying with the recommended list, but there are good reasons for adding or changing that list. I just wanted to know what your reasons were.

I see that you told the father that he could rearrange the order. We really want them to do the tasks in order, so don't announce that. If they do rearrange, that gives us something to think about and maybe even ask them about.

00:53: Dom's physical startle to the sound of the animal fits with the picture I have got from your notes: He is highly sensitive to sounds—at least.

Lotion: His body actually relaxes for a minute, but he keeps moving very fast and there is no sense of calm. His mother's pace of talk also seems fast. It feels as if I was hearing this on a tape that was set a bit fast.

18:28: He shows the instructions and explains. Is this to the camera? Or are you in the room?

He is quite surprised/thrown off by the idea of her leaving. He organizes things by announcing what is going on. Waits a minute, then goes for her. Asks for water? I agree with your notes about his response. It is hard for him and she minimizes the experience.

I'm interested in how much water he drinks as well as the way in which he drinks it—he keeps it in his mouth some time before swallowing it. Does he have swallowing problems?

MIM with father

The fast pace in the beginning here is striking. The father takes charge, but it doesn't settle Dom and he resorts to bringing water—his way of self-soothing and taking charge. The father is very conscious of Dom's fast pace here in the beginning, trying to stop him and slow him down. He manages to take charge, but needs help to find ways to calm him in addition to setting the limit: sit down, uh uh, and gesturing to him with his arm. His fast pace "uhs" don't help, but I totally understand the sense of urgency that this little boy creates.

13:53: What is Dom's silent gesture all about? For the moment, no one is talking and I felt some relief that they weren't as keyed up as they had been.

15:52: I looked for the "mini-temper tantrum." I agree, it's as if he is really frantic to do it his way. What is also interesting is that when his father holds his hand and puts the plaster on the spot that Dom wants, Dom's body for almost the first time relaxes. This would be something to show in feedback (maybe you did)—the difference between the father's verbal and gestural efforts to slow him down and the effect of touch. It also goes along with actually complying with Dom's plan for how it should go, but I do think that calming touch is the way to go. It's as if he finally feels that his father has listened to him. I'll look to see whether this has worked in your sessions.

When the father is out of the room, you come in. Why did you do that? Is this something you generally do or was there something about Dom that made you feel he couldn't cope with his father leaving? Since you were in the room, Dom resorted to his charming ways of engaging you, showing you the plasters and so on.

MIM with both parents

Hand Stack: Once the father gets them organized and all the hands are on top of each other, there is a moment of pause and relaxation that confirms the value of firm pressure for Dom. Very quickly this is lost and the father joins his excitement by tickling. Surprisingly, this allows Dom to settle for a minute afterwards. So, high stimulation may be what he needs, although there are much better ways to provide it than through tickling. The father is certainly lively and the family seems to enjoy high-energy play. This can be positive if they can begin to add the concept of co-regulation and actually staying with and holding sad feelings.

I agree with you that Dom is seldom still and that his behavior conveys a frantic, agitated tone. I found myself not wanting to watch it all. How are the parents coping with this at home?

I'm glad to see that you have tried to explain to yourself—and I assume to the parents—what the origins are of his agitation. Prenatal period with an anxious, depressed mother (did she use drugs?) who wasn't prepared to keep him. Thus a very dysregulated start. Then he just gets settled in one home and is transferred to the adoptive home. At this point, it looks as if these two very clever, very intellectual and very high-energy parents are not open to reading emotional cues, so he probably has not had the co-regulating experience that he desperately needs. Whatever the source of agitation, he desperately needs help to be more relaxed and more trusting.

SESSION 10: PHYLLIS'S FEEDBACK TO STUDENT

This is a very good session. He is much calmer than in the MIMs and the mother is doing quite well supporting you in your effort to make smooth transitions and keeping him calm and focused. She says very little and asks no questions. Good. I appreciate how much energy is required to keep him with you through transitions. You have done an amazing job in this session, especially when I compare it with the MIM sequences with his parents.

I can see your dilemma as you try to make the session calm and yet maintain a pace that keeps Dom engaged. You have done well here. Here are my notes as I watched the video and then went back over your notes.

I see from your notes that you are very aware of his sensory issues. That's good.

I see also that you are working very hard to see his non-verbal signals. You are right to think of them as coming from a much younger child. That should help you—and ultimately his parents—to read him more accurately. This must have been what he desperately needed as a baby but they weren't able to tune in to.

4:03: Wheelbarrow. This is a good choice for a child as fidgety as he is. It is also very nice to add the rhythmic chant with words specifically for Dom.

Feather Blow: The use of the chewy ring makes a lot of sense. Do you need to give him a choice of feathers? I think he will do best if you just decide this sort of thing. It is very nice to see how calm he is during the feather activity, even though he is not very successful at it—using small pillows to catch the feather might help. He doesn't seem troubled by not managing it though.

7:30: He's very ready for the lotion on his leg. You are very attuned to his need here. He turns to look toward the side and you hand him the squashy ball and he gets the chew ring. He manages very well for both legs and hands and then moves on to feet before you are quite ready, but his mother is doing her job well—keeping her hands on his body and supporting him.

9:30: The mother adds a bit of stimulation here, rubbing his head and his cheeks. You comment that it is gentle and that it is new for her. Unfortunately, after a while it seems a bit of an intrusion from Dom's point of view. I wonder whether his mother is feeling a need to be more active in the interaction? But I agree that for a moment he leans back as if really relaxing under her touch. It is good that it doesn't seem to dysregulate Dom. But she goes on rubbing his hair back from his forehead in a way that makes Dom blink each time. Perhaps she thinks she is following your directions about body scaffolding? Show this to her and help her find a more calming way to contribute to his physical experience.

10:24: He is making little hand gestures that suggest more excitement and at 10:46 he impatiently pushes her hands away. It has clearly become too much. Good timing to move on and get his socks on. Well done.

Balance on Pillows, Jump Off: You are right that it's good for him to help set up the pillows. He is calm and purposeful as he does this. The jumping goes well. I kept trying to think of how you could incorporate more intentional activity on his part. You and his mother are lifting his body and providing a lot of good sensory input. I think he would also benefit from actually initiating the jump and feeling the impact as well. Something to try. At the moment, he may need to have all the initiative from you and his mother. He does escape as you and his mother get busy picking up pillows but you get him back very well with the ball.

14:10: Roll over Ball (similar to floating on a raft with therapy ball). Again a very good activity for him. This and the pizza activity seem very calming for him and he stays with it a long time. It must feel good to you and his mother that he can remain so calm and focused. He lets you know when he needs to turn over and it is good that you respond.

19:03: Balloon Tennis. By this point I began to feel that you might be overdoing the sensory stimulation: he is chewing, his mother is rocking him on the ball and you are tossing the balloon. I had the feeling that he would have been content to just rock back and forth with the chewy in his mouth for another little while. No need for the balloon. But I also recognize that you wanted to engage him a bit more. That's important too. This doesn't last long. I wonder whether because he couldn't be very successful throwing from this position, he moved away soon? You are doing a great job in getting him back—rolling him back to the pillows.

Feeding: You are doing very well with transitions: tucking him in to his mother's arms when you have to go for the snack. He seems to be a long way away as he drinks the juice. Very relaxed. Have you found that the reading is important in keeping him quietly with you during feeding? By the end, when you and the mother are chanting the words in rhythm, it felt as if it had gone on a bit long. And the rhythm got faster. It's not clear whether it was the quicker pace of your chant at the end or whether it was just time for him to move, but he starts to get up. That could just be because he had finished the juice, or perhaps because the pace began to speed up.

28:40: Blanket Swing. Another good activity, which lasts for a long time. I was glad that you shifted so the mother could see his face. He seems calm here—does he need the water/cup to remain calm?

Good retrieval after he wanders away. Since we often end sessions after feeding, I'm interested in how you decide when to feed and when to do a few more activities before the end. I understand that you are using Feather Blow at beginning and end as a way of providing structure to the sessions. That makes sense.

Pop the Bubbles: As I watch him with the water cup, I think that the chewy ring is a better soothing object since it doesn't prevent him from using both hands to engage in the play with you.

After his turn, he says, "It's Mommy's turn." I thought he meant that you should blow to her. When you hand it to her, he picks up the water again. Is it possible that he did have a different arrangement in mind and that he had to turn to the water to deal with his disappointment? (I'm reading a lot into this moment!)

Feather Blow: He seems to have a hard time deciding which color feather. Then he's back to the water cup. It certainly is one of his ways of handling moments that don't feel smooth to him.

37:56: He then puts the cup in his mouth and holds his hands out. What a challenge! Made me laugh. I had the same impulse as you: get rid of the water. He does accept your offer of the chewy ring, but only after taking a few more sips. It's interesting that the first half of the session he was content with the chewy ring. He doesn't seem very interested in the Feather Blow, though he does begin to engage with his mother as he blows it to her.

WORK WITH MOTHER: PHYLLIS'S FEEDBACK

I see that you are aware of how much help she needs to achieve the relationship she hopes for and that Dom needs. She is certainly trying hard and has moved significantly from how she was in the MIM. As to feeling that this is her fault, I'm sure you have lots of ways to help her with that, but I imagine that she was faced with a child whose needs are so very different from what she expected—and so very serious in the sensory realm—that she couldn't possibly read his signals and provide what he needed. Her experience would simply have been that he rejected all she tried to do. Shifting to verbal interactions must have been a relief for her. But of course, it doesn't help Dom's underlying needs. Her efforts to stroke and nurture him are very new for her and she will need a lot of guidance to learn how to do it at the right moment and in the most calming way. You can help her with that. For example, the lovely moment when he did lean back and relax after her first stroking. Then by watching the rest of the section, you can point out to her how quickly something lovely becomes too much. Share with her how hard this has been for you too.

I am surprised to read that the mother had told you, just that morning, that she was skeptical about Theraplay. I didn't pick that up. And my view of the session is that it shows a lot of progress. But there is all the more reason to be happy that she managed as much gentle stroking and appropriate support to you during the session.

You are right to be thinking of how to transfer the good relationship more to the mother. But don't push it. Make sure that she is solid and comfortable and able to understand that it is not her fault if he turns away. Help her see the rising tension that leads to his moving away.

I wonder whether you can interact with him as you try out an activity and then shift him to your lap to face his mother so she can do the activity. Would that be a way to transition a bit? I do think that you have made progress so that he is able to lean back against his mother. Help her see what progress that is.

I think it is nurturing to him that you offer the food, that he doesn't have to grab it and hoard it and that you and his mother sit happily watching him eat—sharing a calm moment. You don't need to insist that you or his mother feeds him. It's the moment of relaxation, the food in the tummy and the general appreciation conveyed that is important at the moment.

ACTIVITIES FOR THEM TO SHARE

Do think baby level. Can he do Patty-Cake? This Little Pig, Peek-a-Boo? Could he tolerate hiding with her under a blanket and having you find his knee and so on? Perhaps you need to hide with him and have his mother find his body parts.

Can you make play dough handprints and footprints? The mother could be the one who presses the dough into his palm.

Have a bowl of water with dish soap in it and all blow through straws into it to make bubbles. The bubbles can be picked up in big handfuls and then be dripped into the water. Messy, but might be satisfying.

Have Dom crawl through a cloth tunnel from you to his mother. Or just under a blanket.

Blow cotton balls to each other while lying on tummies. The mother and he could face each other.

That's enough comments. Congratulations. I'm pleased to let you know you have passed this final.

Chapter 16

Foundational Self-Description by Dimension (Session 8) Form Example

This form summarizes what is expected of a student at the Foundational stage of the Theraplay supervision practicum. This is the first stage of supervision practicum and is typically reached after eight or more supervision sessions. For anyone undertaking Theraplay interventions, achieving Foundational status is seen as the minimum requirement.

Aim for an average 3 score, i.e "Demonstrates ability to implement aspect of intervention 30–50% of the time. Beginning to integrate suggestions from supervisor."

MIM ASSESSMENT

Theraplay
INSTITUTE

Administers MIM appropriately:
• Selects appropriate space.
• Provides clear instruction to the family, selecting appropriate activities.
• Asks follow-up questions of the family regarding their experience with the MIM.
MIM analysis:
• Observations support conclusions and plans.
• Intervention plans correspond to MIM analysis that includes specific goals for intervention within appropriate dimensions.
• Session plans reflect understanding of identified goals and are guided by the intervention plan.
• Demonstrates an understanding of who and what needs to change and is able to guide this process through session planning.

MIM feedback appropriate and sensitive:

- Is able to highlight the family/dyad's strengths and illustrate them through video clips.
- Is able to identify areas of concern and empathically explore with caregivers during feedback sessions.

STRUCTURE

- Arranges space and positioning for maximum comfort and support for the child.
- Helps the child focus on and attend to the practitioner or parent.
- Activity choice is appropriate for age/gender/developmental level.
- Leads the child through a variety of organized, interactive playful sequences (e.g. balance between nurture/structure, quiet/boisterous, faster/calmer).
- Helps the child accept structure.
- Helps the child remain regulated.
- Able to help the child regain regulation.

ENGAGEMENT

- Demonstrates openness to connect with the child and create "moments of meeting."
- Draws the child's attention to the adult's face/body and facial expressions/gestures.
- Shares and increases positive affect through the interaction.
- Engages in "serve and return" communication with the child.
- Develops a repertoire of play interactions.

NURTURE

- Notices and acknowledges hurts during session and takes care of them.
- Tailors mode and intensity of nurture to the specific needs of the child.
- Soothes the child when upset.
- Is comfortable with providing touch in its various forms.

CHALLENGE

- Assists the child to tolerate (accept) a variety of new activities.
- Assists the child to develop the ability to transition between activities.
- Assists the child to develop the ability to prolong the interaction.
- Helps the child to experience success.

WORKING WITH PARENTS

- Demonstrates the ability to be attuned to the parents' need in a Theraplay session at a beginning level.
- Provides proper seating.
- Addresses the parent to make them feel involved.
- Steps in to aid the parent if an activity is not going well at a beginning level.
- As the parent demonstrates competence, increases their participation in sessions.

Interpreting:

- Explains clearly to parents the critical aspects of Theraplay sessions and Theraplay principles.
- Demonstrates willingness to explain the reasons underneath the activities to the parents in a supportive manner.

Guiding in session:

- Provides structure for parents to successfully participate in activities with their child.
- Redirects the caregiver as needed to maintain positive interactions with the dyad.
- Includes the parent as much as possible and increases their participation over the course of the intervention.

Assigning homework:

- Provides appropriate assignments to the parent to incorporate into daily/weekly routines with the child.
- Follows up with the parent regarding assignments.
- Able to help parents understand the value of consistency of interaction between sessions.

Dealing with resistance:

- Recognizes and manages countertransference appropriately.
- Provides support and empathy to the parent when resistance is present.
- Maintains the safety of the child in the presence of resistance. Does repair so that the child still feels in favor.

Generalizing:

- Assists parent to take Theraplay skills outside the session.
- Demonstrates willingness to explain the reasons underneath the activities to the parents in a supportive manner.
- Follows the protocol of having consistent contact with the parent as necessary and applicable.

Appropriate modifications for trauma history:

- Understands the effect of the child's trauma and related need for making appropriate accommodations.
- Understands the effect of the child's trauma on the parent.
- Understands the effect of the parent's history of trauma on their ability to parent effectively.

SELF-REFLECTION

Sessions demonstrate clinician's ability to integrate assessment materials:

- Session plans are related to assessment and identified intervention goals.
- Progression of sessions reflects progress towards goal achievement.

Seeks and utilizes supervision effectively and appropriately:

- Is eager to learn.
- Completes required forms and makes specific references to events as they occurred in session.
- Open to suggestions and recommendations of the supervisor.
- Demonstrates an ability to reflect on strengths and challenges within a session and learn from them.

Demonstrates growth across sessions:

- Is able to apply self-reflections to subsequent sessions.
- Integrates feedback of the supervisor in subsequent sessions and as relevant to other families.
- Makes specific references on the session supervision form pertaining to events that happened in their session.

For cohort participants only (the cohort route is when a small group of individuals receive supervision together):

- Actively participates in observations of fellow cohort members, i.e. demonstrates attentiveness to the presenter, asks relevant questions, provides feedback and reflections, is a supportive group member (offers encouraging comments, is willing to share knowledge outside cohort time, etc.).

OVERALL

- Demonstrates understanding of attachment and regulatory theory that underlies Theraplay intervention.
- Demonstrates understanding of the child's underlying physiologic or psychological motives rather than surface behaviors.

Research:

- Is up to date on relevant research in developmental sciences and Theraplay applications.
- Seeks information related to increasing their understanding of current brain, trauma and attachment research to support their work/practice.

Observes contraindications as appropriate:

- Demonstrates flexibility in approach to activities in response to sensory issues, trauma and resistance.

Resources

Chapter 17

What is Theraplay®? A Brief Guide for Parents[1]

---— **CHAPTER PLAN** ---—

This chapter will discuss the following areas:

Theraplay® dimensions

Structure

- Structure in Theraplay®
- Structure checklists
- What does structure look like when it's present?

Engagement

- Engagement in Theraplay®
- Engagement checklists
- What does engagement look like when it's present?

Nurture

- Nurture in Theraplay®
- Nurture checklists
- What does nurture look like when it's present?

Challenge

- Challenge in Theraplay®
- Challenge checklists
- What does challenge look like when it's present?

---

1 All of the checklists and charts in this chapter have been adapted from Norris and Rodwell (2017). The dimension summaries have been reproduced with the permission of The Theraplay Institute.

Keep a good balance between dimensions

This chapter provides a brief overview of Theraplay for use as a tool with parents. Each of the four dimensions is considered in turn with a brief description of the dimension and how it can be helpful. This is then followed by a checklist which could be completed with parents as an aid to discussion. Lastly, a table is provided which illustrates ordinary day-to-day behavior within the dimension.

Theraplay® dimensions

Structure: Safety, organization, regulation

Engagement: Connection, attunement, expansion of positive affect

Nurture: Regulation, secure base, worthiness

Challenge: Support exploration, growth and mastery, competence and confidence

Structure

In the infant-parent relationship: The adult helps the baby become physically regulated. Focus is on the body. Even play activities have a sequence and rhythm. Basic safety, caregiving and play routines set up predictable sequences of organized interaction.

Structure in Theraplay®

The adult is in charge, which leads to reassurance, safety, creation of order, and co-regulation. Teaches the child to be in control of self. Assures the child of order.

Benefits for the child

- Develops their sense of self-regulation and organization.

- Builds capacity to accept appropriate adult rules and limits.

- The child learns that adults are trustworthy and predictable.

- The child develops a strong sense of you as a parent.

Benefits for the parent

- Allows you to have more organized interactions with your child.

- Practice setting appropriate limits.

- Become a confident leader for your child.

- Learn to structure in ways that don't involve words or shouting.

- Stimulate your child at a level that they can handle.

- Communicate to the child: "I am in charge here so you can relax. You are safe with me because I will take good care of you."

Structure checklists
Child checklist

☐ Does your child accept it when you take the lead?

☐ Does your child seem to struggle to know what you want him to do?

☐ Does your child follow your lead (without fear or anxiety)?

☐ Does your child insist on doing things his own way?

☐ Does your child seem to end up being the one in charge?

☐ Do activities seem to end in chaos?

Parent checklist

☐ Do you think you provide a clear lead?

☐ Do you feel mainly in control of your family life?

☐ Do you rely a lot on rewards and threats to influence your child?

☐ Has family life become full of verbal commands or detailed negotiations?

☐ Do you sometimes find it difficult to set limits with your child?

☐ Do you sometimes feel that you could "lose it" with your child?

What does structure look like when it's present?

- You are providing clear guidance which fits with what your child needs and is able to do.

- Your child accepts and seems more relaxed when you take the lead.

Structure: Ordinary life and Theraplay activities

Age	Ordinary life example of adult-led structure	Theraplay activities to promote structure
Infant	Rocking, establishing wake-feed-sleep patterns, holding baby so he/she is comfortable	Mirroring; Patty-Cake; songs with a beginning, middle and end
Toddler	Holding hands to cross a road, saying no, setting routines, providing an age-appropriate environment	Bean Bag Drop; Blanket Run; Jump into My Arms; Play Dough Squeeze
Primary age	Sitting for meals, getting ready for school, joining with a group	Hand Stack; Pop the Bubble; Copy Funny Faces; Follow the Leader; Draw around Hands and Feet; Three-Legged Walk
Teen	Providing a predictable routine and meals, setting house rules, getting child out of bed	Cotton Ball Blow; Measuring; Eye Signals

Engagement

In the infant-parent relationship: The parent is attuned to the baby's state and responds in a way that helps the baby regulate and integrate physical and emotional states. The parent is focused on the baby in an exclusive way, providing sensitively timed soothing and delightful interactions.

Engagement in Theraplay®

The caregiver focuses on the child in an intensive and personal way using what the child says and does to maintain engagement. The child is enticed and drawn out.

Benefits for the child

- Allows the child to experience positive emotions with their parent.

- The child learns about relationships and develops interest in other people.

- The child feels wanted and loveable.

- The child understands that they are capable of interacting in healthy, appropriate ways with others.

Benefits for the parent

- Establish and maintain connection with your child.

- Focus intently on your child.

- Entice your child into enjoying new experiences.

- Have opportunities for playful give and take, which lead to you being able to effectively attune to your child.

- Become more aware of your child's emotional cues.

Engagement checklists
Child checklist

- ☐ Does your child seem to stop you from getting close?

- ☐ Does your child ignore or reject you?

- ☐ Does your child "act silly" when you try to get close or play?

- ☐ Does your child seem to get over-excited when you play together?

- ☐ Does your child find it difficult to attend to you when you play?

- ☐ Does your child seem too serious or find it difficult to relax and have fun?

Parent checklist

- ☐ Do you feel that there is too much distance between you and your child?

- ☐ Do you usually know what your child is feeling, or is it sometimes difficult to tell?

- ☐ Are you usually able to calm your child down when needed?

- ☐ Are you and your child able to be playful together?

- ☐ Do you find yourself becoming too serious or competitive when with your child?

- ☐ Do you find yourself trying too hard to connect with your child?

What does engagement look like when it's present?

- You have delightful "now" moments and genuine fun together.

- You and your child are able to be playful together while still getting things done.

- You are aware of your child's emotional state and you provide just what is needed.

- You are the one who is setting the emotional pace so that your child's feelings, such as excitement, do not become out of control.

- You and your child are "in sync."

Engagement: Ordinary life and Theraplay activities

Age	Ordinary life examples of adult-led engagement	Theraplay activities to promote engagement
Infant	Greeting the baby after a nap, friendly chat during dressing, rocking the baby, developing daily routines of wake-feed-sleep, holding the baby	Peek-a-Boo; Beep and Honk; Pop Cheeks; Hello, Goodbye
Toddler	Involving them with everyday activities in a playful way (being your helper), noticing how they are growing and all the things they can do, singing and playing games that involve changes in pace and surprise	This Little Pig Went to Market; Row, Row, Row Your Boat; Piggy-Back/Horsey-Back Ride; Hide and Seek; Blow Me Over
Primary age	Sharing experiences such as having a meal together, playing at the park, greeting the child after school, having fun together	Check-ups; variations of Hide and Seek; Hand-Clapping Games; Foil Prints; Sticker Match; Create a Special Handshake; Passing Funny Faces; Push Me Over, Pull Me Up; Decorate the Child—with feathers, stickers and face paint
Teen	Staying in touch during the day via phone calls, texts, SMS; noticing their clothes and changing styles; sharing jokes; spending relaxed time together	Mirroring; Passing Funny Faces; Create rhythms with cups; Make up a rap; Foil Prints; Manicure; Cotton Ball Hockey or Ping Pong Ball with straws

Nurture

In the infant-parent relationship: Activities are soothing, calming, quieting and reassuring. They make the world feel safe, predictable, warm, secure. The child develops the expectation that "people will take care of me" and "good things happen to me."

Nurture in Theraplay®

The caregiver meets the child's unfulfilled younger needs, helps the child relax and allows him or herself to be taken care of, and builds the inner working model that the child is lovable and valued.

Benefits for the child

- The child develops a secure base—confidence that they can turn to caring adults for comfort.

- The child feels safer accepting physical care from their parent.

- The child develops understanding that the world is a safe, secure place where their needs will be met.

- The child develops trust in other people.

- The child believes that they are worthy of good care.

- The child learns more about healthy touch and how to be gentle with and respectful of others.

Benefits for the parent

- Become more comfortable providing physical care to your child.

- Develop better understanding of your child's particular sensitivities to certain types of touch.

- Build trust with your child.

- Become more comfortable with touch and/or displaying affection.

Nurture checklists
Child checklist

☐ Does your child accept nurturing touch from you?

☐ Does your child seem to avoid letting you comfort him?

☐ Does your child try to take care of his own needs?

☐ Is your child overly clingy with you?

☐ Does your child seem to reject you?

☐ Is your child able to soothe himself?

☐ Is your child easy or hard to calm down when distressed?

☐ Does your child physically move away when you try to care for him?

☐ Is your child reluctant to share emotions of sadness, anger or hurt?

Parent checklist

☐ Do you feel comfortable with physical affection, such as cuddling your child?

☐ Can you tell when your child is becoming tense, distressed and in need of being calmed?

☐ Do you have a variety of ways to soothe and calm your child when he is distressed or tense?

☐ Is it easy or difficult to soothe your child?

☐ How do you show nurture to your child?

☐ Do you feel in a rush to make your child's hurt feelings go away?

What does nurture look like when it's present?

- You provide nurturing contact (such as touch, calm words and care) to your child, which he accepts.

- You and your child have moments of calmness together when you are able to take care of a need.

- You are able to soothe your child when he is distressed.

- Your child can come to you when he has a stressful problem without fearing that you will become angry or judgmental, or that you will begin to lecture him or try to quickly reassure him.

Nurture: Ordinary life and Theraplay activities

Age	Ordinary life example of adult-led nurture	Theraplay activities to promote nurture
Infant	Feeding, holding, cuddling, changing diapers, bathing and rocking	Feeding; Lullaby; Rocking; Special Kisses (with parent)
Toddler	Bathtime, toweling dry; feeding with a spoon; providing calm bedtime routine, reading stories	Caring for Hurts; Slippery Slip; Personalized Twinkle Song

Primary age	Singing with the child, lotion child after bathtime; playing "dress-up," styling the child's hair	Decorate the Child; Feather Match; Face Painting; Pass a Squeeze; Pizza Massage; Blanket Swing
Teen	Giving the child a manicure, styling hair, shopping for clothes together; giving a foot massage; sitting watching an enjoyable film together; sharing snacks	Lotion or Powder Prints; Playful snack sharing (Donut Challenge); Temporary Tattoos; Trace Messages; Weather Report

Challenge

Challenge in the infant-parent relationship: Activities that help the child extend him or herself a little bit, appropriate to the child's level of functioning. Also allows the child to master tension-arousing experiences.

Challenge in Theraplay®

Activities require a partnership and are not done alone. Encourage the child to take mild age-appropriate risk. Promote feelings of competence and confidence. Also used to redirect resistance.

Benefits for the child

- The child feels confident and competent.

- The child believes that he/she can safely explore and learn new things.

- The child learns to tolerate mild frustration.

- The child accepts and believes positive feedback.

Benefits for the parent

- Learn to collaborate with your child.

- Have fun with your child without becoming competitive.

- Build awareness of your child's triggers and how to prevent/address them in the moment.

Challenge checklists
Child checklist

- ☐ Does your child avoid or seem anxious when trying something new, even when it's really simple?

☐ Does she seem to always need to get things right or perfect?

☐ Does she cope well with frustration?

☐ Does she take risks? Can she slow down when things become too hard?

☐ Can she allow you to help her when she is finding things hard?

☐ Does she say she "can't do" things immediately, or the opposite, that she is the best, the fastest and knows everything?

Parent checklist

☐ Do you sometimes find it difficult knowing what your child can and cannot do?

☐ Does your child find it difficult to handle frustration? Can you find ways to help her?

☐ Do you find yourself being competitive or expecting too much of your child?

☐ Do you find it easy or hard to teach your child new things?

☐ Do you avoid challenging her because you worry about her reaction?

☐ Do you think you sometimes expect too much of her?

☐ Does your child seem very sensitive to failure? Are you able to find ways to help her try?

What does challenge look like when it's present?

- You can understand your child's abilities and the things she finds hard. You are usually able to predict the sorts of things and times when your child may need more support from you.

- You are good at knowing when your child begins to feel stressed and can find ways to help her.

- You can provide enough support for her so that she can focus and attend and have a feeling of something going well.

- You are able to make tasks fit "just right" by choosing something your child can do, and only adding in a little bit of newness (which you know she can do).

- You take pleasure in your child when she makes small steps, whether this is in doing an activity or learning something new in her relationship with you.

Challenge: Ordinary life and Theraplay activities

Age	Ordinary life example of adult-led challenge	Theraplay activity to promote challenge
Infant	Copying games with face and voice; gently moving the baby and bouncing her on a lap; encouraging her to sit or crawl to you	Wriggle in and out of arms
Toddler	Supporting the baby while she learns to walk, playing jumping or climbing games, holding her hand while she balances or walks along a short wall, helping her push her toy	Crawling Race; Red Light, Green Light; Pillow Push; Tug of War
Primary age	Holding her bicycle while she learns to ride; helping her down when she has gone too high; encouraging her when she tries new things	Balancing activities; Balance on Pillows, Jump Off; Feather Blow/Grab; Straight Face Challenge; Balloon Balance; Karate Chop
Teen	Supporting her in her hobbies and celebrating effort and success, noticing when she is finding something hard and finding ways to make the task more achievable for her	Balloon Tennis; Cotton Ball Hockey; Pick up Objects with Toes; Cotton Ball Ping Pong; Balancing Challenges; Newspaper Punch, Basket Toss; Cooperative Races; Thumb Wrestling; Tug of War; Arm Wrestling; Seed Spitting Contest

Keep a good balance between dimensions

It's important to find the right proportion for your unique child at each stage of life. Problems can happen with imbalance between dimensions:

- *Structure* alone does not show the child that he is lovable. Balance structure with nurture.

- *Engagement:* Children need opportunities for joyful play with their parents. Be confident to initiate, lead and structure the play.

- *Nurture* alone does not help children learn the importance of limits, structure, socialization and responsibility. Balance nurture with structure.

- *Challenge:* Meet the child where they are at developmentally; balance developmental challenge with meeting the child's younger (even infant) needs for nurture.

Chapter 18

Theraplay® and Sensory Regulation

─────────────────── CHAPTER PLAN ───────────────────

This chapter will discuss the following areas:

The senses

Some examples of how sensory difficulties impact on attachment relationships

What are the signs that the child is finding things difficult?

Theraplay adaptations®

- Theraplay® adaptations for an overactive child (more likely to go into flight/fight)
- Theraplay® adaptations with a withdrawn passive child (more likely to dissociate or freeze)
- Touch-defensive children
- Auditory processing difficulties
- Easily over-aroused/excited

Ideas around touch

- How does your child respond to touch?

───

This chapter focuses on the adaptations you might need to make in your Theraplay work when children have sensory regulation difficulties. This is summary information and you may need to seek specific specialist advice from a pediatric occupational therapist.

Some children can become overwhelmed by the intensity of interactions and stimulation around them, especially if they have sensory sensitivities. Theraplay is an intense way of working and some adaptations may therefore be needed. Sensory difficulties are common in children who have experienced complex trauma and have additional needs. You will need to monitor their state carefully as you work with them in Theraplay.

The following information will give you some ideas about useful Theraplay adaptations you might make, and two brief checklists about touch are included at the end. The main message is to be curious about:

- what the child may be experiencing

- what sensations they seek out or avoid

- what approaches seem to make things more manageable for them.

If the child has complex difficulties then it is advisable to seek assessment from a qualified pediatric occupational therapist.

When a child becomes overwhelmed within Theraplay, it may be that the intensity of the reciprocal interaction is too intense or that the child has specific sensory sensitivities—or a combination of both (because emotional intensity can activate sensory sensitivities).

Think about the child as having a cup that fills up with all of the sensory and emotional demands of the environment. When the cup is not completely full, the child's nervous system has the capacity to undertake certain tasks (e.g. they may be able to function at school during the morning). However, when they have reached the limit of their tolerance threshold, the cup is in effect overflowing. The child's regulatory state may change significantly (they may not be able to cope with school in the afternoon, for instance, or will explode as they arrive home). When the child is overwhelmed, their muscle tone will tend to drop and motor planning becomes more disorganized. Their arousal levels peak, meaning that they are more likely to be clumsy and uncoordinated, unable to concentrate and liable to emotional meltdowns.

If a child becomes dysregulated in a Theraplay session then it is important to try and work out what was happening before the dysregulated behavior occurred. Was there a lot of touch? Was the child already wobbly when they came into the sessions so that they were then unable to manage the demands of the interaction? Reviewing your video in detail is extremely useful.

The senses

It is helpful to have a basic understanding of sensory regulation and the ways in which an individual's sensory perception can vary.

There are seven main senses: *tactile* (touch), *auditory* (hearing), *taste* and *smell*, *visual* (seeing), *proprioceptive* and *vestibular*. The first five are familiar, but proprioceptive and vestibular systems may be less familiar and there is a further sense, interoception, which is about recognizing how you feel inside (e.g. whether your tummy or bladder are full).

Proprioceptive: Our proprioceptive system makes us aware of our body position and movement, telling us where and what our muscles and joints are doing. This, in turn, helps us to make sense of where we are in the world and our sense of internal self. It is essential for everyday activities such as balance and fine motor skills. This sensory system also helps us feel calm and regulated.

Vestibular: This is our balance and movement system. It helps to keep us balanced, hold us upright against gravity and use both sides of our body, and gives us a physical and emotional sense of where we are in the world. Our vestibular system coordinates movements of the head and eyes, helps us feel the direction and speed of movement and links to auditory processing and regulation.

Sensory integration: When sensations flow in a well-organized manner, the brain can use those sensations to form perceptions, behaviors and learning. When the flow of sensations is disorganized, life can be like a rush-hour traffic jam (Ayres, 2005).

Sensory processing difficulties: These link to a wide range of difficulties in engaging with others and making and sustaining relationships. Sensory processing difficulties impact the following: attachment relationships; sensory sensitivities such as difficulties with touch, smell and sounds; issues with eating and knowing when you are full up; difficulties with toileting, including constipation, soiling, enuresis and frequently needing the toilet; difficulties with attention and regulation; and difficulties with settling to sleep and staying asleep.

Your senses need to be in a state of equilibrium in order to feel balanced, calm, alert, open to experiences and open to relationships. When senses are out of balance, then we can feel "off kilter," overwhelmed and frightened. Sensory processing difficulties can arise due to a wide range of issues (including genetics, illness, medical intervention and early years trauma). Children who have a history of separation, loss, abuse and neglect are more likely to present with a combination of sensory processing and attachment difficulties, and this can result in the child interpreting sensations differently (Bhreathnach, 2013).

Some examples of how sensory difficulties impact on attachment relationships

- Touch can be interpreted as a hurt.

- Sleep difficulties impact the child in all areas.

- Hypervigilance and fear of sensations may be overwhelming, i.e. too much sound, unpredictable movement. This can make being in busy places very difficult and the child becomes overwhelmed.

- Excitement can quickly turn to hyperarousal and lashing out/meltdown.

- Too much talking and auditory information can overwhelm the child and they can disassociate.

- Hypervigilance and fear shut down memory and language centers.

- The child can appear clumsy and break and bump into things. This can be a result of an overloaded nervous system and/or visual perception and motor planning difficulties.

The child's response to sensory sensations can depend on the environment and the emotional context. The trigger can be the attachment relationship if the child has experienced a frightening experience of caregiving in the past. Consequently, the child can respond to different situations with different people and places in a variety of ways.

What are the signs that the child is finding things difficult?

- Reluctance to engage.

- Making noises—sneezing, burping, farting, chewing.

- Avoiding activities—can't, not won't.

- Running off, lashing out, throwing things.

- "Switching off"—shutdown.

- Drop in muscle tone—child may look floppy/clumsy or fall over.

- Widening eyes—muscle tone becomes more tense.

- Falling asleep (after the session) or collapse.

Also look for signs of miscuing. Some children may seem to indicate they are enjoying an activity but you may see elements of the above.

Theraplay® adaptations

The guidance below is adapted with permission from Jennie Forsyth, who is a certified Theraplay practitioner and has undertaken sensory attachment intervention training and supervision with Eadaoin Bhreathnach.

Theraplay® adaptations for an overactive child (more likely to go into flight/fight)

Aim to provide activities that help to down-regulate the child. Here are some suggestions:

- Activities need to include something "heavy" to provide proprioceptive feedback (e.g. balloons may reactivate the child because they are too light, but bean bags will work better).

- Use linear movements (e.g. Blanket Swing) as these movements are calming.

- If the child is getting too over-excited/activated, try a regulating snack (a drink with a straw and crunchy or chewy food) followed by some heavy work activities (e.g. balancing pillows on feet) or activities that provide proprioceptive input (pillow sandwich).

- Listen to crunches (chips and carrots work well).

- Try to avoid activities that include lots of unregulated blowing (blowing a cotton ball, feather, bubbles, etc.).

- Deep, controlled blowing like blowing bubbles and catching them on a wand can be regulating.

- Hot Potato/Cold Potato with bean bags (not a hard ball—the child may be inclined to get over-excited and throw things).

- Make shapes under the blanket with the parent (being under a blanket helps as it blocks out stimulation).

- Crawl under blanket to the parent.

- Weather Report (deep pressure—not light, tickly touch).

- Activities which are exciting and more floor based are "grounding," such as Cotton Ball Blow on tummy and Whose Toes Did I Touch?

Theraplay® adaptations with a withdrawn passive child (more likely to dissociate or freeze)

Aim to provide activities that activate the sensory systems to increase levels of engagement, energy and motivation. Activities need to include elements of movement to decrease inhibition, flat affect and low engagement. For example:

- Blanket Ball Roll (rough sea, calm waters)
- Jump into My Arms
- Motor Boat
- Pirate Song (more active version of Row, Row, Row Your Boat)
- La La Magnets
- Hokey Pokey
- Balloon Tennis
- Cotton Ball Hockey
- Magic Carpet Ride.

Touch-defensive children

- Touch needs to be built up gradually with children who exhibit a trauma-triggered response.
- Try doing a wheelbarrow into the room or a crawling game, or ask them to squeeze or find pegs in high resistance theraputty, before introducing touch to the session. By providing deep pressure to the hands, this will dampen down this sensation and increase tolerance levels. Focus on firm touch—take care during the check-up not to overdo touch.
- Try decorating a cushion or ball with feathers or stickers if the child can not tolerate physical contact.

Auditory processing difficulties

- Keep talking to a minimum and provide clear direction (i.e. "Let's do..."). Use high structure and song to help clarify meaning, such as the Goodbye Song to signal the session has come to an end.

- Be aware that the child may be unsure where the source of the sound is coming from (discrimination difficulty), which may reactivate a trauma-triggered response.

Easily over-aroused/excited

- Keep activities involving lots of free movement and blowing to a minimum.

- Alternate fast and slow activities as these children often want to move, so you will need to offer this to keep them engaged, but too much movement will send them over the top.

- Be careful with games that include throwing.

- Use rhythmic, linear movements rather than spinning as this will excite the child's nervous system even more.

- Music and rhythm help.

Ideas around touch

Healthy touch is essential for healthy development. Within the Theraplay approach, healthy touch is used as a natural part of many activities. Most children will enjoy this and the feeling of closeness and connection it brings. For some children, however, touch can be difficult.

Within Theraplay sessions, you might find that some ways of using touch work better than others and it is important to understand how the child's sensory system is functioning as far as you are able. General guidance is to try keeping touch practical and a natural part of an activity. Observe carefully, keep calm and clear, avoid tickling and teasing and seek specialist advice when needed. The core message from Theraplay is that touch always needs to be kind and safe and should always be for the benefit of the child.

The following brief checklists (Norris and Rodwell, 2017, p.52) could be completed with parents to deepen your understanding about the child's sensitivity to touch. If there are complex issues, seek guidance from a pediatric occupational therapist.

How does your child respond to touch?
Child under-responsive to touch
Touch checklist:

- ☐ Your child can't tell if her face and/or hands are dirty.

- ☐ Your child hugs too hard and often breaks things, like pencils, by pressing too hard.

- ☐ Your child chews or mouths everything, like cuffs and collars on her clothes.

- ☐ Your child constantly touches people and things.

- ☐ Your child drops objects frequently.

- ☐ Your child likes to be barefoot.

If you ticked these then your child may be under-responsive to touch. This means she can't feel things very well and may have to touch more, press hard or push herself against things, to feel that they are there.

Child over-responsive/sensitive to touch
Touch checklist:

- ☐ Your child hates being tickled or cuddled.

- ☐ Your child gets annoyed if somebody "accidentally" touches her.

- ☐ Your child doesn't like having her hair washed or brushed.

- ☐ Your child avoids messy play and doesn't like having things like paint and sand on her hands.

- ☐ Your child is fussy about the texture of her clothes and dislikes labels.

If you ticked these then your child may be over-responsive to light touch. This means that she is very sensitive to touch and it may be painful for her and she reacts to small things as they make her anxious. It may mean that lots of things, like people brushing up against her or being in noisy and busy places, will be hard.

Chapter 19

Sample Session Plans for Different Types of Clients

CHAPTER PLAN

This chapter will discuss the following areas:

Activities focusing on the child

Activities focusing on the parent's issues

When you plan a session, you take a range of factors into account: the child's developmental and chronological age, the issues that they may be having difficulty with, their attitude towards the Theraplay and the corresponding issues regarding their parents. The following examples provide some ideas of the kinds of activities that typically work well in different contexts. In line with the standard sequence of activities, we have included an entrance, check-up, selection of potential goal-directed activities, nurture element and exit. You might not need this number of activities within one session but we wanted to provide a wide choice of activities. Before each session, make an individualized plan for each session specific to the child and your aims.

Activities focusing on the child

For a young child with early trauma who runs around the room/squirms/kicks	
Entrance	Come in holding hands counting 1, 2, 3 Weeeee, or Magic Carpet Ride, Piggy-Back/Horsey-Back Ride—with giddyup and whoooaaa horsey
Check-in	Push Me Over, Land On My Knees (introduce by saying "Did you bring your strong arms? Let me check! See if you can push me over")

cont.

For a young child with early trauma who runs around the room/squirms/kicks	
Possible goal-directed activities	Preparing Pizza Burrito Sushi Roll Cotton Ball Hockey on tummies Hide and Seek (done very calmly and with firm touch) Run to Mommy or Daddy Under the Blanket
Nurture activities	Blanket Swing Feeding Read rhythmic story
Exit	Shoe and Sock Race Go out holding hands counting 1, 2, 3 Weeeee

For a withdrawn/passive/overly compliant child who is frightened	
Entrance	Guess how many steps it will take him to get to seat and then count
Check-in	Counting Fingers/Toes Foil Prints on distal parts of body: bottom of shoe, hand, knee, fist (foil prints can be used as a check-in because you can say "I see you brought your knee, your hand, etc. Let's see if we can make a picture of your hand!")
Possible goal-directed activities	Bean Bag Drop Powder Print—of hands or feet on black felt Paper Toss Feather Pass Hand Stack
Nurture activities	Measuring—with fruit by the foot/licorice string Create a Special Handshake
Exit	Shoe and Sock Race How Many Big Steps?

For a sullen teenager who thinks everything is stupid	
Entrance	Walk in keeping the balloon up, soccer style, i.e. no hands or arms
Check-in (focus on Challenge dimension)	Newspaper Punch, Basket Toss Stupid human tricks (tongue to nose, wiggle ears, flair nostrils, crack knuckles, burp on command, double-jointed, roll tongue, cross eyes, funny accents)
Possible goal-directed activities (Engagement first, then Nurture)	Cotton Ball, Marshmallow, or Newspaper Ball Fight Feeding Alternatives Bubble Tennis
Nurture activities	Foil Prints—of cool things like bottom of shoe, fist, head Lotion Prints—using "cool" lotion like Tommy Hilfiger or Bath & Body Works
Exit	Special Handshake

For a child with major sensory (proprioceptive and vestibular) needs	
Entrance	Piggy-Back/Horsey-Back Ride—with giddyup and whoooaaa horsey
Check-in	Measuring—against wall in different ways: stretched arm really tall, tippy toes, standing on head
Possible goal-directed activities (Structure, focus on regulation)	Push Me Over Row, Row, Row Your Boat Balance pillows on feet and then throw them off on count of three Stand on Pillows, Jump Off—on three Crawling Race Pillow Sandwich
Nurture activities	Blanket Swing Washing Machine Weather Report Twinkle Song
Exit	Shoe and Sock Race Piggy-Back Ride

For a child with early deprivation who needs early engagement experiences	
Entrance	1, 2, 3 Weeeee
Check-in	Counting Fingers/Toes Caring for Hurts or Lotion Prints
Possible goal-directed activities (Engagement, Nurture, Structure)	This Little Pig Went to Market Patty-Cake Peek-a-Boo Bean Bag Drop Pop Cheeks Push Me Over Row, Row, Row Your Boat Hide and Seek Crawling Race
Nurture activities	Special Delivery Feeding Twinkle Song
Exit	Shoe and Sock Race Wheelbarrow—out of the room

For a child who is out of control and acting in a silly/chaotic manner	
Entrance	Magic Carpet Ride—into the room
Check-in	Cotton Ball Hockey on tummies Foil Prints—with aluminum
Possible goal-directed activities (Structure, focus on regulation)	Pillow Sandwich Weather Report—but with a blanket on top of child Burrito/Sushi Roll Build a Fort
Nurture activities	Feeding
Exit	Twinkle Song or humming a song

Activities focusing on the parent's issues

For a parent who is competitive, focused on rules, harsh, authoritarian	
Entrance	Walk in holding hands together taking big steps or jumping child in
Check-in	Special Handshake
Possible goal-directed activities	Powder Prints Passing Funny Faces Pop bubbles together simultaneously (practitioner blows the bubbles) Feather Pass Foil Prints
Nurture activities	Measuring each one of their body parts with licorice or fruit by the foot Weather Report (practitioner does this)
Exit	Walk out holding hands together taking big steps

For a parent who is developmentally delayed, immature or has very weak executive functioning	
Entrance	Big steps walking into the room
Check-in	Lotion or Powder Hand Prints—both parent and child
Possible goal-directed activities (Engagement, Nurture, practitioner providing Structure for both child and parent)	Feather Pass—in a circle with practitioner Passing Funny Faces—in a circle with practitioner Pop the Bubble—with practitioner blowing and parent and child popping together Ring-Around-a-Rosy or Hokey Pokey
Nurture activities	Feeding
Exit	Big steps walking out of the room

Chapter 20

Including Reflective Dialogue in Theraplay®

This chapter will discuss the following areas:

Child is too dysregulated, distressed or angry at the outset of a session

Child overtly tells you a distressing feeling in response to a Theraplay® activity or a Theraplay® activity activates some memory, worry or reaction that needs to be addressed

Child has trauma that is triggered over the course of the week and goes into dissociation or other trauma states

Child gets particularly activated during a certain activity and recalls a non-conscious memory

Parent tells you they did something they regret and they want help talking about it with the child and making a repair

As Theraplay is principally non-verbal, we discourage engaging in conversation during sessions. There are, however, some exceptions and this chapter considers the kinds of situations in which it would be helpful to talk within a Theraplay session.

Practice question:

- When is it actually okay (and even clinically imperative) to talk about issues from the past in Theraplay?

Theraplay is an experiential, physiological, relational modality that stays in the here and now and doesn't rely on words. The basic Theraplay training instructs new practitioners to, at most, acknowledge a feeling or a phenomenon but then find a response within the Theraplay activities to accommodate or respond to that feeling state. The goal is to find a non-verbal way to communicate with the child: "I acknowledge and accept that feeling and I want to make you feel comfortable and show you I can still stay connected to you in whatever feeling you have." But some clients need more than that. Their needs do not present in a linear manner and they may express important themes that it would be insensitive to ignore. We therefore need to consider in what circumstance some additional comments may be useful. This might be: integrating thoughts and feelings, making sense of their narrative, helping them communicate or make meaning of their feelings, making their feelings explicit and providing acknowledgement of those feelings. This chapter provides some scenarios where meaning-making using words may be helpful within a Theraplay session. As we want to emphasize the role of the practitioner here, these scenarios are written using the first person, as if we are in the room with them.

Child is too dysregulated, distressed or angry at the outset of a session

A child comes in so angry that they find any attempt to play or receive nurture a dismissal or provocation of their feelings. For example, a 12-year-old boy came in in a foul and negative mood after having a violent tantrum in the car because he and his mother didn't have time to stop and buy sweets. This boy has regulation issues due to toxic shame. I had set up the Cotton Ball Fight game but the boy was angry, shut down and awash with shame. He hid under the hood of his sweatshirt and we let him be. I spoke to his mother in a prosodic voice about him, saying how it was stressful to keep things together, that he was trying hard all week and then he just exploded, and that he wondered himself why he did it. I wondered aloud whether it may have even scared him that his reaction was so over the top considering he can also be flexible and cooperative at times. It took about 15–20 minutes before the boy was able to peek out from under his hood and accept a drink and begin to interact.

Child overtly tells you a distressing feeling in response to a Theraplay® activity or a Theraplay® activity activates some memory, worry or reaction that needs to be addressed

Eight-year-old Ali had scratched her own arm on purpose after being reprimanded for hurting a child on the playground. Several weeks later I was doing the Caring for Hurts activity, and when we got to the still-healing scratch on her arm, Ali sighed painfully and said, "I don't think that will ever go away." The comment was so laden with painful affect that it was begging to be addressed. So I responded, "Oh, if it never goes away, then you'll always have a reminder there?" "Yeah, it will remind me that I did something bad." We continued the conversation for ten minutes and, with my help, Ali expressed that she felt guilty that she scratched herself, primarily because she felt her mother was worried about her. Ali's mother tried to reassure Ali that she didn't need to worry about worrying her, so I helped the mother just to give empathy and acceptance for Ali's feelings instead of reassurance. This helped Ali to feel more heard by her mother.

Child has trauma that is triggered over the course of the week and goes into dissociation or other trauma states

The parent informs you that something very painful, scary or difficult happened over the course of the week. For example, 12-year-old Adam told his adoptive mother that the only reason she adopted him was so she could be mean to him after his mother didn't let him have a friend over at 9 in the evening. I brought that up towards the end of the session after we had finished the snack, trying to keep my tone curious rather than serious. I asked him if he knew why he sometimes felt that way. Adam couldn't think of a reason or perhaps did not wish to say anything, so I asked permission to take some guesses. Adam agreed, so I guessed, with a curious tone, about whether he sometimes felt that when his mother said no, it felt as if she didn't care about him. Adam nodded in agreement and I normalized this feeling. I helped Adam to understand that, considering his difficult upbringing of being neglected, it sometimes felt terrible and very angering if his adoptive mother said no. I then helped Adam to tell his mother his hard feelings by speaking for him, and his adoptive mother gave him empathy around his hard history.

Child gets particularly activated during a certain activity and recalls a non-conscious memory

This scenario integrates autobiographical narrative. For example, 4-year-old Anna, who was adopted from a foreign orphanage at the age of 1, said she was cold in the session but refused to take any one of the three blankets I had in the office. Earlier in the day, she also said she was hungry but refused any of the dishes her adoptive mother offered. As Anna sat on the couch, she shivered and curled up in a little ball. I guessed that she was trying to show us that she was sad inside because there was a part of her that was still cold and hungry from the orphanage. We had a very productive dialogue of about 15 minutes, wherein Anna listened intently as her mother and I resonated with the sadness, loneliness and fear she must have felt in the orphanage, and that she may wonder sometimes why her adoptive mother didn't come sooner. Her adoptive mother was able to tell Anna how she wished she could have been there at the orphanage to feed her, hold her and keep her warm.

Parent tells you they did something they regret and they want help talking about it with the child and making a repair

An adoptive parent shouted and punished his 11-year-old, Matthew, for sneaking into his sister's bed at night because he was scared to sleep alone. This was despite the fact that Matthew had been abused and neglected until the age of 4 and had many legitimate reasons to be fearful at night. His father had also refused to accompany his son at bedtime to do the comforting bedtime ritual that I had recommended. First, I invited Matthew to say how he felt scared to go up to bed alone and that he was afraid that if he came back down to ask his father for help, his father would have shouted at him. Then I helped the father make some empathic statements like "I can understand that you were scared and it would make sense for you to be scared. I am sorry that I didn't listen to you the first time when you said you didn't want to go to sleep by yourself."

A useful way to conduct these types of conversations is through affective/ reflective dialogue, a concept from dyadic developmental psychotherapy (DDP). DDP (Hughes, 2011a; Golding and Hughes, 2012; Hughes, Golding and Hudson, 2019) relies on many of the same theoretical foundations and concepts as Theraplay and is extremely helpful when combined with Theraplay. The two form the basis for our clinical work.

Chapter 21

What Lies Underneath a Parent's Defensive Statement

CHAPTER PLAN

This chapter will discuss the following areas:

The parent angrily states: "Are you blaming me?"

The parent states: "She just needs to listen!"

The parent states: "How I was raised has nothing to do with this!"

The parent states: "He just needs some medicine!"

The parent asserts: "It's none of your business!"

The parent states: "You don't believe me!"

The parent states: "I was raised this way and I'm okay!"

The parent asks: "Are you saying to just let him do it?"

The parent asks: "How many kids do you have? Do you have adopted kids?"

The parent asks: "Why do I have to do all the changing?"

The parent states: "He needs to learn to respect his parents!"

The parent asks: "How will playing help?"

The parent states: "I can't play/I can't nurture"

The parent states: "My child is manipulating you!"

There are some common statements that parents make in parent meetings that warrant further exploration. This chapter considers some of the possible themes that lie underneath a defensive or self-protective statement and some possible responses. The most useful responses to help parents feel safe are based on Acceptance, Curiosity and Empathy (Hughes *et al.*, 2019).

Keep in mind:

- this is not the time for psycho-education

- make your empathic response come to life so they can feel that you really believe them.

The parent angrily states: "Are you blaming me?"

They may feel:

- responsible for their child's problems

- inadequate

- powerless and ashamed

- that they are supposed to know how to be parents and they are failing—they feel like a failure

- fearful that they hurt their child along the way by doing the wrong thing.

Potential response: Acceptance and empathy—"Thank you so much for telling me that you're worried I'm blaming you. That must feel very hard when you've come for some help. That is not what I think. I think you have been, and are, doing so much. You've doing the very best that you can."

The parent states: "She just needs to listen!"

They may feel:

- helpless/powerlesss/out of control. "I'm the adult/parent and she didn't do it… I don't know what to do! If she doesn't comply, what's going to come next?"

- personally rejected. "My child is rejecting me and the values that are important to me"

- fearful for their child. "I tell you what to do to keep you safe. How can I keep you safe if you don't listen?"

- a failure as a parent. "The world sees me as a bad parent"

- terror and be experiencing the reality that they are not in control. "I can't control the world for my kid or myself."

Potential response: Help the parent grapple with the reality that they do not have control, provide them with emotional support and direct them towards self-care.

The parent states: "How I was raised has nothing to do with this!"

They may feel:

- desperation. "No one understands the real problem and no one can help"

- fearful. They may be in touch with their own real pain that happened in their childhood and fear that this is being transferred in some way to their child

- defensive and need to protect their family of origin. However much they may have been mistreated, there is a deep need to protect one's parents from judgment.

Potential response: Empathy and curiosity—"Just being able to understand what you're bringing to the table can be so helpful. Help me to understand your reactions so that together we can help your child. You come from an important place and I just want to learn more about that."

The parent states: "He just needs some medicine!"

They may feel:

- hopelessness

- and hope that if it's all biological, "then that explains why none of what I have done/will do will work and neither is it my fault"

- exhausted/depleted and as though they haven't been able to help or influence the situation at all. The implication is they have nothing to do with this, but what is actually being said is: "I have everything to do with this because I can't make it better."

Potential response: "You've tried so hard and he has been so resistant to change. I wish there was a magic bullet too. I want to help find all the answers and turn over every rock. But I do think that even if medication would help, your interventions at home also will make a difference."

The parent asserts: "It's none of your business!"

They may be:

- experiencing shame.

Potential response: "Thanks for telling me, you don't want to go there, to think about things that happened in your childhood. We are going to try to find a way to work together. My concern is that if you aren't able to tell me what you're feeling and thinking about, it will only go a certain distance and there will still be work we are missing out on. At the same time, I really appreciate and respect that you're telling me not to go there."

The parent states: "You don't believe me!"

They may feel:

- lonely and isolated

- a failure and full of shame

- a lack of trust in you.

Potential response: "You have been all alone with this and people haven't been listening to you along the way. That has been so hard. But you have kept going on because you are dedicated to your child and I see that. I'm sorry if something I said made you feel as if I don't believe you."

The parent states: "I was raised this way and I'm okay!"

They may be:

- worried that maybe something is wrong with them and that's why the problems have happened.

Potential response: "Thanks for telling me. The way you have been raised and the way you have been operating has made you the person you are today. You are a strong person. You have learned to get things done and soldier on in the face of adversity. I think that's really admirable. I'm guessing that's what you want for your child too. I'm guessing you would like to instill that in him to give him a leg up in this world. (You are showing the parent that you can see their good intention.) Here's my concern, I'm worried that there is a price you had to pay for that upbringing. It seems as though maybe you paid a price? Like feeling lonely? Or not loveable? Or finding relationships difficult? You're hard on yourself, and if there is conflict you retreat. I'm wondering if your child may need something different."

The parent asks: "Are you saying to just let him do it?"

They may feel:

- hopelessness. "This is how it's going to be and I'm going to have to live like this forever"

- a lack of control.

Potential response: "Oh, I apologize. I don't think it's okay for him to mistreat you. Part of what I think is going on for him, when he gets into that mode, is that he has an explosion and he isn't actually aware of his response. (Take care as this could feel to the parent like siding with the child.) Thanks so much for telling me that. I am concerned and want to make your life better. I hear your desperation and am going to be working on that with you. At the same time, if we can't figure out what the underlying issue is, we are going to be doing the same thing over and over again."

The parent asks: "How many kids do you have? Do you have adopted kids?"

They may feel:

- hopelessness. "You don't understand me. And if you don't understand me, then no one will understand me and no one will be able to help me."

Potential response: "You are right that I don't have the same experience. But I have professional experience that might help you a little. More important, however, is that I really want to get to know your experience so that I can help you better. Would you help me just a little bit to understand what it's been like for you?"

The parent asks: "Why do I have to do all the changing?"

They may be:

- completely exhausted.

Potential response: "You don't have to change if you don't want to. I do certainly hear where you are coming from. You're the one who's been doing this for so long (fighting with social workers, school, doctor, etc.) and you're the one who is being asked to change. That must be exhausting. Of course, you're exhausted.

Is there anything that could help take the burden off of you so that you could make more space for your own feelings/needs?" (Explore more help from spouse, friends, respite, self-care, etc.)

The parent states: "He needs to learn to respect his parents!"

They may feel:

- afraid of what will happen to the child if he doesn't respect authority. Jail? End up dead?

- affronted by the child's audacity because they were very afraid of their own parents. Or they are worried that the child will be hurt like they were

- triggered by their child. The child's behavior evokes responses similar to their own authoritarian parents and they are uncomfortable with that. Perhaps they vowed they wouldn't be like their parents.

Potential response: Ask parents, "If he doesn't learn to respect his parents, then what will happen?" (What are they afraid of? Once you uncover their deeper fears, deal with those.)

The parent asks: "How will playing help?"

They may:

- have no experience themselves of playing as a child, so they can't get in touch with the positive results that could come from playing

- fear that you are not taking their worries/concerns seriously

- feel you don't understand how grave their situation is

- be so hurt and they want the child to feel the consequences of the pain he has caused.

Potential response: Explore with curiosity which one of the above resonates most with the parent. Then provide acceptance and empathy.

The parent states: "I can't play/I can't nurture"

They may have:

- a fear of feelings. They feel dead inside

- a fear of being ridiculed and of being out of control

- been traumatized as a child. Play or nurture may be associated in their mind with negative things happening.

Potential response: With curiosity, explore the experience and meaning of play for the parent (as a child) and give empathy. After understanding their fear, consider modifications that may feel more comfortable for the parent.

The parent states: "My child is manipulating you!"
They may feel:

- afraid or out of control. If the practitioner is being duped, then nothing is going to get better

- shame. They have been manipulated by the child and now can't tolerate the thought that they are witnessing it/letting it happen.

Potential response: Acceptance—"Thanks for telling me. Yes, it can feel very mixed up to work with him." Curiosity—"Is that how that feels/felt for you raising him? Are you worried that I'm too gullible or inexperienced to help you? If so, no wonder you're worried."

Chapter 22

Intake Guidelines

This chapter will discuss the following area:

Framework for intake session

- What is the primary reason/problem for which you are seeking intervention at this time?
- Developmental history
- Questions related to the dimensions

This chapter provides a suitable framework for structuring your intake session. The intake session usually includes a combination of history taking and exploration of the parent's perception of the child's difficulties (included here) alongside some reflection, at the end of the intake session, on what Theraplay may have to offer and what the next steps might be in the process.

Framework for intake session
What is the primary reason/problem for which you are seeking intervention at this time?

- Does your husband/wife/partner agree with how you view the problem?
- How does the school/physician view it?
- When did you first became aware of the problem?
- Why do you think your child is behaving in this way?
- Why are you coming for help now?
- Is your child in any other type of therapy (occupational, speech, developmental, physical)?

Developmental history

Please include any information about your child's in-utero experience, birth, early infancy.

If you child is fostered/adopted, please give *all* of your child's placement history, including any details, no matter how small. Do you know anything about the child's birth relatives?

If your child is adopted, how old was your child when he/she first came to live with you? How were his/her eating, sleeping, toileting behaviors in the first year the child was with you?

- Milestones: walking, talking and so on. Toilet training: time, method and attitude.

- Medical history: hospitalizations, illnesses, medications, evaluations, hearing and vision status.

- Disruptions: losses, absences and so on. Problems with separation. Other caretakers, day care, preschool, school experiences.

- Siblings: names, number, position in family, reaction to birth of siblings, current relationships.

Questions related to the dimensions

Structure:

- How do feel about your role in keeping up with the daily routines?

- Do you have clear routines?

- What are the easiest/most difficult things in keeping up with these daily activities—transitions, mealtimes, bedtimes and so on?

Engagement:

- Do you usually know what your child is feeling in a particular situation?

- What makes your child happy?

- What do you enjoy most about being a parent to this child?

- How do you play with your child?

Nurture:

- Does your child show you when he/she is hurt, upset?

- Can you usually help your child calm down when he/she is upset?

- Do you like holding/soothing/cuddling your child?

- If not, what do you think is difficult about it?

- How do you show your child that you care about him/her?

Challenge:

- Do you enjoy teaching your child new things?

- How do you feel (or what do you think) about your role in teaching your child new things?

- Is it easy to know what your child already knows and what not?

- How do you feel about saying no/setting limits to your child?

Conclusion: What are your hopes for your child in the future?

Chapter 23

List of Theraplay® Activities

This chapter includes the up-to-date list of Theraplay activities for dyadic Theraplay. In addition to the 115 from the third edition of *Theraplay: Helping Parents and Children Build Better Relationships Through Attachment Based Play* (Booth and Jernberg, 2010), there are 46 new activities. The activities are organized alphabetically by the Theraplay dimensions: Structure, Engagement, Nurture and Challenge.

Each activity has also been given a suggested appropriate age level:

Young: Chronologically or developmentally young, for example one to three years.

All ages: All ages with appropriate modifications up or down.

Older: Chronologically or developmentally older, for example 8–15 years.

A few activities at the end of each dimension are especially suitable for use with a group of three or more participants, for example when parents enter the session or when more than one child is present. Depending on the way an activity is carried out, it may fit more than one dimension, for example Hand Clapping Games are both engaging and structuring. Many games enjoyed by young children throughout the world (not listed here) can also be adapted and used in sessions with children of all ages. Activities for very young children must be within their physical ability and must make sense to them. Simple activities can be adapted to make them more challenging or more interesting to older children. In order to encourage give and take and extend the child's attention span, you or the parents can take turns with the child and vary the activity whenever possible. Most activities can be adapted for children and parents with physical disabilities.

STRUCTURE

The purpose of structuring activities is to organize and regulate the child's experience. The adult sets limits, defines body boundaries, keeps the child safe and helps to complete sequences of activities.

A word about signals: using signals for when to start will increase the structure in any activity. Start with simple signals, such as "One, two, three, go" or "Ready, steady, go." Advance to more complicated signals, such as listening for a selected word in a series, or watching for a visual signal like a wink or other facial movement. Signals should not be used for every activity as they can slow down the pace or become too predictable and they may take away from the lighthearted tone you want at a particular moment.

Add to It
Older

The adults and child sit in a circle. Start with a simple action, like a wink or a high five. The next player copies that action, then adds to it and so on around the circle. Once everyone has added to the sequence, another person in the circle gets to start the chain of actions again.

Bean Bag Drop
Young

Place a bean bag or soft toy on your own head, put your hands under the child's outstretched hands, give a signal and drop the bean bag into the child's hands by tilting your head towards the child. Take turns. Variations: for a child who cannot catch well, take his hands in yours and bring all four hands together to catch the bean bag. You can also open your hands to let the bean bag fall through.

Blanket Ball Roll
All ages

All members hold tightly to the edges of a blanket. Place a ball in the center and call out which person the group should roll the ball to next.

Cotton Ball Blow
All ages

You and the child hold a scarf or long piece of cloth between you. Place a cotton ball at one end of the scarf and blow it back and forth to the child. An alternative is to place the cotton ball in your cupped hands and blow the ball into the child's hands. Another alternative is to fold up the long sides of a piece of foil (as long as the child's arm or leg) and blow the cotton ball back and forth on the foil tray.

Cotton Ball Hockey
All ages

Lie on the floor on your tummies facing each other (or sit with a pillow between you). Blow cotton balls back and forth trying to get the cotton ball under your partner's arms or off the edge of the pillow. Or cooperate and both blow hard enough to keep the ball in the middle. Make it less competitive but increase the complexity by specifying how many blows can be used to get the ball across the pillow—one blow is easy, but two or three are harder to control.

Count the Squeezes
All ages

The adult and child sit facing each other. The adult holds the child's hands gently and asks her to count the squeezes. Make it more challenging by having the child close her eyes. Another version is for the adult to give a certain number or pattern of squeezes and ask the child to copy the pattern back to them. Make it more challenging by crossing arms before holding hands.

Drawing Around Hands, Feet or Bodies
All ages

Make a picture of the child's hand or foot by drawing it on a piece of paper. Be sure to check on the child's reaction by looking at his face periodically. Full body drawings require the child to lie still for some time and are therefore more challenging and may make the child feel vulnerable; wait to do this until later in the intervention when trust has been established. Be sure to maintain verbal contact with the child as you draw; for example, "I'm coming to your ankle; I'm coming to the tickle spot under your arm."

Eye Signals
Older

Hold hands and stand facing each other. Use eye signals to indicate direction and number of steps to take, for example when you wink your left eye two times, both you and the child take two side steps to your left. If winking is difficult, tilt the head or purse the lips to the left and right. To make it more challenging, add signals for forward and backward movement as well (head back for backward, head forward for forward). You can hold a balloon or a pillow between you by leaning close to each other as you move.

Floating Arms
Young

The child and adult sit on the floor (or chair) both facing outward. Have the child relax into the adult, as if in an easy chair. The child's arms are placed on top of the adult's arms. The adult moves their arms up and down, side to side and in small circles carrying the child's arms along for the ride.

Guess the Steps
All ages
Each player tries to guess how many heel-to-toe steps it will take to measure several areas (i.e. across the room, the length of the mat/rug/couch).

Hand Stack with Variations
All ages
When moving your hand out for a regular hand stack, do some sort of motion before putting your hand on the top again. The other person has to do exactly what you did. Movement ideas are shaky hands, slow hands, upside down hands, fingers spread wide, pointer fingers only.

Hot Potato/Cold Potato
All ages
Everyone sits in a circle. Start the group passing a ball (balloon, bean bag, tissue, etc.) around by placing it into the hands of the child sitting next to you and saying "cold potato." Using gestures and as little language as possible, direct the child holding the ball to place it in the hands of their neighbor in the circle. The group chants "cold potato" every time the ball is passed to a neighbor. Control the pace of passing and chanting so that "cold potato" is passed slowly. After the ball has been passed completely around the circle, start "warm potato" and speed up the pace so that the "warm potato" goes around the circle slightly faster than the "cold potato." The group repeats the passing but, on the third round, they chant "hot potato" and pass the ball quickly. Continue directing the passing, slowing back to "warm potato" and finally "cold potato."

How Many Big Steps?
Young
Each person stands with their feet together. One by one, starting with you, each child takes as many giant lunging steps as they need to get across the room. To increase the challenge, have each child guess how many steps they will need to reach their destination.

Jump into My Arms
Young
Have the child stand on pillows or the couch. Give a signal for the child to jump into your arms.

Jump the River
All ages

Take two pieces of yarn or string and put them parallel to each other. The space in between is the "river." The child jumps across the river to the parent while you are on the side where the child starts from, and then back to you. Based on the child's age and ability, keep moving the strings further and further to make the "river" wider to jump.

Land, Sea and Air
All ages

Determine which part of the floor is "land" and which is "sea." If you are using tape, put down a long piece to mark it off. The area in front of the tape is "sea" and the area behind it is "land." You call out one of three directions: Land, Sea or Air. When you say "Land!" the child jumps into the land area. When you say "Sea!" the child jumps into the sea. When you say "Air!" the child jumps as high into the air as he can. Surprise the players with random commands like "Tornado!" and "Earthquake!" where everyone invents their own movements.

Measuring
All ages

Measure the child's height, length of arms, legs, feet, hands and so forth. Keep a record for later comparisons. Use a measuring tape, yarn or ribbon. Measure surprising things, such as the child's smile, the length of his ears, the circumference of his head, or how high he can jump. You can use fruit tape for measuring, then tear off the length and feed it to the child. "This is just the size of your smile." You thus combine structure with nurture.

Mirroring
All ages

Face the child, move your arms, face or other body parts and ask the child to move in the same way. For a very active child, you can use slow motion or vary the tempo. Take turns being the leader.

Nose-Tongue-Chin
All ages

Give the child these directions one at a time and watch carefully as she plays the game:

Touch your nose and pop out your tongue.

Touch your chin and pull in your tongue.

Touch your left cheek and stick out your tongue to the right.

Touch your right cheek and stick out your tongue out to the left.

Touch your nose and move your tongue to the center.

Touch your chin and pull in your tongue.

Sit across from the child. Take her hand and help her touch your nose, which makes your tongue stick out. Help her touch your right ear, which moves your tongue to the right, then the left ear, which makes the tongue move left. Finally, help her touch your chin, making her tongue pop back in. Once the child understands the game, let her play the game without directing her hands.

Olympic Steps
Older
The child stands on a line to begin. Have the child take a regular-size step and mark the child's heel where he lands. The child then returns to the line and takes the largest step he possibly can—mark at the heel. Return to the line and ask the child to do a broad jump—mark at the heel. For the last turn, the child jumps as far as he can while the parent cheers loudly. See how much further the child can jump when cheered for.

One Potato/Two Potato
All ages
The adults and child sit in a circle facing each other and make hands into fists. Turn fists sideways with thumbs up and fists out in front. The leader puts one fist out in the middle and says "one potato." The person to the right puts their fist on top and says "two potato." This continues with "three potato, four potato, five potato, six potato, seven potato, more." The person on top is the winner and starts the next round of the game.

1, 2, 3 Weeeee
Young
Adults each hold one hand of the child and count "1, 2, 3 Weeeee" while picking up and swooping the child up and over to the designated sitting spot.

Patty-Cake
Young
Hold the child's hands and lead her through the activity. "Patty-cake, patty-cake, Baker's man/Bake me a cake as fast as you can/Roll it and pat it and mark it with a [child's initial]/And toss it in the oven for [child's name] and me!" This is also an engaging activity:

- Use feet or fingertips only.

- Change the pace and ask the child to follow along fast, slow, very slowly.

- Change the tone of the rhythm to loud, soft, whisper.

Peanut Butter and Jelly
All ages

Say "peanut butter" and have the child say "jelly" in just the same way. Repeat five to ten times varying loudness and intonation. Adapt the pair of words to the customs of the country; for example, "fish" and "chips" in the UK.

Pick Up Stick
Older

This game requires three different-size sticks such as chop sticks, popsicle sticks and coffee stirrers. Starting with the largest sticks, press the sticks between you trying to hold them up using only the tips of your fingers. For more of a challenge, try to move the sticks in synchronous motions, such as circles. As an alternative, while standing side by side, you and the child hold a stick between your index fingers (as a pair) and cross the room without dropping the stick. See if the challenge is easier or harder with different types of sticks.

Pillow Sandwich
Young

The child lies on their tummy over a pillow. Place a pillow on the child's back while declaring the ingredients the child likes on a sandwich. After placing one pillow, press down. Add another pillow (topping) until a big stack of pillows is on the child's back.

Play Dough Squeeze or Prints
Young

Place a ball of play dough between the child's hands. Place your hands on the outside of the child's hands and, while looking directly in her eyes, say "Sqeeeeeeze!" as you firmly press your hands and hers into the play dough. This firm pressure can help organize a dysregulated child. You can also use play dough to make finger, hand and footprints.

Pop the Bubble
Young

Blow a bubble and catch it on the wand. Have the child pop the bubble with a particular body part, for example a finger, toe, elbow, shoulder or ear. This is a structured way of playing with bubbles. Bubbles readily capture the interest of young children and can be used as an engaging activity either in this structured form or in a manner that invites more spontaneity (e.g. by having the child pop all the bubbles as quickly as he can).

Red Light, Green Light
Older

Ask the child to do something, such as run, jump, move arms. Green light means go, red light means stop.

Stack of Hands
All ages

Put your hand palm down in front of the child, have the child put his hand on top; alternate hands to make a stack. Take turns moving the hand on the bottom to the top. You can also move from top to bottom. This can be made more complicated by going fast or in slow motion. Putting lotion on hands first makes for a slippery stack and adds an element of nurture. Stack feet, forearms, folded arms and fingers; if a child is wary of touch, stack hands with one to two inches of space between each hand or finger.

Step into My Circle
All ages

Make a circle with your arms held out in front of you low to the ground and have the child step into it. Then rise up, lifting the circle around the child, without touching him. Move the circle level with the child's head and slowly move down and have the child step out. Make it more challenging by holding the circle higher to step into it.

Three-Legged Walk
Older

Stand beside the child. Tie your two adjacent legs together with a scarf or ribbon. With arms around each other's waists, walk across the room. You should be responsible for coordinating the movement. For example, you can say "inside, outside" to indicate which foot to use. Add obstacles (pillows, chairs) to make this more challenging.

Toilet Paper Bust Out
Older

Wrap the child's legs, arms or whole body with toilet paper, paper towels or crepe paper. To let a hesitant child know what is in store, have her hold her arms together in front of her body and wrap them first. On a signal, have the child break out of the wrapping.

Washing Machine
Young

Lay the child on a blanket. Adults pick up the corners of the blanket so that edges rise up but the child is still supported by the floor. Say "Here we go" while starting the machine, and adults sway the blanket back and forth in a "swishing" motion. Tell the child "We need to add some soap" and toss in a few cotton balls on top of the child. Next say "We need to go to a faster washing speed" and bring the opposite arms up and down so that the child rolls a bit in the middle. The next stage is spin. The adults walk around in a circle two or three times. Last is the drying phase. Lay the blanket down and cover the child, leaving his face uncovered. Apply gentle, rhythmic pressure from the shoulders, down the back and legs, stopping at the feet. Apply deep pressure from the top of the arms down. End the game with "hanging the laundry." Each adult takes a hand and peels the child up off the floor until he is standing all the way up on tip toes.

Wiggle Your Body
All ages

Adult and child gently wiggle each body part as you say:

> I wiggle my hands

> I wiggle my feet

> I wiggle my shoulders

> I wiggle my seat

> Now the wiggles are out of me (shake your whole body)

> See how quiet I can be (say this in a whisper).

When parents enter or when there are three or more participants:

Follow the Leader
All ages

All participants stand and form a line holding on to the waist of the person in front of them. The first person chooses a particular way to move and all others copy. The leader goes to the back of the line and the new leader demonstrates a different way to move around the room. This can also be done sitting in a circle and moving only the arms, head and shoulders.

Funny Ways to Cross the Room
All ages
One adult and the child stand at one end of the mat (or play space); the other adult stands at the other end of the mat. The second adult directs the child to come towards her in a certain way, for example hopping, tiptoeing, crawling or walking backwards. The child is greeted with a hug or special greeting on arrival. The first adult then calls her to come back in a specified way. Adult and child can come across the mat together if the child cannot manage alone. With older children, each participant can choose a funny way to cross the room that everyone must try, for example crab walk, elephant walk or scooting.

Hokey Pokey
All ages
Everyone stands in a circle and sings: "You put your right foot in/You put your right foot out/You put your right foot in/And you shake it all about/You do the Hokey Pokey/And you turn yourself around/That's what it's all about/Hokey Pokey!" Arms, heads, whole bodies can be put in to the middle of the circle and shaken. When you do the Hokey Pokey, you dance in whatever way you like, arms in air, with playful, energetic gestures.

Mother, May I?
Older
The parent gives instructions to the child to do something, for example "Take three giant steps toward me." The child must say "Mother, may I?" before responding to the command. If the child forgets, she must return to the starting line. The goal is to have the child come to her parent and get a hug on arrival.

Motor Boat
All ages
Holding hands, everyone walks around in a circle, chanting "Motor boat, motor boat, go so slow/Motor boat, motor boat, go so fast/Motor boat, motor boat, step on the gas!" Gradually increase the speed until it is very fast. Suddenly "put on the brakes!" and start over with the slow tempo. This can also be done with the child and practitioner alone.

Ring-Around-a-Rosy
All ages
Hold hands and walk around in a circle chanting, "Ring-around-a-rosy/A pocket full of posies/Ashes, ashes, we all fall down." All fall down at the end.

Run to Mommy or Daddy Under the Blanket
Young

The child sits on one parent's lap facing the other parent with a small blanket lying on the floor between them. On a signal, both parents lift the blanket and the child runs or crawls under the blanket into the arms of the other parent. This can also be done with the child running between parent and practitioner.

Same, Same, Different Game
Older

This game is set up like Simon Says. One person is the leader and starts with an action and the direction "Same." Any time the leader says "Same," everyone copies the action. When the leader says "Different," other players do anything but the action the leader has chosen. If a player makes a mistake, it is his turn to be the leader.

Simon Says
Older

This is similar to Mother, May I? but with the added challenge that the child must watch out for commands that do not have "Simon Says" as part of the phrase. Thus, when the game is going rapidly, the leader can suddenly omit to say "Simon Says," and the unwary participant may do the action without thinking. If a player makes this mistake, it is his turn to be the leader.

Zoom-Erk-Splash
Older

Everyone sits or stands in a circle. The word "zoom" is passed around the circle quickly by players turning their head and making eye contact with the person next to them. When one person stops the action by saying "Erk," the "zoom" reverses and is sent back the way it came. When the zoom-erk gets stuck in one part of the circle, the person receiving the erk puts his hands together in a diving movement and points his hands to someone across the circle, saying "Splash." The person splashed passes a zoom to the person next to her.

ENGAGEMENT

The purpose of engaging activities is to connect with the child in a playful, positive way, to focus intently on the child and to encourage the child to enjoy new experiences. At all times, it is important to attend to the level of the child's arousal and to modulate it when needed.

Beep and Honk
Young

Press the child's nose and say, "Beep!"; then press their chin and say, "Honk!" Guide the child to touch your nose and chin. Make appropriate beeps and honks as you are touched. The child may be able to supply noises also. Make a special noise when you touch a specific face or body part, for example an elephant trumpeting when you touch a knee. Try to remember which noise goes with which body part when you do a series of touches.

Blow Me Over
All ages

Sit facing the child and, holding hands (you can cradle a younger child in your lap), have the child "blow you over." Fall back as the child blows. Once the child understands the game, you can blow her over.

Butterfly Bubbles
All ages

Ask the child to hold his hands out so that you can blow pretend butterflies (actually bubbles) to sit on his hand before they pop and disappear. Ask the child to decide what the butterfly will look like; he can pick the color, if it has spots or stripes and so on. Slow your breathing down, taking a deep breath before slowly blowing a big bubble. Admire the butterfly together before blowing another. Lower your voice to a whisper to make it as magical as possible.

Check-Ups
All ages

Check body parts, such as nose, chin, ears, cheeks, fingers, toes and knees, to see if they are warm or cold, hard or soft, wiggly or quiet, and so on. Count freckles, toes, fingers and knuckles. Check strong muscles and high jumps.

Counting Fingers and Knuckles
Older

Count from one to five on one hand and then starting with ten on the other hand count down to six. Say with a puzzled look, "Five and six make eleven. Do you have eleven fingers?" Older children will enjoy the joke, younger ones won't get it. You can also count all the knuckles on both hands. Children are often surprised to learn that they have 28 knuckles.

Create a Special Handshake
Older

Make up a special handshake together, taking turns adding new gestures, for example a high five, clasp hands, wiggle fingers and so on. This can be cumulative over several sessions and can be your beginning or ending ritual. It can be used to good advantage when parents join the session.

Dots
Older

Cover the wall with a large piece of butcher paper. Mark a large dot on the paper at one end. Take the child to the other end and blindfold him. Hand the child a marker and help him place his marker on the paper. The adult then gives the child directions (e.g. "Go up, straight, down a little") to help the child navigate his line drawing back to the original dot.

Feather Blow from Straw
Older

Place a feather into straw (the pointy end of the feather in first) at the end away from the mouth. The child blows into the tube towards the adult, who tries to catch the feather. This works well with wider straws those like found with bubble tea. You can also sit side by side and see who can blow the feather further or hit closest to a target on the floor.

Foil Prints
All ages

Shape a piece of aluminum foil around the child's elbow, hand, foot, face, ear or other body part. It helps to place a pillow under the foil and have the child press her hand or foot into the soft surface to get impressions of the fingers and toes. The parent may be called in to guess which print goes with which body part. This is also structuring since it defines body shapes and boundaries.

Goodbye Song
Young

"Goodbye (say child's name), Goodbye (say caregiver's name), Goodbye (say practitioner's name), we're glad you came to play."

Hand Clapping Games
Older

Children of all ages enjoy these games and many have a good repertoire of rhymes and rhythms. You should have a few chants that you know well, for example "Miss Mary Mack" or "A Sailor Went to Sea." You can vary the complexity of the rhythmic pattern and the chant depending on the skill of the child. Always make sure that you first rehearse the clapping pattern slowly so that you can easily get into a satisfying pattern once you add the rhyme.

Heartbeat Rhythm
Young

Have the parent place their ear against the child's chest and listen for his heartbeat. The parent then taps out the heartbeat rhythm on a solid surface. Have the child try and tap out the rhythm with the parent.

Hello, Goodbye
Young

The child sits in the parent's lap facing the parent. The parent supports the child's back with their hands and says "Hello" and then dips the child backwards while saying, "Goodbye." The parent then brings the child back up and says, "Hello." This can be done standing, as well, with the child's legs around the parent's waist. In this position, the downward dip puts the child's face further out of view of the parent.

Hide and Find
All ages

Hide a cotton ball (wrapped candy, a touch of lotion or powder) somewhere on the child (in a cuff or folded sleeve, under the collar, behind the ear). An older child can hide the cotton ball on himself. If the parent or another adult is available, they can find the cotton ball; if not, you can find it. Young children will want to show where the hidden object is. Help parents accept this as the child's eager involvement in the game.

Is the Doggie Home?
Young

Sit facing the child. Put your hand out with fingers loosely together. Ask the child to poke his finger between your pinky and ring finger, asking, "Is the doggie home?" Answer, "No, the doggie is playing soccer" (using activities the child enjoys). The child continues "asking" at each finger door. At the last one, the answer is "Yes, the doggie is home and he gives you a big hug!"

Knock on the Door
Young

This is a simple baby activity. There are many variations in different cultures: "Knock on the door" (tap on the child's forehead); "Peep in" (peek at the child's eyes); "Lift up the latch" (gently push up the child's nose); "Walk in!" (pretend to walk fingers into the child's open mouth or pop a piece of food in).

La La Magnets
Young

Sit knee to knee with the child. The adult takes the child's hands in their hands. Swinging hands back and forth, chant "La La Magnets." The adult then drops hands and calls out a body part that can be touched together (forehead, cheeks, fingertips) and the adult and child put those body parts together. Pull apart and take the child's hands again to continue the game with other body parts.

Mr. Bubble Writing
All ages

Squirt foamy soap (e.g. Mr. Bubble) on a smooth surface like a window or a mirror. Draw something one part at a time and then ask the child to copy it. When done, smear the soap back again and switch the leader, having the child lead if appropriate.

Mountain of Bubbles
All ages

Fill a large plastic bowl two-thirds of the way with water and add several squirts of dish soap. Place it on the floor or on a low table and have everyone sit around it. Each participant is given a straw and told to place the end into the water and blow a mountain of bubbles. Once the bowl is full, players can use their straws to blow the bubbles on top back down by gently blowing at the suds.

Paint a Window
All ages

Mark off an area to be painted (glass window or mirror) with long pieces of tape that go from one side to the other. The taped area will create a mosaic of different shapes. Using tempura paints, create artwork within the taped lines. You and the child alternate filling in shapes between tape lines. You can remove tape for variation of effect.

Peek-a-Boo
Young

Hold the child's hands (or feet) together in front of your face. Peek around or separate the hands (or feet) to "find" the child. A lovely variation is to use a sheer scarf to hide your face or the child's, then pull it off to discover each other.

Piggy-Back/Horsey-Back Ride
All ages

Help the child get onto your back. Jog around the room with the child on your back. The child can give signals such as "Whoa!" and "Giddyup!" The strength of your back determines how old the child can be for this game. All children enjoy it.

Ping Pong Blow
All ages

The adults and child lie on stomachs on the floor, facing each other and holding hands. You blow the ping pong ball to the person on their right and the action continues until the ball goes all the way around the group. With only two players, you can play a version of Ping Pong Ball Hockey, trying to blow the ball under the other person's chin to score points.

Pop Cheeks
Young

Inflate your cheeks with air and help the child to pop them with his hands or feet. The child inflates his cheeks and you pop them in turn.

Popcorn Toes
Young

As you take the child's shoes off, ask if she has popcorn, peanuts, grapes and so forth inside her shoe. Then take the shoe off and discover wonderful toes.

Push Me Over, Land on My Knees
Young

Kneel in front of a standing child (so that the child comes to your eye level) or sit in front of a sitting child. Hold the child's hands. On a signal, have the child push you. As you fall back, pull the child onto your knees and "fly" the child smoothly or bounce the child up and down.

Push Me Over, Pull Me Up
All ages

Sit on the floor in front of the child. Place the child's palms against yours, or put the child's feet against your shoulders. On a signal, have the child push you over.

Fall back in an exaggerated way. Stretch out your hands so that the child can pull you back up.

Row, Row, Row Your Boat
All ages

Sing the familiar song, adding the child's name at the end ("Erin's such a dream"). Small children can be held in your lap. Older children can sit facing you. Clasping forearms rather than hands makes this feel more secure and connected. If another adult is available, the child can be seated between you as if in a boat as you row back and forth. The tempo can be varied from fast to slow and back again to practice regulation. You also can rock from side to side. The second, more exciting verse concludes, "If you see a crocodile, don't forget to scream." Then both scream loudly.

Sticker Match
Young

Put a colorful sticker on the child and have the child put stickers on you or his parent in just the same place until both are decorated in the same way. After the stickers are applied, the child and parent touch matching stickers together, for example nose to nose or elbow to elbow, before removing them.

Sticky Nose
Young

Put a colorful sticker on your own nose. Ask the child to take it off. Or stick a cotton ball on your nose with lotion. Have the child blow it off.

Straw Arrows
Older

Use wide straws and cotton swabs for this spitball-like game. You and the child each take one straw and cotton swabs. Load the straw by inserting a swab in the end closest to your mouth. Give a signal for everyone to shoot the swab across the room. You can see who can shoot the swab furthest, or set up a target to shoot at.

This is the Way the Baby Rides
Young

The adult holds the child on their knees and bounces the child, varying the pace as they move from baby, to lady, to gentleman, to farmer. Another version of this activity is "Trot, trot to Boston, Trot, trot to Lynn, Trot, trot to Boston, All fall in!" Let the child gently "fall" off the adult's lap at the end.

This Little Pig Went to Market
Young
Wiggle each toe as you chant, "This little pig went to market/This little pig stayed home/This little pig had roast beef/This little pig had none/This little pig cried 'Wee, wee, wee,' all the way home." Change the details to fit the particular child, for example "This little pig likes pizza." As you say "all the way home," walk your fingers up the child's arm in a playful way rather than tickling his tummy. With an easily dysregulated child, use firm pressure and a calm approach.

Tissue or Cotton Ball Splat
Older
Line up the adults and child side by side. Place a bowl of water and a box of tissues in front of each person. As quickly as possible, each person removes one tissue at a time, dips it in the water and throws the tissue at the wall (or window). The goal is to get through the tissue box first, keeping as many tissues stuck to the wall as possible. You can use a handful of cotton balls instead of tissues.

Tube Drop
Older
Make a tube from poster board that is about 4 inches in diameter. The adult takes four or five bean bags in their hand. The adult holds the top of the tube up and the tube is positioned downward into the child's hand which covers the bottom of the tube. The adult holds the bean bag at eye level and tells the child to watch his face. When the child makes eye contact, the adult drops the bean bag down the tube and into the child's hand for the child to catch.

Wiggle Toes
Young
Feel for wiggle toes through the child's shoes as a part of greeting and check-up. Remove the shoes to discover the toes.

Zip Zap Magnets
Older
Stand facing the child. Both the adult and child clap their thighs, clap their hands and clap each other's palms while chanting "Zip Zap Magnets." After calling Magnets, the adult calls out a body part and the pair touch body parts together. Speed up the tempo for a more challenging game.

When parents enter or when there are three or more participants:

Blanket Pass
Older

Everyone sits (or stands) in a circle and holds on to the edge of a small blanket, sheet or parachute. Each person takes a turn choosing who they want to pass a soft ball to across the blanket. Everyone must cooperate in lifting or lowering their part of the blanket to make sure that the ball gets to the right person. A variation is to pass the ball around the edge of the circle.

Hide and Seek
All ages

Hide with the child under a blanket or under pillows and ask parents or another adult to find you both. Hiding with the child is important, because it gives you the opportunity to help the child contain the excitement generated by being alone and anticipating the surprise of being found. Parents should be coached to make appreciative comments about their child as they look for him and to find him quickly if he is very young and impatient. A big hug is in order once the child is found.

Hide Notes or Other Objects on the Child for Parents to Find
All ages

One adult hides and the other finds, for example, notes directing the finder to do something with the child ("Pop Sara's cheeks") or to find a cotton ball and give a soft touch, or to find food and feed it to the child.

Magnets
Older

Everyone stands in a wide, loose circle. Each time the leader gives the cue, everyone comes closer and closer until they are touching side by side.

Match the Bean Bags
Young

Give the parent and child five bean bags each. The parent balances a bean bag on the child's body (on the head, shoulder or knee, in the crook of an arm) and the child places a bean bag on the same place on the parent. They take turns dumping the bean bags from the same body part into each other's hands.

Passing Funny Faces
Older

Each person in the circle makes a funny face which is passed in turn to the next person around the circle. Each has a turn to create a funny face.

Progressive Pass Around
Older

Sitting in a circle, one person passes a gentle touch to the next person (such as a nose beep, or pat on the back). The second person passes that touch to the third person plus one of her own. Each person adds a new touch. Everyone helps each other recall the sequence of touches. If a child is wary of touch, this may be done first by doing the touches only on oneself.

Whose Toes Did I Touch?
All ages

Everyone sits in a circle with feet all entwined under a blanket. The person who is "it" touches the lumpy blanket and has to guess whose toes she has touched.

NURTURE

The purpose of nurturing activities is to reinforce the message that the child is worthy of care and that adults will provide care without the child having to ask. Nurturing activities help to calm and regulate the anxious child and enhance feelings of self-worth.

Build a Fort
All ages
Create a fort with pillows and blankets for the child to hide in. Let the child rest in the fort without seeking or finding them.

Burrito/Sushi Roll
All ages
Put a blanket on the floor and have the child lie back along the edge of the blanket. Roll the child over on their tummy while holding the blanket around them so that they are rolled inside the blanket. Describe the ingredients the child likes to place inside, and roll again. Repeat until the child is fully wrapped in the blanket. Then reverse.

Caring for Hurts
All ages
As part of the general check-up for the child's special qualities, notice and care for scratches, bruises, hurts or "boo-boos." Put lotion on or around the hurt, touch with a cotton ball, or blow a kiss. Check for healing in the next session. Do not announce, "Let's see how many hurts you have."

Coming Around the Mountain
All ages
For a child who is too heavy to swing in the blanket, have him sit in the blanket and everyone take a side. Walk in a circle so the child is now moving in a circle while sitting inside the blanket. Sing the song "Comin' Round the Mountain" with much exuberance at varying speeds (to match the speed of the turning of the blanket) and a few "Yee haws!" thrown in! This is more high energy and less nurturing than a blanket swing but still a way to provide an older child with fun in the blanket.

Cotton Ball or Feather Guess
All ages
First demonstrate by touching the child's hand with a cotton ball and a feather; ask the child to notice the difference between the two sensations. Then have the child close her eyes and say where you have touched her and whether you did it with

a cotton ball or a feather. This adds challenge to a nurturing activity. If the child is not comfortable closing her eyes, have her look away.

Cotton Ball Soothe
Young

Have the child relax on pillows or in your arms. You, or a parent, gently stroke the child's face, arms or hands with a cotton ball. Quietly describe the features that you are outlining: rosy cheeks, smiling mouth, upturned nose.

Cotton Ball Touch
All ages

First have the child hold out a hand and demonstrate a gentle touch on one of her fingers, then have her point to or tell you which finger you touched. Have the child close her eyes (or turn her head if closing her eyes bothers her). Touch the child gently with a cotton ball. Have the child open her eyes and indicate where she was touched.

Decorate the Child
All ages

Make rings, necklaces and bracelets with play dough, crazy foam, crepe paper streamers, aluminum foil, stickers and pipe cleaners. Admire what you notice about the child as you place the items on her.

Donut or Pretzel Challenge
Older

Put a donut or pretzel on your finger. See how many bites the child can take before breaking the circle.

Empathy Feeding
All ages

Give the child four or five different foods to be eaten. The parent rank orders the child's preference just by reading the child's facial expression.

Face Painting
All ages

Paint flowers and hearts on cheeks or make the child up like a princess or a prince. Mustaches and beards are interesting for boys and their fathers. A variation on this is to use a soft dry brush and pretend to paint the child's face, describing her wonderful cheeks, her lovely eyebrows, and so forth, as you gently brush each part.

Farmer Picks Carrots
All ages

The parent and child lie on their tummies facing each other. With arms extended forward, the parent and child hold hands between them. The practitioner pretends to be the farmer, who tries to "pick the carrots" for his soup, by gently pulling/yanking on the ankles of both child and parent. But the farmer cannot pull the carrots out of the ground because they are so deeply connected.

Feather Match
All ages

Prepare two sets of five feathers; if they are colored, have the sets match. The parent or practitioner decorates the child with one feather (in the child's hair, tucked into a sleeve, between fingers) and the child places a feather on the adult in the same place. Admire each other.

Feeding
All ages

Have a small snack and drink available for all sessions, but never insist that a child eats. Take the child on your lap or face a seated child. Feed the child, listening for crunches, noticing whether he likes the snack and when he is ready for more. Encourage eye contact. You can add to the interest of the feeding by having two or three kinds of snack—raisins, nuts, biscuits. Have the child close his eyes and guess which snack it is. If the child refuses to let you feed him at first, allow him to feed himself but make yourself a part of the activity, for example by commenting on how long he chews, how loud his chews are, or what you notice about him that lets you know he likes the food.

Feeding Alternatives
All ages

Have the adult use chop sticks to get a treat (usually a gummy treat) to the child's mouth. Have the adult blow a treat across the table into the child's mouth or off the table for the child to catch with their hands. M&Ms and Skittles work well for this. The adult feeds alphabet cereal to the child. For each letter, the adult thinks of something about the child that begins with that letter; for example, A is adorable, L is lovable.

Using long licorice laces, have the adult and child put one end of the licorice in their mouth and place their hands behind their backs. Count to three and the parent and child begin to suck the licorice in to their mouths without using their hands.

Use a chewy snack like gummy bears or fruit leather to provide proprioceptive input and a source of calming.

Sucking a thick drink (yoghurt/milkshake through a straw) is calming and organizing for a dysregulated/anxious child.

Feeding in a Cuddle
Young

Cradle the child in your arms while feeding pudding, applesauce or juice.

Floating on a Raft
All ages

Stack several couch cushions (must be firm) and have the child lie tummy down on top of the stack. Kneel by the pillow stack, holding the stack firmly so it doesn't topple over. Gently rock the child back and forth while guiding her through a narrative: "You are floating on a raft on a peaceful lake, surrounded by trees. A light breeze is gently rocking you back and forth. Overhead you hear birds singing a beautiful song and the sun's rays warm your back." You can add whatever peaceful story you want to tell. Change the wind/rocking directions, suggest a speed boat going by making ripples, making the rocking faster, then slower towards the end.

Hide and Seek Hands
All ages

Cover the parent's eyes and take their hand. Guide them to part of their child's body and have them guess the body part, such as shoulder, elbow, head, feet, toes, nose, cheek. You can also do this with a child hiding under a blanket if the child is comfortable. When the adult guesses correctly you reply, "Wow, Mom/Dad really knows you!"

Lotion or Powder Prints
All ages

Apply lotion or powder to the child's hand or foot and make a print on paper, the floor mat, a pillow, your dark clothing, or on a mirror. If you make a lotion print on dark construction paper, you can shake powder on it and then blow or shake it off to enhance the picture (take care to keep the powder away from the child's face). You can also make a pile of powder on a piece of paper and have the child rub his hand or foot in it to make the print.

Lotioning or Powdering
All ages

Put lotion or powder on the child's arms, hands, legs or feet. You can sing a personalized song as you do this: "Oh lotion, oh lotion on Sarah's feet/It feels so good, it feels so sweet/Oh lotion, oh lotion on Sarah's hands/It feels so good, it feels so grand." Attend to the child's sensory needs by using firm pressure, or choosing powder rather than lotion for the child who has tactile sensitivity.

Love Mark
All ages
Encourage the caregiver to help their child with transitions by playing this game at home. Each time the adult leaves the child, ask the child to pick a special place (cheek, ankle, palm) for the adult to draw a small "love mark." Tell the child that this is a special mark just between the two of you to remind him that you will be thinking of him until your next time together. Make sure to look for the special mark when you return.

Lullaby
Young
Cradle the child in your arms in such a way that eye contact can be maintained. Sing your favorite lullaby or any quiet, soothing song. Add details about the particular child to the traditional words.

Manicure or Pedicure
Older
Soak the child's feet or hands in warm water. Using lotion, massage her feet or hands. Paint the child's toes or fingernails using a variety of colors or letting the child choose the color she wants. Make sure that the child is comfortable having the nail polish remain when she leaves the room. If not, take it off.

Measuring Games 1
Young
Arm Kisses Measure: The child stretches out his arm as far as possible and the adult places kisses up his hand, wrist, forearm and upper arm, counting each kiss along the way. The adult then does the other arm to make sure both arms are the same size

Inch Worm Measure: The adult spreads their hand, putting their thumb at the child's fingertips and stretching their hand as far as it will go. They then move their thumb up to their pinky (creating an inchworm movement with their hand) and then spread their hand again, moving up the child's arm. The adult can measure the length of the child's arm, leg, back, etc.

Measuring Games 2
Young

Lotion Dots: The adult takes some lotion on their fingertip and counts of dabs of lotion on the child's forearm that equal the child's age. The adult then rubs in the counting dots and repeats on the other arm.

Measure with Crepe Paper: Instruct the parent and child to hug each other. Measure the circumference of their hug. Rip the paper and place it on the floor. Instruct the parent and child to hug tighter. Measure with crepe paper again to show that the second piece is shorter.

Paint Prints
All ages

Rub finger paint on the child's hand or foot, using one color or creating a pattern with several colors. It is best to do one hand or foot at a time. Press the painted hand or foot onto paper to make a print. After the prints are made with paint, gently wash, dry and powder the hand or foot.

Powder Palm
All ages

Sprinkle some powder in the child's palm and partially rub it in so that the lines on the palm stand out; notice shapes and letters. Also rub powder into the parent's palm; look for differences and similarities between the child's and the parent's palms.

Powder Trail
Older

Place a small pile of powder on newspaper on the floor. Have the child put his feet into the powder so that they are liberally covered with powder. Have the child walk on the dark mat leaving footprints as he goes. This can be used as a lead-in to having the parents come into a session to find the child who is hidden at the end of the trail of footprints.

Preparing Pizza, Tacos, Hot Dogs or Cookie Dough
All ages

Have the child lie on pillows on his tummy. Kneed his back while describing how delicious the cookie, pizza, taco or hot dog is going to be. Firmly put the appropriate condiments on the pizza or cookie dough.

Rhythm on Your Back
All ages

This is a variation of making shapes on the back for an older child or adolescent. Using both hands, tap out a rhythm on the child's back while sitting behind them. The child then has to repeat it by tapping the same way on the floor. Try giving the child a small wooden drum on which to replay the tapping pattern. The parent is typically doing the rhythm on the back and the practitioner is sitting in front, facing the child.

Slippery, Slippery, Slip
All ages

This is a lotioning activity with an added element of surprise (as well as giving an opportunity to apply firm pressure to the child's body). First, rub lotion on the child's arm or leg. Then, holding firmly, rub well up his arm or leg, saying "Slippery, slippery, slip," and pull toward you, falling backward with an exaggerated motion as the slippery arm or leg escapes. An alternative is to see how quickly the child can pull her hand out from between your two slippery hands and squeeze it back into your clasped hands.

Soft and Floppy
All ages

Have the child lie on the floor and help him get "all soft and floppy." Gently jiggle each arm and leg and let it flop to the floor. If the child has difficulty getting floppy, have him get "stiff like a board" and then let go to be "soft like a noodle." Once the child is relaxed, ask him to wiggle just one part of his body—such as his tummy, his tongue, his big toe.

Special Delivery
Young

As a way of setting up the feeding activity, instruct the parent to sit on the couch or pillow. Pick up the child in a cradle position. Sway the child while singing, "I've got a little [child's name], and she's going to her mommy [or daddy], a-one, a-two and a-threeeeeee, special delivery!" Place the child gently in the parent's lap.

Temporary Tattoos
Older

Apply tattoos or, using washable body paints, draw designs on the child's arms, face or hands.

Trace Messages
Older

Using your finger, trace shapes or simple positive messages on the child's back for her to decipher.

Twinkle Song
All ages

Adapt the words of "Twinkle, Twinkle, Little Star" to the special characteristics of the child. "What a special boy you are/Dark brown hair, and soft, soft cheeks/ Bright brown eyes from which you peek/Twinkle, twinkle little star/What a special boy you are." Touch the parts you refer to as you sing.

Wax Child
All ages

Mold the child as if she is made out of wax, shaping her body parts with a light massage motion while talking about how wonderful each part is. After the child is "molded," she is "painted" with "magic brushes" (use small dry paint brushes); then everyone marvels at what a fine girl she is.

When parents enter or when there are three or more participants:

Blanket Swing
All ages

Spread a blanket on the floor and have the child lie down in the middle. The adults gather up the corners and give a gentle swing while singing a song. At the end, bring the child down for a "soft landing." Position the parents so that they can see the child's face. If the child is fearful of being lifted off the floor, let him remain in contact with the floor as you gently rotate the blanket around in a circle.

Face Painting
All ages

Using washable body paints, parents decorate their child's face with small designs. Older boys with their fathers enjoy making mustaches and beards on each other. The removing of the paint is an opportunity for more nurturing.

Fanning
All ages

After a vigorous activity, one adult or both parents rest with the child in their arms, and the other adult fans with a large pillow, a fan or a newspaper. Watch how everyone's hair blows.

Pass a Squeeze or Touch Around
All ages
Pass a squeeze, a gentle touch, a dab of lotion or a fresh touch of powder from person to person around the circle.

Shoe and Sock Race
Young
Adults race to put kisses on feet and then put the child's shoes back on before the kiss flies away. Ask the parents to see whether the kisses are still there and add new ones when the child goes to bed at night.

Special Kisses
Young
Butterfly Kiss: The parent places her cheek against the child's cheek and flutters her eyelashes so that the child feels the brush of her eyelashes.

Elephant Kiss: Hold both fists in front of your mouth (like a pretend trumpet) and keep one fist by your mouth as you make a kissing noise. Move the other fist toward the child's cheek, completing the kissing noise with a flourish as you touch his cheek.

Eskimo Kiss: The parent and child rub noses.

Note: the practitioner describes the special kisses above or may demonstrate with a gesture; the practitioner makes clear that real kisses are special signs of affection to be shared only by parents and children.

Weather Report
All ages
The adult places a flat hand (palm and fingers) and, pressing firmly but gently, describes the weather while moving hands in the image and rhythm of the weather pattern. For example, it's a warm sunny day: make a repeated large circle on the surface of the back for the sun. The wind is beginning to blow: swoop hands across the back making a swishing noise. Sheets of rain: move hand from top to bottom of the child's back. Use each hand one at a time in a repeated sequence.

CHALLENGE

The purpose of challenging activities is to encourage the child to take age-appropriate risks in order to foster feelings of competence and mastery. These activities are most often done cooperatively with the parent or practitioner. Challenge activities also allow a child to accept Structure, Engagement and Nurture that they might resist in more direct forms.

Balance on Pillows, Jump Off (Cushion Jump)
All ages

Help the child to balance on pillows, starting with one and adding more as long as the child can easily manage. While the child is gaining her balance, hold her around the rib cage, rather than holding her hands. This steadies her and reduces the child's impulse to jump up and down. Once the child is balanced, you can remove your hands and let her experience the feeling of balancing on her own. Then say, "Jump into my arms (or down to the floor) when I give the signal."

Balancing on Body Activities
Older

The child lies on her back on the floor with her feet up in the air. Place one pillow on the child's feet and help her balance it. Add additional pillows one at a time as long as the child is successful. Balance books, bean bags, pillows or hats on the child's head and have her walk across the room.

Balloon Balance
Older

Hold a balloon between you and the child (e.g. between foreheads, shoulders, elbows or hips) and move across the room without dropping or popping the balloon. See if you can do this without using hands.

Balloon Tennis
All ages

Keep the balloon in the air using specified body parts, such as heads, hands, no hands, shoulders. If you choose feet, everyone lies on the floor and keeps the balloon in the air by kicking it gently. To create more structure and focus, choose a goal for how long you can keep it in the air—for example, "Let's see if we can count to 20."

Bean Bag Kick
Older

The adult and child stand facing each other a few feet apart. Balance a bean bag on the child's foot. On the adult's cue, the child kicks the bean bag up in the air and the adult tries to catch it. Count the number caught out of ten tries. Have several rounds to see if they can beat their best score.

Bubble Tennis
All ages
Blow bubbles high in the air between you and the child. Choose one bubble and blow it back and forth between you until it pops.

Catch the Hanky
All ages
Toss a lightweight hanky up in the air and the child tries to catch it before it flutters to the ground. Proceed until everyone has had several chances to toss and catch.

Cooperative Cotton Ball Race
All ages
The adult and child get on their hands and knees at one end of the room. Take turns blowing a cotton ball (or a ping pong ball) to the other side of the room. Try to better your time on repeated trials. A competitive version would be for each to have his own cotton ball and see who can get it across the room first. Parent and child can be teamed up against the practitioner team.

Cotton Ball Pop
Older
The adult and child each take a small pillow and stand facing each other. Push a cotton ball into the center of the pillow hard enough that the pillow folds into itself and the cotton ball is hidden. On the count of 1, 2, 3, pull the sides of the pillow hard and the cotton ball pops up into the air. The child attempts to catch the cotton ball on her pillow. After a few turns, you and the child switch "popper" positions.

Crawling Race
Young
The adult and child crawl on their knees as fast as they can around a stack of pillows, trying to catch the other's feet. Switch direction.

Feather Blow
All ages
The adult and child each hold a small pillow in front of them. The adult blows a feather from their pillow towards the child's pillow. The child must catch it on her pillow and blow it back.

How Many Can You Balance?
All ages
This is a way to use the idea of Bean Bag Drop with an older child. Have the child sitting on the floor. You balance bean bags on various parts of her, such as shoulder, head and on top of extended hands. Have the child stand up and see if they can do it without the bean bags falling off. Then, when the child is standing, ask if she can do a slight hop without any bean bags falling off. Then add another on to her head. Try balancing one on her foot while standing, and so on. You can find various ways to do this with the idea of not dropping the bean bags. At the end, have the child drop the bean bags back into your hands or drop them all to the floor on the count of three.

Karate Chop
All ages
Hold a length of toilet paper or paper streamer in front of the child and have her chop it in half when you give a signal.

Magic Carpet Ride
All ages
Have the child sit on a large pillow or small blanket, holding firmly to the edge. When the child looks at you, pull him around the room. When he breaks eye contact, stop. This works well on a slippery surface, such as a wood or a vinyl floor.

Measuring
All ages
Measure the child's height against a wall and mark it in some way, then measure when she stands on tiptoes and when she jumps up and touches the wall as high as possible. Measure various lengths of jumps on the floor as well.

Newspaper Punch, Basket Toss
All ages
Stretch a single sheet of newspaper tautly in front of the child. Have the child punch through the sheet when given a signal. You must hold the newspaper firmly so that it makes a satisfying pop when the child punches it. Make sure that you hold the paper so that the punch does not hit your chest. To extend the activity, you can add a second or third sheet of paper, have the child use the other hand, and vary the signals. For the basket toss, crush the torn newspaper into balls. Have the child toss a ball into the basket you make with your arms.

Newspaper Soccer Kick
Older
Crumple up five to ten sheets of newspaper into balls. The child sits on a couch with her legs crossed and you kneel on the floor across from her creating a big hoop with your arms. The child on the couch drops a newspaper ball over her foot and tries to kick it towards you. You lunge and make every effort to position yourself to catch the ball in the hoop. The team tries for the best out of ten the first time and then tries to break their record with the second ten attempts. Then have the child close her eyes and try to make a basket by blindly throwing the newspaper ball. You try to catch as many as possible out of ten, and the team works together to beat their last record.

Partner Pull-Up
Older
Sit on the floor holding hands and facing each other with toes together. On a signal, pull up together to a standing position. A variation is to have the partners sitting back to back with arms interlocked. On the signal, they both push up to a standing position. For these activities to work, the partners need to be close in size.

Pick Up Cotton Balls or Other Small Objects with Your Toes
All ages
Start with one or two and increase the number. Once the cotton balls have been picked up, you can add tossing them across the room. You can make this more challenging by having the child hop around the room with the cotton ball between his toes.

Pillow Push
All ages
Place a large pillow between you and the child. Have the child push against the pillow trying to push you over.

Ping Pong Bounce
Older
The adult and child sit on opposite sides of a small table. The child bounces ping pong balls off the table and the adult tries to grab them before they hit the floor (or can catch the ball in a basket). See how many balls they can catch in 30 seconds. Try and beat the score.

Seal Volleyball
All ages
The goal is to keep a balloon up in the air as long as possible but everyone has to use their nose to hit it, not their hands. Players should call their turn out loud so that no one gets hurt going for the balloon.

Seed Spitting Contest
All ages
Feed the child chunks of watermelon or orange or tangerine with seeds. You should eat some too. Both save your seeds. Have the child spit her seed as far as she can. Try to spit your seed as close to hers as possible. Small candies, beans or other small objects can be used as well.

Sock Grab
Older
You and the child sit on the floor with your legs extended and bottoms of your feet nearly touching. Each removes one sock completely and pulls the other sock off the end of the foot just a bit (athletic tube socks work great for this game). On the cue of "Ready, steady, go," each player tries to grab the opponent's sock off their foot using only their toes while at the same time trying to keep their own sock from being grabbed and pulled off.

Straight Face Challenge
Older
The child has to keep a straight face while you try to make him laugh, either by gently touching him (avoid sensitive spots or prolonged tickling) or by making funny faces.

Thumb, Arm or Leg Wrestling
Older
The adult guides the activity, giving starting signals and ensuring safety.

Wheelbarrow
Older
Have the child put her hands on the floor in a push-up position. Stand behind her and clasp her firmly by the ankles or just above the knees. The child "walks" on her hands. This is hard work for the child, so you should stop as soon as it becomes too tiring.

When parents enter or when there are three or more participants:

Cooperative Carrying
Older

Tie four to six strings or ribbons approximately 36 inches in length to a medium or a large rubber band, with equal spacing between the knots. Four to six people each hold one string (or two or three people can each hold two strings) and work together to pick up a paper cup or empty water bottle by pulling the rubber band wide enough to drop it around the object. Once the group captures the object, they can carry it to an appointed place. For more difficulty, stack objects on top of each other. The number of strings can be adjusted to fit the size of the group.

Cooperative Race
Older

There are many ways to organize a cooperative race; for example, taking turns blowing ping pong balls across the room, or kicking balloons. This can be done as a parent-child team against the practitioners, or timed to see how quickly the goal can be reached.

Cotton Ball, Marshmallow or Newspaper Ball Fight
All ages

Divide into two teams. Using cotton balls, marshmallows or newspaper balls, each team throws the balls at the other team trying to get rid of all the balls on their side. Players may set up a "shield" with pillows and throw from behind it.

Cotton Ball or Ping Pong Blow
All ages

Everyone lies on their tummies on the floor. Someone starts the game by naming a person across the circle to whom he intends to blow the cotton ball or ping pong ball. That person names someone else and the ball is blown back and forth across the circle.

Keep Balloon in the Air
All ages

When there are more people, this activity can become quite exciting. You can organize it by taking turns around the circle or by counting how many times the group can keep the balloon in the air before it hits the ground.

Shoe and Sock Race
All ages
The adults race to see who can put the child's shoes and socks back on first.

Tangle
Older
Everyone stands in a circle. One person crosses her arms and takes the hand of someone across the circle, then that person crosses his arms and takes the hand of another person across the circle until everyone is holding hands, deliberately creating a tangle of hands. Participants then untangle without breaking the handholds. It is likely that some people will be facing in and some out when the circle is untangled. It adds to the fun to put lotion on everyone's hands first. Another alternative is to have two participants stand to one side and close their eyes while the tangle is being created. They then direct the process of untangling.

Tug of War
All ages
Divide into teams, for example child and parents versus practitioners. Each team holds on to the ends of a scarf, a blanket or a soft rope, and tries to pull the other team to their side. Make sure that the child has a good grip and that there is nothing to bump into if one team falls.

Tunnels
All ages
The child crawls through a tunnel made of pillows or of kneeling adults to meet you or his parent at the end.

Wiggle In and Out
Young
The child wiggles out of one adult's encircling arms and into the other's arms. This is best with small children and is useful when the child is already wiggling and wanting to get out of your arms.

With gratitude to The Theraplay Institute for allowing the re-publication of these activities.

Glossary

ADHD Attention deficit hyperactivity disorder. A group of behavioral symptoms that include inattentiveness, hyperactivity and impulsiveness.

Affect The biological expression of an emotional state; how emotion is expressed through the voice, body language, eye contact or facial expression.

Affective state The experience of feeling the underlying emotional state.

Affective synchrony The process whereby two individuals are focused on and aware of each other's movements, gaze, body orientation and voice tone in an effort to make sense and share meaning with one another.

Ambivalent A pattern of attachment where the child alternates between clinginess and ignoring, or displaying angry behaviors towards, the parent.

Attachment A biologically driven need for connection with other humans that begins in infancy and continues throughout the lifespan—usually refers to the relationship between a child and their primary caregiver.

Attachment patterns Various ways in which a child's attachment is organized, e.g. secure, avoidant, ambivalent or disorganized.

Attunement The ability of one person to be able to recognize the needs, desires and impulses of another person.

Autonomic nervous system The regulatory system of the body that is responsible for body functions that are not consciously directed, e.g. heartbeat, breathing and digestion. It is made up of the sympathetic nervous system and the parasympathetic nervous system.

Blocked care A state parents can enter when prolonged stress suppresses their capacity to maintain loving and empathic feelings towards their child.

Contraindicated Against the best interests of the client.

Co-regulation When one person supports the other to regulate their affect and associated emotional state, e.g. an adult leading a child into a more regulated state.

Countertransference The unconscious projection of the practitioner's feelings onto a client.

Cultural bias Interpreting or judging people based on one's own cultural standards or assumptions.

DDP Dyadic developmental psychotherapy.

Developmental trauma The impact on a child of repeated experiences of abuse and/or neglect that started early in life and occurred within the family by adults who had the role of caring for or protecting the child.

Didactic approach A style of speaking that focuses on intellectual, cognitive learning, rules and rational explanations that is transmitted in a teacher-like voice.

Dissociating One of the ways in which the brain copes with too much stress, e.g. trauma and abuse. A person may feel detached from their body or numb or disconnected from themselves and the world around them.

Dyad A social group consisting of two people.

Dysregulation A loss of emotional regulation where emotional arousal has reached a point where a person is unable to control or manage their experience.

Emotionally labile Having large, dramatic and frequent shifts in emotion and behavior, from happy to sad, subdued to energetic.

Executive brain systems The structures/mechanisms in the brain which control conscious, logical, planful behaviors. These can be the ability to understand cause and effect, control impulses, organize actions into orderly steps, and delay gratification.

Eye movement desensitization and reprocessing (EMDR) A psychotherapy treatment designed to alleviate the distress associated with traumatic memories.

Fear lens The non-conscious perception that an event that is not inherently dangerous is seen or experienced as threatening or has a potential to harm.

Goodness of fit The relative match between the temperament of two individuals. For example, a naturally easy-going, spontaneous parent with a flexible, easily soothed child will create little strain on the parent-child relationship and there will be a natural goodness of fit. If, however, the child is sensitive, anxious and requires predictability and order in order to remain comfortable, the easy-going, unplanful parent will need to alter their behavior to more closely match the child's need, otherwise there will be a lack of goodness of fit.

Hyperarousal Arousal that is excessively over the upper edge of the window of tolerance associated with intense sensations as agitation, trembling and rapid heart rate, or overwhelming emotions such as rage, terror or panic.

Hypervigilant Inability to relax, and watchfulness for fear-producing events or stimuli, due to continuing internal arousal.

Hypoarousal Arousal that is excessively under the lower edge of the window of tolerance associated with an inability to move, heaviness or numbness, or emotions like despair, hopelessness or an absence of feelings.

Incongruent When an individual responds in a way that is the opposite of what the other person unconsciously expected.

Insecure attachment style Patterns of attachment behavior that reflect varying degrees of a lack of safety in the attachment and may manifest as avoidant, ambivalent or disorganized. Children experience insecure attachment when parents are insensitive or unresponsive to their needs.

Interactive repair The effort made in a relationship to mend a breach in connection, mis-attunement or boundary violation; often used in reference to attachment figures providing interactive repair to soothe an upset infant or child.

Internal working model The internal "maps" that an individual builds up about the world and about herself from her experiences with her primary caregivers in the first 2–3 years of life (Bowlby, 1988). Once established they tend to be fairly resistant to change, since subsequent perceptions are "selected" to fit what is expected.

Intersubjectivity (primary and secondary) Communication between two people within which experience is shared; takes place in a reciprocal relationship where the experience of each person has an impact on, and influences, the experience of the other person.

Intimacy demand The level of relational intensity in an interaction that requires an individual to be able to tolerate the stimulation associated with those vulnerable, exciting or scary feelings.

Limbic system An important part of the mid-brain, implicated in humans' abilities in relationships and attachments, which supports a variety of functions, including emotion, behavior, motivation and long-term memory.

Marschak Interaction Method (MIM) The MIM is a clinical tool unique to Theraplay and is used for structured observation of the interaction between parent and child used to assess the quality of their relationship for the purposes of parent guidance and treatment planning. It consists of a series of simple tasks designed to elicit behaviors in four primary dimensions of Theraplay.

Miscue/miscuing Used in the context of attachment behavior, miscuing is a behavior of a child that, from the outside, indicates one need, whereas internally the child is experiencing a different need. The reason the child shows the opposite behavior to what he is actually feeling or wishes to display is due to the child's unconscious understanding that his parent prefers him not to have that feeling or behavior, so he suppresses that need in order to gain or keep the approval of his parent.

"Moments of meeting" A moment when two individuals, usually through some dramatic shift in attention or emerging understanding, share, typically through gazing, a joined sense of thinking, feeling and sensing the same thing, which brings a deep sense of connection between the two.

Neural system (neural networks) Bundles of neurons that connect one region of the brain or nervous system with another for a common purpose.

PACE An attitude of Playfulness, Acceptance, Curiosity and Empathy—key principles of DDP for engagement and parenting of children who have had relationally traumatic early lives. These qualities are helpful when creating emotional safety and when trying to stay open and engaged with another person.

Parasympathetic nervous system Part of the autonomic nervous system that controls unconscious but critical body functions that occur when the body is at rest, e.g. digestion and slowing heart rate. It can also take us out of connection and into a protective state of collapse.

Polyvagal theory Stephen Porges's polyvagal theory is a theory of the vagus nerve and how it relates to our social behavior. According to the theory, the autonomic nervous system is interconnected with and sensitive to influences that flow from the body toward the brain. The polyvagal theory claims that humans have physical reactions, such as cardiac and digestive changes, associated with their facial expression. Porges argues this theory with observations from both evolutionary biology and neurology. Polyvagal theory has many implications for the study of stress, emotion and social behavior.

Proprioceptive input Sensations from joints, muscles and connective tissues that underlie the body's awareness which can be obtained by lifting, pushing and pulling heavy objects, including one's own weight.

Radical empathy The acting of providing pure empathy in a conversation, without any advice giving or problem solving.

Reciprocal Shared, joint or mutual interaction with each person taking a turn.

Reciprocity The mutually attuned interaction between two people.

Reflective function The ability to imagine mental states in self and others. Through this capacity for reflection, we develop the ability to understand our own behavioral responses and the responses of others as a meaningful attempt to communicate those inner mental states.

Regulation The ability to monitor and modify internal processes; to soothe or intensify our emotions, arousal and sensations until they do not feel uncomfortably low or high, to bring arousal within a window of tolerance.

Relational trauma Interactions with other people, including those with attachment figures, that are experienced as threatening and stimulate dysregulated arousal and animal defense. Relating to the impact of long-term abuse and/or neglect in childhood.

Rupture and repair Referring to the parent-child relationship, this dynamic is where the parent temporarily is not connected to or does the opposite of what the child wishes, in which case the child feels hurt, rejected or displeased with the parent. The parent then quickly repairs by reconnecting with the child through touch, eye contact or another overture that shows the child that she is still in favor with the parent, thereby restoring the harmony between the parent and child.

Sensory processing systems The mechanisms that organize sensation from one's own body and the environment, thus making it possible to use the body effectively within the environment. Specifically, it deals with how the brain processes multiple sensory modality inputs, such as proprioception, vision, the auditory, tactile, olfactory and vestibular systems, interoception and taste into usable information.

Sensory regulation The ability to adjust or regulate the level of alertness in order to respond appropriately to the sensory stimuli present in the environment.

Social engagement system (SES) A set of circuits including the ventral vagal nerve that stimulates engagement with the environment and other human beings through our facial expressions, eye movements, voicebox and turning and tilting of the head; the social engagement system is accessible when we feel safe.

Somatic Affecting the body.

Symbolic play A type of play behavior where a child uses one thing to represent something else.

Sympathetic nervous system Part of the autonomic nervous system that mediates the body's stress (or "fight or flight") response, energizing and mobilizing the body for action.

Synchrony Refers to rhythmic interaction and the mirroring of behavior and emotional states between parent and child.

Transference The unconscious projection of the client's feelings, positive or negative, of a particular person in their lives onto the practitioner (see also "countertransference").

Triad A group of three people.

Vagus nerve A cranial nerve that connects the brainstem to the body and the major nerve of the parasympathetic nervous system, controlling unconscious but critical body functions like heartbeat, breathing and digestion.

Visceral An emotion that is felt very deeply, intuitively, perhaps without rational explanation.

Vitality affect The affects (see "affect" above) of attunement, intersubjectivity and social connection. Refers to subtle, moment-to-moment, qualitative shifts in arousal, energy, flow, feeling and rhythm.

Window of tolerance The zone of optimal arousal level in which a person is able to function most effectively, allowing for the ebb and flow of emotions, and able to receive, process and integrate information and manage the demands of everyday life.

Authors

Vivien Norris, DClinPsy, DipMusicTh, is a chartered clinical psychologist and music therapist. She is also a certified trainer, supervisor and practitioner in both Theraplay* and dyadic developmental psychotherapy. Vivien worked as a clinical psychologist within the NHS in the UK for over 20 years, specializing in therapeutic work with families and in the area of fostering and adoption. She is now Clinical Director of The Family Place (www.thefamilyplace.co.uk), an independent organization providing flexible therapeutic interventions for families. Vivien is co-author of *Parenting with Theraplay* (Norris and Rodwell, 2017) and author of *By Your Side* (www.byyourside.online), a set of resources to support the transition from fostering to adoption. Vivien can be contacted at info@thefamilyplace.co.uk

Dafna Lender, LCSW, is the Director of International Programming for The Theraplay Institute. She is a certified trainer, supervisor and practitioner in both Theraplay and dyadic developmental psychotherapy (DDP). Dafna took her Level One Theraplay training in 1999 and has been practicing Theraplay everywhere she goes since then. Dafna has worked with children and their parents in therapeutic foster care, in residential settings and with children with fetal alcohol syndrome. Dafna teaches and supervises practitioners all over the world in three languages. Dafna can be contacted at dlender@theraplay.org

References

Ainsworth, M. (1969) "Object relations, dependency and attachment: A theoretical review of the infant-mother relationship." *Child Development, 40*, 969–1025.

Ayres, J. (2005) *Sensory Integration and the Child* (25th anniversary edition). Torrance, CA: Western Psychological Services.

Baylin, J. and Hughes, D. (2016) *The Neurobiology of Attachment-Focused Therapy: Enhancing Connection & Trust in the Treatment of Children & Adolescents.* New York, NY: WW Norton & Company.

Bhreathnach, E. (2013) The Just Right State Programme. Available at: www.sensoryattachmentintervention.com/copy-of-training-2.

Booth, P.B. and Jernberg, A.M. (2010) *Theraplay: Helping Parents and Children Build Better Relationships Through Attachment Based Play.* San Francisco, CA: Jossey Bass.

Bowlby, J. (1969) *Attachment and Loss.* New York, NY: Basic Books.

Bowlby, J. (1988) *A Secure Base: Parent-Child Attachment and Healthy Human Development.* London: Routledge.

Brazelton, T.B. (2013) *Learning to Listen: A Life Caring for Children.* Cambridge, MA: Da Capo Press.

Crittenden, P., Dallos, P., Landini, A. and Kozlowska, K. (2014) *Attachment and Family Therapy.* Maidenhead: Open University Press.

Curtiss, P.R. and Warren, P.W. (1973) *The Dynamics of Life Skills Coaching: Life Skills Series.* Prince Albert, Saskatchewan: Training Research and Development Station, Dept. of Manpower and Immigration.

Dunn, W. (2014) *The Sensory Profile 2.* London: Pearson.

Field, T.M. (1990) *Infancy.* Cambridge, MA: Harvard University Press.

Fisher-Borne, M., Cain, J. and Martin, S. (2015) "From mastery to accountability: Cultural humility as an alternative to cultural competence." *International Journal of Social Work Education, 34* (2), 165–181.

Fosha, D., Siegel, D.J. and Solomon, M. (2009) *The Healing Power of Emotion: Affective Neuroscience, Development and Clinical Practice.* New York, NY: WW Norton & Company.

Golding, K. (2008) The Thinking About Your Child Questionnaire, also referred to as Carers Questionnaire. Clinicians and Professionals working with Looked After and Adopted Children (CPLAAC). Available at: https://cplaac.wordpress.com. Initially developed for CPLAAC, currently being validated (personal communication).

Golding, K. and Hughes, D. (2012) *Creating Loving Attachments: Parenting with PACE to Nurture Confidence and Security in the Troubled Child.* London: Jessica Kingsley Publishers.

Hesse, E. (2008) "The Adult Attachment Interview: Protocol, Method of Analysis, and Empirical Studies." In J. Cassidy and P.R. Shaver (eds), *Handbook of Attachment: Theory, Research, and Clinical Applications* (pp.552–598). New York, NY: The Guilford Press.

Hrdy, S. (2009) *Mothers and Others: The Evolutionary Origins of Mutual Understanding.* Cambridge, MA: Harvard University Press.

Hughes, D. (2011a) *Attachment-Focused Therapy Workbook.* New York, NY: WW Norton & Company.

Hughes, D. (2011b) Hopes and Dreams Questionnaire. In D. Hughes, *Attachment-Focused Family Therapy Workbook* (pp.165–172). New York, NY: WW Norton & Company.

Hughes, D., Golding, K. and Hudson, J. (2019) *Healing Relational Trauma with Attachment-Focused Interventions: Dyadic Developmental Psychotherapy with Children and Families.* New York, NY: WW Norton & Company.

Lindaman, S. and Hong, R. (eds) (2020) *Theraplay®—The Handbook of Theory, Applications and Implementation.* London: Jessica Kingsley Publishers.

Lindaman, S. and Mäkelä, J. (2018) "The Polyvagal Foundation of Theraplay Treatment: Combining Social Engagement, Play and Nurture to Create Safety, Regulation and Resilience." In S. Porges, *Clinical Applications of the Polyvagal Theory: The Emergence of Polyvagal-Informed Therapies.* New York, NY: WW Norton & Company.

Lindaman, S. and Norris, V. (2019) The Theraplay Process, based on "The Polyvagal Foundation of Theraplay Treatment: Combining Social Engagement, Play and Nurture to Create Safety, Regulation and Resilience." By Lindaman, S. and Makela, J. (2018) in S. Porges, *Clinical Applications of the Polyvagal Theory: The Emergence of Polyvagal-Informed Therapies.* New York, NY: WW Norton & Company.

Malloch, S. and Trevarthen, C. (2009) *Communicative Musicality: Exploring the Basis of Human Companionship.* Oxford: Oxford University Press.

Norris, V. and Rodwell, H. (2017) *Parenting with Theraplay: Understanding Attachment and How to Nurture a Closer Relationship with Your Child.* London: Jessica Kingsley Publishers.

Ortega, R.M. and Coulborn Faller, K. (2011) "Training child welfare workers from an intersectional cultural humility perspective: A paradigm shift." *Child Welfare, 90* (5), 27–49.

Panksepp, J. (2005) *Affective Neuroscience: The Foundations of Human and Animal Emotions.* Oxford: Oxford University Press.

Perry, B. (2001) "The Neuroarcheology of Childhood Maltreatment: The Neurodevelopmental Costs of Adverse Childhood Events." In K. Franey, R. Geffner and R. Falconer (eds) *The Cost of Maltreatment: Who Pays? We All Do* (pp.15–37). Binghamton, NY: Haworth Press.

Perry, B. (2007) *The Boy Who Was Raised as a Dog: And Other Stories from a Child Psychiatrist's Notebook: What Traumatized Children Can Teach Us About Loss, Love and Healing.* New York, NY: Basic Books.

Porges, S. (2011) *The Polyvagal Theory: Neurophysiological Foundations of Emotions, Attachment, Communication, Self-Regulation.* New York, NY: WW Norton & Company.

Porges, S. and Dana, D. (2018) *Clinical Applications of the Polyvagal Theory: The Emergence of Polyvagal-Informed Therapies.* New York, NY: WW Norton & Company.

Rothbaum, F., Weisz, J., Pott, M., Miyake, K. and Morelli, G. (2000) "Attachment and culture: Security in the United States and Japan." *American Psychologist, 55* (10), 1093–1104.

Salo, S. and Booth, P. (eds) (2019) *Clinical Handbook for the Marschak Interaction Method (MIM).* Available at: www.theraplay.org.

Schore, A.N. (2001) "Effect of a secure attachment relationship on right brain development, affect regulation, and infant mental health." *Infant Mental Health Journal, 22* (1–2), 7–67.

Schore, A.N. (2003) *Affect Dysregulation and Disorders of the Self.* New York, NY: WW Norton & Company.

Schuldberg, J., Fox, N.S., Jones, C.A., Hunter, P., Mechard, M. and Stratton, M. (2012) "Same, same but different: The development of cultural humility through an international volunteer experience." *International Journal of Humanities and Social Science, 2* (17), 17–30.

Siegel, D.J. and Hartzell, M. (2014) *Parenting from the Inside Out: How a Deeper Self-Understanding Can Help You Raise Children Who Thrive* (tenth anniversary edition). New York, NY: Jeremy P. Tarcher/Penguin.

Stern, D. (2000) *The Interpersonal World of the Infant: A View from Psychoanalysis and Developmental Psychology.* New York, NY: Basic Books.

Tarren-Sweeney, M. (2007) "The Assessment Checklist for Children—ACC: A behavioral rating scale for children in foster, kinship and residential care." *Children and Youth Services Review, 29* (5), 672–689.

Tervalon, M. and Murray-Garcia, J. (1998) "Cultural humility versus cultural competence: A critical distinction in defining physician training outcomes in multicultural education." *Journal of Health Care for the Poor and Underserved.* Johns Hopkins University Press, Volume 9, Number 2.

Wampold, B.E. (2015) *The Great Psychotherapy Debate: The Evidence for What Makes Psychotherapy Work* (second edition). New York, NY: Routledge.

Index

Other JKP titles

Vivien Norris and Helen Rodwell

Parenting with Theraplay

Understanding Attachment and How to Nurture a Closer Relationship with Your Child

Forewords by Phyllis Booth and Dafna Lender, The Theraplay® Institute. Illustrations by Miranda Smith

Parenting with Theraplay®
Understanding Attachment and How
to Nurture a Closer Relationship with
Your Child
Vivien Norris and Helen Rodwell
Forewords by Phyllis Booth and Dafna Lender

Paperback: £13.99/$19.95
ISBN: 978 1 78592 209 1
eISBN: 978 1 78450 489 2
208 pages

Theraplay® is an attachment-focused model of parenting that helps parents to understand and relate to their child. Based on a sequence of play activities that are rooted in neuroscience, Theraplay offers a fun and easy way for parents and children to connect. Theraplay is particularly effective with looked-after and adopted children.

By providing an overview of Theraplay and the psychological principles that it is based on, parents and carers will gain an understanding of the basic theory of the model along with practical ideas for applying Theraplay to everyday family life. Through everyday case studies and easy language, parents will gain confidence and learn new skills for emotional bonding, empathy, and acceptance in the relationship with their child.

Dr Vivien Norris is a consultant clinical psychologist, music therapist, certified Theraplay practitioner and supervisor, and the UK Theraplay Training Director. Vivien is also a DDP practitioner who specializes in trauma.

Dr Helen Rodwell is a consultant clinical psychologist and certified Theraplay practitioner. Helen works with looked-after and adopted children and provides supervision and consultation to other professionals, including adoption and fostering social workers.